why sing?

Toward A Theology of Catholic Church Music

Miriam Therese Winter

The Pastoral Press

Washington, DC

ISBN 0-912405-07-4

The Pastoral Press
225 Sheridan Street, NW
Washington, DC 20011
(202) 723-5800

The Pastoral Press is the publications division of the National Association of Pastoral
Musicians, a membership organization of musicians and clergy dedicated to fostering
the art of musical liturgy.

Printed in the United States of America

Cover design by Donald Carlton

Contents

CONTENTS

Introduction

Why Sing? is essentially a doctoral dissertation that was submitted to Princeton Theological Seminary for a Ph. D. in 1983. Although some editorial adjustments were made prior to publication, the approach and at times the style are necessarily conditioned by these considerations.

The purpose of this book is to establish a theological context for contemporary discussions on Catholic Church music. It is hoped that the effort to accomplish this will reveal the need for a clearly constructed theology of Catholic Church music from which theological criteria for governing the use of music in the liturgy might be drawn.

As this study demonstrates, the process of constructing such a theology must surely begin with Church music legislation, which has conditioned music practice from the early Middle Ages into the present time. Although liturgical music has been determined chiefly by regulatory criteria embedded in the legislation, vestiges of theology are bound to be present in the documents or implicit in the rules. Therefore, the theology underlying Church music legislation can be made more explicit by examining the theological foundations of music criteria, past and present. Such an exercise is necessary if the theological enterprise is to evolve in continuity with the tradition of the Church.

The book's central thesis can be expressed in the following terms. A complex of theological assumptions underlies the corpus of music legislation. The present polarization in music practice is essentially a theological problem that is the result of conflicting interpretations of the directives of Vatican II. The theological bases of the Council's statements on music and subsequent criteria for its use cannot be properly articulated if these statements are examined in isolation from other documentation, namely, legislation on the liturgy and decrees on the nature and mission of the Church.

Several hypotheses support this thesis. Roman Catholic Church music is governed by the theological principles of the liturgy in which it functions. A change in liturgical theology necessarily affects its music. Since there has been substantial change in the Church's theology of liturgy as a result of Vatican II, there must have been a theological shift with regard to Catholic Church music which ought to be reflected in the legislation, beginning with Vatican II. To understand this shift, it is necessary to evaluate music legislation in relation to other Conciliar documents, particularly the opening chapters of *Sacrosanctum concilium* with regard to liturgical practice, and *Gaudium et spes*, the pastoral constitution on the Church in the modern world.

Additional assumptions have been operative here. Central among these is the conviction that liturgical music is, of its very nature, *locus theologicus* because of its intimate association with the liturgy, a recognized source of theology. Because musical expressions are time-conditioned, shaped by history and culture and therefore open to development and change, the theology they transmit reflects a variety of perspectives: that of the liturgy and of the legislator and of all those involved in the creation and use of music.

The legislative perspective has dominated Catholic Church music for much of its history, overshadowing, even obliterating, the viewpoints of music makers, those who composed and those who performed. However, the situation is changing. Church music today is shaped by many factors: by a given liturgy and its location, by legislators and musicians, planners and participants of varied backgrounds, ages, and orientations. The theology it mediates most certainly will bear the stamp of all these perspectives. It must be stressed that neither music nor music legislation exists in isolation. Contexts and other contributing factors are integral to its understanding. These are the theoretical foundations on which this book constructs its case.

Structurally, Part One will set the context, Part Two will examine the liturgy and its theological principles, and Part Three, the liturgy's music and its theological bases. As the Second Vatican Council is constitutive of the current status of the Roman Catholic Church and its liturgy, an effort will be made to understand the Council's purpose and the thrust of its deliberations, in order to determine what attitudes influenced its decisions, and why.

Six music documents have been selected for careful analysis. These texts cover the full extent of church music reform and renewal in this century, from its association with the liturgical movement in its beginnings, to its present identification with the pastoral-liturgical mission of the institutional Church. These documents are, therefore, representative of legislative expectations concerning music practice in the pre-Conciliar, Conciliar, and post-Conciliar Church. An examination of their content should yield some understanding of those criteria which have shaped and still shape liturgical music in this country.

I am particularly grateful to Dr. Karlfried Froehlich, Professor of Ecclesiastical History, who guided the dissertation under its original title: *Vatican II in the Development of Criteria For the Use of Music in the Liturgy of the Roman Catholic Church in the United States and Their Theological Bases.* Special thanks go to Mary Ellen Cohn of The Pastoral Press for helping to prepare the manuscript for publication.

I

MUSIC IN THE LITURGY: THE PROBLEM AND ITS CONTEXT

1

Catholic Church Music: An American Perspective

CATHOLIC CHURCH MUSIC TODAY IS BESET BY TENSIONS AND POLARIZATIONS. Perhaps the most critical problem is its failure to achieve unity amid a pluriformity of styles and forms. Instead of a growing tolerance and understanding of differing viewpoints, there is opposition, even antagonism, expressed by proponents of what seems to be two divergent musical streams. It is difficult to define these positions precisely. For now they might be broadly classified as an emphasis on the song of the people and the artist's song. This categorization would eliminate the "folk-song/guitar-song" designation that ordinarily adheres to the former, as well as the criterion of professionalism that usually defines the latter. A word of caution, however, against generalized, premature labeling. Dividing lines are not neatly drawn. Church musicians devoted to the "pursuit of excellence" in "sacred music" recognize and affirm music as a ministry with pastoral implications. On the other hand, protagonists of "pastoral music" continue to provide opportunities for "spiritual growth through musical excellence" and occasions to "claim your art."[1]

That divisions exist and that these are deep can be discerned from a look at the literature of the past twenty years. Music

---

1. Note recent convention themes of National Association of Pastoral Musicians: "Spiritual Growth Through Musical Excellence" (Regional Convention, Philadelphia, 1980), "Claim Your Art" (National Convention, Detroit, 1981).

reviews are particularly revealing.[2] Caustic criticism and a pejorative tone are prevalent in dealing with new church music. There are other signs of entrenchment. In 1971, the Board of Directors of the *Consociatio Internationalis Musicae Sacrae*[3] issued a Memorandum in which it petitioned the Holy See "for an effort of disseminating and reaffirming all information based on the authentic documents" and requested the hierarchy "to disavow explicitly all abuses contrary to these authentic texts."[4] In the spring of 1978, the editors of *Sacred Music* blamed the loss of a Latin repertory and the decline of Church choirs on "two basic errors circulated by the propagandists of the projected reforms," claiming that "these notions are false and cannot be found in any documents coming from the council or from the Holy See," that in fact "the truth is that the direct opposite of these errors can be found clearly enunciated in the Constitution on the Sacred Liturgy, where the use of Latin is commanded and the fostering of choirs and the treasure of sacred music from all ages and in every style, especially Gregorian chant, is ordered for the universal Church."[5] Recently, the editors of that same periodical affirmed their determination "to implement the decrees of the Second Vatican Council, as the council fathers intended." They reiterated their commitment to "fighting against those false interpretations that have followed the council, spread by so-called experts in liturgy, wrongly passed off as the 'spirit of the council' and the will of our bishops ... It is against this propaganda, this deliberate violation of the decrees and wishes of the council that we are at war." Taking their stand for traditional values and against those who lack proper music training, the publication declared itself "at war with those who are disobedient to the Church's directives, and at war with those who promote inferior art."[6]

2. For example, Edward J. McKenna, *Worship* (1978 through 1981); John Ainslie, "English Liturgical Music Since the Council," in *English Catholic Worship* (London: Geoffrey Chapman, 1979), pp. 93–109; James Brieg, "The Hit-and-Miss Parade of Catholic Hymns," *U.S. Catholic* 45 (1980), pp. 28–30.

3. Established by Pope Paul VI in 1963 as a professional organization of specialists and charged with the task of advising him in all matters concerning church music.

4. *Consociatio Internationalis Musicae Sacrae*, "Memorandum of Sacred Music," *Sacred Music* 98 (1971), p. 5.

5. Richard J. Schuler, "True and Sacred," *Sacred Music* 105 (1978), p. 31.

6. Richard J. Schuler, "The Battle," *Sacred Music* 107 (1980), p. 25.

These are serious accusations, for it is around the claim of fidelity to Church teaching that the controversy forms. The issue is not one of fidelity, however, for representatives of opposing views are both quoting Council documents to substantiate their claims. The issue is one of interpretation as it touches on the level of meaning. What did the Council really say about music in its official documentation? What do the texts intend? What does it mean to be faithful to the spirit of Vatican II? Can fidelity to the Council's texts be at variance with fidelity to its essential spirit? What do present laws communicate about content and style and form? What scope is there for interpretation? For variation? For diversity of expression? What guides this interpretation? What is the Church's rationale for contemporary liturgical music and the theological basis for its stance? In short, with regard to its music, what is the mind and spirit of the post-Conciliar Church?

The Council's call for full, active participation by congregations created the context for the present problem. This pastoral goal was closely linked to the need for comprehension, which resulted in a swift transition to a vernacular liturgy throughout the United States. Along with the loss of Latin, there was the loss of all that music in which the Latin language played so integral a part. Gregorian chant and classical polyphony ceased to be the norm or the goal of the average Catholic parish, a traumatic adjustment for professional musicians and all those sensitive to and appreciative of the art treasures of the past. With surprising speed, the style in which musicians had been formed and on which all Catholics had been nurtured, that music sanctioned for centuries by the Church as the only music suitable for the ritual praise of God, disappeared from parish life.

It is not possible here to chronicle the many attempts to fill that musical void. Newly-composed psalms,[7] chants,[8] folk-style songs,[9]

7. Widely used psalms and canticles of French Jesuit Joseph Gelineau, who introduced a new system of vernacular psalmody based on rhythmic stress; psalms of Canadian priest Stephen Somerville.

8. Feast day melodies by Grailville (Loveland, Ohio); plainsong Propers by Sisters of the Most Precious Blood (O'Fallon, Missouri); Mass, Services settings by Dennis Fitzpatrick (Friends of the English Liturgy).

9. So-called "folk music" was especially influential in the United States during the transition phase of the mid-60's. Notable among early contributors to a folk-style vernacular repertory: Sebastian Temple, Paul Quinlan, Clarence Rivers, James Thiem, Ray Repp, Miriam Therese Winter, Ian Mitchell, Peter Sholtes,

hymns,[10] Masses,[11] and choral pieces offered a variety of options to contemporary music practice. The proliferation of new material was a cause for delight for advocates of change, and for deep concern, often revulsion, for many musicians fearful of losing the precious heritage of centuries. There were conferences and congresses, forums to debate the issues, periodicals, publications, and newly-formed organizations devoted specifically to music.[12] There has been much progress during the past twenty years, but serious concerns remain.

Rembert Weakland put the problem succinctly in his remarks to the Church Music Congress meeting in Milwaukee in 1966:

Sister Germaine, Robert Blue, John Ylvisaker, Joe Wise, Sydney Carter, Willard Jabusch, Carey Landry, Jack Miffleton, Tom Parker, and groups such as The Mission and The Dameans. These were soon joined by many others, some of whom gained national prominence (St. Louis Jesuits, Weston Priory). Most maintained a strong local following. A history of this movement has yet to be written.

10. Biblical hymns and psalms of French composer Lucien Deiss; new and traditional hymns available in early hymnals, namely: *The People's Hymnal* (World Library, 1955); *Our Parish Prays and Sings* (1958); *People's Mass Book* (World Library, 1964); *Hymnal of Christian Unity* (G.I.A., 1964); *The English Liturgy Hymnal* (F.E.L., 1965); the Looseleaf Hymnal (combined publication of G.I.A., World Library, Vanguard Music Corp.); hymns included in weekly/monthly missalettes.

11. Among others, C. Alexander Peloquin, Jan Vermulst, Noel Goemanne, Robert Kreutz.

12. The annual North American Liturgical Week, sponsored by the Liturgical Conference; eventually the meetings of the Federation of Diocesan Liturgical Commissions; the Fifth International Music Congress in Chicago-Milwaukee, 1966. In 1965, the Caecilia Society (publication, *Caecilia*) and the Society of St. Gregory (*Catholic Choirmaster*) merged to form the Church Music Association of America (*Sacred Music*) which affiliated with *Consociatio Internationalis Musicae Sacrae (Musica Sacra)*. In 1962, an international group of liturgical musicians gathered to discuss the theory and practice of Christian liturgical music and in 1966 was formally constituted as *Universa Laus*. The Composer's Forum for Catholic Worship was instituted in 1971 to provide good, contemporary music settings for the texts of the liturgy (and went out of existence in 1977.) The National Association of Pastoral Musicians (*Pastoral Music*) was established in 1976 and held its first national convention in Scranton the following year. A special sub-group of the North American Academy of Liturgy (established in 1975, official organ: *Worship*), continues to meet around the topic of liturgical music.

I would like to say that I feel that there are still several gaps that we must work upon to close. The next gap is definitely the gap between musicians and liturgists and theologians throughout the country . . . This is definitely a need, a need for us to come together and to discuss our differences and to find out those points where we think we are apart but are not really so.[13]

There have been significant steps toward closing the gap between liturgists and musicians. To date no theology of Roman Catholic Church music exists to serve as a guide for the interpretation and implementation of the directives of Vatican II. Music previously taken for granted has been subjected to a barrage of questions. It is no longer sufficient to expend energy primarily on implementation. Musicians must move beyond functional, stylistic considerations to probe systematically, from a variety of diverse viewpoints, the deeper theological implications of Vatican II. Recent discussions by scholars on the nature and purpose of liturgical music and the task of liturgical musicians have contributed substantially toward eradicating that theological vacuum inherited after the Council by a Church long accustomed not to reason about its music but simply to obey the law. These discussions have been valuable, but they have not gone far enough. It is time for all who love the Church and who foster the Church's song to set aside distinctions that separate and divide, to enter into dialogue, to try to determine precisely where the artistic and the popular, traditional and contemporary, theoretical and practical, juridical and pastoral, aesthetic and religious, professional and amateur, performer and participant, musician and liturgist converge. It is time for musicians to seriously consider how multiple styles and spiritualities can coexist beneficially in the post-Conciliar Church.

There is need to construct a theological framework as a guide and a stimulus to practice, something for which the post-Conciliar Church is woefully unprepared. Anathemas and collective fiats were not exactly conducive to theological thinking, and centuries of standardization did not prepare the faithful to handle options

---

13. Rembert G. Weakland, In *Sacred Music and Liturgy Reform:* Proceedings of the Fifth International Church Music Congress (Rome: *Consociatio Internationalis Musicae Sacrae,* 1969), p. 253.

with ease. Musicians today are far from agreeing on what constitutes essentials, or how to distinguish qualities that abide from characteristics that change with the times. There may indeed be a definite theological basis to present decision-making, but it is still caught up in polemics that seek to justify personal choice. It is time to articulate clearly those theological positions to which one has given assent and to determine whether they are freely chosen or simply inherited from the past.

On January 3, 1983, Mark Searle, president-elect of the North American Academy of Liturgy, exhorted the members of that Academy to reflect seriously on all aspects of liturgical/pastoral renewal in America since the Council and to make a concerted effort to build up a comprehensive bibliography of scholarly resources in this area. The present bibliography on American Church music consists of a lot of tools for implementation, mainly handbooks and manuals to assist the practitioner in making music happen. There is very little material that even attempts to provide a theological framework for liturgical music practice by addressing the more critical issues systematically and in depth. Some of these issues are: the theological rationale for legislating Church music practice; the sacred/secular issue as it pertains to music for worship; the unique musical requirements of a cathedral liturgy, a parish liturgy, ethnic liturgies, liturgies for special groups on special occasions; the limitations of musical bits and pieces for achieving a true sense of community; an impartial study of the artistic/professional and popular/amateur contributions to Church music tradition; the development of theological criteria for the composition and use of music for worship today. A look at the literature will reveal just how much serious work has yet to be done.

AN OVERVIEW OF THE LITERATURE

The following pages are not concerned with musical repertory, but with the bibliography about Catholic Church music published in this century for Americans. While this survey is limited to material in English, reference will be made occasionally to European works of significance to the dialogue here. Although the research for this chapter has been extensive, it cannot claim to be exhaustive. This examination of the literature reveals the broad developmental trends, both in theory and in practice, of that music used in the liturgy of the Roman Catholic Church since its inception, as well as more detailed information about the dynamics of contemporary reform in America.

Bibliographic material in the form of books or dissertations about Roman Catholic Church music can be classified according to four broad categories: histories, historical and/or canonical studies or monographs, practical manuals or guides, and reflections on music practice.

It is important to note that the designation "Catholic" as it is used in this book is a Reformation term. The history of the development of Church music prior to the sixteenth century is a common Christian heritage, and much valuable information is contained in the writings of Protestant and Eastern Orthodox authors.[14] Vatican II opened the Catholic Church to the benefits of these resources. Consequently, an acceptable bibliography on Catholic Church music can no longer be denominationally exclusive.

Students generally turn to a history of Western music for a perspective on the origins and evolution of Catholic Church music.[15] Those interested in a specifically liturgical history of music have found the resources to be few. When Erwin E. Nemmers published his *Twenty Centuries of Catholic Church Music* in 1949, he noted that to his knowledge there existed only one other similar and far simpler work by a Catholic available in English.[16] That same year, Marie Pierik wrote in the preface to her 32-page booklet, *When the People Sang:*

14. General histories: Edward Dickinson, *Music in the History of the Western Church* (1903); Winfred Douglas, *Church Music in History and Practice* (1937); Millar Patrick, *The Story of the Church's Song* (1962); Russell N. Squire, *Church Music* (1962); C. Henry Phillips, *The Singing Church* (1968); Egon Wellesz, *A History of Byzantine Music and Hymnography* (1949) (1961).

15. Donald J. Grout, *A History of Western Music* (1960); Paul Henry Lang, *Music in Western Civilization* (1941); Hugo Leichtentritt, *Music, History and Ideas* (1958); *The New Oxford History of Music* (1954); Gustave Reese, *Music in the Middle Ages* (1940) *and Music in the Renaissance* (1959); Curt Sachs, *The Rise of Music in the Ancient World* (1943); Oliver Strunk, ed., *Source Readings in Music History* (1950). See also: *New Catholic Encyclopedia* 10 (1967), pp. 97–131.

16. Karl Weinmann, *History of Church Music* (1910). His survey excluded monographs, i.e., R.R. Terry, *Music of the Roman Rite* (1931).

To our knowledge no condensed history of the entire Mass—
Proper and Ordinary—which concentrates particularly on the
participation of the *people* in the early songs of the Church has yet
been presented in English.[17]

In 1961 Alec Robertson published his *Christian Music* as volume
125 of the Twentieth-Century Encyclopedia of Catholicism.[18] Also
in 1961, Helicon Press made available an English translation of
Karl Gustav Fellerer's *Geschichte der Katholischen Kirchenmusik*,
which was first published in Germany in 1949.[19] Although the
Nemmers and Fellerer volumes both predate Vatican II, they
remain the most recent histories of Catholic Church music
currently in print in the United States.[20]

More historical information is available in topical studies.
Twentieth-century scholars have examined in depth the origins of
the Church's liturgical music,[21] the nature of its unique Gregorian
heritage,[22] and the extent of Patristic influence on the attitudes and
practices of early Christians.[23] More recent studies have focused

17. Marie Pierik, *When the People Sang* (Boston: McLaughlin and Reilly, 1949),
p. 7.

18. In England, *Music of the Catholic Church* (London: Burns and Oates, 1961),
volume 117 of the Faith and Facts Books.

19. Karl Gustav Fellerer, *The History of Catholic Church Music*, tr. by Francis A.
Brunner (Baltimore: Helicon Press, 1961).

20. *Geschichte der katholischen Kirchenmusik*, Vol. I (1972), Vol. II (1976), the 900-
page compendium of essays edited by Karl Gustav Fellerer, still awaits
translation.

21. Johannes Quasten, *Music and Worship in Pagan and Christian Antiquity*,
(1929) (1973) translated by Boniface Ramsey (1983); Eric Werner, *The Sacred
Bridge* (1959) (1970); William Sheppard Smith, *Musical Aspects of the New
Testament* (1962).

22. A prolific category. See especially: Justine B. Ward, *Gregorian Chant* (1923);
Dominic Johner, *A New School of Gregorian Chant* (1925); Marie Pierik, *The Spirit of
Gregorian Chant* (1939) and *The Song of the Church* (1947); Egon Wellesz, *Eastern
Elements in Western Chants* (1947); G.B. Chambers, *Folksong-Plainsong: A Study in
Origins and Musical Relationships* (1956); Willi Apel, *Gregorian Chant* (1958); and
the extensive literature in French concerning Gregorian rhythm and interpreta-
tion, notably from Solesmes.

23. Johannes Quasten, *op. cit.*; Theodore Gerold, *Les Peres de l'Eglise et la musique*
(1931); James William McKinnon, *The Church Fathers and Musical Instruments*,
Dissertation, Columbia University (1965); Robert A. Skeris, *Chroma Theou. On the
Origins and Theological Interpretation of the Musical Imagery Used by the
Ecclesiastical Writers of the First Three Centuries* (1976).

on the fundamental principles of liturgical music and their practical application.[24]

Of special interest to this investigation have been those studies involving Church music legislation. Two significant earlier works were developed abroad and are available only in their original Latin and French.[25] Robert Hayburn's doctoral dissertation represents a significant American contribution. His more recent work is a collection of documents from 95 A.D. through 1977, many of which appear for the first time in English.[26]

The majority of Catholic music publications have taken the form of practical manuals or handbooks for the practicing Church musician. When George Predmore first produced his *Church Music in the Light of the Motu Proprio* in 1924, he intended the manual to serve as a guide to those in charge of choirs and, above all, to beginners.[27] His book included a translation of Pius X's *motu proprio* of 1903 with a commentary, recommendations for choirmasters, choirs, and organists regarding proper execution, and lists of approved and recommended music, as well as music that was

24. William Joseph Weiler, *An Investigation of Qualities of Music Essential to the Roman Catholic Liturgy*, Dissertation, Northwestern University (1960); Joseph Gelineau, *Voices and Instruments in Christian Worship* (1964); Charles J. Matonti, *Discovering Principles for the Composition and Use of Contemporary Liturgical Music Through the Study of Selected Requiem Masses*, Dissertation, Columbia University (1972); Mary Alice O'Connor, *The Role of Music in the English Vernacular of the Roman Catholic Church: 1963–1974*, Dissertation, Catholic University (1974); Janet Roland Walton, *The Contributions of Aesthetics to Liturgical-Renewal*, Dissertation, Columbia University (1979); Brian Joseph Sparksman, *The Minister of Music in the Western Church: A Canonical-Historical Study*, Dissertation, Catholic University (1981). The dissertation of Robert Douglas Peterson, *The Folk Idiom in the Music of Contemporary Protestant Worship*, Columbia University (1972) also merits a listing here.

25. Florentius Romita, *Ius Musicae Liturgicae* (1947); André Pons, *Droit ecclesiastique et Musique sacrée* (1958).

26. Robert F. Hayburn, *Pope Saint Pius X and the Vatican Edition of the Chant Books*, Dissertation, University of Southern California (1964); and *Papal Legislation on Sacred Music* (Collegeville: The Liturgical Press, 1979). Note also two studies from Catholic University's canon law series: David Kennedy, *Canon Law and Liturgical Music* (1955) and Brian Sparksman, *op. cit.*

27. George V. Predmore, *Church Music in the Light of the Motu Proprio*. A Guide for the Catholic Choirmaster and Organist (Rochester, NY: The Seminary Press, 1924) and the expanded edition, *Sacred Music and the Catholic Church* (Boston: McLaughlin and Reilly, 1950).

liturgically inappropriate and to be avoided. A revised and expanded edition was reprinted in 1936 and again in 1950. *Singing the Liturgy* by a Sister Marietta was published in 1956 and *Singing in God's Ear* by Dom David Nicholson in 1959. By far the most popular book on the eve of the Council was Paul Hume's *Catholic Church Music* (1960), a commentary on the status of parochial music in which the well-known critic unequivocally denounced, once and for all, those bad but beloved "saccharine" hymns, the mainstay of novenas and the Dialogue Mass with hymns.[28]

Soon after the promulgation of *Sacrosanctum concilium*, the practical handbook designed for popular appeal came into its own. The Liturgical Conference published *A Manual For Church Musicians* (1964) in order to "discuss the implications of the forthcoming vernacular liturgy, and to treat the role of the musician in bringing about a full, active participation by all the faithful in the mysteries of Christ."[29] Written by a team of experts in both liturgy and music, the manual was intended as a reflection on music principles and functions in light of Vatican II, and was directed toward those involved in the renewal of parish worship. A whimsical little book by Omer Westendorf sought to coax the recalcitrant parishioner in the direction of music reform.[30] In 1970 the same publisher produced *Spirit and Song of the New Liturgy*, a comprehensive and theoretically sound handbook for church musicians by liturgist/musician Lucien Deiss. Concerned with the ministerial function of liturgical music as expressed through roles and forms resulting from Vatican II, the revised edition published in 1976 remains without equal among practical guidebooks to date. The 1970's saw an increase in publications for pastoral musicians intent on implementing lay participation in rituals revised according to liturgical norms emanating from Vatican II. Some books were oriented toward the folk style,[31] others ad-

28. Classroom texts and manuals designed for teaching Gregorian chant in the parish are not included in this survey.

29. *A Manual For Church Musicians* (Washington, DC: The Liturgical Conference, 1964), p. 7.

30. Omer Westendorf, *Music Lessons for the Man in the Pew* (Cincinnati: World Library of Sacred Music, 1965).

31. Ed Gutfreund, *With Lyre, Harp, and A Flatpick* (1974); Kent Schneider, *The Creative Musician in the Church* (1976); Timothy Schoenbachler, *Folk Music in Transition* (1979).

dressed a more general approach to music ministry.[32] More recently, the trend is toward the publication of local guidelines by diocesan liturgical commissions.

During the 1960's the Church music forum emerged as an option for national, international, and interdenominational exchange on issues of immediate concern. Some of these gatherings published their proceedings in the form of a book. Repercussions from the Fifth International Church Music Congress sponsored by *Consociatio Internationalis Musicae Sacrae* and The Church Music Association of America in Chicago and Milwaukee in August, 1966[33] linger to this day. Underlying polarizations between liturgists and musicians and among musicians themselves were brought to a head with accusations of manipulation and retrenchment, both having some foundation in fact. In an effort to reestablish a rapport, the Liturgical Conference joined with the Church Music Association of America later that year to conduct a forum that openly addressed the validity of a liturgical music that leaned to the right, to the left, or to the far left, or remained in a central, more balanced, position.[34] *Universa Laus*, an international, interdenominational association of scholars, musicians, and liturgists founded in 1966, published the proceedings of its 1978 meeting for the first time in English for Americans in the form of a book.[35] The National Association of Pastoral Musicians recently published two books, *Pastoral Music in Practice* (1981) and *Music In Catholic Worship, The NPM Commentary* (1982) which are collections of articles first published in its journal, *Pastoral Music*.

Two books might be best described as reflections on music practice, although they are both very different in terms of style and

32. William A. Baumen, *The Ministry of Music. A Guide for the Practicing Church Musician* (1975), Revised by Elaine Rendler (1979); Ralph Middlecamp, *Introduction to Catholic Music Ministry* (1978). Note: the special category of dance is not included in this survey.

33. Johannes Overath, ed., *Sacred Music and Liturgy Reform*: After Vatican II (Rome: *Consociatio Internationalis Musicae Sacrae*, 1969).

34. *Harmony and Discord*: An Open Forum On Church Music, Conducted by the Liturgical Conference and The Church Music Association of America, November 29-December 1, 1966 (Washington, DC: The Liturgical Conference, 1966).

35. *Growing In Church Music*, Proceedings of a Meeting on "Why Church Music?", Conducted by The Society of St. Gregory and *Universa Laus* (Washington, DC: *Universa Laus* English Edition, 1979).

content. *The Performing Audience* by Bernard Huijbers is a provocative, insightful "philosophy on participation of the faithful" that merits a careful reading.[36] *Church Music Transgressed* (1977) by Francis P. Schmitt is basically informational, the past revisited through the author's own personal reflections on "reform." Finally, many post-Conciliar books on liturgical renewal include a chapter on music.[37] The subject is usually addressed from a liturgist's perspective, often in the context of a commentary on *Sacrosanctum concilium* and its implementation.

Catholic Church music periodicals in the United States have traditionally been associated with organizations for which they have functioned as official publications. Five such journals have been significant in chronicling the status of local Church music during the various stages of its development, commenting on and, to some extent, influencing the direction of liturgical music reform and renewal.

Caecilia was the official publication of the American Caecilian Society founded by John B. Singenberger and Msgr. Joseph Salzmann in St. Francis, Wisconsin, in 1873. Patterned after its German counterpart,[38] the American extension of the Caecilian movement also sought to foster reform of sacred music and the revival of chant and Renaissance polyphony through national conventions that offered programs of good Church music performed in cooperation with local choirs. *Caecilia*, a monthly, was first published in 1874, in German, with occasional articles and notices in English. It was not until 1925 with volume 52 that the society produced the first issue entirely in English. By then, support for the journal and its organization had dwindled, and in 1957, the periodical was transferred to a new organization, the

36. Bernard Huijbers, *The Performing Audience*, tr. by Ray Noll *et al* (Phoenix: North American Liturgy Resources, 1974, 1980).

37. Such as: C.J. McNaspy, "The Sacral In Liturgical Music," in *The Renewal of the Liturgy* (1963); Martin Hall, "Music and Pastoral Liturgy, in *Pastoral Liturgy*, ed. by Harold Winstone (1965); George Devine, "Sing to the Lord A New Song," in *Liturgical Renewal: An Agonizing Reappraisal* (1973); Grayson W. Brown, "Music in the Black Spiritual Tradition," in *This Far by Faith* (1977); Joseph Gelineau, "Music and Song," in *The Liturgy Today and Tomorrow* (1978); Miriam Therese Winter, "You Shall Have A Song," in *Preparing the Way of the Lord* (1978).

38. Francis Xavier Witt founded the Caecilian Society in Bamberg in 1868. Pius IX in *Multum ad Movendos Animos*, December 16, 1870, gave it the status of a papal association.

Society of St. Caecilia, and continued as a quarterly for another ten years. With the promulgation of the *motu proprio* in 1903, liturgical music came into its own. The more reactionary Caecelian movement lost its impetus in the States and its annual conventions ceased. Established to develop higher liturgical and artistic standards, the American Caecilian Society had in fact nurtured a nostalgia for a "golden age" of sacred music and, at the same time, promoted the often inferior works of its own members as appropriate contemporary expressions. Its journal reflected these values. Throughout its lifetime, *Caecelia* defended the *motu proprio*'s categories of chant, polyphony, and appropriate modern music tenaciously and uncritically. Francis Schmitt, who edited *Caecilia* in its final years, describes the journal in these words: "... the thing that strikes one who peruses its pages most forcibly is their sameness."[39] One would have to concur with his judgment. Nevertheless, the documentation of music practice in the United States throughout the period of the journal's lengthy existence remains a valuable resource.

Catholic Choirmaster was the offical quarterly publication of the Society of St. Gregory of America, founded in 1914 in Cliff Haven, New York under the inspiration of Nicholas Montani. The society was granted papal approbation in 1915. Established to promote the cause of sacred music according to the provisions of the *motu proprio* of 1903, it elected to do this through a network of affiliated diocesan guilds that came together annually for national conventions. One of its goals was to ensure that "the work of church musicians be enhanced in every possible way" and made attractive though "salaries, working conditions, pastoral cooperation...."[40] In 1920 it published the *St. Gregory Hymnal and Choir Book*, which set a high standard for American Catholic hymnals and saw continuous use well into the post-Conciliar period. In 1928 the society published *The White List* of liturgically acceptable compositions, which functioned as an index of approved music until after the Council.[41] The growing number of summer school and

39. Francis P. Schmitt, *Church Music Transgressed:* Reflections on "Reform" (New York: Seabury Press, 1977), p. 119.

40. Rev. Benedict Ehmann, "Our Spiritual Charter," *Catholic Choirmaster* 34 (1948), p. 98.

41. "The old White List has been abandoned. The new committee will not put its seal of approval (or disapproval) on everything published, but will recom-

workshop alternatives spawned by the liturgical movement led to the decision to terminate national conventions in the 1940's. *Catholic Choirmaster* underwent many changes since its inauguration in 1915. Originally a brochure to advertise new liturgical compositions for G. Schirmer, it was redesigned as a bulletin to report the meetings of the Society of St. Gregory and the progress of liturgical music reform. Around 1939 the bulletin was changed to the status of a periodical. From the start, the Society of St. Gregory had determined that "all subjects of a controversial nature were to be rigorously avoided"[42] while affirming, at the same time, a constructive attitude toward reform. The editors of *Catholic Choirmaster* honored this policy in recording the progress of fifty years of liturgical music in America. In its final Golden Anniversary issue in 1964, editor J. Vincent Higginson predicted that "its purpose and spirit will continue in another new format."[43]

Sacred Music was an attempt to do just that. Monsignor Francis Schmitt, president of the Society of St. Caecilia, and Rev. John C. Selner, as president of the Society of St. Gregory, met with the executives of both organizations at Boys Town, Nebraska, in August of 1964 to effect an amalgamation. *Caecilia* and *Catholic Choirmaster* also merged to form *Sacred Music*, the official publication of the new Church Music Association of America over which Rembert Weakland was chosen to preside. Beginnings were optimistic, even enthusiastic. Prominent and talented musicians from all over the United States expressed an interest in associating with others who were committed to the cause of appropriate music for the worship of God. Rembert Weakland envisioned "an open forum for ideas and knowledge, for opinions and counter-opinions," a conscientious response of those bonded together in a common search "for excellence in Church music, for that which is the best man has to offer musically."[44] From the outset, Weakland acknowledged the problem of alienation.

mend that which it feels to be the best of the compositions appearing for the Liturgy." Rembert G. Weakland, "The Church Music Association of America," *Sacred Music* 92 (1965), p. 2.

42. J. Vincent Higginson, "History of the Saint Gregory Society," *Catholic Choirmaster* 26 (1940), p. 57.

43. J. Vincent Higginson, "Brief History of the Society of St. Gregory," *Catholic Choirmaster* 50 (1964), p. 180.

44. Weakland, "The Church Music Association of America," *op. cit.*, pp. 1–2.

Church musicians throughout this country are much divided among themselves on what should be done, on what is good "Church" music and what is not, and on the path that future Church music should take.[45]

However, he thought that a common commitment to work within the spirit of the Church and its directives would be enough to hold warring factions together. He was wrong. There was far too much division beneath the diversity, and at the fifth international congress in Chicago/Milwaukee in 1966, it all came apart. It may have been too much to ask too soon after the Council, that a new association open to dissent be formed from the remnant of a group that had been closed to controversy, that the radical left mingle harmoniously with those whose heritage was threatened with extinction. The decision to affiliate with the intensely conservative *Consocietas* in Rome was one more step toward the association's eventual demise. It is necessary to situate *Sacred Music* within this context in order to understand its reactionary tone. Editorially, it sided with the *Consocietas* against what it perceived to be a misinterpretation of the mandates of Vatican II. It continues as a voice of protest against many of the current Church music standards and mores.

Musart, first published in 1949, was the journal of the National Catholic Music Educators Association, adjunct to the National Catholic Educators Association before it branched out on its own after the Council. Although its membership was comprised of teachers and liturgists committed to promoting a closer integration between school and church music and to fostering research in music education, it was never a major force in Church music renewal in the United States. The association and its journal ceased in 1976.

Pastoral Music is the bi-monthy journal of the National Association of Pastoral Musicians, an organization of musicians and clergy devoted to the improvement of music at the parish level. Initiated in 1976, the Association seeks to foster the principles of Vatican II through a network of local chapters, regional and national conventions, and a periodical that attempts to bridge the gap between liturgical theologian and parish musician. Past issues of

45. *Ibid.*

Pastoral Music, often thematically oriented, have explored the meaning of music ministry from a pastoral perspective, and raised awareness to a variety of related concerns according to a carefully constructed editorial design. Although committed to serve the average or beginning parish musician, the journal takes the professional musician seriously and is liturgically and theologically sound. A perusal of its articles will yield an accurate reflection of the American Church music situation of the late 1970's and early '80's.

Articles on Catholic Church music have appeared now and then in a variety of periodicals during this century, particularly those oriented toward liturgy. For example, the Liturgical Conference usually dealt with the music question during its annual liturgical week and those proceedings were recorded and published. Its official publication, *Liturgy*, continues to include a perspective on music. *Orate Fratres* (later, *Worship*), the pioneer publication that spearheaded the liturgical movement in the United States in 1926, took ten years to decide "to devote more attention to sacred music," so that music "will no longer be an occasional and temporary guest in its pages" because "it will consequently be our aim to bring to light the 'place' of music in liturgy."[46] It has only partly succeeded in this. While *Worship* did devote considerable space to Erik Routley's comprehensive review of hymnals in the late 1970's and has published articles of substance periodically, Church music is seldom featured. *Liturgical Arts*, since its beginning in 1932, has occasionally included an article on music. Of special note is *Concilium*, a series instituted as a tool for the exploration of theology in the post-Conciliar age of renewal. Introduced in 1964 by associate editors Karl Rahner and Edward Schillebeeckx and directed toward those who carry out pastoral tasks in the Church, *Concilium* has sometimes featured articles on Church music that challenge traditional assumptions. Periodicals that occasionally include a piece on Catholic Church music, far too numerous to mention by name, cover a broad spectrum of audiences and attitudes, of content and style, from the secular *Musical Quarterly* to *Catholic Mind*, *America*, and *Commonweal*. The vast array of material embedded in these volumes offers a wealth

46. Dom Ermin Vitry, "Liturgical Apostolate and Musical Restoration," *Orate Fratres* 10 (1935/36), pp. 54, 56.

of information about the evolution of Catholic Church music in the post-Conciliar Church.

EVALUATION OF THE LITERATURE

What is most striking about this survey is not so much what is present in the literature but what is not. Missing from the American agenda is a systematically articulated theology for Catholic Church music.[47] Although this statement is accurate as it stands, some qualification is in order.

A doctoral dissertation by Alfred Pike entitled *A Theology of Music* was published by The Gregorian Institute of America in 1953. By the author's own admission, the dissertation is not about liturgical music at all but is rather a composer's attempt to evaluate and vindicate great secular music in light of the indifference of the Church. It belongs more in the category of philosophy or aesthetics, as it examines the phenomenon of the art of music from Scholastic premises.

In the twenty-fifth anniversary issue of *Orate Fratres* in 1951, Ermin Vitry tossed this challenge to the future:

> One may confidently hope that a not too distant future will see well-grounded scholars . . . tax their discernment in the interpretation of authentic sources. It will be their task to follow the sinuous path of music in the living tradition of the Church, to outline a theology of sacred music, and to determine the spiritual implications of sung prayer.[48]

It is fitting that Dom Vitry, that venerable pioneer of liturgical song for the people and dedicated chant enthusiast should be the one to

---

47. Protestants in Germany have long been active in this area: Rene Wallau, *Die Musik in ihrer Gottesbeziehung: Zur theologischen Deutung der Musik* (1948); Edmund Schlink, *Zum theologischen Problem der Musik* (1950); Oskar Söhngen, *"Zur Theologie der Music," Theologische Literaturzeitung* (1950), pp. 15–24, *Theologische Grundlagen der Kirchenmusik* (1961) and *Theologie der Musik* (1967); Julius Tyciak, *Theologie in Hymnen: Theologische Perspectiven der byzantinischen Liturgie* (1973). On the Catholic side, Winfried Kurzschenkel in *Die theologische Bestimmung der Musik* (1971) considers developments in Catholic theology and Church music only peripherally.

48. "Music and Prayer," *Orate Fratres* 25 (1951), p. 550.

remind us of the real agenda. The demands of adjustment and change resulting from the Council had to take priority during the past decades, but now that the "how-to's" have been thoroughly addressed, it is time to consider the "why."

In 1976, Robert Skeris published a theological interpretation of the musical imagery of the ecclesiastical writers of the ante-Nicene Church, with an emphasis on the image of Orpheus.[49] His work is a remarkable collection of primary sources, both in their original language and in translation. While he does not address the present situation directly, his commentary on the "new song" motif in late Judaism and early Christianity is an important first step in the construction of a theology of music for worship.

In 1979, Quentin Faulkner proposed a list of topics that seminary music education should cover, classifying them under the categories of Historical-Theological Investigations and Theological Practical Inquiries, stating:

> The mandatory study of music in seminaries should be both practical and theological. It should be the task of major seminaries to ... address from a theological perspective any musical misconceptions or malpractices ... As important as the acquisition of practical skills is, the study of music from a theological perspective is probably even more vital. ... [50]

From a survey of major seminaries in this country, Faulkner learned that there are still no standard guidelines for musical instruction for future priests and that some seminaries still do not have a trained musician on their faculty. Most music education remains on a practical and aesthetical level. While performance and quality are significant concerns that cannot be ignored, Faulkner feels that these must proceed from a thorough grasp of all the theological factors involved. He is right, but his solution is premature. It is not really possible at present to acquaint students with "the historical relationship of the church and music from a theological perspective," nor is it sufficient simply "to let them grapple anew with the questions that have engaged theologians and musicians since the early years of Christianity."[51] Such an

---

49. Skeris, *op. cit.*
50. "Teaching Music to Future Priests," *Liturgy* 24 (1979), p. 36.
51. *Ibid.*

exercise may help students to reflect theologically, which is a value, but it will not yield a proper understanding of the Church's theology of music because it is not possible to teach such a theology when one has not yet been articulated. Much valuable information can be gained from a serious consideration of the issues, but without a specific frame of reference, it may be difficult sometimes to separate opinion from fact.

There have been scattered efforts to come up with some tangible theological substance. In a 1980 master's thesis, Charles Pottie examined the theological meaning of music in Christian worship as expressed in the writings of two contemporaries, Jesuit liturgical musician Joseph Gelineau and the late Protestant hymnologist, Erik Routley.[52] Although representative of very different traditions, these men were selected as church musicians who have consistently tried to approach their task theologically. Both have been deeply involved pastorally in worship and both are widely published. The following are Pottie's conclusions. For Gelineau, who represents a liturgical tradition, the music of worship has theological meaning when it ministers to the liturgical assembly and its liturgical actions by expressing for them faith, hope and love in the God who creates, redeems and makes holy a people in the image of the Son.[53] Routley, who represents the reformed, free church tradition, grounds his theology of worship in the pattern, shape and direction of God's Word as communicated in the sacred scriptures. Music aids in the communication of this Good News in Christ and has a theological dimension when it also speaks of the Word of God—the crucified and risen Christ. Music serves the Word of God, as proclaimed and preached in the church, calling, challenging and enabling the human family to come to its full maturity as sons and daughters of God.[54] Pottie has set a direction that is well worth pursuing. An analysis of the works of those in all traditions who have made a substantial contribution to the development of Christian church music theory and theology is sure to yield valuable data for constructing a basic theology of church music that is ecumenically acceptable.

52. *A More Profound Alleluia! Gelineau and Routley on Music In Christian Worship* (Washington: The Pastoral Press, 1984).

53. *Ibid.* p. 27.

54. *Ibid.* pp. 49–52.

In 1981, Tom Conry penned some lines toward a revisionist theology of liturgical music that calls into question certain prevailing assumptions.[55] Among his nine theses are the following central points. If the mission of the Church is not to preserve the social order nor to conserve a specific ritual tradition but to build, proclaim, and celebrate the Kingdom of God, why does the ecclesial debate continue to revolve around the wrong questions, such as permissible texts and translations? If the object of the rite is not to reenact or recreate a historical event but to educate (catechetize) and inflame with passion (evangelize), how can cultural adaptation help to bridge the gap between two very different times and places, that of Jesus and our own? If the purpose of music and text is not merely to affirm widely held values or to invoke participation but to provoke a decision (*metanoia*) regarding our commitment to the values and person of Jesus and one another, according to what criteria must ritual music be evaluated in order to enable each community to accomplish this goal?[56] There is no doubt that Conry is asking the right questions when he calls upon the Church to focus on the critical issues, but where is the theological guideline to help shape a proper response?

In January of 1983, Edward Foley presented a paper to the music study group of the North American Academy of Liturgy entitled, "Toward A Working Definition of Music in Ritual: A Pre-Theological Investigation" (published by the Pastoral Press, 1984), in which he examines the relationship between music and ritual as a first step toward understanding how music is integral to worship. He garners insights from philosophy, linguistics, and the behavioral and social sciences that depict music as a phenomenon of power, as a form of communication, and as a symbol. This serious attempt to incorporate the data of secular disciplines into the dialogue concerning music and theology is an important step in the right direction. Any theology of church music that arises out of the present time must be firmly rooted in an understanding of the music of this world.

It is clear from the preceding examples that the theological conversation has begun. In addition to the issues cited above,

55. "Toward a Revisionist Theology of Liturgical Music and Text," *Pastoral Music* 5 (1981), pp. 26–31.

56. *Ibid.*, pp. 26–28.

concern for the theological implications of liturgical texts has been part of the dialogue in this country for some time. Many recent writings can claim to be prolegomena to an explicit, systematic theology of Catholic Church music consonant with the culture of today. Such a theology, if ever articulated, would have to take cognizance of what already exists ecumenically, although even here American activity is sparse,[57] and most certainly would develop along ecumenical lines.

Another serious gap has become apparent from this bibliographic survey. Missing from the literature on Catholic Church music is any significant reference to the vast field of biblical scholarship pertaining to early Christian hymns.[58] Aside from a familiarity with the more obvious texts, various theological assertions regarding these and the more cryptic passages have for the most part been ignored. Exegetical analyses of New Testament Christological hymns and credal acclamations have not only not been integrated into the Catholic understanding of Church music development but are not even present in the dialogue.

What is particularly astonishing is the inaccessibility of historical data regarding the evolution of Catholic Church music in America for the period following Vatican II. What exists is either unorganized, inaccurate, or incomplete and, for the most part, must be gleaned from periodicals or proceedings of musical events. In reviewing Francis Schmitt's *Church Music Transgressed*, Richard Schuler concluded:

> The fact remains, however, that someone should write a factual history of the church music of this century... Much of this information is not in writing but remains in the memories of those who made the history.[59]

---

57. Erik Routley, *Church Music and Theology* (1959) and "Theology For Church Musicians," *Theology Today* 34 (1977), pp. 20–28; James R. Carley, "The Theology of Music in Worship," *Encounter* 24 (1963), pp. 365–378; Jay W. Wilkey, "Prolegomena To A Theology of Music," *Review and Expositor* 69 (1972), pp. 507–517; F. Thomas Trotter, "A Theology of Church Music," *The Choral Journal* 14 (1974), p. 15; H. Myron Braun, "Sunday the Musician Was A Theologian," *The Christian Ministry* (1977), pp. 12–16; "Theology of Church Music" in *Key Words In Church Music*, ed. by Carl Schalk (St. Louis: Concordia, 1978), pp. 348–351; Harry Eskrew and Hugh McElrath, "The Hymn and Theology," in *Sing With Understanding* (Nashville: Broadman Press, 1980), pp. 59–71.

58. See Chapter 6, Footnote 6.

59. *Sacred Music* 104 (1977), p. 37.

The need for documentation is evident here.

It is easier to list what the literature lacks than to evaluate what is there. Two concerns leap out from pre-Conciliar literature: legislation and Gregorian chant. During the first half of this century, reflection on church music was dominated by the *motu proprio* of Pius X and its categories of theory and fact. Anniversaries of the decree are occasions to revisit the text again, seldom with any new insight, never with an intention to question its assumptions. Much writing is justification for chant and polyphony or an interpretation of what kind of modern music might be termed appropriate. Commentaries are plentiful; wishful thinking surfaces now and then. There is little really creative thought.

The Conciliar period might be said to extend beyond the duration of the Council, through the revision of rites to the publication of the last of the revised books. This period is strongly influenced by *Sacrosanctum concilium* and the Instructions that follow in its wake. Commentaries and handbooks reflect the need to interpret and to implement, to convince as well as explain. Wide swings of the pendulum between innovation and retrenchment, as well as a bedrock of reasoned order, characterize this time. The vocabulary of the writing echoes the chaos and confusion, the shock and uncertainty, the anger and alienation of a people cut loose from its moorings. Positions are established that will extend the polarization beyond this transitional phase.

The post-Conciliar period is characterized by accommodation to the revised rites and their established texts. At first the literature is preoccupied with instructing and redefining, with establishing norms for participation, and a clarification of roles. Eventually, emphasis on communication shifts to a concern for meaning, and accommodation to culture evolves from accommodation to rite. A tendency to moderation accompanies a trend toward settling in. There is a burst of literary activity with a motif of enculturation. Composers and pastoral musicians are seriously addressed. The literature of late indicates a shift toward more serious thought.

There have been positive additions to the literature of Catholic Church music since the Council, and there are persons deserving of mention as having contributed with some consistency to the challenging of assumptions and the development of thought. Joseph Gelineau and Bernard Huijbers are well known in the

United States. Helmut Hucke is widely read. These men are Europeans.[60] Americans, on the other hand, have not been silent. Since Vatican II, there has been a slow but steady building of a scholarly foundation. Rembert Weakland, musician and liturgist who is presently Archbishop of Milwaukee, is a prominent voice who regularly articulates both problem and potential with authority and consideration. His address to a church music forum in 1967 remains a classic questioning of the state of the art.

> There is no music of a liturgical golden age to which we can turn, because the treasures we have are the product of ages that do not represent an ideal of theological thinking in relationship to liturgy ... Theologically, the problem for the future revolves around the Church's relationship to the world. Music is but one aspect of the whole.[61]

In an address to the Federation of Diocesan Liturgical Commissions in 1973, Patrick Collins pointed out that "every answer is largely conditioned by the question asked," suggesting that ten years after the promulgation of the Council's historic liturgy decree it was time to "review and question the assumptions behind the positions of both church musician and liturgist." His challenge to the assembly:

> I would like to suggest to you a new question, a new ground on which to base the nature of our common colloquy.[62]

The question he poses is this:

> How can we put our knowledge and skills as liturgists and musicians at the service of worshipping communities so that they may express and experience the sacred in a manner best suited to them and in conformity with our faith?[63]

Collins suggests that the real problem is one of faith, and it arises from an assumption concerning the sacred that not everyone

60. See bibliography for selected list of their publications.
61. "Music As Art in Liturgy," *Worship* 41 (1967), pp. 6, 14.
62. "Music and Worship: Thoughts On An Anniversary," *Musart* 26 (Winter, 1974), p. 3.
63. *Ibid.*, p. 9.

shares. This assumption underlies many of the statements on liturgical music in *Sacrosanctum concilium* and in those instructions interpreting the Conciliar decree. Commenting on *Music in Catholic Worship*, the document released by the Bishops Committee on the Liturgy in 1972, which he helped to prepare, Collins admits that "no one on our committee was willing to tackle theologically the relationship between the sacred and the secular as it applies to music in worship."[64] Although there has been some interim progress, it is evident from the literature of the last ten years that this fundamental question still waits to be addressed.

Pastoral Music is the only journal to approach the subject of music and theology seriously and with some consistency. In conceptualizing the overall design of the volumes, publisher Virgil Funk sought to integrate a study of Sacraments and Liturgy of the Hours with an examination of *Music in Catholic Worship* (document of the BCL, 1972) and the role of the minister of music, relating theoretical and theological guidelines to the pragmatics of actual practice. The journal has dealt with a theology of Church music only briefly on occasion, choosing instead to focus on those developments in liturgical theology that influence the practice of music. Limitations imposed by the expectations of its audience prevents topics from being examined systematically and in depth. Nevertheless, these volumes offer considerable foundational information for a constructive theology of music.

Liturgist Nathan Mitchell wrote for the National Association of Pastoral Musicians in 1979:

> Music begins when we become attentive to the voices that are already speaking in an environment. This is why, as every musician knows, there is such an intense and intimate connection between the facts of justice and the facts of bodily life: the relationships of touch and movement, breath and blood, rhythm and repose.[65]

This passage reflects a sense for symbol and integration, for metaphor and meaning, that has recently entered the literature on

---

64. *Ibid.*, p. 8.
65. "A God Who Hears," *Pastoral Music* 4 (Oct/Nov 1979), p. 31.

church music.[66] Such writings, influenced to a large extent by developments in anthropology, ethnomusicology, and aesthetics,[67] give evidence of a growing awareness of the relationship of Church music to the world at large and an effort to interpret the specifics of music for worship in light of the phenomenon of music in general. This is a subject that the Catholic Church in America must continue to address. For the moment, European scholars, particularly Protestants, are a giant step ahead.

Clearly the dialogue concerning Catholic Church music is moving toward a new level of awareness. There have been attempts to introduce a theological perspective. There is, however, no theological guideline whereby standard assumptions might be evaluated and previous conclusions reviewed. This is part of the unfinished agenda of Vatican II. To develop theological criteria for the use of music in the liturgy will not be an easy task, but it can and must be done. This book is intended as a step in that direction, a serious attempt to move toward a theology of Catholic Church music. Its purpose is to raise the question: why sing?—and to establish the question as prior to what is sung and how.

---

66. Such as: Regis Duffy, "Pastoral Music—Its Own Art Form," *Pastoral Music* 5 (June-July 1981), pp. 27–30; Joseph Fitzer, "Instrumental Music in the Liturgy," *Worship* 45 (1971), pp. 539–553; Edward Foley, "On the 'Breath of Dawn' and Other Metaphors," *Pastoral Music* 5 (April-May 1981), pp. 23–25; Joseph Gelineau, "Are New Forms of Liturgical Singing and Music Developing?", *Concilium* 52 (1970), pp. 37–46; *The Liturgy Today and Tomorrow* (New York: Paulist, 1978); and "What No Ear Has Heard. . .," *Music and Liturgy* 5 (1979), pp. 86–93.

67. For example: Susanne K. Langer, *Philosophy In A New Key* (1942) and *Feeling and Form* (1953); Leonard B. Meyer, *Emotion and Meaning in Music* (1956); Alan P. Merriam, *The Anthropology of Music* (1964); Curt Sachs, *The Wellsprings of Music* (1965); Victor Zuckerkandl, *Sound and Symbol* (1969); and others.

II

VATICAN II
AND THE LITURGY:
HISTORICAL OVERVIEW,
THEORETICAL
PRESUPPOSITIONS

2

Vatican II As The Culmination
Of The Liturgical Movement

THE MODERN LITURGICAL MOVEMENT DATES FROM THE EARLY NINETEENTH century. A singular theme encompassing multiple variations, it unfolds as a climactic prelude to the decisions of Vatican II. Generally speaking, it began as a conservative force dedicated to the restoration of the best of Catholic tradition centered in its cult, and it happened "because it was necessary."[1] Liturgical chaos, fostered by an excessive individualism that flourished on subjective devotions, reflected an absence of community that was characteristic of the times. The struggle for community became the basis of a new ecclesiology and the key to liturgical revival. Ritual was thought to be capable of creating a sense of community that could overcome social alienation. The rediscovery of communal forms stressed the conception of the Church as the Body of Christ with an emphasis on community of persons, preparing the way for the People of God to emerge as a foundational image within the hierarchically ordered institutional Church.

This modern liturgical movement falls into three distinctive periods prior to Vatican II. These may be characterized as a nineteenth-century monastic phase, a period of pastoral emphasis, and a period of growing acceptance and legitimation preparatory to the Council.

1. Romano Guardini, in a letter to the bishop of Mainz, 1940. In: The Sacerdotal Communities of Saint-Severin of Paris and Saint-Joseph of Nice, *The Liturgical Movement,* tr. by Lancelot Sheppard (New York: Hawthorn Books, 1964), p. 9.

Dom Prosper Guéranger is generally recognized as the "father of the liturgical movement" for his restoration of liturgical vitality to the defunct monastery of Solesmes in France. The movement that burgeoned from his initiative was rooted in an aesthetic that looked to the patristic period as the Church's "golden age." Guéranger's contributions were many, and he has earned both criticism and praise. Essentially an ultramontanist with a conservative bent, he lacked the vision to comprehend that authentic liturgy must be embodied in contemporary local forms. His tastes were Roman and gothic, with a preference for antiquity over the modern, and mystery (Latin) over comprehension (vernacular), in defiance of the historical-scientific tendencies of the times. Yet his concern to communicate and to educate touched clergy and laity alike through his publications[2] and the model liturgical congregation he had established at Solesmes. His efforts at reform sparked a liturgical revival in Benedictine abbeys throughout Europe.[3] These too were dedicated to the rediscovery of community through the restoration of traditional ritual forms. A clerical and academic emphasis characterized this initial phase of the movement as monasteries turned to archaeology and ancient manuscripts in search of an authentic past. Nevertheless, the success of later pastoral adaptations may be traced to the scholarly commitment and integrity of the movement's pioneers.

Two events after the turn of the century mark the beginning of the liturgical movement's parochial phase, which focused on transmitting liturgical discoveries to the Church at large. The *motu proprio* of Pius X on sacred music (1903)[4] stressed lay participation in the Mass. The address of Dom Lambert Beauduin to the Catholic Congress at Malines (1909) called attention to the importance of the liturgy and stimulated widespread response.[5]

---

2. *Institutions liturgiques* (1840); *Année liturgique*, 6 vol. (1841–1866).

3. In Germany, Beuron and Maria Laach, foundations of Solesmes; in Belgium, Maredsous, founded by Beuron; Mont-César at Louvain and Saint-André at Lophem, near Bruges, both foundations of Maredsous.

4. This decree appears in two places in *Acta Sanctae Sedis* 6 (1903): in Italian, *Tra le sollecitudini*, pp. 329–339 and in Latin translation, *Inter plurimas pastoralis*, pp. 387–395.

5. Beauduin's desiderata: that the Roman Missal be translated and its use promoted widely among the faithful as their chief devotional book; that all piety grow more "liturgical"; that Gregorian chant be fostered according to the pope's request; that choir members make annual retreats in some center of liturgical life.

The movement remained associated with monastic orders, but it took on a different tone. Monasteries became centers of learning oriented toward the parish. They encouraged lay participation and imparted needed skills. Under Beauduin, Mont-César in Belgium hosted liturgical weeks aimed at parish renewal and disseminated a vernacular translation of the missal that received strong popular support. Maria Laach in Germany, best known for its liturgical influence through the *Mysterientheologie* of Dom Odo Casel, was also famous for its liturgical weeks, which appealed particularly to the educated. In Austria, Pius Parsch promoted *Volksliturgie* and popularized an understanding of the calendar through his commentary on the liturgical year. Dom Virgil Michel introduced the liturgical movement to America, inaugurating *Orate Fratres* (later, *Worship*) at St. John's Abbey, Collegeville (Minnesota), in 1926, a publication that spans the movement's development in the States from its beginnings up through the present day. National Liturgical Weeks dating from 1940 brought local liturgists to the forefront, ignited grassroots enthusiasm, and gave the movement in this country its decidedly American stamp.

Intense activity characterizes the third phase of the movement prior to Vatican II. Energy is spent on making liturgy happen on the local level, as parishes grapple with the innovative reality of a return to dynamic traditions. At the same time there are clear signs of digging in and settling down. The movement finally receives official ecclesiastical approval.[6] Centers for liturgical research are established outside the monastic framework.[7] Liturgical congresses occur at intervals.[8] Widespread experimentation focuses on changes in rubrics governing praxis. Legislation increases, chronicling the dynamics of change.[9] What was marginal becomes legitimate, and is incorporated into the system, as movement

As summarized in Louis Bouyer, *Liturgical Piety* (Notre Dame: University Press, 1955), p. 61.

6. Although liturgical initiatives were encouraged, even actively promoted, by Pius X and Pius XI, the liturgical movement received official Church approval with Pius XII in *Mediator Dei* (1947).

7. Notably, the *Centre de Pastorale liturgique* in France (1943); Trier Institute in Germany (1947); the Notre Dame School of Liturgy in the United States (1947).

8. At Maria Laach (1951), Lugano (1953), Assisi (1956).

9. For a list of liturgical legislation prior to and following Vatican II, see Bibliography: Primary Sources.

merges with institution to revitalize the structure and then, as a separate entity, disappear.

LITURGICAL LEGISLATION

As the liturgy, its meaning and practice, took root in geographical centers and began to penetrate the Church, there was a parallel development in official legislation. Rome, of course, moves slowly. Nevertheless, there was movement. A review of the corpus of liturgical legislation reveals an alternating rhythm of initiative and response. Some statements are an invitation or a directive to put a principle into practice, others give permission for deeds or directions that are already a fact.

Pius X (Pope from 1903–1914) can be credited with bringing the institutional Church to the brink of revolution. His statements on Church music,[10] Psalter and Breviary,[11] and the Eucharist[12] addressed issues central to the prayer life of the Church. He initiated active participation by urging that the people be trained to sing the Latin chants. He ordered the psalter to be rearranged and recited in its entirety weekly in the Divine Office, promising a thorough revision of both breviary and missal. He revised the calendar of feasts and seasons, so that Sundays and ferias, appropriate lections and responsories, would be restored to their rightful place. He promoted frequent, even daily reception of the Eucharist and encouraged the participation of children, establishing that first Communion could be taken at an earlier age of discretion than was traditional at the time. These were more than incidental changes. They functioned as change agents, precipitating radical revisions and the search for liturgical integrity that is not yet at an end.

Pius XI (Pope from 1922–1939) is best known to liturgists for his Apostolic Constitution on Liturgy and Gregorian Chant.[13] His

10. *Tra le sollecitudini, motu proprio,* November 22, 1903.

11. *Divino afflatu,* Apostolic Constitution, November 1, 1911; *Abhinc Duos Annos, motu proprio,* October 23, 1913.

12. *Sacra Tridentina Synodus,* Decree of the Sacred Congregation of the Council on daily reception of Holy Communion, December 22, 1905; *Quam singulari,* Decree of the Sacred Congregation on the Sacraments, concerning the age for admission to First Communion, August 8, 1910.

13. *Divini cultus,* Apostolic Constitution, December 20, 1928.

appreciation of liturgy was already evident in his earlier encyclical instituting the new feast of Christ the King.[14] Here he spoke of its teaching power, of how the annual celebration of sacred mysteries was far more effective than official pronouncements of the Church. "Pronouncements speak once; feasts speak every year, in fact forever" and "influence both mind and heart, affecting the whole of [our] nature," stimulating a deeper penetration of the truths God has revealed.[15] In *Divini cultus*, he reiterates the close connection between dogma and the liturgy, reviving the ancient formula, *"legem credendi lex statuat supplicandi,"* which claimed that the standard of faith finds its prior expression in the sacred formulas of the liturgy. During his pontificate the *Missa recitata* or Dialogue Mass became standard practice internationally, another step toward active participation of the laity as the norm.[16]

Pius XII (Pope from 1939–1958) is without doubt the liturgical movement's mentor. Through the exercise of his teaching authority, he fostered the movement's aims, brought to fruition its tentative efforts, and did more than any single person to prepare the way for the conclusions of Vatican II. He gave legitimacy to what was perceived by many as a fringe activity or passing fad, and early in his pontificate, comprehended the deeper theological issues and proceeded to give them voice. He wrote two encyclicals considered to be the classic texts of the liturgical apostolate: *Mystici Corporis* (1943), a statement on the nature of the Church, and *Mediator Dei* (1947), which marks the first time that liturgy was the subject of an encyclical. *Divino afflante Spiritu* (1943), his encyclical promoting biblical studies, formally recognized exegetical progress and the historical-critical approach, encouraged daily reading of Scripture, and prepared the way for the full recovery of the Liturgy of the Word. From the end of World War II until his death, the pontificate of Pius XII is a syllabus of liturgical growth and change: revision of the Psalter (1945), permission for the use of the Chinese language in the Mass (1949), restoration of the Easter Vigil (1951), instruction on art in the liturgy (1952), new discipline for the Eucharistic fast (1953), permission for the

14. *Quas primas*, Encyclical Letter, December 11, 1925.
15. *Ibid.*, art. 25. In R. Kevin Seasoltz, *The New Liturgy* (New York: Herder and Herder, 1966), p. 42.
16. Officially permitted in decree of Sacred Congregation of Rites (S.R.C., No. 4375), August 4, 1922.

celebration of evening Mass (1953), use of English in the celebration of certain sacraments (1954), simplification of the rubrics governing liturgy (1955), the new Order of Holy Week (1955), a compendium on sacred music praxis (1955), the preparation of bilingual Rituals (1956), the validation of con-celebration (1957), permission for the use of Gothic vestments (1957), permission for the vernacular in various parts of the Mass (1958), final thoughts on sacred music and the liturgy (1958).[17] Even before his death he was referred to as patron of pastoral liturgy. In his address to the First International Congress of Pastoral Liturgy at Assisi in 1956, he summarized his thinking: "The liturgical movement is . . . a sign of the providential disposi-tions of God for the present time, of the movement of the Holy Spirit in the Church, to draw [people] more closely to the mysteries of the faith and the riches of grace which flow from the active participation of the faithful in the liturgical life."[18]

It is important to note that popes ordinarily exercise their authority over liturgical matters through the Congregation of Rites, an agency introduced in 1588 to monitor the implementa-tion of the decrees of Trent regarding public worship.[19]

17. For titles, see Bibliography: Primary Sources, under Pre-Conciliar Legisla-tion (Universal): Music, Liturgy.

18. *Vous Nous avez demandé*, Allocution, September 22, 1956. In: Seasoltz, *op. cit.*, p. 234.

19. The work of the Congregation of Sacred Rites fell into two basic categories: worship in general, which included supervision of rites, reform of ceremonies and service books, resolution of controversies, responsibility for feasts of saints; and the processes of beatification and canonization. Once books authorized by Trent were promulgated, liturgical activity centered on response to difficulties, rather than on revision. To offset emphasis on beatification and canonization, Leo XIII added the Liturgical Commission (1891) to codify past decrees and advise the Congregation on liturgical matters, and the Historico-liturgical Commission (1902) to handle historical questions. Pius X added the Commission on Ecclesiastical Music (1904) and restricted the Congregation's activity to worship and the cult of the saints, distinguishing sacramental rites from sacramental discipline, the latter exceeding its jurisdiction. Further reorganization included: the suppression of the three attached commissions (1914); a tripartite structure: for beatification and canonization, for sacred rites, for historical concerns (1930); addition of the Pontifical Commission for the General Restoration of the Liturgy (1948), whose task of revision and reform of liturgical books was assumed by the *Consilium* for Implementation of the Constitution on the Sacred Liturgy (Paul VI, *Sacram liturgicam, Motu proprio*, Jan. 25, 1964) rather than by the Congregation of

Established to ensure strict uniformity, its principal task has been to issue statements in response to problems, particularly those of a rubrical nature. At times it is difficult to distinguish decrees emanating from the office of the Congregation from those of the reigning pontiff, as the Congregation will often prepare and issue statements pertaining to public worship as being in accord with the mind of the pope. Aside from classification, introduction and signature, seasoned readers can identify congregational documents by their content and tone, as these usually reflect the office's mandate to "exercise vigilance that the sacred rites and ceremonies be carefully observed in the celebration of Mass"[20] and ordinarily are concerned with rubrical specifics. Decrees of a more general nature issued by the Congregation as universally binding are listed with the significant legislation promulgated by a pope during his pontificate and are usually included whenever reference is made to papal legislation.

It is also important to mention here that the Code of Canon Law published by Pope Benedict XV in 1918 omitted liturgical law or what might be called the canon law of the liturgy.[21] Consequently, Council documents, papal decrees, and instructions, statements issued by the Congregation of Rites, papers published by episcopal synods, and the official liturgical books (Missal, Pontifical, Ritual, Breviary) remain the prime sources for such legislation.[22] Popes are quite often preoccupied with revising the official books. Indeed, the task of radical revision was one of the first challenges facing Paul VI after the Council. These texts represent the crystalization of the liturgical vision of Vatican II.

Rites. The latter was eventually divided into two congregations, one for the Causes of Saints and one for Divine Worship (Paul VI, *Sacrum Rituum Congregatio*, Apostolic Constitution, May 8, 1969); *Consilium* was absorbed into CDW. Finally, both the Congregation for the Discipline of the Sacraments and the Congregation for Divine Worship were suppressed by Paul VI (*Constans Nobis Studium*, Apostolic Constitution, July 11, 1975) and the present Congregation for the Sacraments and Divine Worship was formed. See *NCE* 12: 518–519.

20. *Codex Iuris Canonici*, can. 253, as quoted in *NCE* 12: 519.

21. Canon No. 1257 contains this reference to liturgy: "It pertains to the Apostolic See alone to order the sacred liturgy and to approve the liturgical books."

22. Students of the liturgy now have available to them a comprehensive vernacular edition of recent liturgical legislation in *Documents On the Liturgy*, Liturgical Press, 1983.

Clearly, then, a full century of intense liturgical development preceded the Second Vatican Council. It was a time of struggle between legitimacy and innovation. Officially, the Church continued to espouse a restrictive stance even as its externals were gradually altered. The tension between tradition and experimentation, always present to some extent, polarized at times into opposing camps. Those who viewed liturgical laws as absolute condemned the deviations of those who accepted the same laws simply as guidelines to praxis. These opposing viewpoints surfaced in the Council during its deliberations.

THE COUNCIL IN PERSPECTIVE

The decision to convoke a Council was serendipitous. Pope John XXIII admitted it was a "sudden flash of inspiration."[23] Three months into his pontificate, his sole concern the "*bonum animarum*," his foremost desire to "meet the spiritual demands of the present time accurately and forcefully,"[24] this interim pope boldly announced his intention to convene the Twenty-First Ecumenical Council of the Universal Church. He anticipated an event directed by the Spirit, a modernization of ecclesiastical legislation according to the "applications the Spirit of the Lord will surely suggest to us as we proceed."[25] He desired "a new Pentecost,"[26] *aggiornamento* (literally, "a bringing up to date"), a genuine renewal that would eventually lead to a reunion of all Christians not yet in harmony with the Apostolic See.

The so-called Apostolic Council of Jerusalem (Acts 15:1–29) is the recognized prototype of the Ecumenical Council. When the leadership[27] met regarding disciplinary matters, they announced a

23. John XXIII, *Gaudet Mater Ecclesia*, Address at the Opening of Vatican II, October 11, 1962. In *The Pope Speaks* (hereafter, *TPS*), vol. 8 (1962), p. 209.

24. John XXIII, *Questa festiva*, Address to the Roman Cardinals, January 25, 1959. In *TPS* 5 (1959), p. 398.

25. *Ibid.*, p. 401.

26. John XXIII, *Humanae salutis*, Apostolic Constitution, December 25, 1961. In *TPS* 7 (1961), p. 360.

27. Peter, James, Paul, and Barnabas are mentioned here. The account in Galatians (2:1–10) includes Titus and John. There is some controversy about whether or not the meeting reported in both sources is the same.

formal decision that was communicated to the churches elsewhere (Acts 15:22–31; cf. 21:25). During the next 250 years, territorial synods[28] met regarding theological and disciplinary matters that called for clarification or decision.[29] It is not until the fourth century and the Council of Nicaea (325 A.D.), however, that the Church celebrates the first of its officially designated universal ecumenical councils.[30]

An ecumenical council is "the solemn exercise of the full, supreme, and universal power of the episcopal college"[31] and is representative of the whole Church. Primary members are all residential bishops in hierarchical communion with the bishop of Rome. The Council possesses a supernatural power to guide, guard, and govern the Church, which is manifested through the natural, legal framework of decisions, decrees, constitutions, and other forms of juridical pronouncements. It is infallible in its teaching with regard to the content of faith, but any disciplinary decrees subject to temporal conditions can be changed by future Councils or popes. The pope alone has the right to convoke, preside over, and confirm an ecumenical council. Without papal confirmation of conciliar decisions, there can be no such Council for the universal Church.[32]

The twenty Councils that preceded Vatican II offer no singular pattern regarding content or style. Conciliar history is marked by controversy, and Council documents are often formulated in reaction to the threat of some external force. Earlier Councils struggled to secure the theological foundations of the Christian faith, articulating Christological and Trinitarian dogmas as safe-guards against the many heresies that challenged orthodoxy and orthopraxis. The later Lateran Councils reflected Rome's penchant for definitive structure while initiating some needed reform. The remaining Councils of the late Middle Ages were essentially

28. Especially in Asia Minor. See NCE 4: 374.

29. Major issues were the fight against Gnosticism, Marcionitism, Montanism, and other heresies, the question of the Easter date, the validity of baptism conferred by heretics.

30. According to Western tradition, there have been 21 such ecumenical councils to date. The East counts only seven, ending the list with Nicaea II (787).

31. NCE 4: 377. The term ecumenical is synonymous here with universal.

32. Ibid., pp. 377–379.

preoccupied with papal authority in the aftermath of schism, reform, the politics of reunion, and the Crusades.

Seeds of conflict sown in earlier centuries continued to germinate well beyond their appointed time, contributing to the concept of Council a climate of uncertainty and mistrust. Conciliarism, for example, sank deep, persistent roots. The perennial challenge to papal primacy and authority gained momentum during the Great Western Schism (1378–1417) when three popes simultaneously claimed Petrine prerogatives, until the contrary development culminated in the final dogmatic solution of papal infallibility defined at Vatican I.

Another factor that prevailed for centuries was the tension between *sacerdotium* and *imperium*, the relation between Church and state. The Emperor Constantine and his successors, who considered themselves Christ's representative and therefore the guardians and champions of the Church, convoked the first ecumenical councils and saw to it that Council decrees were binding by imperial law. Succeeding centuries were eventually able to erase this precedent, but the evolution of a *respublica christiana* and the entanglement of politics and religion left many a mark on conciliar structures and strategies. The principle of *cuius regio, eius religio*[33] which presided at Christendom's demise gave the Reformation a firm foothold and, to some extent, shaped the deliberations at Trent. The agenda of Vatican I (1869–70) was also determined by political factors when the Vatican was invaded while the Council was in session, diverting attention from religious matters to the pragmatic reality of protecting territorial estates. That Council never reconvened.

The effect of these dynamics on the convening of future Councils cannot be minimized. While historical realities change, vestiges of old tensions linger in conciliar precedents. When John XXIII convoked a Council after the silence of one hundred years, he knew that the Church would have to grapple with the ghosts of Councils past.

---

33. Practically speaking, this meant that the population of each geographical territory or estate was either Protestant or Catholic according to the religious persuasion of its local ruler.

THE LEGACY OF TRENT

The Council of Trent stood at a critical turning point in the history of the Church. The tenacious vitality of the Protestant Reformation and the rapidly changing world at large severely threatened the old order. The failure of previous efforts to achieve internal reform had left the Church particularly vulnerable to attack. The ferment within and outside the institution served to shape the Council's agenda, which consisted of safeguarding traditional doctrine and coming to terms with the problem of moral reform.

The Council did not proceed according to a systematic, integrated plan, nor did it reach its conclusions in light of a clearly articulated conception of the Church. Instead, it issued doctrinal and disciplinary decrees and canons in response to the critical concerns of the moment—justification by faith, the importance of scripture and the role of tradition, eucharistic theology and practice, the sacramental system, benefices, monasticism, improper behavior of clerics. After a long and fragmentary duration,[34] the Council ended without achieving its original intent, that of reuniting once again with the Protestants.

The Tridentine era of interpretation and implementation evolved in a manner that often seemed contrary to the true spirit of Trent. Those responsible for implementing the acts of the Council gradually developed an all-encompassing system that bestowed on Trent a singular authority and prestige.

The corpus of the conciliar decisions was presented as exhaustive and definitive; it was to constitute an inexhaustible code of prescriptions for every necessity, gradually elevated to decisive canons to which reference had to be made for all the needs of the Christian life. In this way, although the authority of the council was intransigently determined, isolating it ever more from the preceding productive tradition, there was nevertheless a definite movement toward an ever wider and freer interpretation of its dogmatic and disciplinary decisions. They were interpreted ac-

---

34. The Council lasted 18 years with lengthy adjournments (1545–1563) and witnessed a succession of five popes.

cording to principles and attitudes often different from, and at times even opposed to, those from which the council had taken its inspiration.[35]

Consequently, Trent remained a decisive factor in the life of the Church long after its historic events had ceased, even though its own statements were often overshadowed by subsequent interpolations.

Although the First Vatican Council was the immediate predecessor of Vatican II, the Church stood at the threshold of the latter Council still under the influence of Trent and its interpreters. Through four hundred years, Tridentine spirituality had remained formative of all facets of Catholic piety. Rigid and ill at ease with the changing times, the universal Church was clearly out of step with the modern world. This was most evident in the Tridentine Mass. The solemn spectacle performed before silent masses and overlaid with centuries of accretions bore little resemblance to the dynamic liturgical action of the early Christian Church. Pope John's *aggiornamento* challenged the prevailing rubricist mentality, not to a restoration, but to a genuine renewal that would revitalize the rituals of the Church.

THE FACT OF VATICAN II

At his election, John XXIII stunned the world with the choice of his name.[36] Shortly after, the unpredictable peasant pope surprised everyone again with his intention to convoke an ecumenical council, not in order to complete the aborted agenda of Vatican I, but as a "new day ... dawning on the Church," so that with new enthusiasm, time-honored teaching could be "studied afresh and reformulated in contemporary terms ... in a manner more consistent with a predominantly pastoral view."[37]

35. Giuseppe Alberigo, "The Council of Trent," *Concilium* 7 (1965), pp. 76–77.

36. An earlier Pope John XXIII (1410–15) was one of the three reigning popes during the last phase of the Great Western Schism. Though he continued the succession of popes deriving from the Council of Pisa (1409), the conciliar forces of the Council of Constance forced him out of office and were finally able to end the schism.

When the 2,540 Council Fathers, the *periti* (experts), and the observers of other faith expressions gathered in St. Peter's Basilica on October 11, 1962, history was in the making. Never before in the tradition of the Church had so many of such diversity come together for common cause. For the first time ever, a Council met in complete separation of Church and state, free from the threat of interference by any secular government, free too of the pressure of having to decide doctrinal or other disputes within or outside the Church. It was the first Council in history whose official position was to avoid doctrinal rigidity and condemnation, the first to be essentially and unequivocally pastoral.[38] From its inception, this Council was pervaded with the spirit of its convener, who had established a spiritual alliance with the modern world of technology, created a climate of ecumenical sensitivity and concern, and let it be known to one and all that the pastoral challenge lay in adaptation, in opening windows to the power of the Spirit, and in laying the foundations for reconciliation and peace. Vatican II came to be known, with good reason, as Pope John's Council.

Because John XXIII was attuned to the changed conditions of the world, the Council he called would address an agenda concerning "appropriate adaptation of Church discipline to the needs and conditions of our times."[39] It would be a Council of reform, not reunion, but reform as a first step toward fulfilling his hope for a united Christianity. His commitment to renewal as prerequisite to reunion led to some welcome ecumenical initiatives.[40] After four centuries, a pluriform expression of Christianity was finally accepted in principle as well as in fact. The Council would proceed to treat the Protestant perspective with consideration and respect.[41]

37. John XXIII, *Gaudet Mater Ecclesia, op. cit.,* pp. 213, 215.

38. *Ibid.,* pp. 212–213.

39. John XXIII, *Ad Petri Cathedram,* Encyclical Letter, June 29, 1959. In *TPS* 5 (1959), p. 369.

40. As part of the Council's organizational structure, John XXIII established the Secretariat for Christian Unity, which he later raised to the status of a Conciliar commission under the leadership of Augustin Cardinal Bea. Representatives of various Christian denominations were extended invitations to be present at Council sessions as observer delegates, and accepted.

41. See Council decrees: *Unitatis redintegratio,* November 21, 1964, on Ecumenism; and *Orientalium Ecclesiarum,* November 21, 1964, on the Catholic Eastern Churches, articles 24–29; and John XXIII's Address to the Observer Delegates, October 13, 1962, in *TPS* 8 (1963), pp. 225–227.

Preparation for the Council was extensive and unique. Agenda recommendations solicited from bishops and universities around the world were collected, classified, and synthesized. With the establishment of commissions on a variety of subjects, the introductory phase was brought to a close and the preparatory stage officially began. Preliminary schemata were constructed. Strict procedures were outlined for conducting the Council and for enacting its decrees.[42] When John XXIII addressed the Opening General Congregation of the Twenty-First Ecumenical Council, the "Church's best energies" had already been expended to a degree unparalleled in conciliar history.

The Council Fathers voted to address the schema on the liturgy as the first topic on their agenda. It was a wise choice. Essentials were brought to the forefront with this starting point. Those progressive and reactionary forces at work among the Council members surfaced at the outset and could be dealt with before they had time to polarize and divide. It became clear from the discussions and recommendations that those basic differences encompassed a wide range of perceptions involving not only rubrics but fundamental ecclesiology as well. The initial process of achieving consensus on issues of deepest concern set the tone for the Council as a whole and served as a transition from the Tridentine era into a radically different age. The liturgy schema was a turning point, a bridge between the old and the new. Tendencies articulated in relation to the liturgy became characteristic of the Council itself: a return to origins; the removal of accretions; the rediscovery of essentials; decentralization; adaptation; participation. This could not have happened without the persistent efforts of much that had gone before. The Church's magisterium was in fact indebted to the liturgical movement and all its pioneers.

42. See the following statements of John XXIII: *La Nostra prima*, Address on the Ecumenical Council, June 5, 1960, in *TPS* 6 (1960), pp. 231–239; *Superno Dei nutu*, Apostolic Letter establishing the preparatory commissions, June 5, 1960, *ibid.*, pp. 240–243; *Congregatos Vos*, June 11, 1961 and *Progredientes leniter*, June 20, 1961: Addresses at the opening and closing of the first session of the Central Preparatory Commission, in *TPS* 7 (1961), pp. 241–250; *Appropinquante Concilio*, August 6, 1962, *Motu proprio* establishing regulations for the Council, in *TPS* 8 (1963), pp. 282–288.

3

Sacrosanctum Concilium:
The Liturgy Decree of Vatican II

THE ACCOMPLISHMENTS OF THE LITURGICAL MOVEMENT AND THE EXTENT OF twentieth-century legislation had their influence on the Council Fathers. So much preparatory work had already been done in the theology and praxis of liturgy that closure on the liturgy schema seemed an achievable goal. Dealing with the pragmatics of public prayer would prevent the opening deliberations from slipping over into the purely speculative and, at the same time, would provide an entry into the difficult tasks ahead. As *locus theologicus*, liturgy embodied some of the Council's central themes and, in its surge toward renewal, had helped to rediscover core values inte-gral to its nature and to the Council's task. A new understanding of Christ and the significance of his resurrection; a sense of the history of salvation; an insight into the mystery of the Church as realized in the liturgical assembly; a richer theology of the sacraments, particularly the Eucharist: these were some of the insights foundational to the liturgy which the liturgical movement had already made explicit. A discussion of the liturgy schema meant that critical doctrinal issues would have to be addressed. It seemed a logical place to begin.

The preparatory Pontifical Commission on the Sacred Liturgy appointed by John XXIII constructed the schema on the liturgy from recommendations submitted by the bishops of the world. After several redactions during which the draft was considerably revised and shortened,[1] the document was sent to the General Secretariat for distribution to the Fathers. After the Solemn Opening of the Council, a Conciliar Commission on the Liturgy was elected[2] and the decision was made to place the liturgy schema at the top of the agenda. Discussion began at the Fourth General Congregation and continued through the next fourteen plenary sessions.[3] When put to a vote, the Constitution on the Liturgy was approved in principle by an overwhelming majority, subject to subsequent amendments which were voted on by the Council Fathers just before the First Session was solemnly closed.[4] Approval was given to the amended preface and the first chapter concerning General Principles for Renewing and Promoting the Sacred Liturgy. At the Council's Second Session the following year, the Constitution on the Liturgy was formally approved and promulgated as the first fruits of Vatican II. This document of liturgical reform and renewal, so radically pastoral in orientation, brought the Tridentine era officially to a close.

The Conciliar document on liturgy was promulgated in the form of a Constitution, that is, a permanent law and not simply a decree dealing with concerns of the moment. It is a disciplinary Constitution, not a dogmatic one, containing "dispositions" pertaining to praxis and not dogmatic teachings. Although Church teachings are inherent in the dispositions, these are not defined but simply taught, and the statements containing them represent the *magisterium ordinarium* of the Church.[5] The designation "Constitution" is

1. For a brief history of the schema's evolution, see Thomas Richstatter, *Liturgical Law: New Style, New Spirit* (Chicago: Franciscan Herald Press, 1977), pp. 61–66, 184ff.

2. *AAS* 55 (1963), p. 125. The Council's first act was to constitute the Conciliar commissions. To the 16 members elected to the Liturgical Commission from among the Council Fathers were added eight more nominated by the Pope, a number of *periti* (liturgists, theologians, canonists), the secretary of the Congregation of Rites. Chairman: Cardinal Larraona. Secretary: F. Antonelli, O.F.M. See Joseph Jungmann, *Commentary On the Documents of Vatican II*, Vol 1. (New York: Herder and Herder, 1967), p. 5.

3. For a summary of these discussions, see "A Guide to the Congregations and the Projects," *TPS* 8 (1963), pp. 305–312.

4. For a list of these amendments, see Bonaventura Kloppenburg, "Chronicle of Amendments of the Constitution," *The Liturgy of Vatican II*, Vol. 1 (Chicago: Franciscan Herald Press, 1966), pp. 71–94.

5. Jungmann, *op. cit.*, p. 8.

not entirely accurate, because practical norms are presented only in relationship to the Roman rite. However, since there was conscious agreement by the Council Fathers, with verbal assent from the Eastern and Oriental rites, that norms expressed in terms of a particular rite (namely, the Roman rite) would be understood to have a general application, the document remains a Constitution with principles and norms applicable to the universal Church.[6] The Council was determined to give only broad norms from which concrete application would have to be made by those responsible for implementing its decrees. *Sacrosanctum concilium* provides the broad legal framework for competent juridical bodies to determine what local liturgical practice best exemplifies the basic principles it defines.

The words which precede the Constitution's title are significant: *"Paulus Episcopus, servus servorum Dei, una cum sacrosancti Concilii Patribus. . . ."*[7] The phrase was prefixed to the document prior to its formal approval and promulgation. This statement differs sharply from the practice of previous Councils when decrees were promulgated as apostolic constitutions solely on the authority of the Bishop of Rome. Paul VI was obviously intent on honoring the principle of episcopal collegiality which had arisen early in discussions on the liturgy and would eventually emerge as foundational to the restructuring of authority in the post-Conciliar Church.[8]

Sacrosanctum concilium consists of 130 articles subdivided into seven chapters and an introduction. A declaration on revision of the calendar is appended to the text. Chapter one concerns general principles for the restoration and promotion of the liturgy and general norms for reform and renewal following upon these. Its 42 articles form the basis for a genuine renewal affecting theology and ecclesiology as well as sacrament and rite. Subsequent chapters, in sequence, address the Eucharist, other sacraments and sacramentals, the divine office, the liturgical year, sacred music, and sacred art and sacred furnishings.

---

6. Frederick McManus, *Sacramental Liturgy* (New York: Herder and Herder, 1967), p. 11.

7. *AAS* 56 (1964), p. 97. This phrase rarely appears in translation.

8. McManus, *op. cit.*

Four introductory articles give direction to the whole. The document opens by stating the overall aims of the Council and, by implication, equating these with the liturgy's own aims: to revitalize Christian life; to adapt to the needs of the present those institutions which are subject to change; to foster union among all Christian believers; to strengthen whatever might attract the whole of the human community into the household of the faith (art. 1). It is easy to recognize here the desiderata of John XXIII,[9] which were in accord with the liturgical movement's own long-range goals. The Council's approach to the liturgy is expressed in terms of two key words: reform and promotion. It will first address a renewal of the liturgy in light of a return to its sources, the restoration of neglected values, and the revision of those areas in need of change, before considering ways of promoting the liturgy as central to Christian life.

The Council makes clear at the outset that it will not settle simply for that *instauratio* that suggests a return to past practice without the complementary notion of accommodation to present circumstances and an acceptance of the never-ending development of liturgical forms.[10] In the document's first theological construction, article two elaborates on the fundamental meaning of liturgy in relationship to the Church in the heart of the modern world. This will be examined more fully in this book in chapter four under theology of the Church. It also hints at a more inclusive understanding of the term "liturgy," which hereafter will encompass all the sacraments, the Divine Office, and the sacramentals as well. Finally, article three acknowledges the limiting implications of focusing on the Roman rite in articulating practical norms, while article four affirms the validity of "all lawfully acknowledged rites," valuating not only those already established but giving tacit permission for future rites to evolve. These preparatory articles indicate the spirit in which to interpret the general principles and norms.

9. Articulated in a variety of ways in pre-Conciliar pronouncements, particularly in his *Ad Petri Cathedram*, Encyclical Letter, June 29, 1959, in *TPS* 5 (1959), pp. 359–383; *Princeps Pastorum*, Encyclical Letter, November 28, 1959, in *TPS* 6 (1959/60), pp. 123–145; *Humanae salutis, op. cit.*; and in his address at the opening of the Council, *Gaudet Mater Ecclesia, op. cit.*

10. McManus, *op. cit.*

GENERAL PRINCIPLES AND NORMS

Chapter one lists the general principles for the restoration and promotion of the sacred liturgy according to five categories: the nature of the sacred liturgy and its importance in the life of the Church; the promotion of liturgical instruction and active participation; the reform of the sacred liturgy; promotion of liturgical life in diocese and parish; and the promotion of pastoral-liturgical action. The third category pertaining to liturgical reform offers a series of general norms as guidelines for the restoration of the liturgy. It is impossible to do more than summarize the substance of these principles here. Further analysis of central theological themes will be dealt with later on.

The first category pertains to the nature of the liturgy and its importance in the life of the Church. The Constitution begins by saying that God sent the Son, the Word made flesh, anointed by the Holy Spirit, as Mediator between God and humanity. His own humanity, united with the person of the Word, as instrument of our salvation, achieved perfect reconciliation for us and gave us the fullness of divine worship. Christ achieved his purpose principally through the paschal mystery of his passion, resurrection, and ascension. From his side as he hung wounded on the Cross came forth the sacrament of the Church (art. 5).

As Christ was sent by the Father to preach the gospel to the poor and heal those broken in body and spirit (art. 5), so Christ sent the apostles, filled with the Holy Spirit, to do as he did and to proclaim Christ crucified and risen, so that by means of sacrifice and sacraments they might accomplish what they had proclaimed. Around this the entire liturgical life revolves (art. 6).

By baptism we too are plunged into the paschal mystery to experience his *transitus*, his passage through death to life. Likewise, as often as we eat the Lord's Supper, we proclaim his death, until he comes. The Church has never failed to come together so to celebrate the Pasch, to reflect on those things in Scripture concerning him, to make Eucharist (art. 6).

Christ is always present in his Church, especially in liturgical celebrations. He is present in a variety of modes: in the sacrifice of the Mass in the person of his minister and under the eucharistic species; in the sacraments, by his power; in his Word, for he himself speaks in the Scriptures read in the Church; and whenever the Church gathers to pray and sing, just as he promised (art. 7).

Christ always associates the Church with himself in that action wherein God is glorified and we are sanctified. Public worship is performed by the whole Mystical Body, by both head and members. Since liturgy is an exercise of the priestly office of Jesus Christ, every liturgical celebration is an action surpassing all others in efficacy (art. 7).

In the liturgy our sanctification is signified by signs perceptible to the senses and is effected in a way that corresponds with each of those signs (art. 7). Although of earth, it gives a foretaste of the heavenly liturgy (art. 8). It must be understood that liturgy does not exhaust the entire activity of the Church, which includes evangelization and proclamation. To non-believers the Church announces salvation through God and Jesus whom God has sent. Believers are prepared for the sacraments through a call to faith and penance, are exhorted to observe all that Christ has commanded, and invited to perform good works for the benefit of the world (art. 9).

The liturgy is the summit toward which the activity of the Church is directed and the fount from which all her power flows. Especially from the Eucharist, as from a fount, grace is poured forth upon us; God is glorified and we are sanctified in the most efficacious way (art. 10). For the liturgy to produce its full effects, the faithful must approach it with the proper dispositions, their minds attuned to their voices, cooperative with divine grace. When the liturgy is celebrated, "something more is required than the mere observation of the laws governing valid and licit celebration." It is the duty of pastors to ensure that the faithful take part fully aware of what they are doing, actively engaged in the rite and enriched by its effects (art. 11).

It is the aim and object of all apostolic works that those who are called to faith and are baptized should gather to praise God in the midst of the Church, participate in Christ's sacrifice, and partake of his supper (art. 10). The spiritual life, however, is not limited to participation in the liturgy. Christians are mandated to pray also in secret, to pray without ceasing, and to enter into the daily dying and rising of the Lord (art. 12). Consequently, *pia exercitia* (popular devotions, pious practices) are highly recommended. These, however, should be in harmony with the liturgical seasons. In fact, popular devotions ought to derive from the liturgy and lead persons back to it, since of its very nature, the liturgy far surpasses them all (art. 13).

These principles relating to the nature of the liturgy and its importance in the life of the Church are essentially theological assertions. The formative theology presented in this section centers on Christ, priest and mediator through his *transitus* from death to life, who calls us to share his redemptive task by identifying with the paschal mystery, experiencing his presence among us, and participating in the sacraments as members of his body, the Church. The liturgy, this most efficacious action, is for us both source and summit, whose effective grace enriches the more we are attuned to the rite, whose spirit informs the whole of our spiritual life as it is expressed in devotional prayer. Especially significant is the declaration that santification "is signified by signs perceptible to the senses, and is effected in a way which corresponds with each of these signs" (art. 7). Coupled with the call to full and active participation, the necessity to be properly disposed and aware for the sign to be fully effective, and the observation that it is not enough merely to observe the laws, this indicates a strong shift of emphasis away from the *ex opere operato* mentality of Tridentine sacramentalism toward a more human, more person-oriented spirituality where responsibility for sanctification is shared. It will be beneficial to note the extent to which this theological shift is reflected in *Sacrosanctum concilium* and the Council documents as a whole.

The emphasis in category two is on active participation in the liturgy, particularly of the laity. "All the faithful should be led to that full, conscious, and active participation in liturgical celebrations which is demanded by the very nature of the liturgy. Such participation by the Christian people . . . is their right and duty by reason of their baptism" (art. 14). Full and active participation by all is the primary aim, and this requires instruction. First to be instructed are the clergy, for only when they understand the spirit and power of the liturgy and learn to live liturgically will they be able to fulfill their pastoral responsibility to instruct the faithful (art. 14–19).

The third category, reform of the liturgy, consists of a number of general norms directing liturgical renewal and some specific applications. The section begins with what might be considered the seminal insight of the entire document, a distinction between essentials and time-conditioned traditions. In undertaking the task of restoration, the Church is fully aware that "the liturgy is made up of immutable elements divinely instituted, and of elements subject to change." Having stated this briefly and boldly, the document proceeds to describe exactly what is to be done.

> These not only may but ought to be changed with the passage of time if they have suffered from the intrusion of anything out of harmony with the inner nature of the liturgy or have become unsuited to it. In this restoration, both texts and rites should be drawn up so that they express more clearly the holy things which they signify: the Christian people, so far as possible, should be enabled to understand them with ease and to take part in them fully, actively, and as befits a community (art. 21).[11]

Herein lies the core value of the entire liturgical movement. From this principle, wholly sensitive to the human condition and to the necessity of ritual's embodiment in the culture of its time, the practical norms proceed. These are grouped under four headings: general norms; norms drawn from the hierarchic and communal nature of the liturgy; norms based upon the didactic and pastoral nature of the liturgy; norms for adapting the liturgy to the culture and traditions of peoples.

The first of the general norms introduces a radical change. Authority for the regulation of the liturgy, which has rested solely with the Apostolic See, is extended to include the bishops. Competent territorial bodies of bishops now have jurisdiction to monitor liturgical revision and introduce legitimate change (art. 22). Every effort should be made to retain sound tradition and remain open to legitimate progress. New forms should evolve organically from already existing forms. All liturgical revision should be preceded by a thorough study that is theological, historical and pastoral, and cognizant of what has already been learned from recent liturgical reforms (art. 23). As soon as possible, all liturgical books are to be revised (art. 25). Essential to

---

11. All quotations from *Sacrosanctum Concilium* are taken from the translation published by NCWC, The National Catholic Welfare Conference.

aggiornamento is a living love of scripture, which is to be actively promoted. Its importance to liturgy is stressed (art. 24).

What follows next is a series of norms drawn from the hierarchic and communal nature of the liturgy. The first states that a liturgical service is not a private function, but a celebration of the Church, a "sacrament of unity" expressed by the local Church united and ordered under its bishops (art. 26). Celebrations of a communal nature involving active participation are always to be preferred (art. 27). In liturgical celebrations each person has a distinctive role and should do all and only those parts pertaining to one's office according to the nature of the rite and the principles of liturgy (art. 28). Servers, lectors, commentators, and choir members exercise a genuine liturgical function (art. 29). The laity also participates through sung and spoken responses, actions, bodily attitudes, and silence (art. 30).

Norms derived from the didactic and pastoral nature of the liturgy begin with a rationale that states that liturgy, while worship of God, is likewise for our instruction. God speaks in the liturgy, in the proclamation of the gospel, through visible signs used to signify invisible things. Through prayer, song, actions, the faith of those participating is nourished and their minds are raised to God (art. 33). Therefore, rites should be distinguished by a noble simplicity: short, clear, free of repetition, and easily comprehended (art. 34). The intimate connection between words and rite should be made apparent through a more extensive reading of scripture. The sermon, which is part of the liturgy, should proclaim the *mirabilia Dei* made present in our midst. The ministry of preaching is to be fulfilled with fidelity. Explicit liturgical instruction may be given in a variety of ways, even in short directives at suitable moments within the rite. Bible services, or services of the Word, are to be encouraged, particularly in places where there is no resident priest (art. 35). While Latin is to be preserved as the language of the Latin rites, the use of the vernacular may be extended to readings and some prayers and chants, in the Mass, sacraments and elsewhere, because of its advantage to the people. The competent territorial ecclesiastical authority will determine whether and to what extent the vernacular will be used and will approve translations intended for liturgical use. The Apostolic See will confirm what local authorities decree (art. 36).

Finally, this category on liturgical reform lists norms for adapting the liturgy to the culture and traditions of peoples. A number of policy statements appear in quick succession. No rigid uniformity will be imposed in matters not compromising the essentials of faith or the good of the whole community. The genius and talents of races and peoples are to be respected and fostered. Their customs, insofar as it is possible, will be preserved and sometimes even incorporated into the liturgy intact (art. 37). Provisions shall be made for legitimate variations and adaptations to different regions and peoples, especially in mission lands, when the liturgical books are revised (art. 38). The competent territorial authority will authorize adaptations in sacraments and sacramentals, in liturgical language, music, and the arts, according to this Constitution's norms (art. 39). In some circumstances and places an even more radical adaptation will be needed. The competent territorial authority will recommend to the Apostolic See those elements from local traditions and culture appropriate for use in worship. Qualified persons should formulate liturgical laws in mission areas. These laws should be preceded by adequate experimentation over a given period of time (art. 40).

The fourth category concerns the promotion of liturgical life in diocese and parish. The bishop is to be considered as the high priest of his flock, and the liturgical life of the diocese centered around the bishop should be held in high esteem. Full, active participation in these liturgical celebrations is in fact the preeminent manifestation of the Church (art. 41). Because it is impossible for the bishop always and everywhere to preside over his whole flock, smaller groupings of the faithful established under a local pastor are vitally important and represent the visible Church manifested throughout the world. The liturgical life of these parishes ought to be energetically fostered and efforts made to encourage a sense of community within the parish, especially during the common celebration of Sunday Mass (art. 42).

The fifth and final category of general principles involves pastoral-liturgical action. As zeal for the promotion and restoration of the liturgy is a sign of God's providence and the presence of the Spirit in the Church, some practical approaches are decreed to ensure its progress. It is recommended that competent territorial authority establish a liturgical commission to regulate pastoral-liturgical action, promote studies, and monitor experimentation.

The commission should have access to some kind of institute for pastoral liturgy with the necessary expertise (art. 43–44). In fact, each diocese is to have a liturgical commission under the direction of the bishop, or several dioceses a single commission combining, whenever possible, those separate commissions also recommended for sacred music and sacred art (art. 45–46).

COMMENTARY AND EVALUATION

The general principles explicated in the opening chapter of *Sacrosanctum concilium* are meant to govern the restoration of the liturgy in all of its facets, all of its forms, and to guide its promotion. Consequently, all the remaining articles of the document are to be understood in light of these principles and their derivative norms. The Eucharist, the other sacraments and sacramentals, the liturgy of the hours, the liturgical year, music and art, receive their direction from what is articulated here. Some of these principles constitute a general theology of the liturgy reflective of recent understandings in biblical and liturgical research. Others are more particular, pertaining to the developmental nature of rites and rituals. Related to these principles are some practical and disciplinary norms. On the whole, the manner of implementing these general principles and norms has been left to competent territorial authority. In several instances, particularly with regard to vernacular language and Bible vigils, the gravity of the matter or enthusiasm for a practice has led the Council to spell out the desired reform.

It may be clarifying to summarize those key theological insights recorded in chapter one that governed *aggiornamento* and gave impetus to further change. Reduced to single statements, these comprise the following list. (1) Rediscovery of the centrality of the paschal mystery and our own participation in Christ's passage from death to life. (2) A more accurate understanding of Christ's real presence as mediated through a variety of modes. (3) A realization of the importance of liturgy to the life of the Church and in the life of the Christian community, expressed in terms of the source and summit of activity and power. (4) A rediscovery of the priesthood of all believers and the distribution of ministerial roles. (5) An orientation toward *ex opere operantis*: the rite still effects what it signifies, but it is efficacious to the degree that one is aware, fully involved, and cooperative (not a change in direction, but a shift in emphasis). (6) A closer relationship of the Church to the world as reflected in its ritual, not yet developed theologically here, but hinted at in various principles and norms. These basic theological principles will be returned to later on.

Key insights with far-reaching implications, both theological and practical, include: (1) Liturgy is intrinsically dynamic, for along with immutable elements, it includes elements subject to change. (2) Active participation is of the highest priority, which implies the necessity of educating all the faithful (*laos*) to take responsibility for what is theirs by right. (3) The principle of decentralization marks the end of ritual uniformity with its potential for cultural diversity resulting from locally developed rites. (4) Cultural adaptation/indigenization is an integral liturgical value not simply to be tolerated but sought. (5) Liturgy is not limited to the Eucharist, but includes all the sacraments, the Divine Office, and sacramentals. (6) Spirituality, although informed by the liturgy, is still more inclusive and incorporates other dimensions of action and prayer. (7) The major shift in liturgical theology revolves around a more authentic relationship between signs and what they signify, so that spiritual realities are seen as really incarnate in things of earth. (8) Recovery of scripture will eventually reveal how much of Christianity is rooted in the biblical word, stressing the need for proclamation within and outside the Church. (9) The importance of comprehension cannot be minimized, for people need to celebrate faith's essentials in a language they understand.

Besides positive and pastoral qualities, *Sacrosanctum concilium* has definite limitations. *Periti* commenting on the document admit it is imperfect regarding both content and form. Its most serious defect is the fact that it is largely the result of compromise. A number of points reflect a middle line between rival forces, or a vacillation between two poles.[12] Daring new insights are some-

---

12. For example, the document's ambiguous position on vernacular usage (art. 36, 63). Although the mother tongue is of great advantage to the people, "the use of Latin" is to be preserved. According to the new understanding of episcopal collegiality, territorial ecclesiastical authority can approve regional vernacular translations, but their decisions must be "confirmed" by the Apostolic See. This tension is also reflected in the text's stance on cultural adaptation and

times couched in hieratic language or constrained by a traditional theological framework. Some theological positions are overstated. There was, and still is, disagreement about describing liturgy as source and summit of the Church's action (art. 10). James Empereur speaks to this point.

> Liturgy is not the summit and source of grace-filled life in general, but of the Christian testimony to grace; it is central to what God does in and through the Church as a distinctive community but not necessarily central to his redemptive action in the world.[13]

It can be argued that the aim and object of apostolic work is not solely to draw believers together to praise God in the midst of the Church (art. 10), but to establish the Kingdom by participation in an alienated world's redemption, making present the saving grace of God through initiatives of liberation, justice, and peace. Then, too, the local parish and the role of the priest in the liturgical life of the community are both deemphasized in an effort to undergird with a rationale the bishop's new collegial role. Liturgical celebrations centered around the bishop represent "the preeminent manifestation of the Church" (art. 41). Because this kind of experience is seldom possible, "lesser groupings of the faithful," set up locally under a pastor who takes the place of the bishop, represent the Church's visible manifestation throughout the world (art. 42). Although this position has justification according to Tradition, such an articulation introduces a tension between theology and praxis.

The document's limitations in no way minimize the impact of what has in fact been achieved. *Sacrosanctum concilium* restored a sense of essentials to the liturgy and, faithful to tradition, gave the Church of the twentieth-century the opportunity to articulate its own expression of faith. Summing up the strengths and weaknesses of the Constitution on the Liturgy, Joseph Jungmann concludes with this positive note:

experimentation. Both are values to be encouraged, but with extreme caution. In article 6, the Church's mission is described in terms of both "sacrifice and sacraments," a concession to those who demanded that explicit reference to sacrifice be added to the document's sacramental conception of the Church.

13. James Empereur, "Where We Are At In the Liturgy," in *Modern Liturgy Handbook*, ed. by John P. Mossi (New York: Paulist, 1976), p. 16.

It should be remembered that the reform work of the Constitution represents all that was possible to achieve in 1963, on the part of an assembly of two thousand bishops coming from all the nations of the world, at a time when far-reaching developments are in progress not only in the world, but also in the Church. Many doors have been opened and new perspectives of liturgical possibility have been authorized. We must thank God for the gift that he has given us.[14]

In the words of Cipriano Vagaggini, another Council *peritus*, it was "a great step forward in the toilsome reconquest of Christian essentiality."[15]

14. Joseph Jungmann, "A Great Gift of God to the Church," *The Liturgy of Vatican II*, Vol. 1, ed. by Jovian Lang (Chicago: Franciscan Herald Press, 1966), p. 70.

15. As quoted in Jungmann, *Commentary on the Documents, op. cit.,* p. 7.

4

Theological *Aggiornamento*

A NEW THEOLOGY OF LITURGY EMERGES WITH *SACROSANCTUM CONCILIUM*, this first public articulation of Vatican II, new in the sense of rediscovery and return to original sources in the spirit of the early Church. Its essentials have already been discussed: Christ, *Pascha nostrum*, experienced as really present in word, bread, and community which is gathered, attentive, active, whose faith is enriched and deepened in the celebration of authentic signs. Liturgy is not something the Church does. It is the expression of what the Church is, the historic representation of eternal truths. Immutable truths of faith do not change, only their articulation, as the Church continues to interpret and express its essential meaning at any given time.

This shift in theology of liturgy is rooted in the Church's own self-perception, for liturgy is integrally linked to the nature of the Church. To say that liturgy is the expression or ritualization of the Church's self-understanding implies that there is a connection between the way the Church defines and interprets itself at a given time and the style and substance of its official prayer, that its description of its mission is in fact revelatory of its liturgical expectations. Therefore, ecclesiology has serious consequences for ritual, which is the embodiment of its belief. To fully understand the new liturgy, it is necessary to understand present perceptions of the Church. The following pages will examine Vatican II's theology of Church before proceeding to the underlying theological realities of the Church's sacramental life. In his opening address, Paul VI declared that the theme of the Council's Second Session would be the Church, indicating:

> A thorough investigation must be made into her inner nature, with a view to defining this in human terms, as far as that is possible. . . . It need cause no surprise that the true, definitive and complete notion of the Church as founded by Christ and begun by the Apostles still lacks more precise formulation. . . . It is always possible, therefore, to gain new and deeper insights into its nature. . . . The theological doctrine is susceptible of magnificent development. . . . [1]

THEOLOGY OF CHURCH

When the Council Fathers proceeded to discuss the schema *De Ecclesia* toward the end of the first session, the task was long overdue. A statement on the nature and mission of the Church had eluded Trent's agenda. That Council had been too caught up in the polemics of definition and reform. The need for a clear, public declaration regarding the Church had become acute by the first Vatican Council. Its dogmatic constitution on the Church of Christ was left unfinished (1870) when war broke out, interrupting the Council's deliberations. The four approved chapters of *Pastor aeternus* affirmed that the primacy of jurisdiction over the universal Church belonged by divine right to the bishop of Rome, who was infallible when speaking *ex cathedra* on matters of faith and morals to be held by the universal Church. For centuries the pope had been something more than *primus inter pares*. The *plenitudo administrationis*, the pyramid structure, which had been operative in principle, was now an incontestable fact.

It was essential that Vatican II redress the imbalance created by *Pastor aeternus*, which had presented its position on papal primacy and infallibility out of context, without the foundational reflection on the nature and meaning of the Church and the plenitude of its functions to provide a more accurate picture. Missing was any sense of the pastoral function of the magisterium. The document outlined a hierarchical structure of power and authority supported by theological justification and the traditional anathemas. This

1. *Salvete, Fratres*, September 29, 1963, in *TPS* 9 (1964), p. 131–32.

juridical model of a *societas perfecta* had profound implications for the Church's spiritual life and mission. Several attempts to examine the structure of the Church have come forth from the Holy See during the past century, but it was the encyclical *Mystici Corporis* of Pius XII (1943) that claimed and held attention. A theological milestone, the encyclical focused on the foundational biblical image of the Church as the Mystical Body of Christ, which remained the dominant ecclesiological image right up until the Council.[2]

A primary reason for convoking the Council was clearly expressed before it convened: that the Church might take a hard look at itself, because only by a fresh discovery of its true nature would the Church be able to achieve renewal. Self-awareness and self-understanding must precede any attempts at reform. This became even more apparent during the Council's discussion on liturgy. So many recommendations for change in ritual arose from a changed understanding of the nature of the Church. Collegial authority and pluriformity of ministerial roles, for example, could hardly be reconciled with the ecclesiology that predominated before Vatican II. With all the pastoral and communal emphasis, the title of *De Ecclesia's* opening chapter, "The Nature of the Church Militant," seemed awkwardly out of place. After preliminary discussion during session one, the initial draft was radically revised. It was eventually decided to produce two documents, the one *Ecclesia ad intra*, a dogmatic constitution on the Church's inner nature, the second *Ecclesia ad extra*, a pastoral statement which would speak of the Church's self-awareness in relation to the modern world.

The title change of chapter one to "The Mystery of the Church" symbolized the shift of emphasis in the redacted text based on proposed amendments. The Fathers had affirmed the Christocentric focus of the original draft, but not its approach or spirit.

2. Throughout its history, the Church has been best described by images, usually biblical, rather than by verbal definitions. Paul Minear lists 96 ecclesiological images in his book, *Images of the Church in the New Testament* (Philadelphia: Westminster, 1960). Paul VI alluded to some of these revealing images in *Salvete, Fratres*, op. cit., p. 131, and *Lumen Gentium* expounded on them (art. 6). Vatican II affirmed the richness of the Body of Christ image, but opted for the more dynamic People of God (*LG*, chap. 2) as the dominant image of Conciliar ecclesiology.

John XXIII had insisted that the document not be scholastic in character. Many desired a more pastoral document, one that presented the Church as a community rather than as a society. The Constitution on the Church was considered to be the climax of the Council, but the schema proved disappointing. There was still too much triumphalism, too much fascination with clericalism, not enough of a gospel spirit. One bishop put the concerns clearly into perspective:

> Yesterday the Church was considered above all as an institution, today it is experienced as a community. Yesterday it was the Pope who was mainly in view, today the Pope is thought of as united to the bishops. . . . Yesterday theology stressed the importance of the hierarchy, today it is discovering the people of God. Yesterday it was chiefly concerned with what divided, today it voices all that unites. Yesterday the theology of the Church was mainly preoccupied with the inward life of the Church, today it sees the Church as oriented to the outside world.[3]

The new draft proposed for approval was full of biblical imagery. As the Church's response to the basic question regarding its own existence, it was far more realistic than earlier attempts, yet only a partial articulation, for the existential implications were to be more fully addressed in the pastoral constitution regarding the Church in the modern world. The Dogmatic Constitution on the Church was approved and promulgated November 21, 1964, under the title, *Lumen Gentium*, which points away from the Church to the One whom the Church reflects: Christ the light of the nations who is also the light of the Church.[4]

One must return to biblical sources in order to understand the intrinsic nature of the Church. The New Testament eschatological community of believers, the *Ecclesia (Ekklesia)*, was distinguished from the covenantal *kehal Yahweh* of the Old Testament by its proclamation of Jesus as Lord. *Ecclesia* means both the process of

3. Comment by Bishop Elchinger, as reported by Gerard Philips, "History of the Constitution," in *Commentary On the Documents of Vatican II*, Vol. 1, *op. cit.*, p. 108.

4. A phrase used by John XXIII to sum up the aims of the Council: " . . . *lumen Christi, Ecclesia Christi, lumen gentium.*" *La grande aspettazione*, Radio Message, September 11, 1962, *AAS* 54 (1962), p. 685.

congregating and the congregated community.[5] The Council has managed to recapture this original sense of Church as people coming together, gathering, assembling, by referring to the local community as "assembly" and this entity as "the visible Church constituted throughout the world."[6] This Church, according to Catholic theology, is divinely instituted, for " . . . it was from the side of Christ as he slept the sleep of death upon the cross that there came forth 'the wondrous sacrament of the whole Church.' "[7] "Established in this last age of the world," the Church was "made manifest in the outpouring of the Spirit," and "it will be brought to glorious completion at the end of time."[8]

There has been much ecclesiological reflection during the present century. John XXIII approved of such speculation as part of the continuing project of those committed to the life of the Church.

> The Catholic Church, of course, leaves many questions open to the discussion of theologians . . . For discussion can lead to fuller and deeper understanding of religious truths; when one idea strikes against another, there may be a spark.[9]

The liturgical movement, deeply rooted in a return to essentials, constantly challenged archaic structures, thereby sparking an investigation of the real meaning of the Church and its mission. The Council affirmed this developing ecclesiology and built upon it. Many of the key concepts contained in the Council's declarations on the Church had already become popular: the pastoral approach, the paschal mystery and resurrection theology, the role

---

5. In its secular meaning, *ek-klesia* (those who have been called out . . . summoned together) referred to a meeting of the people for political, not cultic, purposes and meant the actual session. In its religious meaning, *ecclesia* is not something formed once and for all but an event continually repeated, as persons congregate for worship. *Ecclesia* as Church refers both to the universal entity as well as each individual local embodiment which fully represents it. See Hans Küng, *The Church* (Garden City, NY: Image, 1976), pp. 114–124; and K.L. Schmidt, "εκκλησία," *Theologisches Worterbuch zum Neuen Testament III*, ed. G. Kittel (Stuttgart 1933 ff.), pp. 502–539.

6. *Sacrosanctum concilium*, art. 42, hereafter, *SC*.

7. *SC*, art. 5; see also *Lumen gentium*, art. 3, hereafter, *LG*.

8. *LG*, art. 2.

9. John XXIII, *Ad Petri Cathedram, op. cit.*, p. 370.

of the Spirit, the role of the laity, the Church in relation to culture and society, sensitivity to the "signs of the times." Recognition of the Church as mystery, communion, sacrament, had been anticipated by a full generation.[10]

In his classic encyclical, *Mystici Corporis*, Pius XII writes about "the doctrine of the Mystical Body of Christ, which is the Church" (art. 1). He describes the society established by Jesus Christ as "a body," that is, "an unbroken unity" (art. 14) comprised of "a multiplicity of members, which are linked together in such a way as to help one another" (art. 15).[11] *Lumen Gentium* confirms that Christ, through his Spirit, "mystically constitutes as his body" those who are called, and through the power of the Spirit endows the members with "different gifts for the welfare of the Church" (art. 7). "The Church is a mystery," Paul VI proclaimed, "a mystic reality steeped in the presence of God."[12]

Each articulation provides a fuller understanding of the nature of the Church. The Church is the history of the relationship between God and people ... a pilgrimage toward God ... an epiphany or manifestation of God on earth ... the basic sacramental category in which sign and reality coincide and coinhere.[13] The Church is theandric, "*un milieu humano-divin*" in which "the permanent incarnation of the Son of God ... prolongs the presence of the Savior under a visible form and expands it in the domain of the social."[14] The Church is essentially a "kerygmatic

10. See ecclesiology of Dom Virgil Michel in his *The Liturgy of the Church* (1937), and as summarized in the doctoral dissertation of Sister Jeremy Hall, *The Full Stature of Christ* (Collegeville: The Liturgical Press, 1976), p. 201. Also, writings emanating from Maria Laach, especially Odo Casel, *The Mystery of Christian Worship*, tr. by I.T. Hale (Westminster: Newman, 1962) and Romano Guardini, *The Church and the Catholic* (1953); the periodical *Orate Fratres* (later, *Worship*).

11. Passages quoted here were taken from the Vatican translation as printed by *Tipografia Poliglotta Vaticana* and distributed by the National Catholic Welfare Conference (Washington, DC: 1943).

12. *Salvete, Fratres, op. cit.*, p. 131.

13. George Tavard summarizes descriptions of the Church throughout history in *The Church Tomorrow* (New York: Herder, 1965), p. 105.

14. P. Sertillanges, *L'Eglise*, Vol. 1 (Paris: 1917), p. 75, as quoted in Jeremiah Newman, *Change and the Catholic Church* (Baltimore: Helicon, 1965), p. 93.

community . . . a point of encounter with God."[15] It is "a people brought into unity,"[16] a society in the present world which "subsists in the Catholic Church."[17] It is organism and organization, *Gemeinschaft* as well as *Gesellschaft*, "a structural sign" so revitalized that what was once "an instrument of preservation" has become "an agent of transformation."[18] The Church of Vatican II, set up by the life-giving Spirit of Jesus as "the universal sacrament of salvation,"[19] has come full circle. Once filled with disdain for this world as it lived poised in anticipation of another, the Church now finds itself located in the heart of the modern world as *sacramentum mundi*.[20]

By far the most significant contribution to ecclesiology in this century has been the Council's reinterpretation of the Church's stance *vis-à-vis* the world, reflected so forcefully in its pastoral constitution on the Church in the modern world. Fostering "a feeling of deep solidarity with the human race and its history" (art. 1), *Gaudium et spes* set forth "the way it understands the presence and function of the Church in the world of today . . . the world as the theater of human history, its triumphs and failures, the world, which in the Christian vision has been created and is sustained by the love of its maker . . . " (art. 2). Recognizing that "at all times the Church carries the responsibility of reading the signs of the time and interpreting them in the light of the Gospel, if it is to carry out

15. R.P. McBrien, *Church: The Continuing Quest* (New York: Newman, 1970), p. 11, as quoted in Avery Dulles, *Models of the Church* (Garden City, NY: Doubleday, 1974), p. 72.

16. *LG*, art. 4.

17. *LG*, art. 8. The notion of the Church of Christ "subsisting" in the Catholic church is new and has far-reaching ecumenical implications: "Catholic" is no longer an exclusively Roman claim; ecclesial elements of sanctification and truth can be found outside its structure. See Aloys Grillmeier, "The Mystery of the Church," tr. by Kevin Smyth, *Commentary on the Documents of Vatican II*, Vol. 1, *op. cit.*, pp. 149–150.

18. Rafael Avila, *Worship and Politics* (Maryknoll, NY: Orbis, 1981), p. 101.

19. *LG*, art. 48.

20. For Vatican II, the Church as *sacramentum mundi* was a theme repeated in *Lumen Gentium* (art. 9, 48) and *Gaudium et spes* (art. 42). See Jan Groot, "The Church As Sacrament of the World," *Concilium* 31 (1968), pp. 51–66; Thomas O'Dea, "The Church As *Sacramentum Mundi*," *Concilium* 58 (1970), pp. 36–44.

its task," the Council calls Christians to "be aware of and understand the aspirations, the yearnings, and the often dramatic features of the world in which we live" (art. 4). "The People of God . . . led by the Spirit . . . tries to discern in the events, the needs and the longing which it shares with other [people] of our time, what may be genuine signs of the presence or of the purpose of God . . . for faith throws a new light on all things" (art. 11) and, with wisdom, one "is led through the visible realities to those which cannot be seen" (art. 15). Indeed, "this faith should show its fruitfulness by penetrating the whole of life, even the worldly activities of those who believe, and by urging them to be loving and just especially toward those in need" (art. 21).

The pastoral constitution on the Church, the final public declaration of Vatican II, focuses on this theme, noting that human achievements are a sign of God's greatness and the fulfillment of God's design. Far from inhibiting people from getting involved in activities that build up the world, it encourages Christians to do just that (art. 34). The document speaks of the earthly and heavenly city penetrating one another, sharing concerns that are common to both, emphasizing that the Church has much to contribute toward the humanization of this world and its history (art. 40). The Church must strive to " . . . express the Christian message in the concepts and language of different peoples" and to "adapt the Gospel to the understanding of all," in order to present the revealed Word "in suitable terms" and to "foster vital contact and exchange between the Church and different cultures" (art. 44). In fact, the document expressly states:

> the Church needs to step up this exchange . . . [for] it is the task of the whole people of God, particularly of its pastors and theologians, to listen to and distinguish the many voices of our times and to interpret them in the light of the divine Word, in order that the revealed truth may be more deeply penetrated, better understood, and more suitably presented (art. 44).

A strong theme underlying *Gaudium et spes* is the realization that the human person "can achieve true and full humanity only by means of culture" (art. 53). Recognizing the historical, sociological, and ethnological differentiation implied in the term "culture," the document admits that the "heritage of its institutions forms the patrimony proper to each human community" whereby people create "a well-defined, historical milieu . . . from which they draw the values needed to foster humanity and civilization" (53). "There are many links between the message of salvation and culture" (art. 58). Indeed, "there are close links between the things of earth and those things in [the human] condition which transcend the world, and the Church utilizes temporal realities as often as its mission requires it" (art. 76).

What then are the implications for theology and praxis in this firm valuation of the things of this world?

> Theologians are now being asked . . . to seek out more efficient ways . . . of presenting their teaching to modern [persons]: for the deposit and the truths of faith are one thing, the manner of expressing them is quite another. In pastoral care sufficient use should be made, not only of theological principles, but also of the findings of secular sciences, especially psychology and sociology: in this way the faithful will be brought to a purer and more mature living of the faith (art. 62).

A second core passage in *Gaudium et spes* sums up the document's dominant thrust and is central to this investigation. After recalling the precedent that the Church through the centuries and in varying circumstances already "has utilized the resources of different cultures in its preaching" in order to express the message of Christ more faithfully "in the liturgy and in various aspects of the life of the faithful," the passage states:

> The church has been sent to all ages and nations and, therefore, is not tied exclusively and indissolubly to any race or nation, to any one particular way of life, or to any customary practices, ancient or modern. The Church is faithful to its traditions and is at the same time conscious of its universal mission; it can, then, enter into communion with different forms of culture, thereby enriching both itself and the cultures themselves. The good news of Christ . . . takes the spiritual qualities and endowments of every age and nation, and with supernatural riches it causes them to blossom, as it were, from within; it fortifies, completes and restores them in Christ. In this way the Church carries out its mission, and in the very act it stimulates and advances human and civil culture, as well as contributing by its activity, including liturgical activity, to [humanity's] interior freedom (art. 58).

These passages illustrate a definite shift of emphasis in the Church's understanding of its relationship to the world: a this-worldly orientation, a sense of "being in the midst," an incarnation ecclesiology with myriad implications for all of its spiritual life. The entire document, and these excerpts in particular, reads as a climax to the strong social sense that had been developing with some intensity within the Church for a full century as reflected in the social encyclicals of several popes and the Catholic worker/social action/liberation/justice movements so prolific in so many countries during this same period of time. "Just as Christ was in the midst of [people], so too his Church, in which he continues to live, is in the midst of the people ."[21] In his first encyclical letter, *Ecclesiam Suam*, Paul VI addressed the topic of the Church and its present day mission:

> The Church must here and now reflect on its own nature . . . and discover better ways of augmenting the effectiveness and fruitfulness of its contact with the world. For the Church does indeed belong to the world, even though distinguished from it by its own altogether unique characteristics.[22]

Paul Ricoeur contends that the *raison d'être* of the churches is to pose continually the question of ends, of perspective, of well-being and "what for?" in society, to witness to a fundamental meaning in a world devastated by so much meaninglessness. He approaches this challenge on the level of culture, noting that the mythological framework, foundational to all cultures, is no longer believable as it relates to faith in our time, in fact is a scandal of such proportion as to obliterate the "scandal of the cross." Truth incarnate in culture takes on a "disposable believable," he says. "Each epoch requires a disposable believable," and the problem of demythologizing arises at this point, because the present is so culturally remote from the disposable believable of the apostolic age.[23]

21. Pius XII, *Negli ultimi sei anni*, Christmas sermon, December 24, 1945, *AAS* 38 (1946), p. 20; as quoted in Thomas J. Carroll, "Pius XII Envisions the Future," *National Liturgical Week* (1953), p. 164.

22. Art. 18, in *TPS* 10 (1965), p. 258.

23. Paul Ricoeur, "Tasks of the Ecclesial Community in the Modern World," *Theology of Renewal*, Vol. 2: *Renewal of Religious Structures* (New York: Herder, 1968), pp. 243–247.

Vatican II had a similar insight but expressed it in terms of "immutable elements" and "elements subject to change" or "truths of faith are one thing, the manner of expressing them is quite another."[24] To reach this point, the Church had to come to terms with a distinction between essentials and non-essentials, core truths and their time-conditioned presentation, at least in principle. Having done this, the Council Fathers promulgated this "new" ecclesiology, leaving the People of God with the challenge of putting it into practice. Twenty years after the Council, the church is still trying to decide just what this means with regard to specifics, and how and when to apply it.

The integral relationship of ecclesiology and liturgy has been documented by Vatican II. Liturgy "is the outstanding means whereby the faithful may express in their lives, and manifest to others, the mystery of Christ and the real nature of the true Church."[25] Liturgy is, in fact, "the preeminent manifestation of the Church" when the community fully and actively participates according to Conciliar norms.[26] "Liturgical services are not private functions, but are celebrations of the Church," and this "sacrament of unity," which is the Church, is symbolically expressed by "the holy people united and ordered under their bishops."[27] The community assembled for liturgy is a sign, a localized externalization, a self-revelation of the universal Church according to the uniqueness of a particular time and place. It is not the full expression, but only one particular embodiment, one authentic facet that contributes meaning to the whole. Because it is an action of Christ's Body, the Church, every liturgical celebration is "a sacred action surpassing all others."[28] It is "the principal means" of bringing about the Church's mission of salvation,[29] and at the same time "builds up those who are in the Church" and "increases their power to preach Christ and thus show forth the Church."[30]

24. *SC*, art. 21; *GS*, art. 62.
25. *SC*, art. 2.
26. *SC*, art. 41.
27. *SC*, art. 26.
28. *SC*, art. 7.
29. *Apostolicam actuositatem,* Decree on the Apostolate of Lay People, November 18, 1965, art. 6.
30. *SC*, art. 2.

Liturgists have long understood that liturgical awareness contributes to growth in the Church's own self-understanding and that this in turn is reflected in its ritual practice. "It is historically evident that revivals in liturgy or ecclesiology resonate with each other."[31] Liturgy is in fact an "applied ecclesiology, the practical application of what the Church is called to be."[32] It is "dogma in action,"[33] the dynamics of faith mediated without interruption down through the centuries in Christ's Mystical Body, the Church, as the encyclicals *Mystici Corporis* and *Mediator Dei* articulated with such clarity in a way not done before. *Lumen Gentium* sums up this relationship between the liturgy and the Church in eschatological terms:

> It is especially in the sacred liturgy that our union with the heavenly Church is best realized; in the liturgy, through the sacramental signs, the power of the Holy Spirit acts on us, and with the community rejoicing we celebrate together the praise of the divine majesty, when all those of every tribe and nation who have been redeemed by the blood of Christ and gathered together in one Church glorify, in one common song of praise, the one and triune God. When we celebrate the eucharistic sacrifice we are most closely united to the worship of the heavenly Church (art. 50).

SACRAMENTAL THEOLOGY

Sacrosanctum concilium begins its chapter on sacraments and sacramentals with this statement of purpose:

> The purpose of the sacraments is to sanctify [people], to build up the body of Christ, and, finally, to give worship to God; because they are signs they also instruct. They not only presuppose faith, but by words and objects they also nourish, strengthen, and express it; that is why they are called "sacraments of faith" (art. 59).

These lines reflect the change in sacramental theology acknowledged by Vatican II. The arrangement of elements here is not

31. Hall, *op. cit.*, p. xiii.
32. Fred Krause, *Liturgy In Parish Life* (New York: Alba House, 1979), p. 27.
33. William Busch, "About the Encyclical *Mediator Dei*," *Orate Fratres* 22 (1947/48), p. 156.

without consequence. The first priority of the sacramental order is to sanctify persons. The second is the strengthening and edification of the community. The third, finally, is the worship of God. The intent of the Council is not to minimize worship nor to relegate God to last place. On the contrary, it recognizes that God is most fully worshiped when sacraments are celebrated, when individuals are made holy by an experience of Christ in the sign-actions he intended, when the community of believers gives assent through faith to the grace poured out in its midst. The intent is to make clear that the sacraments do not exist primarily for God's benefit. They were instituted for the sanctification of God's people and, as corporate signs, for the building up of the Church. This represents a shift in sacramental emphasis from that which was predominant prior to Vatican II.

Time prevents a recapitulation of the complex evolution of Christian sacrament, from the original meaning of its terminology[34] and the simple signs and gestures of the post-Resurrection communities, through progressive deculturalization to a rigid, uniform rite; and its theological development, which is reflected in the commentary of New Testament writers, the homiletical contributions of the Patristic period, the speculation of the Scholastics, papal legislation, and the canons of Fourth Lateran and Trent.[35] The use of the term at Vatican II adds a welcome dimension to the category of sacrament. It is far more inclusive.[36] It is pastoral and community based. It reflects a respect for culture and local adaptation.

34. From the Latin *sacramentum*, meaning a person or thing constituted by divine right, a function of public authority, such as a consecration or an oath. Its religious use parallels that of the Greek word "mystery," translated *sacramentum*. Two elements are basic to its many meanings in early Christianity: a sacred secret and its manifestation. See: Bernard Leeming, S.J., *Principles of Sacramental Theology* (New York: Longmans, Green & Co., 1956); Karl Rahner, *The Church and the Sacraments* (New York: Herder, 1963); A.-M. Roguet, O.P., *Christ Acts Through the Sacraments*, tr. by Carisbrooke Dominicans (Collegeville, MN: Liturgical Press, 1954).

35. A decree written for the Armenians by Pope Eugenius IV in 1438 gives an account of the seven sacraments and represents the first ecclesiastical synthesis of sacramental doctrine. The Church has never officially defined "sacrament," but guidelines for praxis contained in the canons of Trent (Sessions VII, XIII, XXI, XXII) and *Sacrosanctum concilium* of Vatican II stress essential characteristics.

36. Note the concept of the Church itself as sacrament, already discussed: *SC,* art. 5, 7, 26; *LG,* art. 1, 9, 48; *GS,* art. 42.

The primary purpose of sacraments is that they sanctify. A secondary purpose is that "they also instruct." In fact, "because they are signs they also instruct." Sacraments are both formative and informative. They are occasions whereby Christians experience their faith and its prerogative for the ordering of their lives, and they are also channels for communicating an understanding of the significance of what has been experienced. This instruction is done through the sign actions themselves, for the sacraments instruct "because they are signs," through the modality of signification. They announce what God accomplishes in and through their mediation. For this to be done effectively, the sacramental signs must be easy to understand, that is, they must "express more clearly the holy things which they signify" (art. 21). The Council has returned again to its fundamental rationale for revision and reform.

The statement of purpose in article 59 makes a third doctrinal point. Sacraments "not only presuppose faith, but by words and objects they also nourish, strengthen, and express it; that is why they are called 'sacraments of faith.' " It is an ecclesiastical canon that a valid and fruitful reception of the sacraments presupposes faith in Christ who instituted these graced media and in the power of the sign-actions to effect what they signify. Sacraments are said to confer grace *ex opere operato*, that is, by the force of the action itself, literally, "by the work worked." Symbolic words and actions become instruments of God who, through the sacrament, produces a change in the soul. The effect is due to the divine power, not to the personal merits of either minister or recipient. Sacraments are means of grace "in the case of those who place no impediment."[37] In recent centuries, emphasis has been placed on the minimum proper dispositions necessary for a canonically valid reception. An overemphasis on causality, the intent of which was simply to explain the free dispensation of grace apart from any finite instrumentality, led to a distorted system of "efficacious" rites that "guaranteed grace" for the "recipient," and a misunderstanding of the role of personal faith in the sacramental process. Sacraments were perceived as things that automatically did their job as long as no obstacle prevented them. Sacramental efficacy, however, has always presupposed faith on the part of the

37. Leeming, *op. cit.*, pp. 5–7.

recipient. Not only is faith prerequisite to the sacrament's effect, it is essential for its effectiveness.

Vatican II did not concern itself with sacramental validity. It chose instead to focus attention on the criteria necessary for a fruitful sacramental experience: full and active participation in a ritual that is intelligible, culturally relevant, and up-to-date. Thus celebrated, sacraments are the means whereby grace is poured out upon the community of believers and the "recipient(s)" in its midst. Such "sacraments (signs) of faith" celebrated sincerely become processes whereby a rudimentary assent is nurtured, stretched, and deepened. The grace imparted by the very nature of the sign in turn enables the faithful to receive that grace fruitfully for personal sanctification and the building up of the Body to the greater glory of God. This shift away from a Tridentine preoccupation with validity to a pastoral concern for effectiveness in facilitating sanctification marks a turning point in sacramental thinking.

From this perspective, "it is therefore of the highest importance that the faithful should easily understand the sacramental signs" (art. 59). On the basis of this conclusion, norms for the revision of rites are drawn up in order to "adapt them to the needs of our own times" (art. 62). These norms extend through the remainder of the chapter. They pertain to the use of the vernacular language and to the application of earlier principles to individual sacramental rites.

Two striking additions of theological import stand out in the remaining articles of chapter three. The first involves a broader understanding of the nature of sacrament in an extension of its power to the more inclusive "sacramental." The second is a verbal acknowledgment of the time-conditioned nature of liturgical rites and rituals.

With regard to sacramentals, article 60 is essentially a theological paraphrase of the Church's tradition as contained in Canon 1144 of its 1918 Code of Canon Law. Because the church instituted sacramentals as sacred signs resembling sacraments, these also "signify effects, particularly of a spiritual kind, which are obtained through the Church's intercession" and dispose the faithful to receive the sacraments themselves effectively. The sense of the final phrase of article 60, that through sacramentals "various occasions in life are rendered holy," is transitional to what follows.

Article 61 equates sacraments and sacramentals quite closely, stating that for the well-disposed faithful:

> The liturgy of the sacraments and sacramentals sanctifies almost every event in their lives; they are given access to the stream of divine grace which flows from the paschal mystery of the passion, death, and resurrection of Christ, the fount from which all sacraments and sacramentals draw their power. There is hardly any proper use of material things which cannot thus be directed toward the sanctification of [persons] and the praise of God.

This is indeed a radical return to an earlier patristic understanding of sacrament.[38] While the seven sacraments continue to be distinguished as unique Christ encounters, all of creation is once again validated as potential media of grace. Significant here is the linking of both sacraments and sacramentals under the inclusive *liturgia* (*liturgia Sacramentorum et Sacramentalium*), the prayer of the Church. Both together give access to the grace of the Pasch event from which they draw their power. Together, sacraments and sacramentals sanctify nearly everything of consequence in the lives of the faithful, directing personal and communal sanctification and effecting praise of God. Articles 59 and 61 share a common spirit and were originally sequential. Article 60, in fact, was a later interpolation, added because some Council Fathers insisted that a clearer distinction be drawn between sacrament and sacramental.[39]

Article 62 is a statement of some significance to this investigation.

> With the passage of time, however, there have crept into the rites of the sacraments and sacramentals certain features which have

---

38. The limitation to seven sacraments is a fairly late development; it was declared an article of faith at the Council of Trent (Session VII, Decree Concerning the Sacraments, Canon 1), although there was general consensus on the number seven by the time of Peter Lombard in the twelfth century. Augustine considered many actions and things "visible forms of invisible grace," such as the baptismal font, kiss of peace, creed, Lord's prayer, penitential ashes, salt. These the Church eventually called sacramentals. See: Leeming, *op. cit.*, pp. 553–568, 578.

39. Jungmann, *Commentary On the Documents of Vatican II*, Vol. 1, *op. cit.*, p. 46.

rendered their nature and purpose far from clear today; hence some changes have become necessary to adapt them to the needs of our own times.

This is a frank admission that ritual is and ought to be a product of history and culture. "With the passage of time," despite the Church's propensity for regulated uniformity, the dynamism inherent in ritual activity altered the shape of the rite, not always to its best advantage. Yet ritual is an expression of culture and ought to be perceived as such, which means that intentional changes must be made from time to time to render the action authentic and credible. In the Council's opinion, such is the case in modern times. The assumption clearly implicit here is not simply some inevitable reforms initiated by an external agency, but an understanding of liturgy as possessing its own capacity to be continually updated, if celebrated according to the laws of its own intrinsic nature. The sacramental principle, whereby God has empowered certain natural signs to produce supernatural effects, to be consistently incarnational, must coincide with the signs of the times.

What a change from the Tridentine fixation on rubrics and form. Clearly, a new era of sacramental development has begun. Sacraments are actions, not things. They are ecclesial, not private, grace events, beneficial to the entire faith community. The sacramental process is the movement of that community toward God, nurtured on the way by periodic encounters with the sacred in its midst. The implications of this shift from an individualistic sacramental piety to a community-centered spirituality continues to be explored.[40]

---

40. Of note: Avery Dulles, "The Church As Sacrament," in *Models of the Church, op. cit.,* pp. 58–70; Tad Guzie, *The Book of Sacramental Basics* (New York: Paulist, 1981); Monika Hellwig, *The Meaning of the Sacraments* (Dayton: Pflaum, 1972); Joseph Martos, *Doors to the Sacred* (Garden City, NY: Doubleday, 1981); Joseph M. Powers, *Spirit and Sacrament* (NY: Seabury, 1973); Karl Rahner, "What Is A Sacrament?", *Worship* 47 (1973), pp. 274–284; E. Schillebeeckx, *Christ the Sacrament of Encounter With God* (New York: Sheed and Ward, 1963); Juan Luis Segundo, *The Sacraments Today* (New York: Maryknoll, 1974); George S. Worgul, Jr., *From Magic to Metaphor* (New York: Paulist, 1980).

LITURGICAL THEOLOGY

Much has been written about theology and liturgy during the twentieth century. The dynamic insights of the liturgical movement's pioneers broke through the stereotyped theorizing of centuries to precipitate the radical reorientation of Vatican II. Liturgical theology emerged as a legitimate theological discipline during the decade of implementation that followed, as theorists and serious practitioners probed more deeply into the meaning of the Church's public prayer. To some extent, theology of liturgy and liturgical theology have been used interchangeably, although the latter is the more inclusive term. Since the medieval period, liturgy has meant simply the Mass and the Divine Office. Vatican II redefined it to include all the sacraments and sacramentals, and certain *pia exercitia* as well. Today, it is recognized that liturgical theology embraces a broad spectrum of theological emphases.

At the heart of liturgical theology or a theology of the liturgy is the Eucharist, the Mass. *Sacrosanctum concilium* devotes a separate chapter to a consideration of its essentials. In the opening lines of chapter two, the Eucharist is described as mystery (chapter title), sacrifice, memorial, sacrament, sign of unity, bond of charity, and paschal banquet (art. 47), thereby summarizing the characteristics of a eucharistic theology that has been developing throughout this century. The next paragraph lists the Eucharist's primary effects: that Christ's faithful "be instructed by God's word and be nourished at the table of the Lord's body" so that they be drawn daily "into more perfect union with God and with each other." This is to be achieved through rites and prayers in which the faithful "take part in the sacred action conscious of what they are doing, with devotion and full collaboration," in which they "learn also to offer themselves" by offering the Immaculate Victim with the priest (art. 48). The transition to a contemporary theology reflects here a balance between old and new, for at the heart of the Council's articulation on the Eucharist lies the strength of tradition, reinterpreted and augmented to incorporate new developments according to the principle of organic growth elucidated in chapter one (art. 23). Evident here are rationale and strategies pertaining to the document's basic goals: full, conscious participation by all in the ritual of the Church for the purpose of increased pastoral effectiveness.

The Eucharist is still the *mysterium fidei* it has been proclaimed to be for centuries during that most solemn moment of Consecration in the canon of the Mass, but it is no longer approached as locus of a *mysterium tremendum* before whom the faithful once recoiled and, through feelings of fear and unworthiness, forfeited that frequency of communion that is their heritage. The term "mystery" here is enriched with a meaning contributed by the architects of *Mysterientheologie* and the many subsequent theologians who commented and built upon it.[41] It involves participation in the mystery of Christ, his life, death, resurrection, whereby the events of *Heilsgeschichte* are reenacted, their influence transmitted, and their grace experienced anew in the present time. Through the medium of the liturgy, the power of past events is made present and applicable here and now. Through the mystery of the Eucharist, Christ is really present in the midst of the assembly and, in some mysterious, mystical way, the Church continues as the extension in time of the body of Christ.[42]

Sacrosanctum concilium expresses this understanding of mystery in its chapter on the liturgical year. " . . . Thus recalling the mysteries of redemption, the Church opens to the faithful the riches of her Lord's powers and merits, so that these are in some way made present for all time, and the faithful are enabled to lay hold upon them and become filled with saving grace" (art. 102).

41. From the monastery of Maria Laach: Odo Casel, *The Mystery of Christian Worship* (1932), originator of "mystery-theology"; Columba Marmion, *Christ In His Mysteries* (1924) and *Christ the Life of the Soul* (1925); Anscar Vonier, *Key to the Doctrine of the Eucharist* (1925). Some of Casel's premises were strongly criticized, particularly the relationship he claimed existed between Christianity and the Greek mystery religions. The mystery-theology underlying the Council's own theology of liturgy and Eucharist is the product of redaction and development. See: Louis Bouyer, "Liturgy and Mystery—Dom Casel's Theory Explained and Discussed," in his *Liturgical Piety* (Notre Dame: University Press, 1955), pp. 86–98; Charles Davis, "Odo Casel and the Theology of Mysteries," *Worship* 34 (1959/60), pp. 428–438; Bernard Leeming, "Liturgy and Mystery," *America* 109 (August 17, 1963), pp. 153–55; L.M. McMahon, "Towards A Theology of the Liturgy: Dom Odo Casel and the 'Mysterientheorie'," *Studia Liturgica* 3 (1964), pp. 129–154; Burkhard Neunheuser, "Mystery Presence," *Worship* 34 (1959/60), pp. 120–27.

42. While always a dimension of Christian theology, the notion of the Church as Christ's mystical body took on renewed relevance in the light of mystery theology and, with the Encyclical Letter, *Mystici Corporis* (1943) of Pius XII, emerged as primary image of the pre-Conciliar Church, exerting an influence on the Council's liturgical document.

This is the sense in which *memoriale* is to be understood. Keeping the memory of the Lord's death and resurrection until he comes (art. 47, 102) is not simply an intellectual exercise but a participation—conscious, devout, with full collaboration (art. 48)—in the event itself. That is why baptism is described as being "plunged into the paschal mystery of Christ," whereby individuals "die with him, are buried with him, and rise with him" (art. 6) in an appropriation of Christ's own *transitus* from death to life. That is why Christ chose to sacramentally "perpetuate the *Sacrificium Crucis* throughout the centuries until he should come again," entrusting to the Church "a *memoriale* of his death and resurrection" (art. 47) so that his people might share in it. It is in this sense that the *hostia immaculata* is "offered" by the faithful together with the priest, so that as they "learn also to offer themselves," they may become more and more open to the meritorious power of the mysteries of redemption and are drawn thereby into ever more perfect union with God and God's people through the mediation of Christ (art. 48). What is offered to God along with the substance of the bread is the life of the community and a willingness to be transformed.

Essentially, Vatican II ratified Trent's doctrine concerning the sacrifice of the Mass. However, it did rephrase some of its central constructs (namely, the notion of immolating in an unbloody manner the same Christ who once offered himself in a bloody manner on the altar of the cross), purged it of anathemas, revoked those disciplinary decrees that were reactions to the protest of the times (such as those forbidding the vernacular language and concession of the chalice), and revamped its theological bases. The present statement contains a broader, richer understanding of sacrifice, presented in the context of *convivium paschale*, the sacrificial meal. Theology of sacrifice is now balanced by a theology of the banquet, the sacred meal in which Christ is eaten (art. 47) and true communion is achieved. Sacrificial terms such as altar, priest, victim, immolated, consummated, used to describe the Eucharist prior to the Council, are now joined or replaced by words such as table, meal, banquet, celebrant, celebration, bread broken, wine poured, consumed. Instead of expiation and propitiation, the stress is now on reconciliation and communion, nurture, *viaticum*. The restoration of the supper dimension represents one of the more significant shifts regarding eucharistic theology and practice. The Sacrifice of the Mass is referred to more and more as the Lord's Supper, the Eucharist, with repercussions for piety and praxis. Catholics are now less fearful of approaching the *Coena Domini*. Frequent communion is no longer the exception, but the norm.

The theological rationale once established, the Council proceeds to decree some practical changes so that the Mass "may become pastorally efficacious to the fullest degree" (art. 49). The rite is to be revised and simplified, so that the intrinsic nature and interrelationship of its parts are clear and participation more easily achieved. Accretions of centuries, "elements which, with the passage of time, came to be duplicated, or were added with but little advantage, are now to be discarded," and "other elements which have suffered injury through accidents of history are now to be restored to the vigor which they had . . ." (art. 50). "The treasures of the bible are to be opened up more lavishly, so that richer fare may be provided for the faithful at the table of God's word" (art. 51). It is to be recognized that the Mass is made up of two distinct parts, "the liturgy of the word and the eucharistic liturgy," so closely connected with each other as to form but a single act of worship (art. 56). The homily is to be restored, so that "the mysteries of the faith and the guiding principles of the Christian life are expounded from the sacred text during the course of the liturgical year" (art. 52). The "prayer of the faithful" is also to be restored, so that people might make intercession for the Church and the needs of the world (art. 53). A suitable place may be allotted to the vernacular, particularly with regard to the readings, the prayer of the faithful, and those parts of the ritual which pertain to the people. Reception of the Lord's body at every celebration of the Mass is strongly recommended as the "more perfect form of participation" (art. 55). Under certain circumstances, according to the discretion of the bishops and the guidelines established by the Apostolic See, communion under both kinds may be administered (art. 55). The practice of concelebration is permitted once again (art. 57).

Contrary to the extensive debate carried on at the Council of Trent, Vatican II did not address the issue concerning the manner of Christ's eucharistic presence. Transubstantiation is never mentioned. This in itself is theologically significant and serves to differentiate Vatican II sharply in tone and purpose from the sixteenth century's council of reform. In fact, the notion of Christ's presence is only alluded to in those articles concerning the Eucharist. Everything essential had already been said in the radical assertion of article seven, which enumerated the various modes of Christ's presence: in the sacraments; in his word; when the Church prays and sings; in the Mass, in the person of his minister, but especially under the eucharistic species. It is stressed here that Christ is always present in his Church, especially in liturgical celebrations. Speculation regarding the specific manner in which Christ is really present in the Eucharist was left to future theologians.[43] This is not to imply that the Council was unconcerned about a theology of presence. On the contrary, a conscious effort is made throughout *Sacrosanctum concilium* to foster an awareness of Christ's presence in his mysteries celebrated throughout the liturgical year, in all the sacraments, in the proclamation of his word, and in the midst of the assembly, whenever the People of God gathers for prayer and praise. Such an approach was deemed necessary in order to offset theology's previous fixation on the eucharistic elements as locus of Christ's Real Presence, to the disparagement of other legitimate modes in which he was also "really present." Post-Conciliar discussions on Christ's Real Presence in the Eucharist continue within this broader context.[44]

43. Transubstantiation was the subject of an encyclical, *Mysterium Fidei* (1965), issued by Paul VI at the opening of the Council's Fourth Session as a response to those promoting phenomenological theories of Real Presence and as a gesture toward the more conservative forces in the Church.

44. These include a reinterpretation of transubstantiation, introduction to the more dynamic "transignification" and "transfinalization" to explain how Christ is really present in the Eucharist, and a global perspective with implications for world hunger, justice, and liberation. See: Tissa Balasuriya, *The Eucharist and Human Liberation* (Maryknoll, NY: Orbis, 1979); Charles Davis, "The Theology of Transubstantiation," *Sophia* 3 (1964), pp. 12–24; Regis Duffy, *Real Presence* (New York: Harper & Row, 1982); Tad Guzie, *Jesus and the Eucharist* (New York: Paulist, 1974); Monika Hellwig, *The Eucharist and the Hunger of the World* (Paramus: Paulist, 1976); David N. Power, "Words That Crack: The Uses of 'Sacrifice' in Eucharistic Discourse," *Worship* 53 (1979), pp. 386–404; Joseph M. Powers, *Eucharistic Theology* (New York: Herder, 1967); James Quinn, "Ecumenics and the Eucharist," *The Month* 33, 34 (April, May, September, 1965), pp. 210–16, 272–81, 170–76; E. Schillebeeckx, *The Eucharist*, tr. by N.D. Smith (New York: Sheed and Ward, 1968) and "Transubstantiation, Transfinalization, Transfiguration," *Worship* 40 (1966),

Although chapter three of *Sacrosanctum concilium* on the other sacraments and the sacramentals has already been examined under the category of sacramental theology, it is important to point out here that these are now considered a part of liturgical theology, because the Council has included them within its definition of liturgy. As mentioned earlier, the connection is made explicit in article 61: "Thus, for well-disposed members of the faithful, the liturgy of the sacraments and sacramentals sanctifies almost every event in their lives."

The Council's treatment of the sacraments in chapter three is remarkably different from the dogmatic considerations of the Council of Trent. The approach is wholly pastoral and liturgical. General principles of reform applied to specific sacraments call for a renewal of all rites from a pastoral perspective. In baptism, the adult catechumenate is to be restored with rites to be celebrated at successive intervals. The relationship of confirmation to the whole . of Christian initiation is to be more clearly set forth. The rites, formulas, and ceremonies of the remaining sacraments—penance, anointing of the sick, ordination, marriage—are to be revised in such a way that the grace of these sacraments is more clearly signified. The sacramentals are also to be revised and their circumstances updated to enable the faithful to participate intelligently, actively, and easily. Provision is to be made for certain sacramentals, under special circumstances, to be administered by qualified lay persons, and it is stated that new sacramentals may be added as the need for these becomes apparent. The rite of Christian burial is to reflect more clearly its paschal character and correspond more closely to the traditions of local cultures. This radical reorientation of sacramental understanding is foundational to the entire effort of Vatican II.

Sacrosanctum concilium has also devoted a full chapter to the Divine Office, long a part of the official and therefore liturgical prayer tradition of the Church. The theological mandate for this Liturgy of the Hours is stated at the outset: Christ, high priest of the eternal covenant, "continues his priestly work through the agency of his Church, which is ceaselessly engaged in praising the Lord and interceding for the salvation of the whole world" (art. 83). Traditionally, the office is so devised that "the whole course of the day and night is made holy by the praises of God" (art. 84). When performed correctly by those designated for this purpose, "it is the very prayer which Christ himself, together with his body, addresses to the Father" (84).

Some practical reforms follow. Because the purpose of the office is to sanctify the day, the traditional sequence of the hours should relate once again to the proper time of day, but in a way that is sensitive to the conditions of modern times and the demands of daily life and the active apostolate (art. 88). While the divine office is the public prayer of the Church, it is also a source of piety and should nourish personal prayer. Therefore, it should be prayed attentively and with comprehension (art. 90). To this end, the psalter is to be revised and the psalms distributed over a longer period of time (art. 91); the choice of readings is to be more extensive and accounts of the saints are to accord with the facts (art. 92); vernacular translations may be used whenever the Latin constitutes a grave obstacle to praying properly (art. 101). Lauds and Vespers as morning and evening prayer are to be celebrated again as the two chief hours (art. 89) to which the laity are particularly invited (art. 100). As with other aspects of the liturgy, practical reforms proceed here from pastoral considerations and a desire to make the best of Christian tradition compatible with the expectations of the times.

The document *Sacrosanctum concilium* is both theological and practical. It takes history seriously, acknowledging that theology and experience revitalize one another in meaningful rituals that form, inform, and transform the community of faith prior to the transformation of society. The document, however, is only a guideline. Consequently, much has been left unsaid. It was not the Council's task to make explicit the pluriform possibilities for implementation or to determine precisely how the liturgy might be made effective in a given culture of the post-Conciliar age. This task was left to local liturgists and to the area of liturgical theology under the guidance of local ordinaries.

As a field of exploration and application, liturgical theology is still feeling its way. Cyprian Vagaggini's treatise on the theological dimensions of the liturgy was a valuable compendium prior to the

Council and a useful resource afterward.[45] In 1963, Notre Dame's *Yearbook of Liturgical Studies* published a serious piece that developed a philosophical basis for constructing a liturgical theology.[46] In 1976, a subcommittee of the newly formed North American Academy of Liturgy presented four models for research and teaching in the field, and concluded that a single liturgical theology was neither a possible nor a desirable goal.[47]

The need for a liturgical theology is clearly recognized. Most liturgists will concede that it ought to consist of anthropological, sociological, and psychological components, that its substance as well as its function is integrative and its implementation pluriform. Judging from the literature of recent years, such a liturgical theology is slowly taking shape.[48] According to the dialogue, this theology would have a critical function rather than an explanatory one.[49] Its role would be facilitative, mediating cult to culture and enabling people to discover the appropriate means for hearing and

45. First published in English in 1959, the fourth and present edition was revised and greatly expanded. *Theological Dimensions of the Liturgy*, tr. by Leonard Doyle and W.A. Jurgens (Collegeville: The Liturgical Press, 1976).

46. Charles H. Henkey, "Liturgical Theology," *Yearbook of Liturgical Studies* 4 (1963), pp. 77–107. Suggesting that self-expression into the universe, when directed toward God, is the natural essence of liturgy, Henkey searches for a formal object of such self-expression, which he determines is beauty. Finding that the Scholastic system based on Intellect and Will leaves no room for a liturgical theology, he favors Augustine's three-faculty scheme of Memory, Intellect, and Will, concluding that self-expression into the universe is the formal act of the infused virtue of hope and the formal object of liturgical theology, and that liturgy itself is an act of hope.

47. Joseph M. Powers, "Liturgical Theology I," *Worship* 50 (1976), pp. 307–312. Also, Edward J. Kilmartin, "Liturgical Theology II," *Worship* 50 (1976), pp. 312–315.

48. Walter J. Burghardt, "A Theologian's Challenge to Liturgy," *Theological Studies* 35 (1974), pp. 233–48; Mary Collins, "Critical Questions for Liturgical Theology," *Worship* 53 (1979), pp. 302–17; Peter E. Fink, "Towards A Liturgical Theology," *Worship* 47 (1973), pp. 601–09 and "Liturgy and Pluriformity," *The Way* 20 (1980), pp. 97–107; John Gallen, "American Liturgy: A Theological Locus," *Theological Studies* 35 (1974), pp. 302–11; John Macquarrie, "Subjectivity and Objectivity in Theology and Worship," *Worship* 41 (1967), pp. 152–60; Raimundo Pannikar, *Worship and Secular Man* (London: Darton, Longman and Todd, 1973); Kevin Seasoltz, "Anthropology and Liturgical Theology: Searching For A Compatible Methodology," *Concilium* 112 (1979), pp. 3–13.

49. David N. Power, "Unripe Grapes: The Critical Function of Liturgical Theology," *Worship* 52 (1978), p. 387.

reverencing God.[50] It would seek a proper language of liturgical communication, one that is essentially non-verbal and symbolic, rooted in metaphor, imaginative disclosure, and attitudinal change.[51] If liturgy is indeed the basic language of faith, then liturgical theology has a vital and relevant role to play. Its challenge is to remain attuned to the celebrative, imaginative, and experiential, to resist domination by the cognitive and didactic, that is, to be liturgical as well as theological. That in itself will be a significant contribution to the Church in modern times.

SUMMARY

The post-Conciliar years have been marked by a theological *aggiornamento* in ecclesiology and in sacramental theology. Since Vatican II, this latter category has been absorbed within the scope of the newly emerging discipline known as liturgical theology. The new theological dimensions make more explicit the intimate connection between the Church and its liturgy. A changed perception of the Church and its mission is the basis for the radical revision of all the liturgical rites. The new ecclesiology, heavily influenced by *Gaudium et spes*, the pastoral constitution on the Church in the modern world, has extended the boundaries for liturgical reform and renewal beyond anything the pre-Conciliar Church could have envisioned. The newly revised rites now reflect a Church fully aware of itself as the people of God committed to being a believable sign in the midst of human society. A revitalized community of believers is once again exercising its right to participate in the liturgical action, aware that its cooperation is necessary for the liturgy to produce its full effects. The liturgy of the Church now consists of all the sacraments and sacramentals, and the liturgy of the hours, and possesses the potential to extend its spirituality more deeply into many other aspects of prayer and life. Of all the recent changes in theology and practice, this latter may eventually have the most far-reaching and creative effects.

50. David N. Power, "Cult To Culture: The Liturgical Foundation of Theology," *Worship* 54 (1980), p. 483.
51. Mark Searle, "Liturgy As Metaphor," *Worship* 55 (1981), pp. 98–120.

5

Implementing Vatican II: Liturgical Legislation and Its Implications

VATICAN II ESTABLISHED THE BROAD FRAMEWORK FOR SIGNIFICANT liturgical change, but the real test of its vision lay beyond its jurisdiction. The pastoral challenge of putting its general principles into practice lay with those central agencies responsible for formulating legislation for the whole Church and with territorial episcopal authorities around the world. The Council was followed by a burst of activity on all levels. Rome began immediately to interpret Conciliar data and provide guidelines for the local application of universal norms. Episcopal conferences prepared to petition Rome for confirmation of decrees that exceeded their own authority. Individual Catholics awaited the changes with impatience or dread.

The purpose of this final preparatory chapter is to review the extent of liturgical development after the Council and to come to some understanding of the deeper significance underlying specific changes. This will be approached from the perspective of ecclesiastical legislation and will embrace the following steps. Major liturgical legislation promulgated by the Holy See after the Council will be briefly reviewed. Local implementation of universal legislation and the influence of local initiatives on the decision-making process of the Holy See will be examined from one national perspective, that of the United States. An evaluation of this post-Conciliar period will include an examination of the impact and the consequences of radical ritual change on a Church unaccustomed to diversity and progress; the attitude of the Holy

See toward local and experimental innovations; and current opinions regarding the interpretation of ecclesiastical law. Conclusions relevant to the problem and thesis of this book will be drawn before proceeding to Part Three and an analysis of Church music legislation.

UNIVERSAL LEGISLATION

The pontificate of John XXIII was preoccupied with preparing the way for the ecumenical council he had convoked. Taking his cue from the world around him, his general proclamations were charged with a vision that anticipated change. Liturgical documents from this period are but a prelude to an imminent, more radical period of revision and reform. Decrees concerning ritual references to other faith expressions reflect an ecumenical sensitivity.[1] The omission of the Leonine Prayers after Mass on selected occasions was a step toward eliminating ritual accretions.[2] A new rubrical code for missal and breviary featured a revised calendar for feasts and seasons which restored Sunday to its place of prominence and achieved a more accurate balance between the temporal and sanctoral cycles and the ranking of liturgical feasts.[3] The elimination of rubrical minutiae that had been accumulating for generations resulted in an updated yet dated compendium of the Church's ritual regulations which would serve as a functional starting point for post-Conciliar reform. A return to the liturgical principles of early Christianity is reflected in those changes in the ritual for the baptism of adults, whereby baptism would be distributed in degrees throughout a catechumenate as ritual acknowledgment of progressive stages in the instructional pro-

1. John XXIII, Order Amending the Good Friday Prayers Regarding the Jews, March 17, 1959; Congregation of Rites, Private Decree Regarding Certain Formulas to be Deleted from the Ritual Baptism of Adults, November 27, 1959.

2. Congregation of Rites, Decree on Omission of the Leonine Prayers after Mass, March 9, 1960. These were prayers, usually in the vernacular, ordered to be said after Low Mass by Leo XIII because of the loss of the Papal States, but after the Lateran Treaty of 1928, Pius XI ordered them recited for Russia.

3. John XXIII, *Rubricarum instructum, motu proprio* on the New Rubrical Code, July 25, 1960; Congregation of Rites, *Novum rubricarum Breviarii*, Decree Promulgating the New Rubrical Code, July 26, 1960.

cess.[4] There are hints of *aggiornamento* in permissions granted by special indult or through private response. Vernacular usage is extended in certain cases.[5] A limited acceptance of female lectors is affirmed.[6] The public recitation of the rosary during Mass is discouraged.[7] The importance of the ritual Word is extolled on various occasions, and preachers are exhorted to become familiar with the scriptures, to prepare meaningful homilies offering the "solid nourishment of truth," and to cultivate an authentic ministry of the word.[8] Bit by bit the way is prepared for the change that is to come. Therefore, the apostolic constitution promoting the study of Latin issued just before the Council's convocation took liturgists by surprise.[9] The controversial document extols Latin as an impartial language acceptable to all and, of its very nature, suitable for promoting all forms of culture among peoples. Latin is presented as a living language which is to be preserved or, where necessary, restored as the universal instrument of communication between Rome and the churches of the Latin rite. Its teaching is to be made mandatory in seminaries. No one is to write against its use in the liturgy. Coming as it did on the eve of the Council, the document caused tensions to deepen and polarization to increase.

The task of implementing the decisions of Vatican II fell to Pope Paul VI. He initiated the process with *Sacram liturgiam*,[10] in which he announced the establishment of a special commission[11] to

4. Congregation of Rites, *Ordo Baptismi adultorum*, Decree on Changes in the Roman Ritual, April 16, 1962.

5. Holy Office, Indult granting permission for Epistle and Gospel in the Vernacular in Germany, February 11, 1959; Congregation of Rites, Indult granting permission to omit prior reading in Latin of Holy Week prophecies and Gospel, March 9, 1959; Congregation for the Propagation of the Faith, Indult granting Archdiocese of Calcutta use of vernacular in certain parts of the Mass, July 12, 1961.

6. Congregation for the Propagation of the Faith, Private Response, December 16, 1961.

7. Congregation of Rites, Private Response, February 6, 1960 and May 25, 1960.

8. John XXIII, *Il Signore*, February 10, 1959, and *L'incontro*, February 13, 1961, Allocutions to Lenten Preachers and Parish Priests of Rome.

9. John XXIII, *Veterum sapientia*, Apostolic Constitution, February 22, 1962.

10. Paul VI, *Sacram Liturgiam, Motu proprio*, January 25, 1964.

11. *Consilium ad exsequendam Constitutionem de Sacra Liturgia*, hereafter to be called *Consilium*.

revise the rites, prepare new liturgical books and, in general, to implement in the best possible way the prescriptions of *Sacrosanctum concilium*. Certain norms were to become effective immediately.[12] These included the teaching of liturgy in seminaries, schools of religious communities, and theological faculties; the establishment of diocesan liturgical commissions; a mandatory homily during Mass on Sundays and holy days; the suppression of the Hour of Prime; acknowledgment that members of institutes bound to recite a "little office" or sections of the Divine Office participated in the public prayer of the Church. With regard to territorial episcopal conferences, the document established that the term "territorial" was to be understood to mean "national." These conferences were reminded that the vernacular translations of the Divine Office permitted by *Sacrosanctum concilium* (art. 101) must first be reviewed and approved by the Holy See.

Sacram liturgiam was followed by the first of three major instructions issued jointly by the Congregation of Rites and *Consilium* on general liturgical reform. *Inter Oecumenici* outlined the extent to which *Sacrosanctum concilium* could be implemented before the completion of the revised liturgical books.[13] The duties of bishops' conferences were more carefully defined, the composition and expectation of liturgical commissions described, the close connection between liturgy and pastoral activity emphasized, and the liturgical education and spiritual formation of clerics outlined. Specific changes in the rules for Mass, effective immediately, followed. The opening prayers at the foot of the altar are to be shortened, the Last Gospel and Leonine Prayers omitted. The celebrant is not to repeat the people's parts but may join them in the Ordinary of the Mass. The lesson may be read by a qualified lector. All readings are to be done facing the people. A homily is obligatory on Sundays and major feasts and is recommended at other times. The prayer of the faithful is to be instituted and carried out in the manner described. The secret prayer, the doxology and amen at the end of the Canon are to be chanted or recited aloud. At Low Masses the *Pater Noster* is to be recited by

---

12. That is, at the end of the interim period required by canon law between the promulgation of a decree and the taking effect of its binding force.

13. Congregation of Rites, *Inter Oecumenici*, Instruction on Putting into Effect the Constitution on the Liturgy, September 26, 1964.

priest and people in the vernacular; in sung Masses the people may sing with the priest in Latin. The formula for distributing communion is to be changed to *Corpus Christi* to which the people respond, *Amen!*

Those parts of the Mass which regional authorities may allow in the vernacular, provided their decrees are "approved, that is to say, confirmed, by the Holy See," are listed in the document.[14] Vernacular is also permitted, with approval, for other rites, including their essential forms. An account of the criteria on which translations are based must be forwarded to the Holy See along with any request for vernacular usage. With regard to the Divine Office, clerics not bound to recitation in choir may apply locally for vernacular concessions in case of felt need. Churches should be constructed so as to facilitate the active participation of the faithful. The altar is to be away from the wall to allow the celebrant to face the people. The celebrant's seat should be arranged so that he appears to be truly presiding, avoiding any appearance of a throne. Choir and organ should be positioned so that those who fulfill these functions form part of the congregation. The tabernacle for reservation of the Blessed Sacrament may be placed elsewhere in the Church. In general, these are the major points in *Inter Oecumenici*. The specific ritual changes mandated by the document changed the face of the liturgy.

Many liturgical documents of varying importance appeared in quick succession during the decade that followed.[15] Major legislation was promulgated by Paul VI in the form of apostolic constitutions and letters *motu proprio* and jointly by the Congregation of Rites and *Consilium* as instructions, declarations, or decrees. The arduous task of ritual revision was accomplished in stages over a period of some years.

Shortly after *Inter Oecumenici*, Rome issued an instruction on the use of music in liturgical celebrations.[16] This was followed by the

---

14. These are: readings; prayer of the faithful; Ordinary; Proper antiphons: Introit, Offertory, Communion; what is sung between the lessons; all acclamations, greetings, and dialogue formulas; the formulas: *Ecce Agnus Dei, Domine non sum dignus,* and *Corpus Christi*; the *Pater Noster*, its introduction, and the *Libera nos*.

15. See Bibliography: Primary Sources, for a list of liturgical legislation after the Council.

16. Congregation of Rites, *Musicam sacram*, Instruction on Music in the Liturgy, March 5, 1967.

second of three instructions on general liturgical reform.[17] In order to further develop the participation of the faithful, many bishops had requested more extensive changes than were permitted by *Inter Oecumenici.* While hesitant to compromise the still unfinished revision of liturgical books, Rome nevertheless agreed to the following adaptations: the insertion of one or more intentions for special local needs in the prayer of the faithful; the recitation of the Canon aloud, if opportune; a period of communal reflection after communion; the extension of vernacular concession to the Canon of the Mass and to the lessons of Divine Office, even in choral celebration.

Two major pieces of legislation appeared early in 1969, marking a milestone in the post-Conciliar process of revision and reform. In February, Paul VI issued his *motu proprio* on the reorganization of the Church's liturgical year and the new universal Roman calendar,[18] in which the paschal mystery was once again restored to its central place in salvation history, with Lent through paschaltide the primary liturgical season and Sunday "the original feast day . . . the foundation and kernel of the whole liturgical year."[19] Festivals of the saints were put into proper perspective with the deletion of many names from the universal calendar and their cultic commemoration recommended for local observance in those territories concerned.

Six years after *Sacrosanctum concilium,* the long-awaited Roman Missal revised according to the directives of Vatican II was made available to the universal Church.[20] The Mass had been simplified. Duplications were deleted, missing elements restored. Three new eucharistic prayers, or canons, were added as options. Biblical readings were extended over a three-year cycle, with the addition of a third reading, ordinarily from the Old Testament, on Sundays and major feasts.[21] The responsorial psalm between the readings

17. Congregation of Rites, *Tres abhinc annos,* A Further Instruction on the Correct Implementation of the Constitution on the Liturgy, May 4, 1967.

18. Paul VI, *Mysterii Paschalis, Motu proprio* on Revision of the Liturgical Year and Calendar, February 14, 1969.

19. *SC,* art. 106.

20. Paul VI, *Missale Romanum,* Apostolic Constitution on the New Roman Missal, April 3, 1969; Sacred Congregation of Rites and *Consilium, Institutio Generalis Missalis Romani* and *Ordo Missae,* April 6, 1969. *Editio typica.*

21. See Congregation for Divine Worship, *Ordo lectionum Missae,* May 25, 1969, *editio typica,* second edition, July 24, 1970.

and the greeting of peace before communion were reintroduced into the rite. The commission for revision was deeply concerned about the functional aspect of the rite and not simply a rearrangement of rubrics. The General Instruction that forms an introduction to the missal explains its rationale for reform: to reveal clearly the general structure of the Mass, which consists of the Liturgy of the Word and the Liturgy of the Eucharist "so closely connected as to form one act of worship,"[22] along with introductory and concluding rites; to stress the ecclesial and participational nature of the celebration, and to allow scope for pastoral sensitivity and discernment. To this end, many elements and forms were proposed as options to be selected and rearranged according to individual circumstances. Special ministries specifically for laity were designated and described. Participation and teamwork were anticipated as the norm.

> All concerned should work together in preparing the ceremonies, pastoral arrangements and music for each celebration. They should work under the direction of the rector and should consult the people about parts which belong to them.[23]

The genius of the new Roman rite lay in its flexibility and in the scope for variety possible within the framework of its fixed form. With the completion of the calendar, the new lectionary, and the Missal, the *Consilium* phased out of existence as a separate entity and was absorbed into the Congregation of Rites, marking the end of the initial phase of post-Conciliar renewal and reform.

Two documents picked up on the flexible and pastorally oriented spirit of the new *Ordo Missae*. The first was an instruction on Masses for special gatherings of those who share a common spiritual or apostolic commitment or choose to come together out of a desire for mutual edification, hoping thereby to deepen and intensify Christian life.[24] It offered norms for these celebrations, with a positive acknowledgment of the value of such events. While

---

22. Congregation of Rites and *Consilium*, General Instruction of the Roman Missal, April 6, 1969, art. 8 (*SC*, 56). Eng. tr. approved by National Conference of Catholic Bishops (hereafter, NCCB).

23. *Ibid.*, art. 73.

24. Congregation for Divine Worship, *Actio pastoralis*, Instruction on Masses for Special Gatherings, May 15, 1969.

it was still fairly restrictive, *Actio pastoralis* did at least recognize the need for non-territorial assemblies and their special characteristics.

Several years later, Rome published the Directory on Children's Masses, one of the most refreshing and creative documents to come out of this period. Profoundly pastoral, honoring the educative and formative value of ritual as comprehensible sign, the document adapted the entire Mass rite to the level of children, allowing much scope for authentic and meaningful variation.[25] Those who prepared such celebrations were encouraged to de-emphasize the didactic and to consider the celebration "a special opportunity for making clear the connection between liturgy and life."[26] Concessions were made here that were disallowed anywhere else. The Liturgy of the Word could be celebrated in a completely separate place. If the priest is unable to adapt to the mentality of the children, "there is no reason why one of the adults should not preach a homily to the children after the Gospel."[27] The homily might even take the form of a dialogue with the children. The text of the Roman Missal prayers and other elements of the Mass could also be adapted because, when celebrating with children, "one cannot always insist on absolute identity."[28] Daily Masses with children were discouraged in order to avoid the risk of boredom.

The Congregation for Divine Worship issued its third instruction on general liturgical reform in order to promote the unqualified acceptance of the new *Ordo Missae* with its various options and structured flexibility and to curb those private initiatives that had arisen during the long wait for a revised ritual from Rome.[29] By publishing yet another set of guidelines, it hoped to resume control of all liturgical experimentation. It cautioned priests against any departure from established norms and reminded bishops of their responsibility in this regard. On the whole,

25. Congregation for Divine Worship, *Pueros baptizatos*, Directory for Masses With Children, November 1, 1973.

26. Tr: *TPS* 18 (1974), p. 331.

27. *Ibid.*, p. 324.

28. *Ibid.*, p. 323.

29. Congregation for Divine Worship, *Liturgicae instaurationes*, Third Instruction on the Correct Application of the Constitution on the Liturgy, September 5, 1970.

Liturgicae instaurationes reiterated what might and might not be done, elaborating on those areas for which it felt particular anxiety and concern.

The revised order of the Divine Office touched another area of deep liturgical significance, the sanctification of the day.[30] A special group within *Consilium* labored for seven years to produce the new Liturgy of the Hours, which abolished the weekly cycle and distributed the Psalter over a period of four weeks, expanded the selections from scripture, and included the Fathers and other ecclesiastical writers in the schedule of daily readings. Presented once again as the prayer of the whole human community to which Christ is joined, it recommended that the times, modes, and forms of recitation be adapted to the spiritual situation of those praying, so that the Office could become real personal prayer and the whole life of the faithful a true *leitourgia*.[31]

The post-Conciliar Church was very much concerned about office and ministry and, in 1967, Paul VI restored the permanent diaconate "as a distinct and permanent rank of the hierarchy," with a special grace and character.[32] It was no longer to be regarded as just a step toward the priesthood, but as an office with its own unique dignity and functions, many of them liturgical, open to those male candidates in either the celibate or married state. Several years later, Paul VI reordered certain liturgically oriented offices, abolishing the subdiaconate and establishing that the two remaining offices of acolyte and lector should absorb the subdiaconate's functions.[33] Known as "minor orders" to which candidates were formerly "ordained," acolyte and lector would

---

30. Paul VI, *Laudis canticum*, Apostolic Constitution on Renewal of the Divine Office, November 1, 1970.

31. The Greek term from which the modern English word "liturgy" is derived. Of secular origin, it referred to a public service or office imposed upon the wealthy citizens of ancient Athens for the common good. Its early Christian usage suggests a service performed by the people for the benefit of others. Applied to ritual, it implies active participation on the part of the worshiping assembly, according to designated roles.

32. Paul VI, *Sacrum Diaconatus Ordinem, Motu proprio* on Restoring the Permanent Diaconate, June 18, 1967; see also Paul VI, *Ad Pascendum, Motu proprio* on Clarifying the Role of Deacons, August 15, 1972.

33. Paul VI, *Ministeria Quaedam, Motu proprio* on the Ministries of Lector and Acolyte, August 15, 1972.

henceforth be referred to as ministries to be conferred by "installation" according to a designated rite. The ministries of acolyte and lector were now open to lay Christians, and would therefore no longer be reserved only to candidates for the Sacrament of Orders. Local episcopal authority could even request the recognition of other services as official ministries in the Church if it were pastorally good to do so. This in fact did happen. Before long, Rome recognized the role of the extraordinary minister for the distribution of Holy Communion, recommending that those appointed to this new ministry receive their mandate according to a specially designated rite.[34]

The final phase of post-Conciliar revision brought to completion all the remaining sacramental rites. All of these have been in use for some time now. The new Rite of Baptism for Children honors the various ministries and roles involved in the celebration of this sacrament and allows for suitable adaptations according to a variety of circumstances.[35] For the first time in the history of the Church, there is a baptismal rite especially designed for children. The separate Rite of Christian Initiation of Adults, truly a landmark achievement, features the restoration of the catechumenate and its sanctification by means of periodic liturgical rites.[36] The rite now consists of three clearly distinct stages: becoming catechumens; election or enrollment of names; celebration of the sacraments of initiation. The final stage incorporates the celebration of baptism, confirmation, the Eucharist, and a period of post-baptismal catechesis or *mystagogia*, which reflects a return to the practice of the early Christian church. The entire conversion experience is very closely identified with the paschal mystery of Christ's *transitus* through death to life and is ritualized in relation to the liturgical seasons of Lent and Eastertide.

The new rites for confirmation, ordination, and marriage reflect greater structural clarity.[37] The revised Rite of Anointing and Care

34. Congregation for the Discipline of the Sacraments, *Immensae caritatis*, Instruction on Greater Access to Holy Communion, January 29, 1973.

35. Congregation for Divine Worship, On the Order of Baptism of Infants, May 15, 1969; On the Revised Order of Baptism of Infants, July 10, 1969.

36. Congregation for Divine Worship, On the Order of Christian Initiation of Adults, January 6, 1972.

37. Paul VI, *Divinae Consortium Naturae*, Apostolic Constitution on the Essentials of the Confirmation Rite, August 15, 1971; Paul VI, *Pontificalis Romani*,

of the Sick, formerly called "Extreme Unction," is no longer a sacrament only for those who are at the point of death, but an extension of the Church's pastoral solicitude for those suffering from serious illness or old age.[38] The new Rite of Penance reflects the importance of the mystery and the ministry of reconciliation in three distinct rites.[39] In addition to the rite for reconciliation of individual penitents, there is a rite for reconciliation of several penitents, which emphasizes the ecclesial and communal dimensions of the sacrament by placing individual confession and absolution in the context of a celebration of God's word. There is also a rite for general confession and absolution in accordance with the pastoral norms previously issued.[40] Scope for adaptation includes the option of moving the sacrament from the confessional box to a reconciliation room where, face to face with one another, the priest welcomes the penitent warmly in a comfortable setting conducive to an exchange.

THE IMPLICATIONS OF REFORM

Two foci must be considered when examining the post-Conciliar period of revision and reform: activities in Rome and development on the local or national level in Latin rite localities around the world. Except for the differentiation determined by aspects of culture, personality, and style, any one nation can illustrate the new principles and norms that went into effect after the publication of *Inter Oecumenici*. The principle of decentralization was a key factor in shaping the reform. This was operative in two essential areas: authority and culture.

Although prohibited from making autonomous decisions in all areas of liturgical practice under their jurisdiction, the shift in relationship between central and local authority nevertheless gave

Apostolic Constitution on the New Rite of Ordination, June 18, 1968; Congregation of Rites, Decree on the New Order of Marriage, March 19, 1969.

38. Paul VI, *Sacram Unctionem Infirmorum*, Apostolic Constitution on the Anointing of the Sick, November 30, 1972.

39. Congregation for Divine Worship, Decree on the Rite of Penance, December 2, 1973.

40. Congregation for the Doctrine of the Faith, Pastoral Norms on the Imparting of General Absolution, June 16, 1972.

the bishops more freedom than they had enjoyed since Trent.[41] Some decisions could be made locally. Others had to be confirmed by Rome. The freedom to request changes not yet anticipated by those shaping universal legislation exercised significant influence on *Consilium* and provided the impetus for revision that went well beyond what the central authority had originally intended. *Consilium* often refused permission to individual territorial authorities for specific changes, then incorporated the content of those requests into new legislation.[42] The most obvious effect of decentralization, however, was expressed in terms of culture. The implementation of universal legislation no longer meant rigid uniformity but resulted instead in a pluriform liturgical expression with distinct national characteristics. Adaptation was the key to moving beyond revision and reform to the level of renewal and transformation which the Council documents envisioned and the Church itself desired.

In general, liturgical renewal in the United States proceeded remarkably well. Such a statement of course ignores the untold anguish lurking between the lines. Individuals and groups can document numerous experiences of too little or too much change at a pace that was too slow or too fast, but to address this reality in any detail would be inappropriate here. History can be considered from a variety of perspectives, up close, from a distance, from the viewpoint of an era. It depends on what one is looking for, detail or trends or significant cultural shifts. Looking back upon the post-Conciliar period from the vantage point of the present, one can safely say that genuine liturgical renewal has happened in the United States. Conciliar mandates and recommendations have been effectively implemented. Liturgy to some extent has a decidedly American stamp. If one ignores the disenchanted who have opted out of the structure, it can be said that conservative and liberal elements have been incorporated into the mainstream and that the Church has survived intact.

41. Authority to regulate the liturgy within certain defined limits now lies with national bodies of bishops. *SC*, art. 22.

42. In the United States, a comparison of episcopal and papal documents verifies this process with regard to vernacular concessions and special ministries (acolyte, lector, extraordinary minister of communion). See Bishops' Committee on the Liturgy (hereafter, BCL), *National Conference of Catholic Bishops Newsletter, 1965–1975* (Washington, DC: U.S. Catholic Conference, 1976), pp. 96, 249, 301.

It took a lot of energy, determination, and faith to wrest the Church in the United States from the domination of Tridentine spirituality and to nurture it anew in the spirit of Vatican II. The principles of liturgical renewal, long expounded by local liturgists and eventually supported by the bishops, gradually filtered down to take root in the average American parish. The National Conference of Catholic Bishops had established a standing committee on the liturgy in 1958. After the Council, the Bishops' Committee on the Liturgy played a central role in liturgical adaptation, preparing documents for decision by the bishops, taking initiatives to extend the limits of the criteria for implementation, releasing background statements on various points to educate the public to the reasons for change.[43]

In retrospect, one can say that the swiftness and extent of vernacular adaptation took everyone by surprise. The earliest concessions made on behalf of the people encompassed only the readings and the people's parts.[44] The positive effect of comprehension together with the incongruity of a bilingual ritual led to requests to extend the concession and, within three years, the vernacular was permitted even for the presidential eucharistic prayer with its words of institution.[45] Less than a decade after *Sacrosanctum concilium*, in which controlled vernacular concessions were not so much encouraged as allowed, Latin had disappeared as the ritual language of the Church.[46]

There were many changes surrounding the reception of Holy Communion. A lessening in the eucharistic fast made the sacrament more accessible to many people.[47] Gradual changes altered

---

43. Originally the Bishops' Commission on the Liturgical Apostolate. Renamed BCL in 1967. Newsletter containing official and unofficial material, first published in 1965 as source of information for bishops and liturgy commissions, now enjoys wider circulation.

44. *Inter Oecumenici, op. cit.,* art. 57.

45. *Tres abhinc annos, op. cit.,* art. 28.

46. *SC,* art. 36, 54, 63, 101, 113. With the publication of the Roman Missal, the transition was complete. On November 19, 1969, Paul VI declared to a general audience in Rome: "No longer Latin, but the vernacular, will be the principal language of the Mass." Tr: *TPS* 14 (1970), p. 330.

47. Beginning with Pius XII, the mandatory fast from solid food was shortened from midnight to three hours before the start of Mass (*Christus Dominus,* 1953; *Sacram Communionem,* 1957), to three hours before the reception of communion (Holy Office, *De ieiunio eucharistico,* January 10, 1964) to one hour before reception of communion (Holy Office, *Sul digiuno eucharistico,* December 4, 1964.)

the manner of reception.[48] The restoration of the cup contributed toward the fullness of the sign.[49] Special eucharistic ministers gave the laity a share in distributing Communion and made the sacrament more available to the sick.[50] The debate still continues over the composition of the altar bread.[51]

Certain changes were made with great reluctance. Chief among these concerned the involvement of women. Changes in practice have been slow to effect a change in attitude. At first, women could perform certain services, those occurring outside the sanctuary, at the rector's discretion.[52] Eventually, women were permitted to function as lectors, reading the scripture lessons and announcing the intentions, but were denied installation to the ministry of lector because of their sex.[53] They were, and still are, prohibited from the ministry of acolyte[54] and from the diaconate, which was opened up to lay men. In introducing the role of eucharistic minister, Rome extended to local authority the faculty of selecting candidates according to a designated order of suitable persons. The lay woman was last on this list.[55] The Bishops' Committee on the

---

48. New formula for distribution (Congregation of Rites, *Quo actuosius*, April 25, 1964); option to receive standing (BCL *Newsletter, 1965–1975, op. cit.*, p. 26); option to receive communion in the hand (Congregation for Divine Worship, *En reponse*, May 29, 1969; in the United States, this latter option failed to receive mandatory two-thirds majority vote of NCCB in 1970 and 1973; approved June 27, 1977; implemented November 27, 1977).

49. Permissible on certain occasions (Congregation of Rites, Declaration, March 7, 1965); faculty expanded (Congregation for Divine Worship, *Sacramentali Communione*, June 29, 1970); in the U.S. in January, 1979, the NCCB on its own authority extended faculty to include Sundays and holy days (BCL, *Newsletter, 1976–1980* [Washington, DC: USCC, 1981], p. 145).

50. Congregation for the Discipline of the Sacraments, *Immensae caritatis*, January 29, 1973.

51. *Institutio Generalis Missalis Romani*, April 3, 1969, art. 282–283; *Liturgicae instaurationes*, September 5, 1970, art. 5; Congregation for the Sacraments and Divine Worship, *Inaestimabile Donum*, Instruction, May 23, 1980. For documentation of the exchange between NCCB and the Congregation for the Doctrine of the Faith regarding eucharistic bread, see BCL *Newsletter, 1976–1980*, pp. 219–220.

52. *Institutio Generalis Missalis Romani, op. cit.*, art. 70; *Liturgicae instaurationes, op. cit.*, art. 7.

53. *Ibid.*, art. 66; Paul VI, *Ministeria Quaedam, op. cit.*, art. 7.

54. *Ministeria Quaedam, op. cit.; Liturgicae instaurationes, op. cit.*, art. 7.

55. Congregation for the Discipline of the Sacaraments, *Immensae caritatis*, art. 4.

Liturgy has made every effort to interpret the legislation of Rome in this regard with the greatest possible latitude. Installation to permanent ministries and inclusive liturgical language remain top priority goals.[56]

Rubrical and stylistic change dominated the first phase of liturgical renewal and kept it to the level of reform. Although for some the shift was traumatic and preparation inadequate, people eventually adjusted to praying aloud with some measure of active involvement in a language they could understand, face to face with the priest at the altar, greeted one another with a gesture of peace, received communion standing up, sometimes from one of the neighbors, perhaps even in their own hands. People spoke less and less of "hearing" or "attending" Mass and became accustomed to the new terminology: liturgy, celebration, presidential prayers.

The full, active participation so ardently desired by a pastorally-oriented Council led to a rediscovery of the meaning of ministry and broadened the scope for permanent lay ministries in the liturgy of the Church. The new pastoral liturgy is still in the process of revealing what it means to be pastoral and the ramifications of an active laity fully, freely involved. A change in the ritual's language has led to changes in the text. Pope Paul recognized the potential for this when he met with translators shortly after the Council:

> It may be that the venerability and richness of the Roman speech that the Latin Church has used through the centuries . . . will be partly lost for the sake of pastoral benefits. . . . [57]

56. Two votes on inclusive language failed to receive a two-thirds majority at November, 1979 meeting of NCCB: that the word "men" be deleted from the words of institution; that the celebrant be given the option to substitute inclusive word or phrase for generic term "man" in presidential prayers. Deletion of word "men" from institution narrative approved by NCCB November, 1980 and by Rome, November, 1981. See BCL *Newsletter* XV (December 1979), p. 189; XVII (December 1981), p. 45.

57. Paul VI, Address to the Congress of Liturgical Translators, November 10, 1965. Tr: *TPS* 11 (1966), p. 71.

The International Commission On English in the Liturgy had to make many compromises to produce an acceptable vernacular version of the liturgical texts.[58]

In retrospect the transition has been successful. The revised rituals are being followed with a fair amount of precision and ease, yet it is a fact that the long "interim" period before the appearance of the revised missal proved unsettling to many and left its mark on the American Church. Actions taken provisionally were hard to reverse with the promulgation of the new rules. Customs developed; patterns were established to fill in the lengthy void. A lot of local initiative was exercised while waiting for Rome to speak. Some of it was clandestine but liturgically sound, and included new styles of music, optional songs, prayers, and readings, the use of women lectors, communion in the hand. Such experimentation helped prepare the way for future changes. Other "underground" activities were not always appropriate and concerned Church authority both locally and in Rome. A curb on such activities was inevitable in order to safeguard against capricious change. However, a legitimate desire for more extensive adaptation and innovation nurtured during the interim failed to come to fruition as Rome reverted to a more restrictive posture with the promulgation of the revised liturgical books, shifting the burden of renewal to an orderly implementation of the established liturgical rites. The new rites do allow for local creativity, ensuring some measure of variety and flexibility through various options, a more extensive lectionary, and freedom regarding musical repertoire. Nevertheless, to confine cultural adapation to the limits set by the typical editions was not the Council's intent. At present, permission for

58. Established late 1963 with an episcopal board representing each English-speaking nation, an international advisory board of experienced liturgists, and a Secretariat located in Washington, DC, ICEL had the task of producing the official English translations of Latin texts for liturgical use. The difficulties of translating ecclesiastical Latin effectively and the many cultural linguistic nuances within the commonly-held English language have been continuing challenges. A common ecumenical text was the goal of the North American Consultation on Common Texts (CCT), a group with ecumenical representation, whose work was assimilated by the International Consultation on English Texts (ICET, established in 1969), an international and ecumenical body charged with translating and revising the basic liturgical texts most churches use. In 1970 ICET published *Prayers We Have In Common*. Support for these texts has been inconsistent. They have not been adopted for use in the Catholic liturgy in America.

any deviation from established rites or any controlled experimentation that might challenge those ritual limits must come from
the Holy See.[59]

The demands of a cultural adaptation initiated by the Council
and supported by the revised rites has brought the Church to the
threshold of yet another phase of renewal, one that is characterized by the term indigenization. The Church is only beginning
to discover just what this might imply. Fidelity to the process is
bound to bring local territorial authority up against the limits of
the law. According to *Sacrosanctum concilium*, regulation of the
liturgy depends not only on the authority of the Apostolic See, but
also, "within certain defined limits," on conferences of bishops as
well.[60] The definition of these limits has some direct bearing on the
local Church's ability to be an efficacious sign or sacrament to the
world in which it lives. The Council intended that the liturgy
"remain open to legitimate progress," that "new forms . . . grow
organically from forms already existing."[61] In many ways Rome
has tried to curb this open spirit. There is a perennial tension
between spirit and the law. What was said in another context has
relevance here:

> The historicity of the message and the quest for truth, as is easily
> understandable, will give rise to tensions between tradition and
> innovation. The danger of making historical trappings, transient by
> nature, into a permanent and unchanging reality, and the converse
> danger of letting what the Church has to keep forever flow along on
> the tide of history, are bound to produce divergent and conflicting
> attitudes. One pole of the tension will always be the official
> magisterium, charged with examining and adjudicating; the other
> will come from the respect due to freedom of conscience in
> adhesion to the faith.[62]

At times the spirit of renewal balks before a residue of retrenchment, when the basic freedoms of Vatican II are confronted by
post-Conciliar restraints. Those officially charged with implementing the Council's mandate to change what needed changing

---

59. See *Liturgicae instaurationes, op. cit.*, art. 12.
60. SC, art. 22.
61. SC, art. 23.
62. Jose Setien, "Tensions in the Church," *Concilium* 48 (1969), p. 75.

in order to restore the clarity of liturgical rites gifted the Church with an extraordinary achievement, but this does not mean that the process is complete. Life is always changing, and a liturgy that faithfully expresses life must remain open to change. Indeed, the Council never intended to impose another rigid uniformity, however up to date, but encouraged the genius of various races and peoples to permeate the Church's rites.[63] Should this process be limited to the magisterium or to designated options already prescribed? Statements emanating from Rome during the post-Conciliar period warn against what it considers to be capricious change.[64] How is one to evaluate these in light of Vatican II? Must there be an end to all experimentation in order to prevent some groups from going too far? To what extent is one bound by the negative commentary of the legislator? In this post-Conciliar age of co-responsibility, what is needed is a more enlightened understanding of the community's relationship to liturgy and its law.

There is a growing body of literature on the nature of liturgical law, modes of interpretation, and the obedience it demands.[65] The new liturgy brought new laws, a new style, a new spirit. In fact, says theologian Thomas Vismans, "the first rather drastic innovations in the liturgy, which were announced as the heralds of a series of further innovations, have created a new situation, of which we can hardly grasp the full extent and depth."[66] The Council Fathers inaugurated a new ecclesial polity when they chose to frame their liturgical document in the form of a constitution, a declaration of principle illustrated with practical

63. See SC, art. 37.

64. The list, too extensive to note here, includes various types of documents from Paul VI, the Congregation of Rites, and Consilium.

65. See especially: Peter E. Fink, "Liturgy and Pluriformity," The Way 20 (1980), pp. 97–107; John M. Huels, "The Interpretation of Liturgical Law," Worship 55 (1981), pp. 218–237; Walter J. Kelly, "The Authority of Liturgical Laws," The Jurist 28 (1968), pp. 397–424; Frederick R. McManus, "Liturgical Law and Difficult Cases," Worship 48 (1974), pp. 347–366; Ladislas Orsy, "The Interpreter and His Art," The Jurist 40 (1980), pp. 27–56; Thomas Richstatter, "Changing Styles of Liturgical Law," The Jurist 38 (1978), pp. 415–425 and Liturgical Law: New Style, New Spirit (Chicago: Franciscan Herald Press, 1977); R. Kevin Seasoltz, New Liturgy, New Laws (Collegeville: The Liturgical Press, 1980); Thomas Vismans, "Liturgy Or Rubrics?", Concilium 12 (1966), pp. 83–91.

66. Vismans, ibid., p. 85.

norms, anthropological in its approach and concern, and not to be interpreted in the usual juridical manner.[67] The Constitution itself states that "when the liturgy is celebrated, something more is required than the mere observation of the laws governing valid and licit celebration."[68] What is required of liturgical celebration is that an actively engaged community is "enriched by its effects."[69]

Thomas Richstatter sees the rediscovery of the laity as a factor radically influencing the new style of liturgical law, which is shaped by norms drawn from the liturgy's communal nature as the Constitution states.[70] In the exercise of its liturgical ministry, the assembly gives flesh to ritual structures, attempts to make them pastorally functional, shares responsibility for the celebration's design by selecting its optional elements. Officially, the first stage of post-conciliar liturgical renewal concerned the restoration of liturgical texts. Practically speaking, a haphazard yet wholly dynamic stage of interim legislation and experimentation preceded this, giving rise to some practices that were then incorporated into the new rites and initiating a pastoral awakening that would facilitate their implementation. The current critical stage concerns "the translation of these texts into living worship for the Church."[71] This too involves a certain dynamism and a degree of enculturation, for the texts are not simply formulas to be applied but represent a ritual experience to be embodied, ensuring diversity and variety within a given community as well as among the countless communities within the universal Church.

There are still other stages, however, because there are other aspects of liturgical renewal that have yet to be addressed. These include the rediscovery of *pia exercitia* for which there may or may not be existing rites or texts; the development of a more extensive system of sacramentals to complement the present sacramental system; the search for rites and rituals to meet the spiritual needs of the people of God in the present time. All of these areas are dimensions of liturgy as it is understood by the Council and are touched on in *Sacrosanctum concilium*. All have been neglected in

67. *Ibid.*, pp. 86–87; Walter Kelley, *op. cit.*, pp. 411–412.

68. *SC*, art. 11.

69. *Ibid.*

70. Richstatter, "Changing Styles of Liturgical Law," *op. cit.*, pp. 422–423; *SC*, art. 26–32.

71. John Gallen, "American Liturgy: A Theological Locus," *op. cit.*, p. 301.

the struggle to implement the Eucharistic liturgy, the sacraments, and more recently, the Liturgy of the Hours. It is in these former areas that the people themselves have failed to exercise their pastoral responsibilities. While it is true that leadership has directed its attention to established rites, as in the past, it is equally true that the people have done likewise. There is no doubt that a more enabling style of leadership would have done much to facilitate an awkward laity's exploration of further possibilities, but the fact that their participation has been limited to the official rites, primarily the Eucharist, is not wholly the fault of the leadership. Taking initiative is an expectation of shared responsibility in the post-Conciliar Church. Rome has concentrated on producing the official liturgical books. That has always been, and still is, Rome's primary responsibility. How guardianship over those books is exercised is still an unsettled question, but it must not distract the Church at large from addressing the yet unfinished business of the Council: those areas of liturgy in which greater pastoral freedom and creativity can be exercised and must be exercised if the fullness of liturgical life envisioned by Vatican II is to be achieved.

Rome elected to prepare the liturgical books and then enforce their strict observance as the proper sequence of liturgical renewal. Earlier liturgical praxis, however, long preceded its codification into books. It is ironic that a Church so dedicated to a return to its origins would embrace so definitively such a reversal of primitive Church experience. Custom, experience, usage preceded the formulation of laws. Even today, the 1918 Code of Canon Law acknowledges that "custom is the best interpreter of laws" (Canon 29).

All time-conditioned structures, no matter how flexible or pluriform, are subject to the maxim, *semper reformanda*. Vatican II gave the Church at large an active share in that process of reform. Kevin Seasoltz speaks of the principle of personal and conscious responsibility on which all of *Sacrosanctum concilium* is based. "Worship cannot be legislated, for it is the free and loving response of the whole person to a loving God."[72] The minister's responsibility is to contribute to the enrichment of all who take part in the celebration, not simply to assure a faithful observance

72. Seasoltz, *New Liturgy, New Laws, op. cit.,* p. 205.

of norms. In fact, pastoral considerations may sometimes demand that the minister go beyond the norms in order to bring the liturgy to life.[73] In this lies the new law and new spirit, that they may have life and have it to the full. To achieve this means keeping the pastoral and juridical characteristics of the new liturgy poised in creative tension. This challenge falls to all Christians, those in the parish as well as those in Rome. A Church in which "the liturgy daily builds up those who are within into a holy temple of the Lord, a dwelling place for God in the Spirit,"[74] could hardly settle for less.

From the perspective of its documentation, how does the post-Conciliar period measure up against such a criterion? What might be said of the overall spirit of both the legislation and the legislators responsible for shaping reform? It would be foolish as well as unfeasible to presume to do justice to an undertaking of such magnitude at a chapter's end. Nevertheless, these preliminary reflections would be incomplete without attempting this task.

Any such evaluative consideration must address feelings as well as facts. It is a fact that Paul VI was mandated to initiate, and accomplish, a movement of reform and renewal unparalleled in the history of the Church. He was faced with changing the structures of a Church that for four full centuries had been carefully programmed against change. Nurtured for most of its existence by a single cultural style, the Latin-rite Church in the twentieth-century was, nevertheless, intellectually and culturally diverse, conditioned by those scientific tendencies characteristic of the modern age, globally extended, spiritually entrenched, with liberal and conservative emphases, often indifferent, occasionally intense. The seeds of participation, adaptation, had to be thrown into the heart of this melting pot. Paul had to satisfy all factions, or at least avoid their alienation, and be sensitive to both old and new. It would have been enough simply to keep the Church free of schism. But together with those under his jurisdiction, Paul VI managed admirably to accomplish the Council's goals. The liturgy has been reformed according to the fundamental principles articulated at Vatican II. The rites have been revised so that they

73. *Ibid.*, p. 207.
74. *SC*, art. 2.

are biblically based, theologically sound, pastorally-oriented, traditional, yet up to date. The renewal of the life of the Church, rooted in its life of prayer, has definitely begun. This post-Conciliar period accomplished more than stylistic changes. There has been fundamental, ontological change. Paul's own evaluation concludes: "So let us not talk about a 'new Mass,' but rather about a 'new era' in the life of the Church."[75]

What can be said of the feelings behind the facts of change? The documentation gives clues to a deep-seated ambivalence in implementing the reform. Without a doubt, the Holy See was committed to the liturgical renewal mandated by Vatican II. What this meant, how it was communicated, contributed another dimension to the facts of the reform. From the outset, it was clear that every significant initiative must pass the judgment of Rome, which retained the right to approve or deny requests for change.[76] Experimentation was forbidden, except for that which came directly under Rome's control. Concern about "disciplinary irregularities in communal worship that have occurred in various places . . . that are wholly at odds with the precepts now in force in the Church" led to the condemnation of all unauthorized innovation.[77] Clergy and faithful were urged "not to give in to unbridled and freewheeling experimentation, but rather to perfect and execute the rites prescribed by the Church."[78] With the publication of the official books, this attitude was emphasized.

> The time has come now to put an end to all activities which disrupt the community (such activities are pernicious, whatever the ideology behind them!). Let us respect the norms which governed the work and let us implement in its totality a liturgical reform

75. Paul VI, Address on the New Mass Rite, November 19, 1969. Tr: *TPS* 14 (1970), p. 329.

76. One of the main controversies surrounding Paul's *motu proprio Sacram liturgiam* concerned this point of approval. The initial text was published in *L'Osservatore Romano*, January 29, 1964, and contradicted *Sacrosanctum concilium*, which had authorized regional conferences of bishops to choose and approve vernacular texts. The revised, official document was less definite, but subsequent interpretations placed the source of approval for translations and experimentation in general in Rome.

77. Paul VI, *Iuvat Nos*, Address to *Consilium* on Obstacles to Liturgical Renewal, April 19, 1967. Tr: *TPS* 12 (1967), p. 112.

78. *Ibid.*

which We approved in accordance with the decisions of the council.[79]

The Apostolic See assumed the responsibility for interpreting and protecting the spirit of Vatican II. Fear of a desacralization destructive to authentic worship led Rome to tighten the reins.

> This danger must be repulsed. Individuals, periodicals and institutions which may be under its spell must be won over again to the cause of the Church and its support. The norms and teachings of the Council must be defended.[80]

This dismissal of those who, perhaps in all sincerity, rearranged the rubrics to achieve what they perceived to be the Council's ends, established a clear dichotomy between those who, without deviation, followed the rules, accepting Rome's definition of renewal and its prerogative of ultimate control, from those who did not. This delineation was a significant byproduct of post-Conciliar reform.

There is no doubt that Paul VI dearly loved the liturgy. Even before his election, as Archbishop of Milan, he fostered the liturgical movement's aims.[81] This love of the Church's ritual together with fidelity to tradition and commitment to the Council's aims permeate his writings, along with his struggle to achieve a balance between conflicting forces, to incorporate both old and new. As a result, documents from this period often give mixed signals. It is easy for those in retrospect to quote a Paul of their choosing, one who is moving forward in the vanguard of reform, another who is carefully protecting what he values from the past. The following passages illustrate this point.

> Learn to be open to the spirit of renewal that is sweeping the world and penetrating into ecclesiastical regulations too.... [82]

79. Paul VI, Address to the Secret Consistory, June 27, 1977. Tr: *TPS* 22 (1977), p. 276.

80. Paul VI, *Iuvat Nos, op. cit.*, p. 113.

81. Giovanni Battista Cardinal Montini, "Liturgical Formation," *Worship* 33 (1959), pp. 136–164.

82. Paul VI, *Non possiamo tacere*, Address to Pastors and Preachers, March 1, 1965. Tr: *TPS* 10 (1965), p. 229.

Taken by itself this could well serve as a support for the liberal wing of the reform. However, it is followed immediately by:

> ... but, at the same time, learn to defend yourselves against the dizzy whirl of arbitrary innovations, of suggestions derived from a current brand of ideas which are not approved by the Church, and not supported by experience. Remember: *ex fructibus eorum!*[83]

Obviously, there is more to Paul's understanding of openness to the spirit of renewal than what at first appears. To a general audience at the beginning of the post-Conciliar period, he said:

> We must all change our customary outlook on sacred ceremonies and religious practice ... a new spiritual pedagogy has been born of the Council; this is its great innovation.[84]

To the *Consilium* entrusted with the specifics of renewal, he offered guidelines that include this statement:

> And if we are to have innovations, we should prefer those which make available to us the treasures left by the great epochs of Christian piety, rather than those of our own devising. But this does not deny the Church the right to express herself in modern terms, to "sing a new song," if the Holy Spirit's influence really is at work within her to inspire it.[85]

The careful perusal of other documents strengthens the portrait of a Paul who struggled to keep in balance what he knew ought to be done and what he might perhaps have preferred. It seems that Paul could deal fairly easily with the change that he himself managed, but had to struggle mightily with the implications of that change. This tendency toward duality further complicates an understanding of a complicated time. Perhaps mixed signals were necessary in order to coalesce a Church comprised of such extremes. It did assure that both sides were represented where the critical decisions were made. What makes this point particularly

---

83. *Ibid.*

84. Paul VI, Address to a General Audience, January 13, 1965. Tr: *TPS* 10 (1965), p. 193.

85. Paul VI, *Ecce adstat Concilium*, Address to *Consilium*, October 13, 1966. Tr: *TPS* 12 (1967), p. 10.

germane is the fact that what was said and done during this period has to a large extent become "normative" for future developments. Many who seek to understand the meaning of the Council look to the documents that implemented, and to a large extent interpreted, its principles and aims. It is crucial that one be able to distinguish the feelings from the facts.

The Church of the twentieth-century owes an enormous debt of gratitude to its leadership for bringing it to the present intact. Very tangible ritual accomplishments are a monument to history of the Paul whose papacy was servant to the phenomena of change. From Paul himself comes an appropriate epitaph for his time:

> Everything is moving, changing, evolving, everything is racing towards a future in which we are already living in our dreams.[86]

SUMMARY AND CONCLUSIONS

In summary, the implementation of the liturgical vision of Vatican II as articulated in *Sacrosanctum concilium* proceeded on two levels. The central level sought to provide the interpretive and legislative framework for local application of the Council's broad directives and norms. At the same time, national entities began to introduce the specifics of change into the local diocese and parish.

In Rome, Paul VI established a special *Consilium* to work along with the Congregation of Rites in implementing the Council's decree. Their primary responsibility consisted in the revision of the liturgical books, which meant the arduous task of simplifying the Church's established rites and rituals according to new criteria and norms. *Consilium* issued three major instructions on the liturgy. The first two clarified the type and extent of liturgical adaptation permissible during the interim period prior to the completion of the revision of the official books and anticipated some of the more permanent changes. The third instruction marked the close of the so-called interim phase of experimentation and implementation.

---

86. Paul VI, Address on the Church in a Changing World, October 28, 1970. Tr: *The Teachings of Pope Paul VI 1970*, (Washington, DC: USCC, 1971), p. 369.

The new Missal made available in 1969 reflects the best of the Council's expectations: a wholly vernacular rite restored to an earlier structural integrity, with a viable Liturgy of the Word enriched by an expanded lectionary and a required homily; a built-in flexibility provided by various options; opportunity for local adaptation and enculturation through songs, commentary, and prayers; and scope for full, active participation by the assembly according to designated roles. Before long, some of those roles were recognized as officially instituted lay ministries with rites of installation, namely, the ministries of acolyte, lector, eucharistic minister. The permanent diaconate was restored. The revision of the Liturgy of the Hours and the remaining sacramental rites was completed.

In America, liturgical reform and renewal has made a good beginning and continues to develop along positive lines. To a large extent, the American experience is paradigmatic of progress in a number of other nations, particularly Western Europe. Early enthusiasm hastened the availability of a completely vernacular liturgy and the full, responsible participation of the laity. The general thrust of development has centered on setting certain national guidelines for parish application and the production of numerous pastoral aids for all those involved in liturgical design and action. The renewal continues to reflect a strong pastoral emphasis. In the States, more and more attention is being paid to minority concerns. There is a growing sensitivity to inclusive language, to the special needs of the handicapped regarding full liturgical participation, to the rich ethnic composition of parish communities in this country and the need for a more diverse cultural expression. There has recently been a nationwide study of the Order of the Mass and a concerted effort to lessen the number of scheduled Masses to match more realistically the actual attendance patterns. Communication among levels remains open, facilitated by the Bishops Committee on the Liturgy, which relates to diocesan worship offices through the Federation of Diocesan Liturgical Commissions. In November 1983, the American bishops through the BCL issued a statement on prayer and worship to mark the twentieth anniversary of *Sacrosanctum concilium* entitled "The Church At Prayer—A Holy Temple of the Lord." While many bishops have written pastoral letters on the liturgy to the people in their dioceses, this was the first time that the American bishops as a body issued a pastoral statement specifically addressing worship and prayer. "Catholics need to know from their bishops that the liturgical reform of the last two decades has been a positive sign in the development of a deeper spiritual life in our country," to hear them "affirm our liturgical life and point us in newer directions for ongoing education and growth in a vibrant liturgical spirituality."[87]

Without a doubt, twentieth-century Roman Catholic liturgy has been marked by phenomenal change, both in its theology and in its ritual. The sheer scope of this change has been overwhelming, as the amount of data presented here indicates.

Liturgical reform and reorientation have evolved from fundamental theological shifts concerning the nature of the Church. Only recently conceived as an organization hierarchically structured, the Church has rediscovered its communal nature and the centrality of the people of God who participate in the priesthood of all believers. For centuries preoccupied with its universal character uniformly ordered, the Church has loosened its rigid control to allow for pluriform manifestations incarnate locally. Long concerned with protecting its divinely instituted heritage from profanation, the post-Conciliar Church is coming to grips with the facts of its humanity: conditioned by time, rooted in culture, caring about this world while awaiting with hope the world that is to come.

These theological shifts have had profound implications for the Church's ritual expression. Liturgy is not simply a collection of rites to be performed and perpetuated but actions to be experienced, the doing of which constitutes the concrete manifestation of the Church. Liturgy is what the Church is and believes. Therefore, it must be believable: the signs themselves must be credible and meaningful, the whole experience capable of effecting a transformation of the individual, the community, and the world. Liturgy now is more closely linked to life, and like life, it is constantly changing. This sense of dynamism conveys a richer sense of presence: God permanently in our midst, reason enough for the community's wholehearted participation in the keeping of a feast.

---

87. Archbishop Oscar H. Lipscomb of Mobile, who coordinated the document's preparation. BCL *Newsletter* XVIII (December 1982), p. 46.

Edward Schillebeeckx points out some difficulties confronting the post-Conciliar Church in its efforts to maintain and enliven "the spirit of Vatican II."

A careful watch will need to be kept to ensure that no misunderstanding arises around the considerable change of meaning given by Pope Paul VI in his address during the public session of 18 November 1965 to the concept of *aggiornamento* compared with the significance attached to it by Pope John XXIII. To quote Pope Paul: "Henceforth aggiornamento will mean to us: enlightened penetration into the spirit of the Council and the faithful application of the directives so happily and firmly outlined by the council." Before and in the early stages of the council, *aggiornamento* meant throwing open the doors and setting out on a journey of discovery. But in the meantime the council has reached definite decisions, so that from now on the *aggiornamento* is channelled. Herein also lurks the danger of a "post-Vatican catholicism," just as the Council of Trent led to a rigid "post-Tridentine Roman catholicism". . . . The criterion of every *aggiornamento* is the apostolic spirit of holy scripture, of which every council—Vatican II included—can only draw an historically situated profile.[88]

It is inevitable that the further the Church gets from the historical events of Vatican II, the more it will come to rely on individual perceptions and interpretations of both the event and its meaning as the basis of its own decision-making. As through a prism, the Council's vision acquires a kaleidoscope of nuances when refracted through the experience of those who try to put that vision into practice. *Aggiornamento* is a dynamic concept, the liturgy itself is a living entity, and both are wide open to the influence of human agency. *Aggiornamento* is never really finished. The liturgy is never finally renewed. The vision is never wholly incarnate in any one time or place. Yet the vision is transmitted with integrity when the dynamics of faith are firmly rooted in the perennial truths of revelation and find their focus in the living, risen Word made flesh. There will always be tension between the concerns of the central administrative level, charged with the guardianship of tradition, and the needs of the individual local community, but such tension can also be looked upon as the Church's creative

88. Edward Schillebeeckx, *Vatican II: The Real Achievement,* tr. by H.J.J. Vaughan (London: Sheed and Ward, 1967), pp. 83–84.

struggle to keep in balance a diverse people's fidelity to One who is, after all, beyond understanding.

A profound pastoral orientation is deeply embedded in the vision of Vatican II: a pastoral conception of the Church struggling to be a believable sign in the midst of the modern world, a pastoral liturgy in which all ritual expression is evaluated in terms of its effects. The Council envisioned such a pastoral spirit permeating all aspects of Church polity and practice, yet in the post-Conciliar Church it must be admitted that pastoral reform itself has not always been handled in a pastoral way. During the present phase of *aggiornamento*, the Church must come to terms with its greatest challenge, that of learning to be truly pastoral, and this can only be done effectively when all levels and factions become more sensitized to one another's point of view. There is a legitimate need for order, for coordination and regulation, for the protection of a legacy entrusted to us from the past, but there is also scope, in matters of lesser consequence, for a relaxation of the rules. There is a legitimate place within tradition for elements of ritualization arising out of present need, but there is also a danger in reducing a reenactment of the myth to the confines of a subjective piety. It is not easy to achieve a balance without relinquishing something of value, but the Church, having restored pastoral functions and defined itself in pastoral terms, would do well now to focus its energies on the finer points of a full pastoral identification in all areas, particularly in its liturgy.

Such a wholistic approach arises out of the Council's own understanding of liturgy as encompassing far more than the eucharistic rite and the Liturgy of the Hours. A fair balance between continuity and innovation has already been accomplished in the Church's official revisions of these rites. The same might be said of the other sacraments as well. The area that has remained undeveloped since the Council is that broad spectrum of possibilities included in the phrase *pia exercitia*. Traditionally, the people have expressed their creativity and spontaneity in the area of popular devotions, and pious practices have flourished throughout Christian history. The Council did not intend to eliminate this rich source of piety when it stressed the centrality of the Eucharist with its liturgy of the Word; rather, it wanted to ensure that such emphases did not substitute for the essentials, and that they be derived from the liturgy and its spirit.

Today, liturgical life in America consists almost exclusively of a periodic participation in the sacraments, thereby failing to achieve an integration of liturgy and life, which was the Council's intent. Such an integration needs the support of relevant popular devotions with deep liturgical roots in order to achieve a wholistic liturgical spirituality. Rosaries, novenas, Stations of the Cross, and processions once met a definite need. Pious practices that flourished before the Council were disparaged in an effort to reorient the community liturgically and theologically, and those that were appropriate have not yet been recovered. New practices have not yet arisen. It is uncertain which devotions today will fulfill the desire of families and small, intentional communities to experience Christ present in their midst. The Liturgy of the Hours, revised and restored to the people in order to fill this need, is not really catching on. Bible or Word services, popular at the time of the Council and in certain Third World nations today, have not taken root in American culture. Consequently, the eucharistic liturgy is made to bear the full pastoral burden of creative involvement on the part of the people, and this is a primary cause of much of the present tension. A eucharistic emphasis that features a daily availability along with a mandatory weekly participation makes it difficult to develop viable alternatives. But without such alternatives, the whole thrust of the Council regarding genuine liturgical renewal remains incomplete. The rediscovery of this area and its development within the framework and spirit of liturgy will have profound implications for the life of the Church, its catalogue of rituals, and its music.

III

VATICAN II AND THE USE OF MUSIC: AN INTERPRETATION

6

Papal Legislation on Music

FROM ITS INCEPTION, THE CHRISTIAN CHURCH EXPRESSED ITS NEW-FOUND faith in song. Scriptural documentation,[1] exhortations,[2] hymn fragments,[3] and acclamations,[4] as well as evidence from external sources,[5] testify to the early stages of a tradition of music in Christian worship.

Along with evidence of the use of song in the liturgy of the primitive Church are indications of the leadership's preoccupation with that song and an emerging theology of music. In fact, New

1. Acts 16:25; 1 Co 14:26
2. Eph 5:18–19; Col 3:16; Jas 5:13
3. Eph 5:14; 1 Tim 3:16; Phil 2:6–11; Heb 1:3; Rev. 4:11; 5:9, 2–13; 19: 1–2, 6
4. Amen, alleluia, hosannah; also, doxological and ter-Sanctus formulae embedded in New Testament literature, all remnants of the musical heritage of the synagogue.
5. The first definite piece of evidence outside the canonical writings regarding Christian liturgical song is recorded in a letter by the younger Pliny to the Emperor Trajan in the year 112 A.D.: "They [the Christians] insisted however that their whole crime or error came to this: they had the custom of meeting on a certain fixed day, before daybreak, to sing a hymn, alternating among themselves, to Christ as God. . . . "

In Justin's letter to the Emperor (around 150 A.D.): "We have learned that the only honor worthy of him is, not to consume by fire the things he has made for our nourishment, but to devote them to our use and those in need, in thankfulness to him sending up solemn prayers and hymns for our creation and all means of health, for the variety of creatures and the changes of the seasons . . . " (*Apology* I 13,2).

Testament hymn fragments are extant today only because theological commentaries have ensured their preservation and transmission. Authors of canonical epistles and books quoted hymns and expounded on them. These hymnic citations reveal little about the nature of early musical expression beyond the fact that it was Christological and credal.[6] There is no factual information at all regarding sound, style, or mode of execution that might enable a musical reconstruction. Theologically, however, the material is revealing. The texts selected for citation, their placement within a literary context, the nature and extent of textual redactions and accompanying commentary reflect the rudiments of a theology that continues to develop with the maturing Church.

Biblical studies are revealing more and more about the significance of the early Church's song in the shaping of its thought. Luke's placement of the Magnificat (perhaps a Maccabean war hymn)[7] on the lips of Mary at the beginning of his Gospel may indeed be a conscious device for signaling the advent of a new and messianic age of justice for the oppressed.[8] According to some scholars, the Prologue of the Gospel of John is a Logos hymn which has contributed much to an understanding of that book and to the Church's understanding of Jesus.[9] The cosmic redeemer

6. General studies: Josef Kroll, *Die Christliche Hymnodik* (Darmstadt: Wissenschaftliche Buchgesellschaft, 1968); R.P. Martin, *Worship in the Early Church* (Westwood, NJ: Fleming H. Revell Co., 1964), pp. 39–52; Jack T. Sanders, *The New Testament Christological Hymns* (Cambridge: University Press, 1971); Gottfried Schille, *Frühchristliche Hymnen* (Berlin: Evangelische Verlagsanstalt, 1965); William Sheppard Smith, *Musical Aspects of the New Testament* (Amsterdam: Uitgeverij W. Ten Have N.V., 1962); David M. Stanley, "*Carmenque Christo Quasi Deo Dicere,*" *Catholic Biblical Quarterly* 20 (1958), pp. 173–191; Bruce Vawter, "The Development of the Expression of Faith in the Worshipping Community: In the New Testament," *Concilium* 82 (1973), pp. 22–29.

7. Paul Winter, "Magnificat and Benedictus—Maccabean Psalms?", *Bulletin of the John Rylands Library* 37 (1954), pp. 328–47.

8. Raymond Brown, *The Birth of the Messiah* (Garden City, NY: Doubleday, 1977), pp. 355–66; Richard Cassidy, *Jesus, Politics and Society* (Maryknoll: Orbis, 1978), p. 21f; Douglas Jones, "The Background and Character of the Lukan Psalms," *Journal of Theological Studies* 19 (1968), pp. 19–28.

9. Raymond E. Brown considers the Prologue "an early Christian hymn, probably stemming from Johannine circles, which has been adapted to serve as an overture to the Gospel narrative of the career of the incarnate Word." In: *The Anchor Bible*, vol. 29: *The Gospel According to John: I–XII* (New York: Doubleday, 1966), p. 1f. Not all would agree.

hymn of Colossians suggests a variety of meanings, such as the reconciliation of Christianity to a radically different worldview, perhaps even the legitimacy of appropriating secular song.[10]

Theologizing in relation to music, although fragmentary and brief, is present in the New Testament literature. Paul extemporizes to the Corinthian community on the necessity of singing with comprehension in his excursus on praising in tongues.[11] The authors of Ephesians and Colossians similarly equate song with the fullness of Christ's Spirit and the obligation of giving thanks.[12] The liturgical hymns in Revelations, the texts and their contexts, are replete with a theological imagery unique to the New Testament corpus. Consistently, however, the thoughts and feelings of the composers themselves and the singing, celebrating communities recede into oblivion behind the perspectives of those who chronicled the period and commented on it.

A more definite theology of music takes shape in the writings of the early Fathers. Musical imagery abounds.[13] The ideal community is one that resonates in perfect harmony, whose accord is a hymn to Christ.[14] Joined to the hymn of the universe, the Christian

---

10. Ernst Käsemann, "A Primitive Christian Baptismal Liturgy," *Essays on New Testament Themes* (London: SCM, 1964), pp. 149–68; Eduard Lohse, "Pauline Theology in the Letter to the Colossians," *New Testament Studies* 15 (1969), pp. 211–20; Ralph Martin, "An Early Christian Hymn (Col 1: 15–20)," *Evangelical Quarterly Review* 36 (1964), pp. 195–205; Charles Masson, "L'hymne christologique de l'épitre aux Colossiens I, 15–20," *Revue de Theologie et de Philosophie* 36 n.s. (1948), pp. 138–42; Otto Piper, "The Savior's Eternal Work: An Exegesis of Col. 1:9–29," *Interpretation* 3 (1949), pp. 286–98; James M. Robinson, "A Formal Analysis of Colossians 1: 15–20," *Journal of Biblical Literature* 76 (1957), pp. 270–87; Eduard Schweizer, "The Church As the Missionary Body of Christ," *Neotestamentica* (Zwingli Verlag Zürich/Stuttgart, 1963), pp. 317–29; Bruce Vawter, "The Colossians Hymn and the Principle of Redaction," *Catholic Biblical Quarterly* 33 (1971), pp. 62–81.

11. 1 Co 14:13–19

12. Eph 5:17–20; Col 3:12–17

13. See Robert A. Skeris, *Chroma Theou* (Altötting: Verlag Alfred Coppenrath, 1976): A study on the origins and theological interpretation of the musical imagery used by the ecclesiastical writers of the first three centuries, with special reference to the image of Orpheus.

14. Ignatius of Antioch: " . . . Your accord and harmonious love is a hymn to Jesus Christ. Yes, one and all, you should form yourselves into a choir, so that, in perfect harmony and taking your pitch from God, you may sing in unison and with one voice to the Father through Jesus Christ" (*Ephesians* 4:1–3).

is participant in a cosmic choir of praise.[15] Creation is compared to a well-tuned instrument plucked by the Master player who orchestrates the human spirit and the harmony of the spheres.[16] Ignatius of Antioch, Clement of Alexandria, Tertullian, Athanasius, Eusebius, Ambrose, Augustine, and John Chrysostom are some of the early Church leaders who employed musical imagery and delivered discourses on the meaning of music and its relationship to Christian experience in the heart of a pagan world.[17]

There is also a discordant note creating a counterpoint to the positive attitudes of this period. A persistent negativity prepares the way for the legislative strictures of the early Middle Ages and subsequent millenium. Concern for the propriety of Christian music makes itself felt.[18] Church leaders begin to exercise a more definite control. There is rejection of dance and the use of

---

15. Origen: "We address our hymns of praise to the supreme God alone and to his only-begotten Son, the divine Logos. And we sing praise to God and to his only-begotten Son, as do also the sun, moon, and stars, and all the heavenly host. For all these form a divine choir and with just men sing the praise of the supreme God and his only-begotten Son" (*Contra Celsum* VIII 67).

16. Athanasius: " ... just like the plectrum in harmony, so man himself, become as it were a psaltery and totally responsive to the Spirit, serves and observes the intents and purposes of God with all his bodily limbs and all his movements." (*Epistola ad Marcellum* 28) And: "Just as a musician tuning his lyre and skillfully combining the bass and the sharp notes, the middle and the others, produces a single melody, so the wisdom of God, holding the universe like a lyre, draws together the things in the air with those on earth, and those in heaven with those in the air, and combines the whole with the parts, linking them by his command and will, thus producing in beauty and harmony a single world and a single order within it. ... " (*Oratio contra gentes* 42)

Also, Clement of Alexandria: "By the power of the Holy Spirit He arranged in harmonious order this great world, yes, and the little world of man too, body and soul together; and on this many-voiced instrument of the universe He makes music to God, and sings to the human instrument ... The Lord fashioned man a beautiful, breathing instrument, after his own image, and assuredly He Himself is an all-harmonious instrument of God, melodious and holy, the wisdom that is above this world, the heavenly Word" (*Protreptikos* I 5/3–4).

17. See especially Robert Skeris, *op. cit.*, for specific references to musical imagery.

18. "If anyone belonging to the theater come, whether it be man or woman ... or one that plays on the pipe, on the lute, or on the harp at those games, or a dancing master, or a huckster, either let them leave off their employments, or let them be rejected" (*Didascalia* VIII 32/9).

instruments, of rhythms and sounds identified with pagan religious feasts and bacchanalian festivals.[19] A genuine concern to guard the Church of God against seductive influences drives the leadership to be cautious and protective of the status quo. There are warnings. There are threats. Finally, there are laws.

Church leaders have been continually concerned about the music of the community and have shown a tendency early on to exercise control. It is uncertain precisely when or how expressions of concern culminated in clerical domination, but it is a fact of history that the music once guided by the living leadership's views became guarded by its laws. Theological reflection receded behind the force of legislation. From the early Middle Ages on, Christianity's music was conditioned by prohibitions and sanctions, by prescriptions and directives, by regulations and rules.

The purpose of this chapter is to give some indication of the scope and content of that ecclesiastical legislation which has set the conditions for the theory and practice of Roman Catholic Church music throughout the greater part of its history. Such an overview will establish the context for an analysis of specific documents and their interpretation in subsequent chapters. Decrees of popes, General Councils, and the Congregation of Rites fall within this category and are generally classified as papal legislation.[20] While the entire corpus of music legislation has been examined, only the more significant documents from each histori-

---

19. Clement of Alexandria: "For if people occupy their time with pipes, and psalteries, and choirs, and dances, and Egyptian clapping of hands, and such disorderly frivolities, they become quite immodest and intractable, beat on cymbals and drums, and make a noise on instruments of delusion . . . The one instrument of peace, the Word alone by which we honor God, is what we employ. We no longer employ the ancient psaltery, and trumpet, and timbrel, and flute, which those expert in war and contemners of the fear of God were wont to make use of also in the choruses at their festive assemblies . . . " (*Pedagogus* II 40, 1/2; 4, 42, 1/3).

And from Augustine: "Once upon a time, not many years ago, imprudent dancers intruded into similar places . . . Here we celebrate the holiness and the festival of the martyrs—here there shall be no dancing . . . " (Address #311).

20. Because Conciliar decisions must be confirmed by the pope to be official and binding, and Congregational legislation falls under the jurisdiction of the pope. In this chapter, only major decrees of the Congregation of Rites will be considered.

cal period will be mentioned here. A more comprehensive chronology of major legislation and significant supplementary documents is recorded in the bibliography.[21]

While tradition implies that Roman Catholic Church music has always been closely regulated, it is not possible to extend the reach of formal legislation back into the ante-Nicene period. The earliest official document of a legislative character pertaining to music is attributed to Leo IV (847–855). Nevertheless, there is some indication that even during the apostolic period music came under the jurisdiction of the Church.[22] There is tangible evidence (but no legislation per se) that music was to some extent officially regulated from the fourth century on. The interest of the popes,[23] commentaries of Church Fathers,[24] and decrees of Church Councils[25] indicate the extent of ecclesiastical concern. Surprisingly, the achievements of Gregory the Great (590–604), a major figure in the history of Catholic Church music, are known primarily through supplementary sources.[26] He himself left no legislation

21. Robert Hayburn, *Papal Legislation On Sacred Music* (hereafter, *PLSM*), has been a valuable resource for the more elusive earlier documents and the only translation available for many of the later ones.

22. For instance, Paul's injunction: 1 Co 14:15,40.

23. The *Liber Pontificalis* (critical ed. L. Duchesne, 2 vols., 1886–92; commentary, J.B. Lightfoot, *Apostolic Fathers* I, 1890, pp. 303–25), a collection of early papal biographies, contains an apocryphal letter from Jerome to Damasus relating how the latter as pope (366–84) "gave order to sing the psalms by day and by night in all the churches." (vol. I:213) Celestine I (422–32) "ordered that the 150 psalms be sung before the Sacrifice" (*LP* I:238), introduced antiphonal and responsorial psalmody and the Introit into the Mass, and founded a *Schola cantorum* in Rome as a model for the cultivation and composition of plainsong. Leo the Great (440–61), described in *Liber Pontificalis* as "excellent in song" and as having "instituted the yearly chant" (I:238), designated specific chants for each day of the liturgical year, and founded a monastery to observe the canonical hours and to maintain the chant in the papal basilica. *The New Oxford History of Music* II, ed. Dom Anselm Hughes (1955), pp. 95–6. Hayburn, *PLSM*, pp. 2–3. There are many other examples of papal interest in music.

24. See: Skeris, *op. cit.*; McKinnon, *op. cit.*

25. Council of Chalcedon (451) prescribed whom singers might marry (Canon 14). Of interest is the Council of Laodicea (ca. 367), which determined who could sing in the Church (Canon 15) and what the singer could wear (Canon 22). As a regional council, its decrees fall outside the scope of papal legislation.

26. Some of these sources: Bede the Venerable (b. ca. 670), called father of English history, praises Putta, bishop of Rochester, "for his knowledge of the Roman chant which he had learned from the pupils of St. Gregory." (*Historia*

regarding those actions attributed to his pontificate, the codification of the chant and the subsequent imposition of Roman chant
on the universal Church. A letter to Bishop John of Syracuse, in
which he defends the singing of the Alleluia in Masses outside of
Paschaltide and his custom of varying the *Kyrie Eleison* on Sundays
and feasts, is one of the few written records Gregory has left
concerning the nature of his liturgical reforms.[27]

THE MIDDLE AGES

The bull *Una Res* (ca. 850) of Leo IV, the first tangible piece of
papal legislation on music, records the extent to which the
Gregorian tradition[28] had already taken hold in the Church.
Writing to Abbot Honoratus of the monastery of Farfa (near

Ecclesiastica IV:2, *PL* 95:175) A direct connection of the pope's name with music or
plainsong is absent from Bede's life of Gregory. However, another indirect
reference occurs in the same source (V:20). See Dom Paul Meyvaert, "Bede and
Gregory the Great" (Mount Holyoke College, The Jarrow Lecture, 1964), pp. 7–
8. Also, André Pons, *Droit ecclesiastique et Musique sacrée*, tome 1, *La reforme de Saint
Gregoire le Grand* (St-Maurice, Suisse: 1958).

Egbert, Archbishop of York (d. 766), writes in *De Institutione Catholica*: "We in
the English Church for our part always observe the first month's fast in the first
week of Lent, in response to the authority of our lawmaker St. Gregory the Great,
who so ordered in the copy of his Antiphonary and his Missal which he sent us
through our teacher, the blessed Augustine." (*PL* 89:441)

Pope Leo IV (847–55): "This most holy Pope Gregory was a very great
worshipper of God . . . he produced the music We speak of, which We sing in
Church and elsewhere, produced many works of musical art for the stirring up or
moving more intensely of human spirits. . . . " (*Una Res*, British Museum, codex
no. 8873, fol. 168.)

John the Deacon of Rome (b. 824) writes in his *Vita Gregorii Magni*: " . . . he
compiled for the sake of the singers the collection called Antiphoner, which is of
so great usefulness. He also founded the School of Singers who to this day
perform the sacred chant in the Holy Roman Church according to instructions
received from him." (*PL* 75:90)

Translations of texts cited here from Hayburn, *PLSM*, pp. 6–9.

27. *PL* 77:956.

28. Chant selections were compiled and codified during the pontificate of
Gregory the Great (590–604). This Roman collection containing melodies from
the East as well as Western compositions came to be known as Gregorian chant
and its use was made mandatory in the Latin Church. Other Latin chant
traditions: Ambrosian, Gallican, and Mozarabic.

Rome) regarding deviations from standard practice, Leo upholds the norms with the full authority of his office.

> A most unbelievable report has reached Our ears ... namely, that you find distasteful the beauty of Gregorian chant, which the Church in her tradition of singing and reading has decreed and carried on ... We command under sentence of excommunication that, in the singing and readings in your churches, you carry them out in no other way than that which Pope St. Gregory handed down, and we hold that you cultivate and sing this tradition always. ... [29]

In addition to threatening Honoratus with excommunication, Leo concludes with the warning:

> If, which we hardly believe, anyone should try, now or in the future, in any way whatever, to lead you back or turn you aside to any tradition besides the one which we gave you ... We declare by Our authority and also the authority of all Our predecessors that he shall remain in perpetual anathema for his presumptuous audacity. [30]

The document *Docta Sanctorum Patrum* of John XXII (1324–1325) is the most important piece of music legislation to come out of the medieval period. It gives a concise yet vivid description of the techniques of the Ars Nova, first, by cautioning against doing violence to the words, and secondly, by castigating those who propagate sensuous practices in preference to the musical heritage of the Church.

> Certain exponents of a new school, who think only of the laws of measured time, are composing new melodies of their own creation with a new system of notes, and these they prefer to the ancient, traditional music. [31]

29. Hayburn, *PLSM*, pp. 8–9.

30. *Ibid.*, p. 9.

31. *Corpus juris canonici*, ed. a. 1582 *cum glossa (in aedibus populi Romani, iussu Gregorii XIII)*, (Leipzig: Ed. Aem. Friedberg, 1879–1881), 1:1256–1257. In Hayburn, *PLSM*, p. 20. He describes the melodies as "sung in semibreves and minimas and with gracenotes of repercussion ... broken up by *hocheti* or robbed of their virility by *discanti, tripla, motectus*, with a dangerous element produced by certain parts sung on texts in the vernacular."

Decrying the confusion such composers cause by their ignorance of the modes, the traditional foundation upon which past writers have built, the pope reveals the reason why the new music is causing such concern:

> The mere number of the notes, in these compositions, conceal from us the plain-chant melody, with its simple, well-regulated rises and falls which indicate the character of the Mode. These musicians run without pausing, they intoxicate the ear without satisfying it, they dramatize the text with gestures and, instead of promoting devotion, they prevent it by creating a sensuous and innocent atmosphere . . . Consequently, We and Our Brethren (the cardinals) have realized for a long time that this state of things required correction. And now We are prepared to take effective action to prohibit, cast out, and banish such things from the Church of God.[32]

The prohibition is not absolute, however. The document concludes with a statement permitting the new music on occasion, but stipulating the conditions for its use.

> We do not intend to forbid the occasional use—principally on solemn feasts at Mass and at Divine Office—of certain consonant intervals superimposed upon the simple ecclesiastical chant, provided these harmonies are in the spirit and character of the melodies themselves, as, for instance, the consonance of the octave, the fifth, the fourth, and others of this nature; but always on condition that the melodies themselves remain intact in the pure integrity of their form, and that no innovation take place against true musical discipline; for such consonances are pleasing to the ear and arouse devotion, and they prevent torpor among those who sing in honor of God.[33]

The concern of John XXII regarding figured music was well founded, for polyphonic developments of the Ars Nova were threatening the Gregorian tradition with extinction. A simple tonal expansion of the Gregorian melodic line had begun several centuries earlier when two parallel voice parts were superimposed upon the chant to create harmonic intervals of a fourth, fifth, and

32. Hayburn, *PLSM*, p. 21.
33. *Ibid.*

octave. The liturgical melody and text, or *cantus firmus*, remained the core of all such organum, parallel as well as the freer descant style. Gradually, individual voices ceased to be linked harmonically to the *cantus firmus* but were given melodic and then rhythmic independence. The twelfth-century school of St. Martial in Limoges promoted a polyphonic art of this nature, which gave impetus to vertical composition in the West. With the organa of the Notre Dame School of Paris, the center of interest shifted from the Gregorian *cantus firmus* to the polyphonic composition. No longer a determining factor, the *cantus firmus* in fact became an alien element and was completely eliminated from the new *conductus* form. Chant-linked organum and the free *conductus* were followed by the polyphonic motet which flourished from the twelfth century. By the fourteenth century, multi-textual, multi-lingual, multi-rhythmic motets of freely composed contrapuntal voices were commonplace.

For John XXII, harmonic ornamentation of the chant melody remained a legitimate option for solemn feasts, but the new art, which had eliminated the liturgical link between the polyphonic style and ecclesiastical music, was reprehensible. More than ever, chant became the sign of liturgical legitimacy and an authentic ecclesiastical style. With this first papal decree on polyphony, the Church limited the scope of contemporary artistic expression within the official rites. The impetus for this decision came from current and widespread abuse and the prohibition was directed against inappropriate developments. However, this public proclamation against stylistic innovations within a popular art form in use within the churches has usually been interpreted as a stand against artistic development itself and a mistrust of popular invention. It is important to remember that the traditional chant was in danger of disappearing and liturgical texts had become incomprehensible. The pope's comments must be read in light of this overriding concern.

A decree emanating from the Council of Basel (1431–1447), convoked by Eugene IV to secure union with the Greeks, merits mention here, as it lists some other abuses characteristic of medieval music on the eve of the Reformation.

> The abuses now existing in some churches whereby the Credo which is the symbol and profession of our faith, is not sung in its entirety, or the Preface or Pater Noster is omitted, or worldly songs

or ballads are sung . . . are hereby abolished, and it is decreed that those found guilty of such violations in the future, be duly penalized by their superiors.[34]

THE TRIDENTINE ERA

The Council of Trent said very little about music in its official decrees, although the impact of the Council on subsequent attitudes and Church practice was substantial. Its primary declaration was more of a summary statement after considerable discussion had ensued among the delegates near the Council's close. It might be helpful to sketch the main lines of this discussion that underlies the legislation of Trent.

Many of the issues debated in committee were similar to those raised in a report sent by Nausea Blancicampianus, bishop of Vienne in France, to Paul III two years before the Council. Presuming a reunion with the protesting churches, his first recommendation was "to do away with those German songs, which they use very much in their churches," or "it will not be possible for long to have unity."[35] His second concern was for the source of liturgical texts. "Nothing may be read or sung in Church unless it is taken from Sacred Scripture, or is at least in accord with it. . . . "[36] A third section detailed five specific areas of abuse by cathedral canons responsible for chanting the Divine Office, namely, musical ignorance; use of inaccurate music books; the tendency "rather to roar than to sing in the choir" and to omit prescribed parts of the service "for the sake of the harmonies of songs or organ music;" their manner of singing the chant; the occasional use of questionable music and vernacular texts not taken from sacred Scripture.[37] The bishop concludes his comments on music with a warning to singers to adhere to Sacred Scripture in the choice of chants and to "cut out those things which in their order and time are not worthy and fitting praise to God."[38]

---

34. Canon 12. Tr. in H. J. Schroeder, *Disciplinary Decrees of the General Councils* (St. Louis: Herder, 1937), p. 478.
35. Hayburn, *PLSM*, p. 26.
36. *Ibid.*
37. *Ibid.*
38. *Ibid.*, p. 27.

These issues were not addressed until twenty years later, when the question of music was discussed in committee and then in the general sessions of the Council. It is interesting to trace the legislative statement on music through schema redactions to its final articulation. On August 8, 1562, the following statement concerning music was included in the schema on abuses to be avoided in the Mass.

> Therefore it must be discussed whether that type of music which is now practiced in figured modulations and which delights the ears more than the mind and which is seen to excite the faithful to lascivious rather than to religious thoughts, should be taken away from the Masses. For in this type of music profane things are often sung, as for example that of the hunt (*caccia*) and the battle (*battaglia*).[39]

When the final compendium of abuses to be avoided in the Mass was drawn up, the statement read:

> The type of music in divine services is reduced to the norm which Pope John XXII prescribed in his work *De vita et honestate clericorum*, and it should be sung so that the words are more intelligible than the modulations of the music.[40]

Council discussion concerning these abuses began September 10, 1562. A committee of deputies recorded the following concerning canon 8:

> In the case of those Masses which are celebrated with singing and with organ, let nothing profane be intermingled, but only hymns and divine praises. If anything is to be sung with the organ from the sacred services while they are in progress, let it be recited in a simple clear voice beforehand so that no one will miss any part of the eternal reading of the sacred writings. The whole plan of singing in musical modes should be constituted not to give empty pleasure to the ear, but in such a way that the words may be clearly

39. *Ibid.*

40. *Ibid.* The text here is referring to *Docta Sanctorum Patrum*, the decree on music cited earlier, which John XXII included in book 3, chapter 1 of his *De vita et honestate clericorum*.

understood by all, and thus the hearts of the listeners be drawn to the desire of heavenly harmonies, in the contemplation of the joys of the blessed.[41]

The actual legislation of the Council concerning music proceeded from three separate sessions.

At the Twenty-Second Session, September 17, 1562, the Council voted to include the following summation of previous texts and discussions in its Decree Concerning The Things To Be Observed And Avoided In The Celebration of Mass:

They shall also banish from the churches all such music which, whether by the organ or in the singing, contains things that are lascivious or impure; . . . "[42]

In context, that sentence continues and concludes: "likewise all worldly conduct, vain and profane conversations, wandering around, noise and clamor, so that the house of God may be seen to be and may be truly called a house of prayer."[43]

At the Twenty-Third Session, July 15, 1563, the Council passed the reform decree on the Sacrament of Orders, which includes this recommendation regarding the education of clerics: "they shall study grammar, singing, ecclesiastical computation, and other useful arts. . . . "[44]

At the Twenty-Fourth Session, November 11, 1563, the reform decree that became official includes this decision regarding the qualifications and duties of those clerics promoted to cathedral churches:

All shall be obliged to perform the divine offices in person and not by substitutes; also to assist and serve the bishop when celebrating and exercising other pontifical functions, and in the choir instituted for psalmody, to praise the name of God reverently, distinctly and devoutly in hymns and canticles.[45]

---

41. *Ibid.*
42. H.J. Schroeder, *Canons and Decrees of the Council of Trent* (St. Louis: Herder, 1941), p. 151.
43. *Ibid.*
44. *Ibid.*, p. 176.
45. *Ibid.*, p. 202.

After prescribing for suitable behavior and dress, the decree continues:

> With regard to matters that pertain to the proper manner of conducting the divine offices, the proper way of singing or modulating therein, the definite rule for assembling and remaining in choir, the things necessary for those who minister in the church, and such like, the provincial synod shall prescribe for each province a fixed form that will be beneficial to and in accordance with the usage of each province. In the meantime, the bishop, with the aid of no less than two canons, one chosen by himself, the other by the chapter, may provide in these matters as he may deem expedient.[46]

The question of chant and its use was apparently discussed again in the session of November 23, 1563 in conjunction with the needs of female religious. The decree under consideration recommended that the Divine Office "should be continued by them in high voice" rather than by professional substitutes; that they "leave to the Deacon and Subdeacon the office of chanting the Lessons, Epistles, and Gospels;" and that they "abstain from singing either in Choir or elsewhere the so-called 'figured' chant."[47] These suggestions were never included in the official canons of the Council.[48]

During the closing Oration delivered at the final session on December 3, 1563, Bishop Jerome Ragazonus enumerated the Council's achievements and included this reference to music: "... you have banished from the temple of the Lord the more effeminate singing and musical compositions...."[49]

The real consequences for music came soon after the Council ended. The *motu proprio Alias nullas constitutiones*, which Pius IV issued on August 2, 1564, established a congregation of eight cardinals to implement the decrees of the Council. Music reform began with the Papal Choir at St. Peter's where fourteen singers were dismissed.[50] It was at this time that polyphonic music was

46. *Ibid.*
47. Hayburn, *PLSM*, p. 29.
48. In Hayburn's presentation of the legislation of Trent, it is difficult at times to separate preliminary discussion from the final canonical decrees.
49. Schroeder, *op. cit.*, p. 261.
50. Hayburn, *PLSM*, pp. 29–30.

seriously evaluated, and the search for a model that was lucid and supportive of the text resulted in a preference for the Palestrinian style. Significant for the course of music legislation was the institution of the Congregation of Rites by Sixtus V in 1588 to ensure uniformity in ritual practice. It became the primary source of interpretation for ritual legislation, issuing official instructions, local dispensations, and reams of rescripts to safeguard the music and the rubrics of the rites.

Legislation for the remainder of the sixteenth century is preoccupied with the publication of new chant editions as a result of the revision of liturgical books initiated by the Council.[51] In 1577, Gregory XIII entrusted to Giovanni Palestrina and Annibale Zoilo, a composer of the papal chapel, the task of adjusting the music to fit those textual corrections.[52] Instead of minor adjustments, the two radically altered the traditional melodies according to their own criteria. The completed Gradual, which caused an uproar in the musical world because of its violation of the ancient chant, was never published. Private editions of the chant compiled from other sources began to proliferate, and in 1592, Giovanni Battista Raimondi, founder of the Medicean Printing Company, petitioned Rome for permission to publish an official edition. Determined to print the manuscript rejected some years before, he contracted with Palestrina to continue the project, but the composer died before it was completed. A scandal involving Ignio, Palestrina's son, who tried to sell Raimondi a fraudulent manuscript he claimed to have been prepared by his father, the subsequent lawsuit, and papal involvement in the complex process of litigation, is all documented by Rome and makes interesting reading.[53] The end result was the printing of the Medicean Gradual in 1615. Raimondi had been granted an exclusive fifteen-year privilege to print the official books,[54] but the publication of an edition that had so modified the melodies as to mutilate the very structure of the ancient chant caused Paul V to withdraw those briefs that had spoken favorably of the project. Although the printing privilege remained, he refused to make the

---

51. *Missale, Breviarum, Rituale, Pontificale.*
52. Brief: October 25, 1577.
53. See Hayburn, *PLSM*, pp. 46–57.
54. Congregation of Rites, January 21, 1594 and March 29, 1594; bull of Paul V, May 31, 1608. In Hayburn, *PLSM*, pp. 46, 47, 58.

book mandatory for the churches. This Medicean edition was to become the source for the official Ratisbon edition of the chant in the nineteenth century.

In addition to chant books and their publication, much Tridentine legislation concerns the Confraternity of Music in Rome, a society of musicians who eventually gained monopoly on music production and the regulation of music standards in that city.[55] The most significant piece of music legislation to come out of the seventeenth century was *Piae sollicitudinis* issued by Alexander VII, April 23, 1657, to the churches in Rome. It contains a vivid description of abuses prevalent in Roman churches and prescribes, under pain of excommunication, that nothing be sung except "those compositions which have words which are prescribed in the Breviary and Missal" or "selected from Sacred Scripture, or the Holy Fathers of the Church," and banishes from the churches "music which imitates dance music and profane rather than ecclesiastical melody," demanding that choirmasters take an oath to uphold these prescriptions.[56]

Annus qui, the lengthy encyclical of Benedict XIV promulgated February 19, 1749, is a major document on church music and the most comprehensive treatment of the subject during the Tridentine era.[57]

The primary topic of concern, musical chant and the use of musical instruments, is introduced with a warning.

[Musical chant] has now been introduced into the churches and is commonly accompanied by the organ and other musical instruments. Let it be executed in such a way as not to appear profane, worldly or theatrical. The use of the organ and other musical instruments is not yet admitted by all the Christian world.[58]

---

55. Sixtus V, *Confirmatio erectionis Confraternitatis Musicorum*, April 24, 1585; Urban VIII, Decree, November 20, 1624 and December 9, 1626.

56. *Bullarium diplomatum et privilegiorum Romanorum Pontificum*, 24 vols. and appendix (Turin: *Augustae*, 1857–1872), 16:275. In Hayburn, *PLSM*, p. 76.

57. *Bullarium Magnum Romanorum* XVIII, pp. 9–24.

58. Hayburn, *PLSM*, p. 95. For this document, Hayburn has used the translation of the Daughters of St. Paul, *The Liturgy* (Boston: St. Paul Editions, 1962), pp. 46–78.

The text reflects on churches that do not use the organ, after the example of the Pontifical Chapel, and then draws this preliminary conclusion:

> ... leaving aside the dispute that sees the adversaries divided into two fields: those who condemn and detest in their churches the use of chant and musical instruments and on the other hand those who approve and praise it, there is certainly no one who does not desire a certain difference between ecclesiastical chant and theatrical melodies, and who does not acknowledge that the use of theatrical and profane chant must not be tolerated in Churches.[59]

The discussion that follows develops both sides of the question, listing adversaries and proponents of the use of instruments. Under the former, Thomas Aquinas is mentioned as one who absolutely did not approve of harmonic chant and musical instruments in Church. The list of those who favor such music is much longer and includes Cardinals Bellarmine and Cajetan, who speak out particularly in defense of the organ. The text explains that the Council of Trent considered eliminating such music from the churches, but through the intervention of the Emperor Ferdinand, the decree was softened to prohibit only that music which suggests anything lewd or impure. Suarez[60] is noted as defining organ to mean not only that instrument so named, but other musical instruments as well. Consequently, "he concludes that once the organ is used in churches, other musical instruments may also be used."[61]

A section on theatrical music, which is forbidden in Church, is followed by a lengthy exposition on motets, in which individuals and Councils are quoted regarding the importance of understanding the words.

The Council of Cambrai (1565): "What must therefore be sung in choir is destined to instruct the faithful: it must therefore be sung in such a manner as to be understood by the mind."[62]

---

59. Hayburn, *PLSM*, p. 96.
60. Francisco de Suarez (1548–1617), an eminent Jesuit theologian.
61. Hayburn, *PLSM*, p. 98. Footnote 22 in the text points out that St. Isidore had said earlier that "the word organ generally indicates all musical instruments." (p. 107)
62. *Ibid.*, p. 101.

The Council of Cologne (1536): " . . . the most important part is made up precisely of the recital of the words of the prophets, the apostles, the Epistle, the Creed, the Preface or the act of thanksgiving and the Our Father . . . these texts like all others must be sung clearly and intelligibly."[63]

The first Council of Milan (1565): "Let chant and music be serious, devout, clear, suitable to God's house and to divine praise; executed in such a manner that those who listen to it understand the words and be moved to devotion."[64]

The Council of Toledo (1566): " . . . let bishops who allow the practice of melodic variations in the musicians' choirs in which voices are mixed according to different orders, insure that the words of the psalms and of the other parts generally sung do not remain incomprehensible and suffocated by a disordinate uproar. As for the use of so called organic music, let the words of these sung parts always be understood and the minds of the listeners inclined to praise God more through the pronunciation of the words than with the melodies of a curious compòsition."[65]

By way of summary, the text returns again to musical instruments, to clarify its intent regarding figured music and to make some observations about instrumental music. Its position on figured music is reflected in the following text.

> We need to fix the limits between Church chant and music and that of the theaters. We must state the difference between the two because in our days figurative or harmonic chant accompanied by the playing of instruments are adopted both in theaters and in churches.[66]

The discussion on instrumental music focuses on three main points: musical instruments which may be tolerated in churches; those instruments which are generally used to accompany chant; and the use of instruments independently of chant, that is, in orchestral playing. After quoting several opinions favoring or forbidding various individual instruments, the document includes

63. *Ibid.*, pp. 101–102.
64. *Ibid.*, p. 102.
65. *Ibid.*
66. *Ibid.*, p. 103.

its own list of those that are acceptable and those that are not. Surprisingly, brass, woodwind, and strings seem to fall into both categories, indicating that no one classification is objectionable in itself but rather, as the text states, what must be excluded from worship are "in general all instruments that give a theatrical swing to music."[67] Instrumental performance must be directed toward achieving worship goals.

> As to the manner of using those instruments which may be admitted with sacred music, We only warn that they be used exclusively to uphold the chant of the words, so that their meaning be well impressed in the minds of the listeners, and the souls of the faithful moved to the contemplation of spiritual things and urged to love God and divine things all the more.[68]

It is clear that instrumental accompaniment is acceptable in worship when it meets the criteria outlined above and is prohibited only when it fails to perform responsibly.

> However, if the instruments continue to be played and stop only once in a while, as is the custom today, to give time to listeners to hear the harmonic modulations—the vibrating emotions, vulgarly called trills—if for the rest they do nothing else but bother and drown out the choir voices and the meaning of the words, then the use of the instruments does not reach the desired end; it becomes useless, rather, it is forbidden and condemned.[69]

The document concludes its discussion of instrumental music with some statements concerning orchestral music.

> Finally, we speak of orchestral music. Where its use has been introduced it may be tolerated as long as it is serious and does not, because of its length, cause boredom or serious inconvenience to those who are in choir, or who are celebrating at the altar, during Vespers and Mass.[70]

---

67. *Ibid.*
68. *Ibid.*
69. *Ibid.*, p. 104.
70. *Ibid.*

In defense of his position, Benedict XIV again quotes Suarez, thereby offering the contemporary reader a clearer understanding of what was meant by permissible orchestral music.

"It is to be understood from this that in itself the practice of inserting in the Divine Office the playing of the organ without singing is not to be condemned, as long as the music of the instruments be soft, as is often the case during Solemn High Mass or between the psalms of the Divine Office. In these cases such playing is not part of the Office, but adds to the solemnity and veneration of the Office itself and to the elevation of the spirit of the faithful so that they be more easily moved and disposed to devotion. But as no vocal chant is associated with this playing, it is necessary that the said chant be serious and suitable to excite devotion."[71]

The encyclical's main concern is stressed in the final paragraphs: the elimination of abuse in those churches violating the principles of figured and instrumental music as outlined above, and the prohibition of sumptuous theatrical concerts held in church buildings, particularly during Holy Week, which is the most intolerable abuse of all.

Annus qui is a remarkable document. It reads with precision and clarity and is particularly notable for its balanced presentation of divergent points of view. The number of sources quoted in defense of each position and a summary of previous legislation relating to certain key issues make the document a veritable encyclopedia of information pertaining to the tradition.

What is especially remarkable is the kind of information this document conveys. The use of figured music and instrumental music is common in the churches of the eighteenth century and, according to Pope Benedict XIV, this fact is neither surprising nor particularly disturbing. A stand is taken against abuse, but the pope is careful to distinguish between what is actually prohibited and what is not. Accompanied chant is acceptable when it serves to enhance the words and inspire devotion. Purely instrumental music is also allowed when it is performed appropriately and leads to prayer. It is recognized that opinion differs on these issues, and

71. *De Religione*, Book III, chap. XIII, n. 17, as cited in Hayburn, *PLSM*, p. 104.

an effort is made to present both sides fairly. All are encouraged to unite against a common enemy, a theatrical style of music that has invaded some churches in both accompanied vocal and purely orchestral forms.

The list of those on record in favor of instrumental music is surprising and includes cardinals and councils prominent during the period following the conclusion of the Council of Trent. Such testimony serves to strengthen the opinion that Trent did not speak out against the musical styles of that period but against abuses within all of the styles or forms, against "all such music which, whether by the organ or in the singing, contains things that are lascivious or impure. . . . "[72] *Annus qui* suggests that Benedict XIV came closer to capturing the spirit of that Council than did some of his predecessors responsible for implementing what it had decreed. It also indicates that the abuses decried by Trent were still prevalent nearly two centuries later, laying open to question the effectiveness of reform.

Finally, the more inclusive understanding of the term "organ" warrants further investigation. Isidore, Suarez, and Benedict XIV say that the term has meant other instruments as well. Just how extensive was this understanding is impossible to determine without a careful and focused research. Such a study could yield important information for interpreting documents pertaining to organ accompaniment during the period following the Council of Trent.

Annus qui is such a unique and significant document, one wonders where it has been all these years and why it has not been prominent in the dialogue of this century. The Daughters of St. Paul and Robert Hayburn have done musicians a service by making it available to the American Church in translation.

In 1830 Pius VIII approved the statutes of the Italian Society of St. Caecilia,[73] in effect inaugurating a movement for church music reform of considerable significance in the nineteenth century. Many documents touch on this reform, which spread through Italy, Germany, and the United States, but for the most part, papal documents in the second half of the century become embroiled once again in the question of the chant.

---

72. Schroeder, *Canons and Decrees, op. cit.*, p. 151.
73. *Bullarii Romani continuatio summorum pontificium*, 10 vols. (Prati: Aldina, 1856), 9:139. In Hayburn, *op. cit.*, pp. 115–121.

The circumstances whereby the Ratisbon edition became the official chant edition of the Church from 1870 to 1900 are intriguing and complex. The publication was the result of a confluence of forces: the conviction of Franz Xavier Haberl, founder of the Ratisbon School of Music (1874), that he had somehow discovered the only extant copy of the original Medicean Gradual which he believed to be the authentic work of Palestrina; the desire of the Congregation of Rites for an official chant edition based on the Medicean source along with an exclusive thirty-year printing right as economic guarantee; and the determination of Frederick Pustet to be the publisher so privileged. He obtained that permission and engaged Haberl to compose the missing chants. The project was approved by a commission and printed, page by page, to the delight of Pius IX and his successor, Leo XIII. Decrees of praise were issued and the work defended against the growing criticism of editors and scholars challenging the volume's authenticity in light of Solesmes research into ancient manuscripts. The legislative activity pertaining to the Solesmes challenge to the Ratisbon edition and the latter's defense is too extensive to even summarize adequately here and forms the basis of Robert Hayburn's doctoral dissertation.[74] The end result was a legislative reversal. In light of the evidence Solesmes had amassed through an exhaustive comparison of all extant manuscripts, Rome could no longer continue to promote the Ratisbon edition as the only legitimate, authentic chant of the Roman Church.[75] Support for Solesmes spread even to Rome, where Jesuit Angelo De Santi, musician and confidant of the future Pius X, was influential in the change of attitude there. With *Nos quidem* of Leo XIII,[76] Solesmes was exonerated. The Pustet privilege was not renewed, and the more questionable actions of Roman legislators were consigned to the papal archives.[77] Unfortunately, however, the chant controversy did not end with the close of the century. It simply shifted to another front.

74. Hayburn, *Pope Saint Pius X, op. cit.*
75. Congregation of Rites, Decree, April 14, 1877; Brief, November 15, 1878; *Romanorum pontificum,* April 10/26, 1883; and *Quod Sanctus Augustinus,* July 7, 1894.
76. Issued May 17, 1901. In *Rassegna Gregoriana* (1902), col. 5.
77. The decree, *Romanorum pontificum* of April 10, 1883 confirming the authenticity of the Ratisbon edition is omitted from the official *Decreta authentica*

TWENTIETH-CENTURY REFORM

Pope Pius X (1903–1914), who issued more music decrees than any other pope in history,[78] gave impetus to the liturgy and liturgical music reform that has dominated this century. His *motu proprio* on sacred music, *Tra le sollecitudini*, issued November 22, 1903, was a decisive turning point in music history and remains a major referent to this day.

As a seminarian and young cleric, Giuseppe Sarto sustained a love of music through a variety of activities,[79] which included an interest in the work of Solesmes, and as bishop, first of Mantua, then Venice, he sowed the legislative seeds that would bear fruit during his later pontificate. In 1893, the newly created cardinal of Venice responded to a general request sent by Leo XIII for suggestions for some new legislation on sacred music.[80] In collaboration with his friend Angelo De Santi, who actually wrote the material Sarto submitted, he prepared the now famous *votum* of 1893 which, in its broad outline and specific articulations, is nearly identical to the *motu proprio* of 1903. The first two sections of general considerations and particular observations, which comprise a study of the principles underlying sacred music and a recapitulation of the origin and development of its reform, serve as a preliminary rationale to the document's main agenda. It is part three that is so closely related to *Tra le sollecitudini*.[81] Cardinal Sarto continued to promote church music reform in Venice,[82] and in 1895, issued a pastoral letter on sacred music, his last major proclamation on the subject before ascending to the papacy in 1903.[83]

---

of the Congregation of Rites. See letters of Leo XIII praising Solesmes, then conditioning that praise in Hayburn, *op. cit.* pp. 175–176.

78. Hayburn contends, "more than all the popes together." In *PLSM*, p. 195.

79. He taught chant, organized a parish choir, copied manuscripts.

80. The pope planned to update *Ordinatio quoad sacram musicam* (1884) with a second instruction, which he issued in 1894.

81. For a point by point comparison of similar passages, see Hayburn, *PLSM*, pp. 223–231.

82. He initiated a chant course at the seminary, established alternating choirs for the psalmody of Vespers at the Cathedral, prohibited the presence of women in choirs and pianos or noisy instruments in church.

83. *Documenta pontificia ad instaurationem liturgicam spectantia* (1903–1953) (Rome: *Edizioni Liturgiche*, 1953), p. 1. Tr. in Hayburn, *PLSM*, pp. 213–218.

The *motu proprio* on sacred music was among the first official acts of the new pope, promulgated within the early months of his pontificate. The Congregation of Rites underscored the obligatory nature of this legislation in a decree issued January 8, 1904.[84] In a second *motu proprio, Col nostro,* issued April 24, 1904, Pius X called attention once again to a perennial concern, the chant of the Church.[85] There is documentary evidence of Angelo De Santi's participation in all four of the major formulations of Pius X, including *Tra le sollecitudini.*[86] Yet there is little doubt that these documents accurately reflect the mind of Pius X and are not simply the construct of De Santi appropriated by the pope.[87] Pius X turned his attention at once to the reform of music in the city of Rome,[88] but a considerable portion of his pontificate was concerned with facilitating a new chant edition and making peace with the monks of Solesmes.

For an official Vatican edition of the chant based on authentic sources, Pius X turned to Solesmes, entrusting the monks with the task of preparing the manuscripts for publication. *Col nostro* established a papal commission to oversee the project. Dom Joseph Pothier and Dom André Mocquereau, protagonists of divergent chant interpretations, saw their differences escalate into deeper division as the project progressed.[89] Further polarization within the Commission itself regarding proper criteria for evaluating authenticity came to a head over the question of chant

84. *Decreta Authentica* 6 (ap. 1), 48. Tr. in Hayburn, *PLSM,* pp. 253–254.

85. *ASS* 36 (1903), p. 586. Tr. in Hayburn, *PLSM,* pp. 256–257.

86. Letters of Cardinal Sarto to Angelo De Santi, July 9 and July 30, 1893; De Santi's letter to Dom Mocquereau, January 4, 1904. Tr. in Hayburn, *PLSM,* pp. 203–204, 219–220.

87. Don Lorenzo Perosi recalls these words of Pius X to the Roman Music Commission on July 24, 1904: "How can they say that I let myself be influenced by people of these days? I have for twenty years pushed the restoration of sacred music in other places." *Rassegna Gregoriana* (July-August 1904), col. 404, in Hayburn, *PLSM,* p. 236.

88. Pius X, *Il desiderio,* Letter to Cardinal Respighi, December 8, 1903.

89. Pothier supported a free oratorical rhythm which had its basis in the Latin text; Mocquereau held that chant rhythm was derived from the music itself, independent of the text. Mocquereau directed the monks of Solesmes in the task of revision, Pothier was made head of the papal commission charged with approving their work.

development, and higher authority intervened.[90] In a series of actions which, to this day, reflect questionable motives and authorization, Cardinal Merry Del Val, prefect of the Congregation of Rites, tilted the balance in favor of the proponents of art over antiquity, mandated the 1895 edition of Dom Pothier as the model for the official books, and terminated the involvement of Dom Mocquereau and the monks of Solesmes in the project.[91] The official Vatican edition of the chant *Graduale* was published in 1905 and made obligatory for the universal Church. Publication of the remainder of the books continued to 1912. From 1905 on, Pius X struggled to reincorporate the monks of Solesmes, so that they might once again edit the chant they had done so much to restore to vitality. In 1913, he succeeded, conferring a responsibility which Solesmes still continues to fulfill.

The Code of Canon Law (1918), promulgated by Benedict XV who succeeded Pius X to the papacy in 1914, contains a single reference to music. After stating in the spirit of Trent that "all music, whether instrumental or vocal, which contains anything lascivious or impure, must be entirely kept out of the churches," the canon concludes with this all-inclusive statement: "The liturgical laws concerning sacred music shall be observed" (Canon No. 1264).[92]

Pius XI (1921–1938), an ardent supporter of Church music, issued *Divini cultus sanctitatem* (December 28, 1928), an apostolic constitution on liturgy and liturgical music in the spirit of Pius X. Extolling the arts, particularly music, as ministers in the service of the Church, he confirmed the principles and practices legislated by his predecessor and added some recommendations of his own. Regarding the chant, he emphasized training in method and performance, so that the singing required by the liturgical rites might be executed with beauty and precision and this knowledge

90. Solesmes held that the only legitimate chant tradition is one which does not contradict the sources from which it came, implying continuity of transmission. Others favored artistic variants as representing a true development of the Gregorian tradition.

91. Letters to Dom Pothier, April 3 and June 24, 1905. In Hayburn, *PLSM*, pp. 263–265.

92. The new *Codex Iuris Canonici* promulgated January 25, 1983 contains no reference to the liturgical laws of music.

imparted to all. He called for the formation of choirs similar to those that flourished during the height of the polyphonic age and encouraged the formation of *scholae puerorum*, even in the smaller churches. He praised the human voice as the most perfect instrument, yet allowed the use of the organ as it was part of the tradition. Active participation was seen as a necessity, so that "the faithful taking part in sacred ceremonies should not do so as mere outsiders or mute spectators, but as worshipers thoroughly imbued with the beauty of the liturgy."[93]

The liturgical achievements of Pius XII (1939–1958) have already been enumerated in chapter two. His contribution to liturgical music legislation falls within that category but warrants some comment here.

The pope of pastoral liturgy was also the pope of pastoral music. His writings reflect enthusiasm for the initiatives of his predecessor Pius X, a dedication to tradition, and an openness to the best of what is new. In *Mediator Dei* (1947), his major encyclical on the liturgy, Pius XII exhorts Church leaders:

> ... to promote with care congregational singing, and to see to its accurate execution with all due dignity, since it easily stirs up and arouses the faith and piety of large gatherings of the faithful. Let the full harmonious singing of our people rise to heaven like the bursting of a thunderous sea and let them testify by the melody of their song to the unity of their hearts and minds. ... [94]

In the same document he also cautions that "one would be straying from the straight path ... were he to disdain and reject polyphonic music or singing in parts, even where it conforms to regulations issued by the Holy See" (art. 62). He promotes the Gregorian tradition, proposing it to the faithful "as belonging to them also" (art. 191), yet insists that "it cannot be said that modern music and singing should be entirely excluded from Catholic worship" (art. 193). Years later he articulated the essentials of his philosophy of church music:

93. Hayburn, *PLSM*, p. 331.
94. Article 194; other music references in *Mediator Dei*: articles 21, 24, 62, 105, 106, 108, 109, 150, 191–193.

No change in the principles, which, as essential, have permanent force, but their further advance and development in form, in a loyal application of those same principles to the circumstances and needs of today.[95]

His approach to music is inclusive, yet always within the framework of the rules. Throughout his pontificate he encouraged the recovery of the people's song and, at the same time, remained aware of liturgical music as an art form with a long and rich tradition.

Pius XII is best remembered by musicians for *Musicae sacrae disciplina*, issued December 25, 1955, his only encyclical that year and the last before his death.[96] His intention was to confirm and update the landmark decree of Pius X, and the document is rich with insight into the mind of Pius XII concerning a subject which he admits "has always been very close to our heart."[97] Pius XII was an articulate writer with a brilliant intellect who researched his topics thoroughly. His encyclical on music reflects his grasp of the subject, which he develops from a variety of perspectives. This topic of contemporary concern is first set within the context of biblical and ecclesiastical tradition, then examined from the perspective of aesthetics, and finally developed from a pastoral point of view. It places strong emphasis on the spiritual and catechetical value of religious song for fostering a sense of community within and apart from the liturgy. Cardinal Tardini, in his memoirs of Pius XII published after the pope's death, gives us a clue on how to evaluate his documents. Pius XII did not like to displease anyone. If he had to communicate a negative decision or a reprimand, he made every effort to "sugar the pill," as the pope himself expressed it.

> Taking the document which had been prepared, he would eliminate one or another clause that he found too strong, insert some more pleasing expressions, add a few words of praise. The resulting pill

95. *Mit Wohlwollen*, Letter to Cardinal Innitzer of Vienna, October, 1954, in *TPS* 2 (1955), p. 79.

96. *AAS* 48 (1956), pp. 5–25. Tr: *TPS* 3 (1956), pp. 7–23 and Seasoltz, *TNL*, pp. 218–233.

97. Seasoltz, *TNL*, p. 218.

was so skillfully sugar-coated that the patient, on reading the document or being received in audience by the Pope, would sometimes absorb *the sugar* with relish and not even notice he had swallowed the pill.[98]

Later on in the same volume, Cardinal Tardini gives us yet another assist in understanding the mind of Pius XII through his writings.

In Pius XII's style there is a rich profusion of phrases and clauses, as though he were trying to analyze even the most hidden recesses of his thought. At times, he is like a jeweller intent on showing to others the changing tints and manifold facets of a precious gem. The precious gem is there, but it will be found only on a careful reading of the texts. In the profusion of this elegant phraseology, there are, indeed, a number of sentences which could not be clearer, more incisive, nor more powerful. In this we have the substance and kernel of Pius XII's thought, while the rest are, to a great extent, a development, an amplification, and an ornamentation of these essential thoughts.[99]

Tardini gives some examples by way of illustration to encourage others "to do more careful research and make even happier discoveries."[100]

What are the "precious gems" embedded in the elegant phraseology of *Musicae sacrae disciplina*? What are the bitter pills sugar-coated to facilitate acceptance? There seems to be a "gem," in fact, a "sugar-coated pill," for both professional musician and representative of the people's song. For the professional:

The artist who is firm in his faith and leads a life worthy of a Christian, who is motivated by the love of God and reverently uses the powers the Creator has given him, expresses and manifests the truths he holds and the piety he possesses so skillfully, beautifully and pleasingly in colors and lines or sounds and harmonies that this sacred labor of art is an act of worship and religion for him. It also effectively arouses and inspires people to profess the faith and

98. Domenico Cardinal Tardini, *Memories of Pius XII,* tr. by Rosemary Goldie (Westminster, MD: Newman Press, 1961), p. 74.
99. *Ibid.,* p. 87.
100. *Ibid.*

cultivate piety. The Church has always honored and always will honor this kind of artist (art. 28, 29).

Pius XII stresses that there will always be a place for the professional musician in the life of the Church. However, the musician's creativity is not for the sake of the art or solely for the artist, but must be an act of worship that is pastorally efficacious. It is not enough simply to create musical masterpieces to enrich the Church's treasury. Such treasures must also enrich the prayer life of the worshiping community. To the proponents of popular hymns and songs, he writes:

> ... these sacred canticles, born as they are from the most profound depths of the people's soul, deeply move the emotions and spirit and stir up pious sentiments. When they are sung at religious rites by a great crowd of people singing as with one voice, they are powerful in raising the minds of the faithful to higher things (art. 63).

The pope's enthusiasm for popular hymns and singing is tempered only by the constraint of existing rules. Religious hymns and songs are to be cultivated and collected. Their value and integrity is affirmed, and suggestions are offered for extra-liturgical use, as well as limited use in the liturgy. However, he is careful to keep the boundaries intact. They should be sung at the proper time and place. For both professional and amateur, there is affirmation and restraint.

The document reflects the pontiff's lifelong career as a diplomat, one who is accustomed to warring factions and who knows how to draw both sides closer together. It reflects the characteristics of one who is known for standing with the people in difficult times, one totally dedicated to the cause of making peace. The encyclical is situated just prior to the Council, when talk of a vernacular liturgy with its consequences for the traditional repertoire was particularly intense. Pius XII was preparing both sides for the future, for the loss of some cherished values as well as a limit to expectations for change. It is important to recall that there was no hint of a possible Council at the time of his writing, and those sweeping changes, less than a decade away, were beyond his imagining. Nevertheless, the document, though rooted in tradition, is very forward looking. It is like a bridge pulling the past into the future, the culmination of all Pius X had envisioned and more than he had hoped for, the basis for an eventual restructuring of traditional practice to meet the expectations of post-Conciliar times.

Three years after the encyclical on music, the Congregation of Rites issued an Instruction On Sacred Music and the Sacred Liturgy, *De Musica sacra*,[101] a lengthy piece stressing the prescriptions already imposed by *Musicae sacrae disciplina*, *Mediator Dei*, and *Tra le sollecitudini*. As an Instruction which, in principle, is not concerned with establishing new legislation but rather with making existing laws practically applicable, *De Musica sacra* attempts to show how music and liturgy can and should be celebrated. As the last significant statement on music before the Council, it is a concise summary of the progress of reform during this century and reflects the status of Catholic Church music legislation and practice on the threshold of Vatican II.

VATICAN II RENEWAL

The ten articles that comprise chapter six (*"De Musica sacra"*) of *Sacrosanctum concilium* represent a new phase in the history of Catholic Church music. They are the new frame of reference for all subsequent legislation. Joseph Jungmann admits there was some astonishment among Council members that the subject of music would comprise a separate chapter almost equal in length to the chapter on the Eucharist.[102]

Preparation of the text was beset with tensions, and the schema that was finally presented to the Council for discussion was largely the result of compromise. The subcommission charged with preparing the initial draft had consisted of experts in music who were intent on safeguarding the interests of tradition. When the text was submitted for preliminary review, the Preparatory Commission added a strong pastoral-liturgical emphasis. Jungmann relates that criticism of the final draft was so strong among

---

101. *De Musica sacra et sacra Liturgia*, September 3, 1958. *AAS* 50 (1958), pp. 630–663. Tr: *TPS* 5 (1959), pp. 223–250.

102. *Commentary on the Documents, op. cit.*, p. 76.

Council members that the text had to be thoroughly revised by the Council Commission.[103] A comparison of preliminary and approved texts of Article 113 illustrates the extent of the change.

The preliminary text for Article 113 reads:

> The noblest form of liturgy is the solemn service in the Latin tongue with the participation of the people; the people and the choir should be led on to such a celebration stage by stage; hence the bishops' conferences should be able to decree that individual chants could be rendered in the mother tongue.[104]

This version proposes the solemn Latin High Mass as the most noble expression of the liturgy. The vernacular is perceived simply as a stage preparatory to the full acceptance of this highest ideal. The Preparatory Commission had accepted this articulation as the only way to get vernacular song on the agenda. Large groups of bishops, particularly those from Africa and Chile, objected strongly to this preference for Latin, which merely tolerated the vernacular as a preliminary and therefore temporary stage. The article was amended and the Council overwhelmingly approved the present articulation.[105]

When the first version of Article 113 failed to gain acceptance, there was concern that all of the Latin tradition might be lost in the groundswell of support for the vernacular. Instead of remaining the norm for the people, traditional music and its preservation became the responsibility of choirs. The phrase "cathedral churches" was added to the text of Article 114, because cathedrals have traditionally been centers of artistic expression and the guardians of classical styles. This amendment strengthened the traditional tone of the text, but the pastoral tone was also strengthened with the added reference to chapter one concerning the people's participation. The final text of Article 114 reflects a carefully balanced compromise between two distinct points of view.

Schillebeeckx refers to these two points of view in an essay following the Council's first session. He speaks of the fundamental difference between the world of ideas, or "essential thinking,"

---

103. *Ibid.*
104. *Ibid.,* p. 77.
105. *Ibid.,* p. 78.

which regards the mysteries of faith and human life as abstract essences to be formulated with precision, and the world of pastoral experience, or "existential thinking," which is conditioned by the data of everyday life.[106] Council decisions emerged from the struggle between these two distinct mentalities. In chapter six, this struggle is very apparent. Schillebeeckx also expresses this difference in terms of keeping the faith pure and keeping the faith alive.[107] In musical terms, it was a struggle between maintaining the tradition intact for a few and allowing the values of that tradition to come alive for many.

It took until March 5, 1967 before *Musicam sacram*, the Instruction for implementing the Council's decree on music,[108] was finally formulated and communicated to the universal Church. The long wait for official direction contributed to the ambiguities and tension of that interim period as many proceeded to implement Conciliar directives according to criteria of their own. The Instruction, consisting of sixty-nine articles, is a lengthy piece of legislation that remains the last and latest official document on Church music promulgated by Rome.[109] All local legislation and practice must coincide with the guidelines articulated here.

Since the Council shifted responsibility for implementation of liturgical norms to local ecclesiastical authorities, Americans now look to the National Conference of Catholic Bishops for guidance. In 1968, the Bishops Committee on the Liturgy published "The Place of Music in Eucharistic Celebration" in its January–February *Newsletter*. Although of unofficial status, the document precipitated much comment, both by those who favored its vision and those who feared the freedom it implied. Four years later, the document had been rewritten and released by the Bishops Committee on the Liturgy under the auspices of the National Conference of Catholic Bishops as guidelines for the use of music

---

106. *Vatican II: A Struggle of Minds* (Dublin: Gill and Son, 1963), pp. 10–11.

107. *Ibid.*, p. 32.

108. *AAS* 59 (1967), pp. 300–320. Tr: *TPS* 12 (1967), pp. 173–186.

109. Other post-Conciliar documents that make reference to music: Paul VI, *Sacram Liturgiam* (1964), *Ecce adstat Concilium* (1966); CR and *Consilium, Inter Oecumenici* (1964), *General Instruction on the Roman Missal* (1969); Congregation for Divine Worship, *Actio pastoralis Ecclesiae* (1969), *Liturgicae instaurationes* (1970), *Pueros baptizatos* (1973). See bibliography for details.

in the Catholic Church in America.[110] A revised edition was issued in 1983 with textual changes of an editorial nature to add clarity and to incorporate inclusive language.[111] A supplement entitled *Liturgical Music Today* was prepared and released for the tenth anniversary of *Music in Catholic Worship*.[112] Today, these two documents represent the official position of the American bishops on the use of music in the liturgy.[113]

CONCLUDING REMARKS

It is difficult to summarize a chapter that spans twenty centuries and is already in summary form. What has been presented here is only a glimpse of some of the legislation of some of the popes and councils from some of the more significant periods in church music history. The texts selected are representative of the issues, but are far too few in number to allow one to do more than highlight major trends.

The first tangible piece of music legislation does not appear until the ninth century, but there is strong evidence of centralization for several centuries prior to that. Well before the corpus of music legislation formally establishes Rome's jurisdiction, it seems that the music standards set by the Apostolic See and disseminated throughout the Empire were perceived as normative for the Latin rite.

---

110. *Music In Catholic Worship* (1972), United States Catholic Conference, 1312 Massachusetts Avenue, N.W., Washington, DC 20005.

111. *Music in Catholic Worship* (1983), USCC, as above. A closer analysis of both versions (1972 and 1983) may eventually reveal that one or more of the editorial adjustments represent a substantive change.

112. NCCB, *Liturgical Music Today*, A statement of the BCL on the Tenth Anniversary of *Music in Catholic Worship*, September 28, 1982. Available from the United States Catholic Conference.

113. Other statements on music have appeared in the BCL *Newsletter* from time to time, such as, "Musical Tones for English Texts," December 1965; "The Role of the Choir," "The Use of Music for Special Groups," "The Salaries of Church Musicians," April 1966; "Statement on Masses in Homes and on Music," February 1967; "Copyright Violations," December 1967 and May 1969; "Letter to Composers of Liturgical Music," November 1980; "New Directions for Liturgical Music," May 1981; "Dance in the Liturgy," (reprint of an essay from *Notitiae* 11 [1975], pp. 202–205), April 1982.

Major events in church music history are not always chronicled in the legislation. The establishment of the Gregorian tradition through the redaction and codification of selected chants; the beginnings of polyphony and its early evolution up to its first critical, increasingly secular stage; the rebirth of ecclesiastical polyphony in its classical, sixteenth-century form: legislation is reticent about these developments. Documents indicate legislators are less concerned with announcing new possibilities than with correcting deviations and maintaining fidelity to a tradition once the new pattern is the norm. Twentieth-century legislation reflects some trend-setting characteristics in the area of popular participation, but with the exception of *Tra le sollecitudini* of Pius X, music legislation is seldom in the vanguard of *aggiornamento*, although it is continually promoting reform.

Several broad conclusions can be drawn from the legislation surveyed here. The first observation is somewhat surpising. Papal legislation on music is not always as restrictive as is popularly believed. On closer examination, a number of documents are seen to be concerned primarily with eliminating abuse, not with stifling creativity. Unfortunately, the suppression of creativity is often a byproduct of the Church's determination to protect its ritual from profanation. Part of the problem regarding acceptable musical repertoire stems from confusion regarding the nature of "abuse." Except for a persistent abhorrence for the theatrical throughout the centuries, there is no agreement, even among legislators, on what constitutes an abuse. What is abusive to some can be inspiring to others. Polyphony, hymnody, the organ, other instruments, popular song: all have been considered by legislators as both positive and negative influences at one time or another, as *Annus qui* has so clearly shown. At the heart of the problem is the fact that it has been the prerogative of each pope to decide what is or is not an abuse, what is or is not profane and therefore offensive and to be condemned. Nowhere in the literature is there any evidence of a clear theological guideline for making such choices. Rather, it appears that the primary referent, aside from personal predilection, is papal precedent.

Along these lines, it has been clarifying to search out precisely what kind of music was prohibited by the Council of Trent. Contrary to popular impression, no musical style or form was actually forbidden. The condemnation of figured music that dominated the committee sessions was never incorporated into the final decree. Trent made only one statement, which was subsequently written into the 1918 Code of Canon Law, a request to banish from the churches any music containing things that are lascivious or impure. In itself, this is not a prohibitive statement, but a legitimate effort to protect the tradition from violation. However, since it was included in the decree as a summation of previous texts and discussions, those who implemented the decree at the conclusion of the Council often interpreted its intent in light of this more restrictive context. Consequently, instead of eliminating only lascivious elements, certain legislators sought to eliminate what they considered to be lascivious styles, repertoires, instruments, and texts. Not all of the popes reacted this way.

On the other hand, much of the legislation lacks vision, is constrained and conservative and politically expedient. This is particularly true whenever Church leadership becomes preoccupied with the reform of the official books. Rigidity in this area can usually be traced to curial interventions. Indeed, there is a sense that the overall impression of papal legislation rendered so far would be less positive if the present survey had included a representative sampling of the multitude of rescripts issued by the Congregation of Rites. After examining the more general legislation of the popes and the specific *decreta* of the Congregation, it is clear that the more restrictive atmosphere attributed to music legislation in the last few centuries has been generated primarily by the latter body, which was instituted two decades after the close of the Council of Trent for the purpose of guarding the tradition and maintaining a uniform rite.

The corpus of papal legislation bears witness to the vitality of artistic expression which, time and again, refuses to give in to the pressure of legislative restraints. There is a sense of movement and development through the centuries which, despite efforts to bar some of its manifestations from the sanctuary, often succeeds in encompassing both Church and society, challenging distinctions between the two.

Prior to the modern liturgical movement, the legislation is eloquent in its silence about the people and their song. Until quite recently, antagonists in the legislation were the proponents of ecclesiastical chant on the one side, and of artistic, polyphonic music on the other. For all practical purposes, the legislation considered these latter the people, but they are in fact the professionals: the choir director, the choir, the organist, the instrumentalist, the composer. Until recently, these were the ones who challenged the establishment, who threatened the integrity of tradition. In the aftermath of the Reformation, however, a new voice emerges within the legislation, the voice of the silent masses, whose song is variously described as modern music, religious song, popular song, hymn. These are labeled "the people," and the former become "the artists." For a time, there is evidence of a tripartite interest within the legislation, each fostering a separate emphasis, each entity distinct: the establishment, the artists, the people. With Vatican II, the equation changes, and that is the biggest surprise of all.

A most curious phenomenon of the post-Conciliar period is the shift in understanding concerning the professional musician. Practically overnight, the artist has emerged as the guardian of tradition, the symbol of perfection of form, representative of the establishment. But as we have seen, the corpus of music legislation prior to Vatican II records a different image. The professional has always been one to be watched, his or her creativity kept in check, in the best interests of tradition. Through the centuries, professional music has drawn forth from the hierarchy a whole catalogue of complaints directed against real or imagined abuse. With the advent of vernacular liturgy, however, tradition receives a new champion, and there is a reversal of roles. The professional musician becomes the custodian of the Church's musical heritage. The struggle for validation has been long and difficult, yet the struggle is not really over. It has simply taken another form. The artist is still not fully accepted, but the opponent is no longer the establishment, for the artist now is the establishment. The new opponent is the people, and the new threat is the people's song.

7

Criteria for the Use of Music
in the Liturgy

THE PURPOSE OF THIS CHAPTER IS TO LIFT UP CRITERIA FOR THE USE OF MUSIC
in the liturgy both before and after Vatican II, as established by the
major music legislation of this century, and to evaluate those
criteria in order to determine the effect of the Council on the
music of the Catholic Church. Of particular interest here is the
music of the American church.

Unless otherwise specified, the term "criteria" as used in this
and the following chapter is understood to mean those regulatory
norms or legal standards that govern music practice. My premise is
that music ought to be governed by theological criteria clearly
articulated and understood, from which practical guidelines are
drawn. As a step toward articulating those theological criteria, the
present chapter will name and evaluate regulatory criteria of a
practical nature in effect before and after Vatican II. The following
chapter will address the theological bases underlying those
regulatory norms. Six key documents form the basis for this
analysis: *Tra le sollecitudini* (1903), *Musicae sacrae disciplina* (1955),
De Musica sacra (1958), Chapter Six of *Sacrosanctum concilium*
(1963), *Musicam sacram* (1967), and *Music in Catholic Worship*
(1972).[1]

---

1. Throughout this chapter, these documents will be referred to as: *TLS, MSD,
DMS, SC, MS, MCW*. Ordinarily, citations from *MCW* will be taken from the 1983
edition of the 1972 document.

The six documents to be analyzed are representative of the pre-Conciliar, Conciliar and post-Conciliar periods of twentieth-century music legislation. The Instruction *De Musica sacra* is essentially an expansion of the earlier encyclical by Pius XII. Together with the precedent setting *motu proprio* of Pius X, it documents a progression of development during the period prior to the Council. The Instruction *Musicam sacram* is Rome's interpretation and application of Conciliar directives. Chapter six of *Sacrosanctum concilium* and this Instruction mark a decisive turning point from pre-Conciliar to post-Conciliar practice. The 1972 statement by the American bishops is characteristic of the post-Conciliar age. The regulatory criteria extracted from these documents will provide the data for a theological evaluation in chapter eight.

Significant change has taken place in the liturgy in this century, particularly as a result of Vatican II. This chapter will investigate the change that has taken place in legislating the liturgy's music in order to determine to what extent this change is or is not in harmony with the liturgy's own theological and ritual change. Are the new criteria more pastorally oriented? Do they reflect changing roles and ministries? To what extent are they supportive of the newly emerging people's song? These are some of the questions that will be asked of the texts.

GENERAL PRINCIPLES

Each of the documents under consideration prefaces its practical data with some theoretical reflection, yet each handles its material in a somewhat different way. *Tra le sollecitudini* opens with a section entitled General Principles (*Principia generalia*), *De Musica sacra* with General Concepts (*Notiones generales*), *Musicam sacram* with General Norms (*De quibusdam normis generalioribus*). Pius XII's encyclical has no subdivisions but is one continuous reflection. In *Music in Catholic Worship,* as in *Sacrosanctum concilium,* music criteria flow from the principles of liturgical celebration. In all the documents, music is placed in the context of the liturgy and its theology, and theoretical principles are often interwoven throughout the body of the text.

Consistent among twentieth-century legislators is the conviction that "the Church has always recognized and favored the progress of the arts" (*TLS*, 5) and given "the highest honor and praise . . . to liturgical music" (*MSD*, 35) whose tradition is "greater even than that of any other art" (*SC*, 112). Scripture, the Fathers of the Church, and previous popes are cited as having "bestowed praise upon sacred song" (*SC*, 112; *MSD*, 5–20) to establish that music has been "greatly esteemed throughout the Church's history" (*MSD*, 83). Musical progress is recognized and affirmed. "Under the auspices of the Church, the study of sacred music has . . . gradually progressed from the simple and ingenuous Gregorian modes to great and magnificent works of art" (*MSD*, 16), yielding "a treasure of inestimable value" (*SC*, 112). There is a genuine expectation that the art of music "will be developed and continually perfected" (*MSD*, 83) today as in the past. The Church, it is said, has always admitted to the service of worship "everything good and beautiful discovered by genius in the course of ages," provided it has "the needed qualities" and is in harmony with "the liturgical laws" (*TLS*, 5; also, *SC*, 112).

The documents are also unanimous in their preference for a sung form when Eucharist is celebrated with the people.

> Liturgical worship is given a more noble form when the divine offices are celebrated solemnly in song, with the assistance of sacred ministers and the active participation of the people (*SC*, 113; *MS*, 5).

Prior to the Council, there were two kinds of Masses: the *Missa in cantu* ("sung Mass") and the *Missa lecta* ("read Mass") (*DMS*, 3). The *Missa in cantu* was either a *Missa solemnis* or the simpler *Missa cantata*. At the time of Pius X, the Solemn High Mass, High Mass, and Low Mass were three distinct rituals. Then the *Missa lecta* evolved stylistically to include the *Missa recitata* (Dialogue Mass with congregation) and the so-called *Betsingmesse* (Dialogue Mass with hymns). These distinctions were incorporated into the 1958 Instruction's degrees of congregational participation (for the *Missa in cantu*, art. 25–26; the *Missa lecta*, art. 29–31). The 1967 Instruction states that "the distinction between solemn, sung, and read Mass, sanctioned by the Instruction of 1958, is retained," and offers its own degrees of participation for greater pastoral effectiveness (*MS*, 28). The American document of 1972, however, introduces a radical change.

> While it is possible to make technical distinctions in the forms of Mass—all the way from the Mass in which nothing is sung to the Mass in which everything is sung—such distinctions are of little significance in themselves; almost unlimited combinations of sung and recited parts may be chosen (*MCW*, 51).

The centuries-old tradition regarding the sung Ordinary and sung Proper as foundational to the High Mass is interpreted anew. "The former distinction between the ordinary and proper parts of the Mass with regard to musical settings and distribution of roles is no longer retained" (*MCW*, 51). In addition, the four-hymn "Low Mass" format, an accommodation of the vernacular to the pre-Conciliar Latin Mass, "is now outdated" (52). In the American Church, those distinctions between Solemn High Mass, High Mass, and Low Mass that had determined degrees of solemnity "have become obsolete and should no longer be used. The present emphasis is not on the solemnity of form or on parts that must be sung, but on the active participation of the assembly in the liturgical celebration."[2] Indeed, "many and varied musical patterns are now possible within the liturgical structure" (*MCW*, 50). The style of each liturgical celebration is governed by pastoral considerations (*MCW*, 39).

THE NATURE OF MUSIC

Music, "the science or the sense of proper modulation,"[3] is "among the many and great gifts of nature" with which God has gifted God's people (*MSD*, 4). Speaking of all the arts in general, including music, Pius XII validates religious art in terms of faith itself, denying to the artist devoid of belief "that inward eye with which he might see what God's majesty and worship demand of

---

2. BCL *Newsletter* 9 (May 1973), p. 375.
3. Augustine, *De origine animae hominis* I, 2: *PL* 33, 725, as quoted by Pius XII in *MSD*, 5.

him," and to the artist's works "the piety and faith that befit God's temple" (*MSD*, 27). On the other hand, one who is firm in faith and motivated by God's love "expresses and manifests the truths he holds and the piety he possesses so skillfully, beautifully and pleasingly in . . . sounds and harmonies" that the artistic experience, an act of worship for the artist, effectively inspires others to piety and faith (*MSD*, 28). Not everyone would link the criterion of faith so inflexibly to the nature of religious art, in this case, music for worship. Yet the documents agree that in the Church's celebrations of faith, "music is of preeminent importance." (*MCW*, 23)

In reading twentieth-century legislation, one is struck by the casual and unexplained acceptance of the designation "sacred," which prefaces all references to music for use in the liturgy. Pius X's landmark *motu proprio de musica sacra* made the term a permanent part of the Church music vocabulary. More recent documents have failed to examine the burden of past assumptions that this term carries into the present. Indeed, *"sacra"* says something about the nature of the *"musica"* that it conditions. Precisely what it says, or would hope to say, will be considered in the following chapter.

Relationship to Liturgy

Pius XII would apply his standards for religious art more strictly to music, because "sacred music enters more intimately into divine worship than many other liberal arts," which merely prepare a setting, whereas music "has an important place in the actual performance of the sacred ceremonies and rites themselves" (*MSD*, 30). The Council went a step further and declared the tradition of music to be "greater even than that of any other art" (*SC*, 112). According to Pius XII, "the dignity and force of sacred music are greater the closer sacred music itself approaches to the supreme act of Christian worship" (*MSD*, 34), which is the Eucharist. Or, in the words of the Council Fathers, "sacred music is to be considered the more holy in proportion as it is more closely connected with the liturgical action . . . " (*SC*, 112).

In 1903, Pius X made a decisive statement about the nature of sacred music, describing it as *"pars integrans solemnis liturgiae"* (*TLS*, 1). The phrase has become an accepted part of the tradition ever since.[4] The 1958 Instruction recognized sacred music as being "closely linked to the liturgy," reserving to "sacred chant" the distinction of being "an integral part of the liturgy itself" (DMS, 104). Specifically, "everything which the liturgical books require to be chanted . . . is an integral part of the liturgy" (DMS, 21). So close is the connection, that "instructions on sacred music and sacred liturgy cannot be separated" (DMS, 104). The Conciliar Constitution expands the principle, relating the preeminence of music to the fact that "as sacred song united to the words, it forms a necessary or integral part of the solemn liturgy" ("necessarium vel integralem liturgiae solemnis partem"; SC, 112). The American document affirms that "as sacred song united to the words" music forms an "integral part of solemn liturgy" (MCW, 23, 1972 edition). The word "necessary" does not appear in this statement, but it has been added to the 1983 edition ("necessary or integral") to more accurately reflect the conciliar constitution's original articulation. Several questions arise. Was the omission of "necessary" from the 1972 document intended as a substantive statement or was it simply a stylistic deletion? Are "integral" and "necessary" unequivocally equated or is there a distinction in meaning or emphasis between the two terms? The 1982 Supplement to this document states that the Church's liturgy "is inherently musical" and music should therefore be appreciated as "a necessarily normal dimension of every experience of communal worship."[5] The Supplement distinguishes between music that simply accompanies ritual action as an enrichment (LMT, 9) and "the sung prayer" which is "a constituent element of the rite" and consequently "the integral mode by which the mystery is proclaimed and presented" (10).

Pius X gave impetus to a second principle pertaining to the nature of sacred music that has informed the tradition of this century. Objecting to that inappropriate use of music which overshadowed the liturgy itself, he reminded the Church that liturgy is not subservient to the music, as if it were its handmaid ("quasi musicorum sit ancilla"; TLS, 23),[6] but the contrary. Pius XII

---

4. See Chapter 8, pp. 205–212.

5. BCL, *Liturgical Music Today*, art. 5 (hereafter, *LMT*).

6. Pius XI elaborated on this in *Divini cultus sanctitatem* (hereafter, *DCS*), declaring the arts *"ancillae nobilissimae divino cultui inserviant,"* AAS 21 (1929), p. 35.

referred to sacred music as "the servant . . . of the sacred liturgy" ("*cultum sacrum minus*"; *MSD*, 30). Vatican II introduced the expression "*munus ministeriale*" and opted to describe the nature of liturgical music in terms of its "ministerial function" (*SC*, 112).

Following the lead of the Conciliar Constitution, the American document stresses the sign dimension of music in the liturgy. Music is, in fact, preeminent "among the many signs and symbols used by the Church to celebrate its faith" (*MCW*, 23). How music, by its very nature, can be sign or symbol is best explained by examining how it functions within the liturgy precisely as liturgical sign. In brief, Christians gather to "express our faith . . . and, by expressing it, renew and deepen it" (1). Such "faith in Christ and in one another" is "expressed in the signs and symbols of celebration" (4), which are "vehicles of communication and instruments of faith" (7). Music, by its very nature, has the capacity to "unveil a dimension of meaning and feeling, a communication of ideas and intuitions that words alone cannot yield" (24).

Qualities

> Sacred music should consequently possess, in the highest degree, the qualities proper to the liturgy, and precisely sanctity and goodness of form from which spontaneously springs its other character, universality (*TLS*, 2).

These qualities required of Catholic Church music—*sanctitas, bonitas formarum, universalitas*—are reiterated by Pius X himself and appropriated by his successors. *Musica sacra* must be holy (*sit sancta*) and exclude anything that savors of the profane (*TLS*, 2; *MSD*, 42). It must be true art (*sit ars vera*). It must be universal (*sit universalitas*); (*TLS*, 2; *MSD*, 45). Additional qualities can be gleaned from those passages in the encyclical of Pius XII praising compositions rightly ordered: "an artistic purity and richness of melody," which render the best of the tradition "completely worthy of accompanying and beautifying the Church's sacred rites" (*MSD*, 53), "virtue and purity" (44). To be fruitful and effective, popular religious hymns must be "in full conformity with the doctrine of the Catholic faith" and must "express and explain that doctrine accurately"; must "use plain language . . . simple melody . . . be free from violent and vain excess of words . . . short . . . easy . . . manifest a religious dignity and seriousness"

(63). The 1967 Instruction cautions that new melodies for vernacular texts must attain "a sufficient maturity and perfection" (*MS*, 60). The American document speaks of "the quality of joy and enthusiasm" (*MCW*, 23) that music transmits to community worship and also raises awareness to technical qualifications. Music intended for use in the liturgy must be "technically, aesthetically, and expressively good" (26). A musical judgment can and must be exercised by those qualified to do so. "Musicians must search for and create music of quality for worship" (27). In enumerating the qualities inherent in music for worship, Church leaders have been primarily concerned about the quality of that music. The American Church is convinced that "only artistically sound music will be effective in the long run" (*MCW*, 26), and insists that music be "good" (29). Earlier documents would insist that music be "perfect" (*DMS*, 60a).

THE PURPOSE OF MUSIC

The purpose of music in the liturgy is "the glory of God and the sanctification and edification of the faithful" (*TLS*, 1). The Council decree concurs (*SC*, 112). It is there "to add greater efficacy to the text" in order that "the faithful may be the more easily moved to devotion and better disposed to receive the fruits of grace" (*TLS*, 1). Such music has long been at the service of the faithful, facilitating a "more effective nourishment of spiritual life" among them (*MSD*, 1) in order "to lead them to higher things" (5) by "turning their minds piously to God through the works it directs to their senses" (27). At the same time, it "increases the honor given to God" (32), for "its purpose is to express in human works the infinite divine beauty of which it is, as it were, the reflection" (25). Prior to the Council, the "lofty purpose of sacred music" consisted in contributing daily to "greater splendor in the celebration of divine worship" by seeking to "beautify and embellish the voices of the priest who offers Mass and of the Christian people who praise the sovereign God" (1, 31). The purpose of maintaining the chant as the song of the Church was to ensure that "the unity and universality of the Church may shine forth more powerfully every day" (46). According to *Music In Catholic Worship*, the purpose of music in liturgy now is to "assist the assembled believers to express and share the gift of faith that is within them and to nourish and strengthen their interior commitment of faith" (*MCW*, 23).

Function

According to Pius X, the principal function of music in the liturgy is "to clothe with befitting melody the liturgical text proposed for the understanding of the faithful" (*TLS*, 1). The post-Conciliar Church continues to recognize the capacity of music to "heighten the texts so that they speak more fully and more effectively" (*MCW*, 23). For some time its function has also been that of "accompanying with beautiful sound the voice of the priest . . . answering him joyfully with the people who are present and enhancing the whole liturgical ceremony with its noble art" (*MSD*, 34). The Council describes "the ministerial function supplied by sacred music in the service of the Lord" in this way: "it adds delight to prayer, fosters unity of minds, or confers greater solemnity upon the sacred rites" (*SC*, 112). The American document builds on the Council's insight into music's ministerial function:

> The function of music is ministerial; it must serve and never dominate . . . It imparts a sense of unity to the congregation and sets the appropriate tone for a particular celebration (*MCW*, 23).

The 1982 Supplement develops this understanding further:

> The various functions of sung prayer must be distinguished within liturgical rites. Sometimes song is meant to accompany ritual actions. In such cases the song is not independent but serves, rather, to support the prayer of the assembly . . . The music enriches the moment . . . At other places in the liturgical action the sung prayer itself is a constituent element of the rite . . . the integral mode by which the mystery is proclaimed and presented (*LMT*, 9, 10).

As mentioned earlier, music in liturgy functions essentially as a sign whereby the celebrating community seeks to "give bodily expression to faith" so that its faith might be fostered and nourished (*MCW*, 5, 6).

Use

Traditionally, the use of music in the liturgy has been determined by expectations of the rite and by the needs of the faithful.
As the means whereby God's word has been ritualized, it has
been used as the mode of transmission for essential texts, making
it an "integral part" of the rite (SC, 112). Music has been used also
for the sake of the congregation, because through music "prayer is
expressed in a more attractive way, the mystery of the liturgy . . . is
more openly shown, the unity of hearts is more profoundly
achieved . . . minds are more easily raised to heavenly things" (MS,
5). "Always and everywhere," writes Pius XII, "sacred song and
the art of music have been used to ornament and decorate
religious ceremonies" (MSD, 6), "to increase the glory of the
sacred rites" (15) and "the magnificence of divine worship"
(53).

A key word in Catholic Church music history is "solemnity." It
sets the style and tone of the liturgy, influences other criteria to lift
up all elements in the direction of a grand display. Celebrations
"may be solemnized by singing," feasts are "given due solemnity"
through the appropriate use of music (MS, 44). "Each feast and
season has its own spirit and its own music," the American
document explains, and "great feasts demand more solemnity"
(MCW, 19). Communities "will want to sing more on the great
feasts" because "important events . . . suggest fuller programs of
song" (20).

Songs have long been used by religious educators as "effective
aids" of evangelization to "foster and increase faith and piety"
(MSD, 67) or as a source of "spiritual consolation" (45). The
traditional chant has been the means whereby "the faithful,
wherever they may be, will hear music that is familiar to them and
a part of their own home" (45). In addition to "fostering the devotion of the faithful" (MS, 46), music "clearly demonstrates the
'ecclesial' aspect of the celebration" (42) and is used to emphasize
this dimension. The American document and its supplement stress
that music to be used in liturgical celebration must be subjected to
a threefold judgment: musical, liturgical, and pastoral (MCW,
25–41; LMT, 29), and that "the pastoral judgment governs the use
and function of every element of celebration" (MCW, 39). The
pastoral judgment asks: "Does music in the celebration enable

these people to express their faith, in this place, in this age, in this culture" (39)? "Will it help this assembly to pray" (*LMT*, 29)? The prototype of the 1972 statement appeared in the 1968 edition of the BCL *Newsletter* under the title, "The Place of Music in Eucharistic Celebrations."[7] It included two statements that were not retained in the document. "The primary goal of celebration is to make a humanly attractive experience."[8] "Music, more than any other resource, makes a celebration of the liturgy an attractive human experience."[9] Nevertheless, *Music In Catholic Worship* continues to affirm that the signs and symbols of celebration must indeed be "humanly attractive" (7). Efforts to ensure that music is appropriate to the liturgy contribute toward that goal.

PRACTICAL NORMS

The documents under consideration regulate music practice. Consequently, to a large extent, they are comprised of operational norms. Preceptive or directive, broadly regulatory or rubrically specific, these norms touch on all aspects of music making, including the preservation of core values and their transmission. The criteria embedded in each of the documents have set the standards and served as guidelines indicative of the times. The two Instructions, in particular, are compendia of the official Church's expectations regarding the use of music in its liturgy immediately before and after Vatican II. Because the coverage is so detailed and extensive, only the major elements can be dealt with here.

MUSIC MAKING

There are many facets to music making, elements of style and form, the quality of its creation and recreation, the extent to which it is expressive of the culture in which it resides. Twentieth-century legislation set the norms in all these areas and monitored adaptations.

7. Volume 4, January–February, 1968, pp. 113–119.
8. *Ibid.*, p. 114.
9. *Ibid.*, p. 115.

Style

Those qualities proper to liturgical music "are possessed in the highest degree by Gregorian chant" (*TLS*, 3). It is, therefore, to be "restored in the functions of public worship" and regarded as "the supreme model for sacred music" (3). Convinced that the Roman style of chant was illustrative of the highest standards of liturgical music, Pius X established the following rule:

> The more closely a composition for Church approaches in its movement, inspiration and savor the Gregorian form, the more sacred and liturgical it is: and the more out of harmony it is with that supreme model, the less worthy it is of the temple (3).

He insisted that Gregorian chant "be cultivated by all with diligence and love, according to the Tridentine prescriptions" (25). By the time Pius XII wrote his encyclical in 1955, however, there was less talk of restoration and more of preservation.

> It is the duty of all those to whom Christ the Lord has entrusted the task of guarding and dispensing the Church's riches to preserve this precious treasure of Gregorian chant diligently and to impart it generously to the Christian people (*MSD*, 44).

The 1958 Instruction states the conditions of mandatory use. Where the rubrics require that certain parts of the liturgy be chanted by the priest and his celebrants with responses from the choir and the people, these "must be chanted exclusively in Gregorian chant, as given in the 'typical' editions. Accompaniment by any instrument is forbidden" (16b). In all other parts of the liturgy, "unless there are mitigating circumstances, it is preferable to use [Gregorian chant] instead of other kinds of sacred music" (16). The Council affirms its primacy but does not mandate its use.

> The Church acknowledges Gregorian chant as specially suited to the Roman liturgy: therefore, other things being equal, it should be given pride of place in liturgical services (*SC*, 116).

The 1967 Instruction specifies that "in sung liturgical services celebrated in Latin . . . other things being equal," Gregorian chant "should be given pride of place" and sung as preserved "in the 'typical' editions" (*MS*, 50a). However, as suggested by *Sacrosanctum concilium* (117) "it is also desirable that an edition be prepared consisting of more simple melodies, for use in smaller churches" (*MS*, 50b).

In addition to Gregorian chant, "the qualities mentioned are also possessed in an excellent degree by the classic polyphony" (*TLS*, 4). Because "classic polyphony approaches closely to the . . . supreme model of all sacred music . . . it has been found worthy of a place side by side with the Gregorian chant" (4). Here, too, a specific style is recommended, that of the Roman school which, according to liturgical standards, reached its zenith in the sixteenth-century compositions of Pierluigi da Palestrina (4). Consequently, Pius X legislates that classic polyphony "be restored largely in ecclesiastical functions, especially in the more important basilicas . . . and other ecclesiastical institutions in which the necessary means are usually not lacking" (4). Pius XII cautions:

> . . . great prudence and care should be used . . . to keep out of the churches polyphonic music which, because of its heavy and bombastic style, might obscure the sacred words of the liturgy by a kind of exaggeration, interfere with the conduct of the liturgical service or, finally, lower the skill and competence of the singers to the disadvantage of sacred worship (*MSD*, 57).

The pre-Conciliar Instruction allows the use of polyphony in all liturgical functions, provided "there is a choir which knows how to perform it according to the rules of the art" (*DMS*, 17). While acknowledging that "this kind of sacred music is more suitable to the liturgical functions celebrated in greater splendor" (17), it recommends that "ancient compositions of sacred polyphony which are still buried in archives, should be diligently sought out . . . steps taken for their fitting preservation" and "their publication either in critical editions or in adaptations for liturgical use" (49). The Council did not limit its recommendations to Gregorian chant. "Other kinds of sacred music, especially polyphony, are by no means excluded from liturgical celebrations, so long as they accord with the spirit of the liturgical action . . . " (*SC*, 116).

In his *motu proprio*, Pius X allowed that "modern music is also admitted in the Church," since "it, too, furnishes compositions of such excellence, sobriety and gravity that they are in no way unworthy of the liturgical functions" (*TLS*, 5). Nevertheless, "as modern music has come to be devoted mainly to profane uses, greater care must be taken with regard to it" (5). Those "compositions of modern style which are admitted in the Church may contain nothing profane" (5). In fact, care must be taken that they "be not fashioned even in their external forms after the manner of profane pieces" (5). The pope spoke out against the theatrical style prevalent in nineteenth-century Italy. He described it as "diametrically opposed to the Gregorian chant and the classic polyphony, and therefore to the most important law of sacred music" (6),[10] because its intrinsic structure, rhythm, and conventionalism adapt badly to liturgical forms (6). The 1958 Instruction adds that "modern sacred music" intended for liturgical use "must be pious and preserve a religious character" (*DMS*, 7), must be "composed in conformity with liturgical laws and the rules that pertain to sacred music" (50), and must be "in accord with the dignity, seriousness, and sanctity of the liturgy" (18).

Pius XII writes at great length about the hymn, which belongs to the people and is rightly called religious. He locates it in the earliest tradition of the Church and engages in an enthusiastic recital of its positive features. "The tunes of these hymns which are often sung in the language of the people, are memorized with almost no effort . . . the mind grasps the words and the music" (*MSD*, 37). Consequently, these hymns "can exercise great and salutary force and power on the souls of the faithful" (36). The pope urges Church leaders "to foster and promote diligently popular religious singing of this kind," to encourage experts in the field "to gather hymns of this sort into one collection . . . so that all of the faithful can learn them more easily, memorize them and sing them correctly" (66). He notes the limitations of the popular style, its appropriateness "during non-liturgical services" and "outside churches at various solemnities and celebrations" (36). The Instruction *De Musica sacra* concurs with the pope's recommendations, stating that "popular religious song may be freely

10. In Seasoltz, *The New Liturgy*, pg. 6, *sacrorum musicorum legibus* is translated as "the most important law of all good music."

used in pious exercises" (19), that it "has a place in all the
solemnities of Christian life, whether in public or in the family,"
and "is sometimes admitted in liturgical functions themselves"
(51).

The Instruction also identifies another kind of music, "religious
music," as a distinct classification.

> By "religious music" is meant any music which, either because of
> the intention of the composer or because of the subject and purpose
> of the composition, is likely to express and arouse pious and
> religious sentiments and is therefore "most helpful to religion"
> (10).

Such music, however, "is not meant for sacred worship" and
therefore "is not permitted in liturgical functions" (10). Yet it
"should be greatly esteemed and assiduously cultivated" since it
"tends to arouse religious sentiments in those who hear it and to
foster worship" and is therefore quite appropriately called "religious music" (54). "The proper places for performing works of
religious music are concert halls or auditoriums, but not churches"
(55). The Instruction then proceeds to outline in detail the rubrics
required should such a concert be permitted to take place in a
church, such as, permission from the proper authorities (in
writing), removal of the Blessed Sacrament (if at all possible), the
selling of tickets and distribution of programs (to take place
outside the church), the recommendation that the concert conclude with some pious exercise (Benediction preferred) (55).

The Council does not really address the question of modern
music, except by implication. The 1967 Instruction assigns all non-
liturgical music to the area of "popular devotions," particularly to
"celebrations of the Word of God" where they can "foster a
religious spirit and encourage meditation on the sacred mystery"
(MS, 46). The American document of 1972 states that "in modern
times the Church has consistently recognized and freely admitted
the use of various styles of music as an aid to liturgical worship"
(MCW, 28). Indeed, since the Council, "there has arisen a more
pressing need for musical compositions in idioms that can be sung
by the congregation and thus further communal participation"
(28). The following statement is characteristic of Catholic Church
music in the United States today:

We do a disservice to musical values, however, when we confuse the judgment of music with the judgment of musical style. Style and value are two distinct judgments. Good music of new styles is finding a happy home in the celebrations of today. To chant and polyphony we have effectively added the chorale hymn, restored responsorial singing to some extent, and employed many styles of contemporary composition. Music in folk idiom is finding acceptance in eucharistic celebrations. We must judge value within each style (*MCW*, 28).

Perhaps the single, most formative influence on the style of Catholic Church music has been that of liturgical language. "The language of the Roman rite is Latin," wrote Pius X in 1903 (*TLS*, 7). Alternatives were out of the question. "It is therefore forbidden to sing anything whatever in the vernacular in solemn liturgical functions" (7). By preserving the Latin language, Pius X ensured the primacy of Gregorian chant and classical polyphony. In 1955 Pius XII confirmed that "the law by which it is forbidden to sing the liturgical words themselves in the language of the people remains in force . . . " (*MSD*, 47). However:

> Where, according to old or immemorial custom, some popular hymns are sung in the language of the people after the sacred words of the liturgy have been sung in Latin during the solemn eucharistic sacrifice, local ordinaries can allow this to be done "if, in the light of the circumstances of the locality and the people, they believe that [custom] cannot prudently be removed"[11] (47).

The 1958 Instruction reaffirms that "the rule forbidding the chanting of liturgical phrases in the vernacular has no exceptions" (*DMS*, 14a). Latin is still "the language of liturgical functions," that is, unless the liturgical books "explicitly permit another language" (13a). There are "special exceptions granted from this law on the exclusive use of Latin in liturgical functions" and these "remain in force, but one may not give them a broader interpretation or transfer them to other regions without authorization from the Holy See" (13c). In the *Missa lecta*, priest and people "may use only the Latin language" when participating directly in the authorized texts. However, after the prescribed parts are completed, "if the

11. The 1918 *Code of Canon Law*, canon 5, is quoted here.

faithful wish to add some popular prayers or hymns to this direct liturgical participation, according to local custom, this may be done in the vernacular" (14b). It is to be understood by all that "the language of Gregorian chant as a liturgical chant is solely Latin" (16a).

The Council shifted the decision regarding language to the local national level, stating "it is for the competent territorial ecclesiastical authority . . . to decide whether, and to what extent, the vernacular language is to be used" (and for the Holy See to confirm their decisions) (*SC*, 36). "In Masses which are celebrated with the people, a suitable place may be allotted to their mother tongue" (54). In the 1967 Instruction, the emphasis regarding language shifts. "Where the vernacular has been introduced into the celebration of Mass, the local Ordinaries will judge whether it may be opportune to preserve one or more Masses celebrated in Latin—especially sung Masses . . . " (*MS*, 48). And:

> Pastors of souls, having taken into consideration pastoral usefulness and the character of their own language, should see whether parts of the heritage of sacred music, written in previous centuries for Latin texts, could also be conveniently used, not only in liturgical celebrations in Latin, but also in those performed in the vernacular. There is nothing to prevent different parts in one and the same celebration being sung in different languages (51).

With the completion of the new Roman Missal, the use of the vernacular language is no longer the exception but the norm.

> Thus, in the great diversity of languages, one unique prayer will rise as an acceptable offering to our Father in heaven, through our High Priest Jesus Christ, in the Holy Spirit.[12]

Pope Paul VI addressed a general audience on the implications of this change. "No longer Latin, but the vernacular, will be the principle language of the Mass." In losing Latin, "we lose the centuries-old idiom of Christianity . . . and thus we shall lose a large portion of that wondrous and incomparable reality, Gregorian chant, which is both artistic and spiritual." What would justify such a loss? "We are sacrificing an inestimable treasure,"

---

12. Paul VI, *Missale Romanum*, April 3, 1969. Tr: *TPS* 14 (1969), p. 169.

but "our understanding of prayer is worth more than the regal antique garments in which it has been clothed. More important is the participation of the people. . . . "[13]

Previous norms virtually ensured that traditional music would survive intact. For a time, new norms threatened those very forms with extinction. "The musical tradition of the universal Church is a treasure of inestimable value," Vatican II decreed, and that "treasure of sacred music is to be preserved and fostered with great care . . . " (SC, 112, 114). The American document insists that "the nature of the liturgy itself will help to determine what kind of music is called for" (MCW, 30), whether music suitable for "a more informal style of celebration" (17) or an occasion with "more solemnity" (19), whether "the new musical settings" or "the best of the old music," that is, the "rich heritage of Latin chants and motets" (27).

> Flexibility is recognized today as an important value in liturgy. The musician with a sense of artistry and a deep knowledge of the rhythm of the liturgical action will be able to combine the many options into an effective whole . . . [to] enhance the liturgy with new creations of variety and richness and with those compositions from the time-honored treasury of liturgical music which can still serve today's celebrations (76).[14]

Form

The Tridentine Mass had a set form from which there could be no deviation. "The different parts of the Mass and the office must retain, even musically, that particular concept and form which ecclesiastical tradition has assigned to them" (TLS, 10). The Ordinary had to be through-composed to "preserve the unity of composition proper to their text" (11a).

> It is not lawful, therefore, to compose them in separate pieces, in such a way that each of such pieces may form a complete compositon in itself, and be capable of being detached from the rest and substituted by another (11a).

13. Paul IV, Address On the New Order of Mass, November 19, 1969. Tr: TPS 14 (1970), p. 330.

14. The 1972 version of the text begins "Flexibility reigns supreme."

For those texts rendered in music, "the order in which they are to be rendered, being determined for every liturgical function, it is not lawful to confuse this order or to change the prescribed texts for others . . . " (*TLS*, 8; *DMS*, 21a). Ordinaries and Propers were precisely ordered, because the rite required that "all of their parts should be diligently and carefully arranged to produce their salutary results in a fitting manner" (*MSD*, 40). Not only was it "strictly forbidden . . . to alter or omit or improperly repeat words" (*DMS*, 21a), but it was also "strictly forbidden to omit, wholly or in part, any liturgical text which should be chanted" (21b), unless there was "reasonable cause" not to chant a given text, in which case a "monotone (*recto tono*)" substitution was permitted (21c).

In the 1967 Instruction, the rules are far less rigid. Options are allowed. "There is no reason why some of the Proper or Ordinary should not be sung in said Masses. Moreover, some other song can also, on occasions, be sung at the beginning, at the Offertory, at the Communion and at the end of Mass" . . . but "they must be in keeping with the parts of the Mass, with the feast, or with the liturgical season" (*MS*, 36).

With *Music In Catholic Worship*, the emphasis clearly shifts. There is still that concern for structure and form, perhaps more so than ever before, but a rediscovery of the nature of each ritual component has resulted in a reorienting of values within the infrastructure of the rite. "The choice of sung parts, the balance between them, and the style of musical setting used should reflect the relative importance of the parts of the Mass (or other service) and the nature of each part" (*MCW*, 31). The liturgy now requires choices. Each celebration is different, and those responsible for planning the music "must have a clear understanding of the structure of the liturgy," know what has "primary importance . . . know the nature of each of the parts of the liturgy and the relationship of each part to the overall rhythm of the liturgical action" (42). New criteria have been established to provide for the principal classes of texts: proclamations, acclamations, psalms, hymns, and prayers. One must now ask, "Does the music express and interpret the text correctly and make it more meaningful? Is the form of the text respected" (32)? The Supplement confirms that "the musical form employed must match its liturgical function" (*LMT*, 11).

Music In Catholic Worship is preoccupied with explaining the nature of the different genres and providing guidelines for their correct execution. A clear rationale accompanies practical recommendations.

> The acclamations are shouts of joy which arise from the whole assembly as forceful and meaningful assents to God's Word and Action. (53) In the eucharistic celebration there are five acclamations which ought to be sung even at Masses in which little else is sung: Alleluia; "Holy, Holy, Holy Lord"; Memorial Acclamation; Great Amen; Doxology to the Lord's Prayer (54).

Those parts preceding the liturgy of the word "have the character of introduction and preparation" (*MCW*, 44). Therefore, "the entrance song should create an atmosphere of celebration" (61) in order "to help the assembled people become a worshiping community and to prepare them for listening to God's Word and celebrating the Eucharist" (44). The responsorial psalm is a "unique and very important song" in response to the first lesson, with 900 refrains in the new lectionary's effort to match the psalm's content to the scripture's theme (63). In responding, the people accept God's Word, "involving themselves in the great covenant of love and redemption . . ." (45). The eucharistic prayer is the center of the entire celebration, "a statement of faith of the local assembly . . . affirmed and ratified by all those present through acclamations of faith: the first acclamation or Sanctus, the memorial acclamation, and the Great Amen" (47). Communion is the climax, "prepared for by several rites . . . accompanied by a song expressing the unity of the communicants" (48). As the document explains, the ordinary chants "may be treated as individual choices. One or more may be sung, the others, spoken" (64). Today, "many new patterns and combinations of song are emerging in eucharistic celebrations" (75).

> Experience with the 1967 statement makes it clear that mere observance of a pattern or rule of sung liturgy will not create a living and authentic celebration or worship in Christian congregations. That is the reason statements such as this must take the form of recommendation and attempts at guidance. In turn, this demands responsible study and choice . . . (*MCW*, Introduction).

Performance

In the performance of the sacred liturgical rites this same Gregorian chant should be most widely used and great care should be taken that it should be performed properly, worthily and reverently (*MSD*, 44).

Both before and after the Council, Church leaders have expressed concern that liturgical music not only be rightly done but well done. In establishing a special commission to watch over the music executed in churches, Pius X wrote: "Nor are they to see merely that the music is good in itself, but also that it is adapted to the powers of the singers and be always well executed" (*TLS*, 24). This applies to all who participate in the singing. "The priest celebrant and the sacred ministers, besides an accurate observance of the rubrics, should endeavor to execute their sung parts as correctly, distinctly, and artistically as they can" (*DMS*, 94). Clerics assigned to cathedrals or other large churches "must strive with all care and attention to become ready and able to perform the sacred chant and liturgical functions perfectly" (111). In fact, "whenever it is possible to choose the persons who will celebrate liturgical functions, it is better that those be preferred who are recognized for their singing ability," particularly "for the more solemn liturgical functions or for those in which the chant is more difficult or when the function is to be transmitted by radio or television" (95). Polyphony may be sung at Mass if "there is a choir which knows how to perform it according to the rules of the art" (17). Those who are drawn to popular songs are encouraged to "sing them correctly" (*MSD*, 66).

The 1967 document echoes the earlier Instruction. "Whenever, for a liturgical service which is to be celebrated in sung form, one can make a choice between various people, it is desirable that those who are known to be more proficient in singing be given preference" (*MS*, 8). Then a concession is offered.

If, however, a choice of this kind cannot be made, and the priest or minister does not possess a voice suitable for the proper execution of the singing, he can render without singing one or more of the more difficult parts which concern him, reciting them in a loud and distinct voice (8).

The American document agrees. "What he cannot sing well and effectively he ought to recite" (*MCW*, 22). Above all, time must be spent in preparation. "If capable of singing, he ought, for the sake of the people, to rehearse carefully the sung parts that contribute to their celebration" (22).

Since the Council a new criterion is in effect concerning the use of music.

> In selecting the kind of sacred music to be used, whether it be for the choir or for the people, the capacities of those who are to sing the music must be taken into account (*MS*, 9; also, *MCW*, 15, 79).

Previously it was held that "in view of the nature of the sacred liturgy, its holiness and its dignity, the use of any kind of musical instrument [in fact, any kind of musical contribution] should in itself be perfect" (*DMS*, 60a). The American statement quotes Augustine in support of another view: "Do not allow yourselves to be offended by the imperfect while you strive for the perfect" (*MCW*, 27)[15]

Preparation

Pius X reflects Rome's concern for adequate preparation of those involved with sacred music, particularly its priests. For seminaries, he proposed that "care be taken to touch on those points which regard more directly the principles and laws of sacred music . . . with some particular instruction in the esthetic side of the art" (*TLS*, 26). He supported higher schools of sacred music and believed it was "of the utmost importance that the Church herself provide for the instruction of its masters, organists and singers." (28) Pius XII emphasized music instruction in seminaries and in religious houses of study (*MSD*, 75), suggesting that those especially talented be given an opportunity to cultivate their gifts (76). The 1958 Instruction agreed with the pope's emphasis and, in addition, added a lengthy section on the necessity of music education for all levels of the faithful, from primary and secondary schools on through university (*DMS*, 106–108). It too praised those institutes and associations estab-

---

15. No source given.

lished to foster a love and study of Church music (*DMS*, 117; *MSD*, 79–80).

Vatican II agreed that "great importance is to be attached to the teaching and practice of music in seminaries, in the novitiates and houses of study of religious of both sexes, and also in other Catholic institutions and schools" (*SC*, 115). For this reason, "teachers are to be carefully trained and put in charge of the teaching of sacred music" (115). Higher institutes of sacred music should be founded, whenever possible (115). *Musicam sacram* stresses "the formation of the whole people in singing . . . together with liturgical instruction, according to the age, status and way of life of the faithful," beginning with earliest elementary school education (18). The Instruction recommends that diocesan, national, and international associations of sacred music assist with "this technical and spiritual formation" (25). *Music in Catholic Worship* does not address the question of education specifically, but the document itself reflects a serious concern for instruction, and the pastoral processes it encourages with regard to liturgical celebration are inherently educational.

Adaptation

Pius X recognized the value of indigenous music traditions, each with its own national or cultural distinction. In discussing the quality of universality, characteristic of sacred music as he defined it, he conceded that "every nation is permitted to admit into its ecclesiastical compositions those special forms which in a certain manner constitute the specific character of its native music . . . " (*TLS*, 2). But he added this important qualification:

> . . . these forms must be subordinated in such a manner to the general characteristics of sacred music that nobody of another nation may receive, on hearing them, an impression other than good (2).

Pius XII noted that "many of the peoples entrusted to the ministry of the missionaries take great delight in music," concluding that "it is not prudent, then, for the heralds of Christ, the true God, to minimize or neglect entirely this effective help in their apostolate." Unlike his predecessor, Pius X, he did not condition the use of indigenous forms with criteria for universal acceptance, but recommended that "preachers of the Gospel in pagan lands should sedulously and willingly promote in the course of their apostolic ministry the love for religious song which is cherished by the men entrusted to their care," in order that the truths of their new faith might be "sung in a language and in melodies familiar to them" (*MSD*, 70). *De Musica sacra* was careful to distinguish between "peoples endowed with human culture [*humana cultura*], sometimes centuries old and very rich, and peoples who still lack a high level of culture" (112), when it established the following rules:

(1) Priests who are sent to foreign missions should have a sound training in the sacred liturgy and sacred chant.

(2) If peoples are involved who have a highly developed musical culture of their own, the missionaries should endeavor, with due precautions, to adapt the native music to sacred use. They should organize pious exercises in such a way that the native faithful can express their religious devotion in the languages and melodies of their own people.

(3) ... in the case of a less civilized people ... missionaries should take special care not to extinguish that religious spirit but rather, after having overcome superstitution, render it Christian especially by means of pious exercises (112).

The Council was particularly attuned to enculturation.

In certain parts of the world, especially mission lands, there are peoples who have their own musical traditions, and these play a great part in their religious and social life. For this reason due importance is to be attached to their music, and a suitable place is to be given to it, not only in forming their attitude toward religion, but also in adapting worship to their native genius ... (*SC*, 119).

Missionaries are to be trained in music so that they might become "competent in promoting the traditional music of these peoples" (119). It is recognized that "adapting sacred music for those regions which possess a musical tradition of their own, especially mission areas, will require a very specialized preparation [by] the experts." The primary concern will be "to harmonize the sense of the sacred with the spirit, traditions and characteristic expressions proper to each of these peoples." This will require "sufficient knowledge both of the liturgy and musical tradition of the Church, and of the language, popular songs and other characteristic expressions of the people . . . " (*MS*, 61). Such an indigenization process does not concern only *pia exercitia* but the liturgy itself, and it is not restricted to so-called "mission" areas. The recent Supplement released by the BCL in America urges that "the rich diversity of the cultural heritage of the many peoples of our country today must be recognized, fostered and celebrated." It is not yet sufficiently realized that "the United States of America is a nation of nations, a country in which people speak many tongues, live their lives in diverse ways, celebrate events in song and music in the folkways of their cultural, ethnic and racial roots" (*LMT*, 54). The document offers this criterion for the future:

> Liturgical music today must be as diverse and multi-cultural as the members of the assembly. Pastors and musicians must encourage not only the use of traditional music of other languages, but also the composition of new liturgical music appropriate to various cultures. Likewise the great musical gifts of the Hispanic, Black and other ethnic communities in the Church should enrich the whole Church in the United States in a dialogue of cultures (55).

MUSIC MAKERS

"The Church in the United States today needs the services of many qualified musicians as song leaders, organists, instrumentalists, cantors, choir directors and composers" (*MCW*, 77). To this list of those involved in the parish ministry of music must be added the celebrant (presider), the choir, and the congregation (assembly).[16]

The Congregation

When Pius X chose "to restore the use of the Gregorian chant by the people," he did it "so that the faithful may again take a more active part in the ecclesiastical offices," believing that this was what

16. In America today, there is a preference for "presider" and "assembly."

"they were wont to do in ancient times" (*TLS*, 3). Pius XII, in his encyclical on the liturgy, exhorted the faithful "to sing their hymns and chant their songs of praise and thanksgiving to him who is King of Kings. . . ."[17] Commending those who try to make the liturgy an act in which all who are present share, he suggested that the faithful join in the High Mass responses and chants or, on other occasions, "sing hymns suitable to the different parts of the Mass."[18] Years later, he was still convinced that "hymns can be a powerful aid in keeping the faithful from attending the holy sacrifice like dumb and idle spectators," particularly "when these hymns are properly adapted to the individual parts of the Mass" (*MSD*, 64). The 1958 Instruction organized the active participation of the faithful according to progressive degrees of involvement. In the solemn Mass, the first degree entailed chanting the liturgical responses, the second degree, the parts of the Ordinary, the third degree, the Propers of the Mass (*DMS*, 25). In the "low Mass," the first mode of participation was either interior or external according to regional custom, the second involved prayer and song in common, the third was comprised of four degrees: (1) the easiest liturgical responses; (2) those responses which the rubrics assign to the acolyte; (3) recitation of the Ordinary parts of the Mass; (4) recitation of the Propers (29–31).

Vatican II was committed to ensuring that "whenever the sacred action is to be celebrated with song, the whole body of the faithful may be able to contribute that active participation which is rightly theirs" (*SC*, 114). To this end it decreed that "religious singing by the people is to be skillfully fostered, so that in devotions and sacred exercises, as also during liturgical services, the voices of the faithful may ring out" (118). For the sake of the assembly, the subsequent Instruction allowed structural changes in the rite that had been set for centuries:

> In order that the faithful may actively participate more willingly and with greater benefit, it is fitting that the format of the celebration and the degrees of participation in it should be varied as much as possible, according to the solemnity of the day and the nature of the congregation present (*MS*, 10).

---

17. *Mediator Dei*, November 20, 1947, art. 24. Tr: *NCWC*, p. 13.
18. *Ibid.*, art. 105, p. 39.

The Instruction insists that congregational singing is to be carefully promoted, beginning with the simpler responses and acclamations and culminating in a complete participation in all those parts that pertain to the people (16). The degrees of participation for the *Missa cantata* have been redesigned (28–31). The goal of all these new rules and rubrics is the rediscovery of "a whole congregation expressing its faith and devotion in song" (16).

Today the assembly itself is the determining factor in the kind and amount of music used in the liturgy. Musical decisions are guided by a pastoral criterion: music must be suitable to the needs of the faithful who sing it (*MCW*, 40), and "meaningful for a genuinely human faith experience for these specific worshipers" (41).

The Choir

The choir, central to eucharistic celebration throughout the Church's recorded history, has retained its significance in this post-Conciliar period, but the nature of its role has changed. At the turn of the century, Pius X wrote: "With the exception of the melodies proper to the celebrant at the altar and to the ministers . . . all the rest of the liturgical chant belongs to the choir of levites" who, as "singers in the church, even when they are laymen, are really taking the place of the ecclesiastical choir" (*TLS*, 12). For this reason, "only those are to be admitted to form part of the musical chapel of a church who are men of known piety and probity of life," who "by their modest and devout bearing during the liturgical functions show that they are worthy of the holy office they exercise" (14). They should "wear the ecclesiastical habit and surplice" and "be hidden behind grating," avoiding excessive exposure to public view (14).

All three documents before the Council encourage the establishment of *scholae cantorum*, particularly in the principal churches (*TLS*, 25, 27; *MSD*, 73; *DMS*, 99). "It is highly desirable" that even "parish churches . . . have their own permanent musical choir . . . which is capable of giving true ministerial service" (*DMS*, 99). A "boys choir," often praised by the Holy See, is "still more important to sacred and religious singing" and should be the goal of every church (114). The Council agreed that "choirs must be diligently promoted, especially in cathedral churches" (*SC*, 114).

The 1967 Instruction reaffirms the *schola cantorum* (or *capella musica*) "because of the liturgical ministry it performs," and clarifies its role: "to ensure the proper performance of the parts which belong to it ... and to encourage the active participation of the faithful in the singing" (*MS*, 19). Large choirs such as those credited with "preserving and developing a musical heritage of inestimable value" should now be reserved for celebrations "of a more elaborate kind" (20). The nature of the choir is no longer ecclesiastical but "it is a part of the whole congregation" and its placement in the church should reflect this change (23). The American document concurs that "a well-trained choir adds beauty and solemnity to the liturgy and also assists and encourages the singing of the congregation" (*MCW*, 36).

> At times the choir, within the congregation of the faithful and as part of it, will assume the role of leadership, while at other times it will retain its own distinctive ministry ... will sing works whose musical demands enlist and challenge its competence (36; BCL *Newsletter*, 18 April 1966).

The Church's attitude toward women in ministerial roles is reflected in its legislation, particularly on the question of choirs. According to the rationale of Pius X, "singers in church have a real liturgical service ... therefore women, as being incapable of exercising such an office cannot be admitted to form part of the choir or of the musical chapel" (*TLS*, 13). Yet there is appreciation for the feminine sound, so "whenever, then, it is desired to employ the acute voice of sopranos or contraltos, these parts must be taken by boys, according to the most ancient usage of the Church" (13). Pius XII, quoting previous decrees of the Congregation of Rites, conceded:

> Where it is impossible to have schools of singers or where there are not enough choir boys, it is allowed that "a group of men and women or girls, located in a place outside the sanctuary set apart for the exclusive use of this group, can sing the liturgical texts at solemn Mass, as long as the men are completely separated from the women and girls and everything unbecoming is avoided"[19].

19. *MSD*, 74, quoting CR, Decrees No. 3964, 4201, 4231.

In the absence of a typical choir, the 1958 Instruction allowed that even "a choir of the faithful is permitted, whether 'mixed' or entirely of women or of girls," positioned "outside the sanctuary or communion rail" with a separation of the sexes (*DMS*, 100). It specified, however, that "the laity of male sex ... when they are appointed by the competent ecclesiastical authority ... to execute sacred music ... exercise a direct but delegated ministerial service ... " (*DMS*, 93c). And "it is only permitted that, in case of necessity, a woman be used as director of the song and prayers of the faithful" (96a). The Council made an oblique reference to the participation of women in the ministry of music with its comment, "Composers and singers, especially boys, must also be given a genuine liturgical training" (*SC*, 115). The 1967 Instruction says:

> The choir can consist, according to the customs of each country and other circumstances, of either men and boys, or men and boys only, or men and women, or even, where there is a genuine case for it, of women only (*MS*, 22).

The practice is retained that "whenever the choir also includes women, it should be placed outside the sanctuary" (*presbyterium*) (23). A statement released by the BCL, February 14, 1971 on the "Place of Women in the Liturgy," reflects current practice in the United States:

> With the exception of service at the altar itself, women may be admitted to the exercise of other liturgical ministries. In particular the designation of women to serve in such ministries as reader, cantor, leader of singing, commentator, director of liturgical participation, etc., is left to the judgment of the pastor or the priest who presides over the celebration, in the light of the culture and mentality of the congregation.
>
> ... ministries performed by women, such as leading the singing or otherwise directing the congregation, should be done either within or outside the sanctuary area, depending on circumstances or convenience.[20]

---

20. BCL *Newsletter* 7 (April–May, 1971), p. 278.

The Cantor

The role of cantor was restored to the list of post-Conciliar liturgical ministries primarily to serve the needs of the revitalized assembly. Precursor to the cantor was the pre-Conciliar "commentator," introduced to "explain the rites" and to "direct the external participation of the faithful—their responses, prayers, and songs" (*DMS*, 96). The role was eliminated with the vernacular. *Musicam sacram* recommended that "provision should be made for at least one or two properly trained singers, especially where there is no possibility of setting up even a small choir." Such a singer could "lead and support the faithful" in some simple musical settings and would even be desirable in churches with choirs as an alternative to the whole ensemble (21). *Music in Catholic Worship* agrees that "an individual singer can effectively lead the assembly, attractively proclaim the Word of God in the psalm sung between the readings and take his or her part in other responsorial singing" (35). While not a substitute for the choir, "a trained and competent cantor can perform an important ministry" (35). The 1982 Supplement clarifies the role:

> Among music ministers, the cantor has come to be recognized as having a crucial role in the development of congregational singing. Besides being qualified to lead singing, he or she must have the skills to introduce and teach new music, and to encourage the assembly. This must be done with sensitivity so that the cantor does not intrude on the communal prayer or become manipulative (*LMT*, 68).

It is not always clear that "the cantor's role is distinct from that of the psalmist, whose ministry is the singing of the verses of the responsorial psalm and communion psalm" because "frequently the two roles will be combined" (69).

Instrumentalists

The documents speak of instruments far more than of those who play them. These passages also pertain to musicians by way of implication. Pius X wrote in 1903: "Although music proper to the Church is purely vocal music, music with the accompaniment of the organ is also permitted" (*TLS*, 15), provided it does not delay or interrupt the chant (17). Pius XII spoke of the organ's special qualities, how "it adds a wonderful splendor and a special magnificence to the ceremonies of the Church . . . moves the souls of the faithful . . . gives minds an almost heavenly joy . . . lifts them up powerfully to God and to higher things" (*MSD*, 58). The 1958 Instruction agreed that the "pipe organ has been and remains the principal solemn liturgical musical instrument of the Latin Church" (61). The Council retained this conviction, declaring the pipe organ "the traditional musical instrument . . . to be held in high esteem" (*SC*, 120; also, *MS*, 62). The pre-Conciliar Instruction included numerous and detailed regulations about the use of the organ, when it could be played and when it had to remain silent (*DMS*, 29, 81–84), how it should be played (66), and where it should be located (67). An organ intended for liturgical use "must be equipped with tones that befit religious use . . . be duly blessed and . . . be diligently cared for as a sacred object" (62). The harmonium was permitted "on condition that its tonal quality and amplitude of sound makes it suitable to sacred use" (63), but the electronic organ was only temporarily tolerated with the explicit permission of the Ordinary until a pipe organ could be procured (64). Organists were exhorted to "reflect on the active part they play in giving glory to God and edifying the faithful" (65). The later Instruction repeated many of these points, but far more succinctly (*MS*, 62–67).

"In special cases, within due limits . . . other instruments may be allowed," but only with permission of the Ordinary (*TLS*, 15). Pius X surrounded the use of instruments with prohibitions: "the piano is forbidden," also "noisy or frivolous instruments such as drums, cymbals, bells and the like" (19), and "bands" (20). Only rarely, with consent of the Ordinary, one might admit "a number of wind instruments" to be played in "a grave and suitable style" (20). Pius XII allowed other instruments to be called upon, "so long as they play nothing profane, nothing clamorous or strident" (*MSD*, 59). He personally favored "the violin and other musical instruments that use the bow" because "they express the joyous and sad sentiments of the soul with an indescribable power" (59). The 1958 Instruction agreed, adding that "those instruments which by common consent are suited only for profane music must be absolutely prohibited" (70). Suitable instruments ought to produce their sound with gravity, "with a sort of religious chastity," avoiding "the clangor of profane music" (*DMS*, 68b).

Vatican II decreed:

> Other instruments may also be admitted for use in divine worship, with the knowledge and consent of the competent territorial authority . . . on condition that the instruments are suitable, or can be made suitable, for sacred use, accord with the dignity of the temple, and truly contribute to the edification of the faithful (*SC*, 120).

The 1967 Instruction added that "the culture and the traditions of individual peoples must be taken into account" in permitting the use of instruments, forbidding "those instruments which are, by common opinion and use, suitable for secular music only" (*MS*, 63). The American bishops have been much more lenient in the use of instrumental music. "Song is not the only kind of music suitable for liturgical celebration" (*MCW*, 37).[21] In the United States, "musical instruments other than the organ may be used in liturgical services, provided they are played in a manner that is suitable to public worship." Unlike past laws, "this decision deliberately refrains from singling out specific instruments," preferring to let the circumstances of the celebration determine use (*MCW*, 37). Recently, the BCL released the rationale underlying its criteria for instrumental use:

> Church music legislation of the past reflected a culture in which singing was not only primary, but was presumed to be unaccompanied (chant and polyphony). The music of today, as indeed musical culture today, regularly presumes that song is accompanied. This places instruments in a different light. The song achieves much of its vitality from the rhythm and harmony of its accompaniment. Instrumental accompaniment is a great support to an assembly in learning new music and in giving full voice to its prayer and praise in worship (*LMT*, 57).

In addition, "instrumental music can also assist the assembly in preparing for worship, in meditating on the mysteries, and in joyfully progressing in its passage from liturgy to life." Used in this

21. The 1972 text uses "singing" instead of "song."

way, instrumental music is far "more than an easily dispensable adornment to the rites." Rather, it is truly "ministerial" (58).

Composers

Pius XII addressed this word to composers of sacred music. "All who use the art they possess to compose such musical compositions" exercise "a true and genuine apostolate" and will receive "the generous rewards and honors of apostles" (*MSD*, 38). For this reason, "they should hold their work in high esteem not only as artists . . . but also as ministers of Christ the Lord," and their conduct and lives should reflect "the dignity of their calling" (39). Composers of sacred music "should possess sufficient knowledge of the sacred liturgy . . . know Latin . . . have a sound training in the art of sacred and of profane music" and in "the history of music" as well (*DMS*, 98a). Composers, and all musicians, have a special responsibility to "give good example" because "they directly or indirectly participate in the sacred liturgy" (97).

The Council stressed that composers "be given a genuine liturgical training" (*SC*, 115) and addressed this directive to them.

> Composers, filled with the Christian spirit, should feel that their vocation is to cultivate sacred music and increase its store of treasures. Let them produce compositions which have the qualities proper to genuine sacred music, not confining themselves to works which can be sung only by large choirs, but providing also for the needs of small choirs, and for the active participation of the entire assembly of the faithful (121).

Composers are reminded that texts must conform to Catholic doctrine and "should be drawn chiefly from holy scripture and from liturgical sources" (121). *Musicam sacram* made some specific recommendations concerning the composer's task (54–61), giving priority to texts involving both priest and people, encouraging a respect for tradition so that "'new forms may in some way grow organically from forms that already exist,' and the new work will form a new part in the musical heritage of the Church, not unworthy of its past" (*MS*, 59, citing *SC*, 23). The requirement that "new melodies to be used by the priest and ministers must be approved" underscores the shift from papal control to regulation "by the competent territorial authority" (MS, 57). In 1972, the American document stressed a "pressing need for musical compositions in idioms that can be sung by the congregation and thus further communal participation" (MCW, 28; BCL Newsletter, 18 April, 1966). "For the composer . . . there is an unprecedented challenge" to "enhance the liturgy with new creations of variety and richness" (MCW, 76). Some specific recommendations appear in a recent document from the BCL:

> For you, musicians who compose, the responsibility is equally clear: to be well-trained and sensitive to the liturgy, to provide musical settings for the approved liturgical and scriptural texts, and to prepare music for hymn texts that enhance those moments of communal worship where they can be incorporated.[22]

Two important working principles are proposed: that they "compose to assist the assembly" and "respect the liturgical texts."[23]

Closely related to the question of composition are the issues of ownership and copyright. The 1958 Instruction reiterated Vatican policy by stating that "the Holy See reserves to itself all rights of use and ownership of all the Gregorian melodies contained in the liturgical books of the Roman Church and approved by it" (DMS, 57). The purpose of this policy was to ensure that the authentic Gregorian chant in the typical editions would "be reproduced only by editors who have proper authorization, accurately and completely, as regards both melodies and texts" (59). While local ecclesiastical authority holds the copyright for approved translations of official texts, the influx of newly composed music encouraged by the Council and accepted for liturgical use thrust the Church into a situation for which it was unprepared. In 1967, the Music Advisory Board of the BCL released a statement appealing to "those engaged in parish music programs throughout the country to curb and discourage" the practice of "indiscriminate and unauthorized use of copyright materials," declaring that "it is absolutely illegal and immoral to reproduce—by any means—

---

22. "Letter to Composers of Liturgical Music," November 23, 1980, in BCL Newsletter 16 (December, 1980), p. 238.
23. Ibid.

either the text or music or both of copyrighted materials without the written permission of the copyright owner."[24] A second statement in 1969 reported that the practice of unauthorized reproduction "not only continues but has increased in parishes throughout the country" with the result that "authors, composers, and publishers lack incentive to employ their talents and efforts in the field of Church music because of meager and inadequate financial remuneration."[25] *Music in Catholic Worship* exhorted parish musicians to obey the copyright laws so that "composers and publishers receive just compensation" (*MCW*, 78). The situation has improved. The much publicized infringement suit of Dennis Fitzpatrick against the Archdiocese of Chicago undoubtedly has done a lot to raise awareness of rights and responsibilities in this area.[26]

MUSIC MINISTRY

Even before the Council, Pius XII wrote:

> All who use the art they possess to compose such musical compositions, to teach them or to perform them by singing or using musical instruments . . . should hold their work in high esteem not only as artists and teachers of art, but also as ministers of Christ the Lord and as his helpers in the work of the apostolate (*MSD*, 38–39).

As a result of the apostolic letter *Ministeria quaedam* (Paul VI, 1972), the American bishops agreed at their November 1973 meeting to ask Rome to permit in this country the liturgical institution of ministers of music. It was felt that the formal acknowledgment of this role through commissioning and investiture in a service of public prayer would enhance the place of music in the liturgical celebration and confirm a distribution of roles. The BCL explains that the ministry of Church music is a liturgical ministry which includes a number of functions distinct enough to deserve formal

24. "Copyright Violations," BCL *Newsletter* 3 (December 1967), p. 109.
25. "Statement on Copyright Violations," BCL *Newsletter* 5 (May 1969), p. 177.
26. See *Pastoral Music* 6 (June–July 1982), p. 4.

recognition: psalmist, cantor, leader of song, director of music, organist.[27] "These are the pastoral musicians, whose ministry is especially cherished by the Church" (LMT, 63). There has been no noticeable response from Rome.

Although the 1958 Instruction reads, "It is desirable that the organists, choir directors, singers, musicians, and all others engaged in the service of the Church offer their works of piety and of zeal for the love of God, without any recompense," the same Instruction already recognizes that "should it be that they are unable to offer their services gratuitously, Christian justice and charity demand that ecclesiastical superiors give them just pay" (DMS, 101). The post-Conciliar Church, praising those "many generous musicians who have given years of service despite receiving only meager financial compensation," strongly recommends that "every diocese and parish should establish policies for hiring and paying living wages to competent musicians" (MCW, 77). The latest document from the BCL confirms that "the musician's gifts must be recognized as a valued part of the pastoral effort, and for which proper compensation must be made" (LMT, 66). While explaining why some members of the community "are recognized for the special gifts they exhibit in leading the musical praise and thanksgiving of Christian assemblies," the Supplement to Music in Catholic Worship reminds the Christian community that "the entire worshiping assembly exercises a ministry of music" (63).

CONCLUDING COMMENTS

Before concluding this chapter, it is important to say a word about the legislative context of the criteria articulated here and to point out those broad shifts in emphasis that have occurred in this century as reflected in these documents.

The motu proprio of Pius X was written "of his own initiative" because "chief among the anxieties of the pastoral office" was, for him, the responsibility of "maintaining and promoting the decorum of the house of God" (Preface). As a response to "abuse in

27. "Ministers of Church Music and Catechists," BCL Newsletter 10 (February 1974), pp. 411–412.

connection with sacred chant and music," the document was promulgated with "the force of law" intended for "a juridical code of sacred music" and "its scrupulous observance" was imposed on all (*Ibid.*). It is surprisingly short—considering its impact and the numerous times it has been cited—clearly organized, and succinctly written. The liturgical rationale for music reform is stated in its Preface.

The encyclical of Pius XII is twice the length of the *motu proprio*, descriptive, florid, more theoretical than practical. Written so that the former "'legal code of sacred music' may be confirmed and inculcated anew, shown in a new light and strengthened by new proofs," it reflects the thinking of a liturgically innovative pope as well as a continuity with tradition (3). While references to liturgy occur in various places throughout the document, there is no special section with a specifically liturgical emphasis, no doubt because Pius XII expected this reflection on music to be read in relation to his previous legislation on liturgy, particularly *Mediator Dei*.

The 1958 Instruction by the Congregation of Rites, by far the longest document in this series, is entitled *De Musica sacra et sacra Liturgia*, reflecting an awareness that "sacred music and sacred liturgy are so closely linked that laws and norms cannot be given for one while ignoring the other" (Introduction). Although the two are addressed separately as music "and" liturgy, an effort is made to combine the principal points of previous legislation on liturgy and music under one cover, namely, *Tra le sollecitudini, Divini cultus sanctitatem*, and *Mediator Dei*. In this context, the recommendations of *Musicae sacrae disciplina* are given practical application.

Sacrosanctum concilium aims at a true integration of music and liturgy, inasmuch as the principles and norms of chapter one are clearly meant to be constitutive for the document as a whole. Not all the items pertaining to music are confined to chapter six. As a Conciliar constitution, its directives are binding on the universal Church, yet its broad principles and norms are designed to be given pluriform local application. As the declaration of an ecumenical council abrogating all previous laws contrary to its spirit, the decree as a whole marks a legislative turning point in Church music history, restoring to the bishops the authority to legislate local practice, restoring to the people the right of active participation, radically altering standard repertoire as a result.

Chapter six is the shortest of the documents analyzed here. Because it is a separate chapter, there is a tendency among musicians to consider the Council's music statement independently of its context, which would be contrary to the document's intent.

The Instruction *Musicam sacram* was stalled in committee and underwent a number of redactions before it was finally published in 1967 through the combined efforts of *Consilium* and the Congregation of Rites. Commentators generally agree that the document reflects the struggle between conservative and progressive tendencies. Some would hold that the final result was a rather reluctant adjustment of the 1958 Instruction to the demands of the Council. Others point out that its shift in emphasis from a preoccupation with rubrics to a concern for principles is truly Conciliar. This latter evaluation seems closer to the truth. The Instruction represents an effort to make the Council's general norms more practically applicable. Recommendations regarding music appear in their liturgical contexts.

Music in Catholic Worship is similar in length to *Musicam sacram* (only *De Musica sacra* is longer) but radically different in content and tone to all that has gone before. It represents a major landmark in Church music legislation in America because, for the first time, Americans now follow a document different from the one issued by Rome. Legislatively, it is a concrete application of the principle of liturgical decentralization instituted by the Council and was prepared for Americans because the Instruction from Rome (*Musicam sacram*) was felt to be insufficient. Compared to previous decrees regulating the use of music, this document reflects a much more informal approach to legislation, both in its style and in the manner in which it came into existence. Many people participated in its preparation: the Music Advisory Board of the Bishops' Committee on the Liturgy, the music committee of the National Federation of Diocesan Liturgical Commissions, the full BCL, which gave its approval. It was published by the BCL as a guide for all those who celebrate and plan liturgies, with the hope that it might "be of use to the bishops and their liturgical commissions" (Introduction), and not as a legal document. It was not fully accepted at first, but after a decade of use, it has become the primary frame of reference concerning music in worship in

America, setting the standards for present practice, and is considered the official statement in this regard.

Like *Sacrosanctum concilium, Music in Catholic Worship* opens with theological principles that govern the entire document. This is the statement's strength. Right at the beginning, it provides a rationale for understanding the place of music and its ministry within worship and gives some basis for the importance of musical options and cultural relevance. The specific directives regarding music are genuinely pastoral and presented in a way that is both informative and flexible. The document is uniquely suited to the culture to which it speaks.

As valuable as this document has been and continues to be for the American Church, it does not represent the ideal statement. Several serious limitations prevent its recommendation as a model for the structuring of post-Conciliar church music.

The first limitation pertains to both structure and content. The opening theological principles mentioned above are presented as the first of six major sections under the general heading, Music in Catholic Worship. These sections are entitled:

I. The Theology of Celebration
II. Pastoral Planning for Celebration
III. The Place of Music in the Celebration
IV. General Consideration on Liturgical Structure
V. Application of the Principles of Celebration to Music in Eucharistic Worship
VI. Music in Sacramental Celebrations

Such an arrangement makes it difficult to perceive that those first theological principles should inform all aspects of church music theory and practice. The text itself fails to make the association clear. On closer examination, the principles of celebration to be applied to music (V) are seen to be ritual principles of a formal nature determining song patterns and genre, and not the theological principles articulated in section one. The very fact that theological considerations are confined to a separate section hinders an integration with the very subject they should be informing. The fact that this section is entitled "the theology of celebration" only strengthens the impression that liturgical music borrows its theological agenda from the liturgy and has yet to consider a theology of its own. In this document, music is addressed essentially in terms of anthropological principles and principles of technique which call for the exercise of rational judgment and sound management skills, not from a perspective of a theology of church music. Although it makes an important contribution in an area of vital concern, *Music in Catholic Worship* lacks critical reflection and fails to integrate liturgy, music, and theology in a coherent, cohesive statement.

A second limitation concerns the decision to issue a supplement to the 1972 document (*Liturgical Music Today*, 1982) to accompany a revised edition of the original (*Music In Catholic Worship*, 1983), instead of a new and much needed statement reflecting the development of liturgical music in America since Vatican II. *Liturgical Music Today* is a second practical yet poorly integrated manual for church musicians that underscores the need for critical reflection in the area of church music today. The very fact that this document no longer addresses the subject under the title of music in worship but as liturgical music only creates confusion. Finally, both documents are totally oriented to service music for the Church's official rites. Neither one addresses the question of alternate celebrations within a broader understanding of liturgy. While this in itself does not lessen their value, it is important to remember that these statements do not represent the full range of possibilities for liturgical music in America today.

In examining the evolution of criteria for the use of music from 1903 to the present, the following trends must be noted.

First, there is a shift from the juridical to the pastoral, from a preceptive to a directive approach, clearly reflected in the documents, but the need for some kind of legislative framework is never entirely eliminated. *Tra le sollecitudini* was issued as a juridical code and its scrupulous observance was imposed with the full force of ecclesiastical law. The Instruction *De Musica sacra* concludes with the reminder that His Holiness Pope Pius XII ordered that it be exactly observed by all to whom it applied. The post-Conciliar Instruction *Musicam sacram* states: "it is hoped that pastors of souls, musicians and the faithful will gladly accept these norms and put them into practice" (4). The Bishops' Committee on the Liturgy presented *Music in Catholic Worship* as background and guidelines which it hoped would be useful to the bishops, their liturgical commissions, and all who celebrate or plan liturgies. This shift away from the juridical and preceptive is also noted in the vocabulary of the texts. Words such as "forbidden" and "permitted" and "must" prominent in pre-Conciliar documents give way to "desirable" or "recommended" or "may."

There is a shift from liturgical absolutes to an awareness of pastoral needs, some would say a bit too far in the direction of popular taste. *Tra le sollecitudini* forbade any vernacular singing whatever in solemn liturgical functions and insisted that the liturgical texts be sung precisely as prescribed in the books. In *De Musica sacra*, the prescription regarding solemn liturgical functions is still preserved, but there is already a solid tradition of dialogue Mass with hymns in certain cultures. With *Musicam sacram*, degrees of participation are maintained and Latin is encouraged, but vernacular singing is allowed with approval for the benefit of the people. *Music in Catholic Worship* removes all distinctions between degrees of participation and the High Mass/Low Mass categories. What is sung is determined primarily by the needs of the participating congregation, and the pastoral judgment becomes paramount.

There is a definite shift from a preoccupation with elements of style at the beginning of the twentieth century to a concern for the formal structure and various musical genres of the rite in the post-Conciliar Church, although concerns about musical style remain deeply embedded in the consciousness of musicians. An aesthetic preference for Gregorian chant and classical polyphony promoted by Pius X is supported by Pius XII, but the latter indicates a growing appreciation for other styles of musical expression, particularly the song of the people (the hymn), which has limited liturgical use. *Musicam sacram* reflects a preference for traditional categories, but *Music in Catholic Worship* is unconcerned about questions of style. It promotes good music in any style and is more concerned about explaining the variety of musical forms now necessary for a proper understanding of ritual music.

Finally, there is a shift away from the set patterns formerly imposed by the rite to a variety of musical options, but these are still limited by the structural principles of the rite. *Tra le sollecitudini* allowed no deviation whatever from the prescribed patterns of the Ordinary and the Proper parts of the Mass, and this approach held firm until after the Council. *Musicam sacram* offered some variety in its degrees of participation and its wider definition of kinds of music permissible in liturgy. *Music in Catholic Worship* encourages variety with its many options: any part of the liturgy can be said or sung in any style at any time, with or without instrumentation. The singing of acclamations is emphasized, liturgical seasons and levels of solemnity are to be honored, and all music selected is to be conditioned by pastoral concerns.

8

Theological Bases for the Use of Music in the Liturgy

THE PRECEDING CHAPTER FOCUSED ON THOSE PRACTICAL CRITERIA THAT have conditioned the use of music in the liturgy. At present, music practice is regulated, not by clear theological criteria arising from a theology of church music, but by norms of an external nature guided, to some extent, by principles drawn from liturgical theology. Legal or regulatory norms without a sound theological foundation are inadequate for setting church music standards. In the absence of a church music theology, one must look to the theological bases of regulatory criteria, aware that changes in music practice may be indicative of changing theological orientations.

The purpose of the present chapter is twofold: to articulate the theological bases behind the criteria for the use of music in the liturgy of the Catholic Church and to show to what extent these have changed as a result of Vatican II. The theological bases under consideration are those theological orientations or emphases underlying practical criteria regulating music use.

That there are theological bases for the use of music can be concluded from deductions already drawn. The liturgy is *locus theologicus* (see Chapter 3). Music, therefore, as integral to the liturgy (see Chapter 7), reflects theology.

That the theological bases for the use of music have changed since Vatican II can be similarly assumed. Since music is governed by the theological principles of the liturgy in which it functions, a change in liturgical theology necessarily affects the theology of its music. There has been a substantial change in the liturgy and liturgical theology as a result of Vatican II. Consequently, there should also be a change in music and its theology. Chapter 7 illustrated the change in criteria for music use. The task of the present chapter is to articulate underlying theological change.

Music legislation has been the primary focus for describing those changes in music practice resulting from Vatican II. The shift in music theology precipitated by the Council ought to be reflected in that same legislation. Therefore, the six major documents that formed the basis for chapter 7 will serve as primary sources here. This legislation will be examined for theological data and information indicative of theological trends. Such material may be implicit in the criteria or clearly stated in their contexts. In dialogue with previous chapters and supplementary sources, this chapter will conclude with an attempt to articulate the dominant theological themes underlying Catholic Church music legislation before, during, and after Vatican II.

THEOLOGICAL INDICATORS

In order to get at the theological foundations of Catholic Church music, it is wise to turn first to the several key phrases descriptive of music that occur consistently in the documents and emerge as primary indicators of theological intention here. At the very least, *musica sacra, pars integrans,* and *munus ministeriale,* concepts central to Catholic Church music, offer such theological clues. The three are interrelated, but *musica sacra* comprises both content and context for this analysis, so it will be considered first.

MUSICA SACRA

What exactly is *musica sacra?* In five of the six documents under consideration, the phrase has the status of a title.[1] But nowhere in

---

1. Pius X, *Tra le sollecitudini, Motu proprio, Instructio De Sacris Musicis* (1903); Pius XII, *Musicae sacrae disciplina* (1955); CR, Instruction, *De Musica sacra et sacra Liturgia* (1958); Chapter VI, *"De Musica sacra"* of *Sacrosanctum concilium* (1963); CR and *Consilium,* Instruction (1967), known as *Musicam sacram* from its opening words.

the legislation is there any indication of where the phrase originated or any definition of precisely what it means. It appears in the *motu proprio* of 1903 as an authoritative label for a designated repertoire and so it has remained.

Helmut Hucke equates the term with the English phrase, "Church music."[2] While it may be argued that *musica ecclesiastica* differs from traditional assumptions concerning *musica sacra*, this disassociation of music from the "*sacrum*" may in fact be closer to the designation's original intent.

The medieval Church knew only the *cantus*, at first the *cantus planus*, eventually *cantus gregorianus*, which functioned also as the *cantus firmus* in organum and eventually polyphony. *Cantus ecclesiasticus* distinguished Gregorian chant and polyphony from *cantica secularia*. *Musica* was an inclusive term, embracing the rules of the *cantus* and musicology, as well as music making and all existing repertoire. Ecclesiastical chant and secular chant were expressions of one music and both were governed by the same philosophical, theological, and artistic principles. In the sixteenth century this unity was ruptured by the advent of "worldly" music. Church music remained *musica ecclesiastica* or *musica sacra*. "Sacred" linked music to the *sacrum*, the liturgy, not to indicate that music in itself was "holy," but that it was used for a holy thing.[3]

In 1605, Claudio Monteverdi promoted a new style of music which he called the *seconda prattica* to distinguish it from the ancient polyphonic style, the *prima prattica*.[4] The madrigal was representative of this new *musica humana* or *musica spirituale* which, while sometimes suitable for devotions, was not liturgical because of the choice of text. This new genre precipitated that split between Church music (*musica divina*) and other music that has lasted to this day. The polyphonic motet with approved texts fixed by the Council of Trent remained characteristic of liturgical music or *musica ecclesiastica*. Once freed from the limitations imposed by the Church, the new music evolved to a variety of forms and styles that were legitimate in their own right. Those that were not profane or secular were designated "religious" music, but never *sacra* or *liturgica*.

2. Helmut Hucke, "Changing Concepts of Church Music," *Growing In Church Music* (Washington, DC: *Universa Laus*, 1979), p. 18.

3. *Ibid.*, p. 23.

4. Nicolas Schalz, "*La Notion de 'Musique sacrée,'*" *La Maison-Dieu* 108 (1971), pp. 33–34.

Some attribute the term *"musica sacra"* to composer and theoretician Michael Praetorius, who used it as a title in the first volume of his book, *De musica sacra et ecclesiastica* (1614), to distinguish between sacred and profane music, not in reference to style but as an acknowledgment of two different repertoires. The term was popular at first among theoreticians,[5] but it did not come into general use until much later, gaining prominence in the nineteenth century in conjunction with the movement for Church music restoration and Caecilian reform. In reaction to the advances of classical instrumental music, former Baroque extravagance, and Romanticist excess, *"musica sacra"* came to represent all that was best and seemingly lost with the traditional *stile antico*: the *gravitas* of the Palestrinian motet, the noble simplicity of *a capella* singing, the "sacred" chant inseparably linked to the liturgical ("sacred") rite. In seeking to reorient the music of the Church to the best of its tradition, the Caecilian movement contributed significantly to the evolution of the notion *"musica sacra"* and its eventual adoption by the twentieth-century Church. It fostered the stylistic distinction between sacred and profane music inherited from the Baroque era and identified authentic Church music with the music of the past. It supported the sacralization of a specific historical repertoire and one particular style, namely, that of the Roman school, exemplified in Gregorian chant and the polyphony of Palestrina. It promoted the notion of a universal musical language in the mandatory Gregorian model.[6] All of these emphases carried over into the twentieth century through the sponsorship of Pius X.

It was not until the late nineteenth century that the term *musica sacra* entered official Church legislation. The first papal document to use it was the Instruction *De musica sacra* issued July 7, 1894 by the Congregation of Rites during the pontificate of Leo XIII. This was the document for which Cardinal Sarto had prepared his famous *Votum* of 1893, identical in so many passages to *Tra le sollecitudini*. It is no surprise, therefore, that *musica sacra* entered ecclesiastical legislation definitively with the *motu proprio* of 1903.

---

5. Giovanni-Battista Doni, *Dissertatio de musica sacra*, 1740; Martin Gerbert, *De cantu et musica sacra*, 2 vol., 1777–1779.

6. Schalz, *op. cit.*, p. 38.

Pius X contributed substantially to an understanding of *musica sacra* and, by so doing, radically altered its meaning. The qualities and functions he attributed to *musica sacra* have had far-reaching implications. For the first time, *musica sacra* is defined as an integral part of the liturgy (*pars integrans solemnis liturgiae*). No longer merely decorative, its principal office (*praecipuum munus*) is to enhance the text of the liturgy in order that it might add "greater efficacy to the text" (*verba intelligentiora*). *Musica sacra* itself participates in the glory of God and the sanctification of the faithful (*gloria Dei et sanctificatione Christifidelium*), the general object of the liturgy. Its tendency to "increase the decorum and the splendor of the ecclesiastical ceremonies" is affirmed, and solemnity becomes the measure of the perfection of liturgical form (*TLS*, 1).

Certain qualities are declared characteristic of authentic *musica sacra*. For the first time in the long history of its transmission, the *sacra* of *musica sacra* becomes integral to the phrase. The music itself must be *sacra*, not only in its content, excluding any nuance of profanity, but also in its manner of execution. A specific repertoire is designated *sacra* and a particular genre (form, style) is declared to be the supreme model of the *sacra*. Music becomes a repository and a measure of holiness to the extent that it is in harmony with the Gregorian model. Succeeding popes perpetuated this principle, although emphasis gradually shifted to a conformity with the Gregorian spirit and not with elements of style. The 1958 Instruction, implementing the encyclical of Pius XII, extended the scope of *musica sacra* to include *musica sacra moderna, musica sacra pro organo, cantus popularis religiosus,* and *musica religiosa,* along with the traditional *cantus gregorianus* and *polyphonia sacra* (*DMS*, 4). The 1967 Instruction added *musica sacra pro aliis admissis instrumentis* to the above (*MS*, 4b). Vatican II declared that the source of the *sacra* is not in the music but rooted in the liturgy. "*Musica sacra* is to be considered the more holy in proportion as it is closely connected with *actio liturgica*" (*SC*, 112). The 1967 Instruction understands *musica sacra* to be music "created for the celebration of divine worship" and therefore "endowed with a certain holy sincerity of form" (4a). The Third Instruction on the Liturgy states that music used in the liturgy, or *musica sacra*, must have qualities of holiness and good form.[7] Both Instructions cite Pius X as the

---

7. CDW, *Liturgicae Instaurationes*, September 5, 1970, art. 3c.

source of their emphases. This proclivity toward a "holy music," music in which the *sacra* is inherent by design or by association, persists in the legislation until *Music in Catholic Worship*, where it becomes a sign of what the assembly itself experiences and expresses.

Two other qualities, one aesthetic, one sociological, attributed to *musica sacra* by Pius X, have theological implications. The fact that *musica sacra* must be *ars vera* put the movement for the restoration of Church music on a collision course with the aims of the liturgical movement, not in principle, but in practice. *Tra le sollecitudini*, an *Instructio De Sacris Musicis*, is acknowledged as the inauguration of the modern liturgical movement, yet its emphasis on artistic principles and perfection of musical form and perform-ance was in direct conflict with its liturgical goal of getting people to sing. For a time, the two thrusts were reconciled in a theology that stressed the benefits of singing artistically, but even before the Council, the partnership fell apart. This preoccupation with artistic values has remained a constant in this century, surfacing in the Council's concern for the *thesaurus musicae sacrae* and its awarding to Gregorian chant *principem locum* in the liturgy. The final quality attributed to *musica sacra* by Pius X was an attempt to extend the *musica traditio* uniformly to every culture. The fact that *musica sacra* must be *universalis* ignored the principles of anthropology and ethnomusicology and was finally challenged directly by the Council's *Gaudium et spes*.

One restriction associated with the *musica sacra* of Pius X has obvious theological implications, the fact that its performance by an ecclesiastical choir has been reserved exclusively for males. The lifting of this restriction in post-Conciliar America was coincident with a change in nomenclature and the method of evaluating music. Today, *musica sacra* is simply "music in Catholic worship." It consists of no predetermined repertoire, but admits any and all music that can be successfully validated by a threefold musical, liturgical, and pastoral judgment, which would indicate that it has the appropriate aesthetic and functional qualifications and proper-ly serves both the liturgy and the assembly. *Music In Catholic Worship* does refer several times to "sacred song," but only when quoting previous legislation (*MCW, 23, 35, 36*). Its 1982 supple-ment prefers to use the term "liturgical music" for all instrumental music, song, and chant used in the official rites.

Shortly after the Council, Rembert Weakland addressed this issue:

> We are still plagued by the question: What are the elements that make music sacred? What elements make it worldly or profane? . . . It is a false question. There is no musical element that is either secular or sacred by nature. Such a distinction places a false dichotomy in the way God made this world that does not exist.[8]

Previously, certain stylistic principles intrinsic to the music were felt to be reflective of the sacred:

> . . . a rhythm that avoids strong pulses; a melody whose physiognomy is neither so characteristic nor so engaging as to make an appeal in its own behalf; counterpoint, which cultivates long-breathed eloquence rather than instant and dramatic effect; a chromaticism which is at all times restricted in amount and lacking in emotionalism; dissonance, used only when it is technically necessary or in the interest of text emphasis; and modality which creates an atmosphere unmistakeably ecclesiastical.[9]

Three new developments have contributed to a widening of the meaning of *musica sacra*: the inundation of secular culture with new styles and sounds that "have begun to seep into the sanctuary . . . a thaw in the attitude of theologians, church officials and indeed some church musicians toward at least some of these new expressions"; and "the recent multiplication of life-styles among people in close geographical proximity."[10] Today, the problem of standards is paramount, but criteria are hard to articulate when *musica sacra* now includes music previously unsuitable for worship. The category of *musica sacra* may have been expanded, but its semantic carries a connotation of outdated models and raises the suspicion of theological irrelevance. On another occasion, Rembert Weakland wrote:

8. Rembert Weakland, "The Sung Mass and Its Problems," *Proceedings of North American Liturgical Week* 26 (1965), p. 242.

9. Archibald T. Davison, *Church Music: Illusion and Reality* (Cambridge: Harvard University Press, 1952), pp. 37–38.

10. Quentin Faulkner, "What Is 'Sacred Music'?", *Music: The AGO Magazine* (September 1978), p. 55.

There is no music of a liturgical golden age to which we can turn, because the treasures we have are the product of ages that do not represent an ideal of theological thinking in relationship to liturgy.... The Romantic period made a false aesthetic judgment ... that has found its way into official documents.[11]

Helmut Hucke explains how "a new *musica sacra*, which many regard as a theological statement, is emerging from avant-garde circles in the world of music."[12] This new *musica sacra* "has nothing in common with the traditional forms of Church music." Quoting a contemporary theologian and composer, he describes it as a "*musica sacra* without taboos" that perhaps will "provide music for a form of worship in the church of the future," a music that would have regained "its original eschatological character."[13] Hucke concludes with the observation that "music is taking on an entirely new dimension and is confronting liturgists with quite different questions."[14]

Quentin Faulkner comes full circle with a definition he feels "all camps might be able to live with," which is: "Sacred music is music which is potentially sacramental."[15] What differentiates his designation of music as a potentially "holy thing" from that of Pius X is the acknowledgment that all music, like all of creation, has this capacity. Prerequisites are a rootedness in the fixed content of revelation and the capacity to nurture in faith. "A piece of 'sacred music' ought to be capable of revealing new insights, of communicating in hearing after hearing that which is sacred."[16]

David Johnson points to this paradox: there is "music which is generally *called* sacred and music which actually causes the earnest, diligent worshiper to have sacred thoughts." Such transcendent experiences do not always occur in the assigned places, so that "a secular composition ... not associated with the church or with sacred endeavors, might move a listener so intensely" that "the music which transported him so deeply is,

11. Rembert Weakland, "Music As Art in Liturgy," *Worship* 41 (1967), p. 6.

12. Helmut Hucke, "Towards A New Kind of Church Music," *Concilium* 62 (1971), p. 94.

13. D. Schnebel, "*Musica sacra onhe Tabus*," *Melos* 35 (1968), pp. 371–376, as cited in Hucke, *ibid.*, pp. 94–95.

14. *Ibid.*, p. 95.

15. Faulkner, *op. cit.*, p. 56.

16. *Ibid.*

indeed, actually sacred because of its effect on him."[17] He draws the following conclusion:

> The quality of sacredness exists in the ear of the listener, just as beauty exists in the eye of the beholder. The significant difference is that we do not require that beauty effectively cause any change in us. But most of us, at least ministers and church musicians, hope that our musical efforts help, in some small way perhaps, to draw people closer to God so that their lives may actually be changed.[18]

This expectation is in accord with the concerns of the American bishops who conclude their 1972 statement with a similar goal, which was affirmed in 1983:

> Styles of music, choices of instruments, forms of celebration—all converge in a single purpose: that men and women of faith may proclaim and share that faith in prayer and Christ may grow among us all (84).

The preceding citations illustrate the diversity of the dialogue concerning this very important issue today: is there or is there not a legitimate *musica sacra* and, if so, of what does the *musica* consist, and what is the nature of the *sacra*. For most of the past century, the sense of "holiness" consisted of sanctity of form, and aesthetic criteria posed as theological statements. Stylistic standards which developed from a fundamental aesthetic were mistaken for theological criteria and imposed with the force of law, until Vatican II located the locus of the *sacra* in the liturgy itself. Because of its shaky foundation, the whole notion of a *musica sacra* has lost credibility in the post-Conciliar Church resulting, at times, in a rejection of all prior standards except subjective ones. But is the notion of a *musica sacra* really outmoded, or does the problem lie in the fact that our understanding of the *sacra* is not broad enough? The debate continues on the level of anthropology and aesthetics, but the issue is a theological one. Quentin Faulkner's sacramental approach touches on a possible solution to the problem, but he does not go far enough.

---

17. David Johnson, "What Is Sacred Music?" *Musart* 23 (1971), p. 21.
18. *Ibid.*

Vatican II restored to the notion of *musica sacra* the primacy of its connection to the liturgy, and it also redefined liturgy in a far more inclusive way. An answer to our dilemma lies deeply embedded in an integration of these two facts. The concept of *musica sacra* originated in relation to the eucharistic rite, and it has remained firmly bound to the rite both in our understanding of it and in fact. Reform of the term itself has not yet approached *aggiornamento*, for a broadening of the concept has focused on expanding the scope of music styles, forms, media, repertoires that might legitimately be used in the rite. The first step toward *aggiornamento* for *musica sacra* is to liberate the concept from the limitations of its exclusive association with the official liturgical rites.

Music is a gift of God, a vehicle of the *sacra* it is supposed to reveal to us. So described, it is a sacramental, and as such, is liturgy. In this sense, which fully reflects the spirit of Vatican II, *musica sacra* is *musica liturgica*. As liturgy, as sacramental, *musica sacra* has the capacity to gain "access to the stream of divine grace which flows from the paschal mystery," thereby sanctifying the events of daily life and effectively praising God (*SC*, 61).

Music functioning as a sacramental would necessarily have some standards. These, however, should flow from criteria determining sacramentals, not primarily from what is or is not aesthetically appropriate. This brings the method of discernment to a theological level. Sound theology is cognizant of anthropological and other concerns, but in structuring a *musica sacra*, theological principles should come first. Music as a gift of God must be used and used well. Quality is of the essence, but not in an ontological way. Sometimes the best music will simply have to be the best that we can do.

Liturgy not only transforms, it educates, through an authentic faith expression that impresses on the community the essentials of its beliefs. The Church has done little to foster this educational dimension because it has been too caught up with the symbolic and the sociological aspects of the rites. It is not enough just to clarify the signs without stressing what they signify. Music has the capacity to be an educational vehicle, once an educational ethos and methodology is made clear. This calls for criteria that are theologically based. The power of *musica sacra* may well be as sacramental sign.

PARS INTEGRANS

That music is an integral part of the liturgy has stood as an uncontested principle since it was first officially stated by Pius X in 1903. Precisely how it is integral, by nature or function or association, is not completely clear.

Pius X introduced the notion somewhat parenthetically. "Sacred music, as an integral part of the solemn liturgy, participates in its general object, which is the glory of God and the santification and edification of the faithful."[19] He simply articulated what was, to him, a self-evident fact. Because music is integral to the liturgy and because "its principal office is to clothe with befitting melody the liturgical text," it fulfills a particular purpose, which is "to add greater efficacy to the text" (1). The functional presence of music in the liturgy is directed to a specific end, to enhance the text, its meaning, its efficacy, in order that the faithful might be better disposed to benefit from the mysteries celebrated.

Sacrosanctum concilium emphasizes the importance of this relationship of music to text by stating that the musical tradition of the Church is preeminent among all the arts because "as sacred song united to the words, it forms a necessary or integral part of the solemn liturgy."[20] The *musica sacra* of tradition is considered *pars integrans* because it is "united to the words," which are integral to the liturgy. The 1958 Instruction had already alluded to the prominence of ritual texts. "Everything which the liturgical books require to be chanted by the priest and his ministers, or by the choir and people, is an integral part of the sacred liturgy" (*DMS,* 21). Later on in the text, this emphasis reappears. "Sacred music is closely linked to the liturgy; sacred chant is an integral part of the liturgy itself."[21] *Musica sacra* is linked to the rite. *Cantus sacer* is integral to it. This is an important distinction. Not all *musica sacra* is *pars integrans,* only the *cantus* which transmits the necessary ritual texts. It appears that this intimate, inseparable connection between

19. "*Musica sacra, prout pars integrans solemnis liturgiae, huius particeps est finis . . .* " (*TLS,* 1).

20. " *. . . quod ut cantus sacer qui verbis inhaeret necessariam vel integralem liturgiae sollemnis partem efficit*" (*SC,* 112).

21. "*Musica sacra arctissime cum Liturgia connectitur; cantus vero sacer integre ad ipsam Liturgiam pertinet*" (*DMS,* 104).

essential texts, the Latin language, and the chant is the source of the *pars integrans* of liturgical music.

Helmut Hucke, however, intimates that the *musica sacra* of Pius X encompassed only polyphony, not Gregorian chant, that the validation of art music and the aggrandizing of chant were two separate thrusts.[22] The fact that Pius XI in *Divini cultus* refers to the *motu proprio* as being concerned with both Gregorian chant and sacred music, and that the 1958 Instruction maintains that distinction, tends to support this interpretation. According to Hucke, those principles pertaining to sacred music articulated by Pius X were designed to ensure that art music used in the service of the Church would be appropriate. Because abuses were prevalent, it was necessary to point out that liturgy was not "at the service of the music, for the music is merely a part of the liturgy and its humble handmaid" (*TLS*, 23). Therefore, artistic music should have the qualities of "holiness" and "goodness of form," in fact, be representative of "true art" (2).[23] In this context are to be understood those references to music increasing "the splendor of the ecclesiastical ceremonies" (1) and the necessity to "exclude all profanity not only in itself, but in the manner in which it is presented . . . " (2). The latter comment, especially, is less applicable to chant. This approach would explain the stress on Gregorian chant as "the supreme model for sacred music," and the insistence that "a composition for church" be in harmony with the chant's movement and inspiration. It would make sense of the lengthy excursus on art and artistic principles as the context for comments on sacred music in *Musicae sacrae disciplina*. There Pius XII wrote that "these laws and standards for religious art apply in a stricter and holier way to sacred music because sacred music enters more intimately into divine worship" and, for this reason, the Church must "prevent whatever might be unbecoming to sacred worship or anything that might distract . . . " (30).

The theory raises some questions. Why did the phrase *pars integrans* become so closely identified with Gregorian chant and not with polyphony? The literature leaves no doubt that this was

---

22. Helmut Hucke, "The Roman Instruction on Music in the Liturgy," *Concilium* 32 (1968), p. 122.
23. *Ibid.*, p. 123.

indeed the case. It may be because the notion of music as integral to the liturgy arose simultaneously with the restoration of the chant, and that the chant was so obviously liturgical that its value simply overshadowed the other emphasis. Liturgists striving for a recovery of the Word stressed its liturgical rightness because of its association with the word and its capacity to mediate the genius of the Roman rite. Musicians emphasized its artistic merits, the integral relationship between melodic and textual accents, the beauty of its interpretation, the challenge of performing it well. An emphasis on liturgical solemnity, the struggle for an authentic chant edition, and the recovery of artistic integrity all coincided, and chant became paradigmatic of the ideal liturgical music. It was *pars integrans*.

The Council acknowledges the preeminence of Gregorian chant in the liturgy and in tradition. Because it is "specially suited to the Roman liturgy"—it is *pars integrans*—"other things being equal, it should be given pride of place in liturgical services" (116). The Council also affirms polyphony and recommends that the treasury of sacred music be preserved and fostered. Above all, the Council emphasizes the primary importance of the assembly's active participation through song, and to this end, religious singing is to be fostered, instruments are to be admitted, new compositions are to be written, instruction is to be imparted, ritual language is to be evaluated and necessary changes are to be made. There is no mention of the new music being *pars integrans*—the opening statement was made in relation to the traditional music of the past—although music is still presented as necessary, even integral, to the "more noble form" of liturgical worship. If liturgical music remains *pars integrans*, it will no longer be so simply because of its association with the text, because its relationship to the text—that unique union between word, melody, rhythm, accent which centered in a specific language and repertoire—has changed. Prior to the Council, music was integral to the liturgy because, by transmitting liturgical texts, it performed an essential service for the rite. Today, music also performs an essential service for the assembly, enabling the assembly to participate in the liturgical action. Since such participation is integral to the very nature of liturgical celebration, it may well be that music is *pars integrans* mainly because of its ministerial function. Is it essential that such music be associated with a text?

Pius X stated that "the music proper to the Church is purely vocal music . . . " (*TLS*, 15). History bears witness to this. "Singing is the primary point of departure for Christian ritual music" because it is "bonded to the biblical and sacramental word."[24] Rembert Weakland points out that Roman Catholic Church music has "always tended to be logogenic in nature and to exclude pathogenic elements."[25]

> Logogenic music is that which is word-inspired, or word-born. It consists in heightened speech patterns. It adds tone to word but hardly admits of a musical logic that is not word-determined. Pathogenic elements in music are those born of the attempt to use musical elements directly for emotional expression. . . . The meeting ground of the two presents a fascinating esthetic problem.[26]

Weakland points out that Christian musical esthetics absorbed logogenic elements from Platonic musical esthetics which influenced the early Fathers. Joseph Fitzer writes:

> To perform music without a text, without, so to speak, a set of commands or directions for the powers of music, was to introduce the irrational. . . . Thus it came about that philosophers and theologians tried to reduce music to the inflection of words, or, failing in that, sought to ban excessive indulgence in instrumental music. . . . [27]

Throughout the Hellenistic world and the ancient Near East "the message is clear: without words music has no honorable meaning."[28]

> The power of music freed from the word is an unwelcome power . . . And primitives knew well the enchanting power of music, knew well that a *carmen* could be a *charm*. Like all the powers of nature music had to receive a religious blessing, that is, a formula

24. Document prepared by *Universa Laus*, "Music in Christian Celebration" (1980), art. 5/1.

25. Weakland, "The Sung Mass and Its Problems," *op. cit.*, p. 240.

26. *Ibid.*

27. Joseph Fitzer, "Instrumental Music in the Liturgy," *Worship* 45 (1971), p. 543.

28. *Ibid.*, p. 544.

of words attesting to its re-creation as religious. Surprisingly to the twentieth-century Christian, perhaps, the primitive and Platonic distrust of wordless nature became part and parcel of Christianity; the result was the Roman Ritual.[29]

Yet one cannot dismiss a Hebraic connection, one deeper than the obvious appropriation of an essentially logogenic psalmody from the synagogue service of the word. In Hebrew, *dābār* meant more than spoken word. It meant action, event. It covered both word and deed. It possessed a dynamic power of its own. Like the word of the Lord which came to the prophets, "the word of God has power to heal people" (Ps 107:20) and "it shall accomplish what I want" (Is 55:11).

We must remember that in Hebrew outlook a word once spoken had a quasi-substantial existence of its own.[30]

The whole of this *logos* theology was caught up and transmitted to Christianity in the Gospel of John, particularly in the *Logos* hymn of the Prologue. The liturgy has always been intimately associated with God's word, enabling the power of past events recorded in scripture to come alive in the present through ritual reenactment. So vital was the word to the liturgy, that only the chant, its musical medium, was considered liturgical music.[31] This early identification of music with the word evolved to a preoccupation with the text, and finally, with the preservation of a language. "The language of the Roman Church is Latin. It is therefore forbidden to sing anything whatever in the vernacular in solemn liturgical functions . . . (*TLS*, 7). The liturgical text must be sung as it is in the books without alteration . . . " (9).

There is a polarity between *verbum* and *melos*, a tension between the intellectual and the emotional. Weakland warns that "logogenic tendencies in origin do tend to become intellectualized, pathogenic origins do tend to ecstatic and rhapsodic forms."[32]

29. *Ibid.*

30. Raymond E. Brown, *The Gospel According to John* (New York: Doubleday, 1966), p. 521.

31. The classification according to music *of* worship (liturgical chant), music *for* worship (polyphony), and music *at* worship (other forms) persisted for some time. See Karl Gustav Fellerer, *The History of Catholic Church Music* (1961).

32. Weakland, "The Sung Mass," *op. cit.*, p. 241.

Indeed, "the liturgy as a celebration of Christians is concerned with the communication of content, with interpretation, and with history."[33] Yet music with words is "music in a mixed state. . . . Instrumental music, on the other hand, is music in a pure state, music on its own terms: music, and only music. Only when music is freed from the word can it be present in its full power."[34] Augustine attests to the sheer, ecstatic power of the *jubilus*:

> What does singing a "jubilation" mean? It is the realization that words cannot express the inner music of the heart. For those who sing in the harvest field, or vineyard, or in work deeply occupying the attention, when they are overcome with joy at the words of the song, being filled with such exaltation, the words fail to express their emotion, so leaving the syllables of the words, they drop into vowel sounds—the vowel sounds signifying that the heart is yearning to express what the tongue cannot utter.[35]

Universa Laus draws this conclusion:

> In certain cases, a musical act may constitute a rite in itself: e.g. the ringing of bells or music for meditation. In other cases it may be integral to a rite: e.g. a procession or an action without singing. Music can make a moment become an event, give a certain quality to the course of time in celebration, signify a feast, provide an aid to contemplation; and in the end become itself an act of prayer.[36]

At the time of the Council, Joseph Gelineau spoke of music as "an integral, though not necessary, element in Christian worship."[37] Liturgist Robert Hovda insists, "It should be made clear that music does not constitute a *sine qua non* for liturgy . . . liturgy can be a complete community and esthetic experience without song."[38] That music is organically linked to the liturgy, an integral element of its expression, few would deny. But to be "of the essence" is one

33. Bernard Huijbers, "The Nature of Liturgical Music," *Music and Liturgy* 4 (1978), p. 51.

34. Fitzer, *op. cit.*, p. 543.

35. *Enarr.* Ps. 32.

36. *Universa Laus* Document, *op. cit.*, art. 6/4.

37. *Voices and Instruments in Christian Worship*, tr. by Clifford Howell (Collegeville: Liturgical Press, 1964), p. 46.

38. "Music," *Liturgical Arts* 38 (1970), p. 43.

thing. To be "essential" or "necessary," *sine qua non,* constitutive of, inevitable in the sense that one cannot do without, is another. Chapter six of *Sacrosanctum concilium* insists on active participation by the assembly "whenever the sacred action is to be celebrated with song" (114). This suggests the possibility of a liturgy without music. The decree also points out that liturgical worship "is given a more noble form" when "celebrated solemnly in song" (113), a qualitative statement about form, not essence. Nobility of form is equated with solemnity, and solemnity has traditionally been equated with music and expressed in terms of degrees: a lot of music, a little music, or none at all. The American documents continue to support the principle of progressive solemnity (*MCW,* 19–20; *LMT,* 13). However, the 1982 supplement, *Liturgical Music Today,* leans heavily in the direction of having some music at every liturgy. It refers to music as "a necessarily normal dimension" of communal worship (5). "The gospel acclamation, moreover, must always be sung" (17; 1981 *Introduction: Lectionary for Mass,* 23).

This emphasis on music as "normal" to every liturgy reflects the present trend in the United States toward an understanding of music as "normative" to liturgy. "Increasingly we realize that music is not only intrinsic to liturgical prayer but that it is liturgy at its best!" For this reason, "musical liturgy is ideal liturgy. Musical liturgy is the norm for our practice."[39] In Europe they are asking "whether this presence is necessary because of theological reasons, or whether it responds to basic anthropological exigencies."[40] This is the question the Church in America should be asking. The following passage indicates why.

> No one can maintain that a Mass without song is less perfect than one with song. Rather, it is more just to encourage the "state of singing," the openness to expression, as a human condition favorable for celebration, for a liturgy-as-feast. But every Christian reunion must find its own paths toward a feast, to celebrate God in spirit and in truth, to *psallere sapienter.*[41]

39. John Gallen, "Musical Liturgy Is On the Way," *Pastoral Music* 1 (1976), p. 11.

40. Gino Stefani, "Does the Liturgy Still Need Music?" *Concilium* 42 (1969), p. 71.

41. *Ibid.,* p. 86.

This is a strong anthropological statement supporting the right of each assembly to determine the nature of its own response, but what is the theological rationale for such a claim? The opening sentence indicates the misunderstanding that can arise in the absence of a theology. Music as integral and necessary to liturgy continues to receive strong aesthetic and anthropological justification, and regulatory criteria lean heavily on principles drawn from these areas. With the loosening of the inseparable bond between liturgical music and ritual text, and the wider definition of liturgy and forms of liturgical expression, theological reasons for such a claim are no longer clear.

The *pars integrans* issue underscores the need for a theology of church music as the basis for determining criteria for using music in the liturgy. Such a theology would surely address the following consideration: music is *pars integrans* as a vehicle for God's Word, albeit translated and updated, and as a vehicle for the assembly's response to and assimilation of that Word. The theological basis is twofold. First, the Logos, the Word-made-flesh, not as justification for a logogenic, text-bound music caught up in words, but a music that is Word-inspired and caught up in Word-events. Second, the *Ecclesia*, the assembly, where music can prepare for a deeper experience of God's presence and an integration of Word and life, for when two or more gather in his name, a whole lot more can happen beyond the ritual keeping of a feast. Rooted in the biblical Word and in the assembly of believers, music can help make connections and foster an integration of the two. When this happens in the liturgy, music is *pars integrans*.

MUNUS MINISTERIALE

The most significant notion to emerge from the Council with regard to music is described in *Sacrosanctum concilium* as "the ministerial function supplied by sacred music in the service of the Lord."[42] This *munus ministeriale* has radically altered the liturgy's whole approach to music, affecting everything from language to genre, repertoire, and style.

42. " ... *munus Musicae sacrae ministeriale in dominico servitio pressius illustrarunt"* (*SC,* 112).

Since Pius X, music has been understood to have a supportive role, evolving with the changing liturgy from a position of subservience (*ancilla*) to service or ministry (*munus ministeriale*). The *munus ministeriale* of music is twofold: it serves both the liturgy and the assembly. These are not two independent functions, but rather two aspects of a single ministry "in the service of the Lord." In the fulfilling of its ministerial function, music becomes *sacra* and is *pars integrans*, achieving its purpose as articulated by Pius X and confirmed by the Council, which is "the glory of God and the santification of the faithful" (*TLS*, 1; *SC*, 112).

Music has much to contribute in its ministry to the liturgy. First of all, it serves the ritual experience as a whole. "Liturgical worship is given a more noble form when the divine offices are celebrated solemnly in song . . ." (*SC*, 113). When so celebrated, "with the ministers of each degree fulfilling their ministry and the people participating" (*SC*, 113; *MS*, 5), the whole character of the rite is affected.

> Indeed, through this form, prayer is expressed in a more attractive way, the mystery of the liturgy, with its hierarchical and community nature, is more openly shown, the unity of hearts is more profoundly achieved by the union of voices, minds are more easily raised to heavenly things by the beauty of the sacred rites, and the whole celebration more clearly prefigures that heavenly liturgy which is enacted in the holy city of Jerusalem (*MS*, 5).

The same document continues a bit further on:

> It should be borne in mind that the true solemnity of liturgical worship depends less on a more ornate form of singing and a more magnificent ceremonial than on its worthy and religious celebration, which takes into account the integrity of the liturgical celebration itself, and the performance of each of its parts according to their own particular nature (11).

Besides contributing a solemnity to certain ceremonies, music adds a pastoral dimension to ordinary parish liturgies when it "sets the appropriate tone for a particular celebration," for "the quality of joy and enthusiasm which music adds to community worship cannot be gained in any other way" (*MCW*, 23).

Specifically, the ministry of music is very intimately associated with the liturgical texts. Pius X stated that "its principal office is to clothe with befitting melody the liturgical text proposed for the understanding of the faithful" (*TLS*, 1). At first glance, this statement seems innocent enough, but in fact it is explosive, containing within it the source of the twentieth-century's tension between music and the liturgy: ritual (and artistic) integrity and popular comprehension. The two halves of the phrase parted early on, each taking a separate route toward a common goal. Much was made of the chant's intrinsic ability to provide the perfect melody for the text. Much was also made of the fact that this contributed little to the faithful's understanding. The Council finally reconciled the demands of the rite with the needs of the assembly by means of the *munus ministeriale* of music, but it had to effect some radical changes in the liturgy in order to do so. The perennial problem of musical artistry and integrity is as yet unresolved.

Before the Council, the rite had priority, and the primary function of music was to serve its texts: to support them, clothe them, enhance them, reveal their deeper meaning. To some extent, the fulfillment of this function benefited those who were initiated into the intricacies of language and style. For example, *"Hodie, Christus natus est,"* the *Magnificat* antiphon of Second Vespers of Christmas, and *"Resurrexi, et adhuc tecum sum, alleluia,"* the Introit for Easter Sunday morning, are exquisitely revelatory in their haunting modal and melodic settings. But it cannot be denied that pre-Conciliar music, particularly the chant, often concealed far more than it revealed, failing to communicate to the masses, keeping the sacred Mysteries all too mysterious, and at times perpetuating a questionable theology among the unsuspecting. Not until the vernacular did people realize the extent to which the well-known, well-loved sequence, *"Dies Irae,"* had them cowering before an avenging God, forewarned by David and the pagan Sibyl, both of whom the *Saint Andrew Daily Missal* addressed as "prophets." Lucien Deiss points out that the Introit for the Feast of Several Martyrs was "plainly a song of vengeance," in which the congregation called out to the Lord to "repay our neighbors sevenfold" in order to "avenge the blood of your saints. . . . "[43] If, as

---

43. Lucien Deiss, *Spirit and Song of the New Liturgy* (Cincinnati: World Library Publications, 1976), p. 5.

Pius X indicated, the ultimate aim of music was to increase the efficacy of the text in order that grace might more fully abound among those enlightened, it did this rather poorly. It enhanced the mystique of the ritual instead of releasing the power of God's word, communicating theological nuances the word did not always intend. The key, of course, was the language. Once the rite was free to say what it meant, it had to mean what it said.

Since the advent of vernacular, it is no longer enough for music to be beautiful or to contribute to ceremonial splendor. Music "should heighten the texts so that they speak more fully and more effectively" (*MCW*, 23). Today, music has a real responsibility to the text. Current legislation puts serious questions to the music. "Does the music express and interpret the text correctly and make it more meaningful? Is the form of the text respected? . . . Each has a specific function which must be served by the music chosen for a text" (*MCW*, 32). Since the Council, the function of music is as closely linked to form as it is to text. The different forms should be reflected in the music. There are acclamations, processional songs, responsorial psalms, Ordinary pieces, and songs that are supplementary, as well as antiphons, dialogues, and litanies. These can be set as psalms, hymns, chants, songs, or short responses or refrains. "The various functions of sung prayer must be distinguished within liturgical rites." At times the function of music is "to accompany ritual actions" in which case it "is not independent but serves, rather, to support the prayer of the assembly" (*LMT*, 9). At other times, "the music does not serve as a mere accompaniment, but as the integral mode by which the mystery is proclaimed and presented" (10). The *munus ministeriale* as it pertains to the liturgy is guided by these two criteria: "beyond determining the moments when song is needed, the musical form employed must match its liturgical function" (11). In fact, "the nature of the liturgy itself will help to determine what kind of music is called for, what parts are to be preferred for singing and who is to sing them" (*MCW*, 30).

Vatican II insisted that ritual music does more than serve the rite. The American bishops agreed:

In addition to expressing texts, music can also unveil a dimension of meaning and feeling, a communication of ideas and intuitions which words alone cannot yield (*MCW*, 24).

In this it serves the assembly.

> Music should assist the assembled believers to express and share the gift of faith that is within them and to nourish and strengthen their interior commitment of faith" (23).

Yet in all of this "the function of music is ministerial; it must serve and never dominate" (23). It submits to the pastoral judgment that "governs the use and function of every element of celebration" when it asks, "does music in the celebration enable these people to express their faith, in this place, in this age, in this culture?" (39).

> In liturgy, music fulfills a certain number of anthropological functions, relating both to individual and to group, that are the same as those met with in society as a whole . . . the use of music for emotional expression, group solidarity, as a ceremonial symbol. . . . [44]

The Council affirmed these functions, calling "holy" that music in the liturgy which "adds delight to prayer" and "fosters unity of minds" (SC, 112). Beyond practical functions, "there is also the symbolic function which opens up a space and a freedom for the heart of a believer." Indeed "the liturgy expects of music that it will signify the other side of human realities."[45]

> Like every symbolic sign, music "refers" one to something beyond itself. It opens the door to the indefinable realm of meanings and reactions. Taken in terms of faith, music for the believer becomes both the *sacramentum* and the *mysterion* of the realities being celebrated.[46]

When music really functions, it is far more than functional music, for "it can release us from the literal—the literal sense of words

---

44. *Universa Laus* Document, *op. cit.*, art. 7/1.
45. Joseph Gelineau, "What No Ear Has Heard . . .," *Music and Liturgy* 5 (1979), p. 92.
46. *Universa Laus* Document, *op. cit.*, art. 7/4.

and the literalness of thought—it can carry us towards a transparency of mystery."[47]

> Ritual music is never put on for its own sake . . . nor merely for practical ends . . . nor even just so that the rite may be accomplished. In the final analysis, ritual music is always aiming at the whole human individual and his or her encounter, in the believing assembly, with the God of Jesus Christ.[48]

Ever since the Council, the assembly must decide at every celebration just what it will sing, and why. Yet through all the changes of this century, music remains at the service of the Lord. Its liturgical and pastoral integrity enables it to be an authentic mediating structure for the interventions of grace. Ultimately, its *munus ministeriale* is to be revelatory of God's Word, to function as a bridge between transcendence and the transformation of the heart.

> If the musician can go beyond his [or her] chosen art to fuse music with the church's ritual, allowing music to be the handmaid of the Holy Spirit, then there is great hope that through the liturgical experience the Christian assembly will be "struck to the soul" . . . that it will be somehow changed in Christ.[49]

THEOLOGICAL FACTORS

Actuosa participatio is the key to understanding the changes in liturgical practice that resulted from Vatican II. It is also the primary factor in underlying theological change. *Actuosa participatio* and a *sensus communitatis* were instrumental in the restoration of the *Ecclesia orans* and the rearticulation of ancient values in contemporary terms. These two developments in liturgical theology have had a significant impact on the music of the Catholic

---

47. John Michael East, "The Challenge of Vatican II to the English Tradition," *Music and Liturgy* 4 (1978), p. 151.

48. *Universa Laus, op. cit.,* art. 7/5.

49. Daniel A. Kister, "A Musical-Liturgical Artistry in the Mass," *Worship* 41 (1967), p. 464.

Church and have done more perhaps than anything else to alter its repertoire. It is important, therefore, to take the time to consider them briefly here.

ACTUOSA PARTICIPATIO

A main objective of the Church music reform inaugurated by Pius X was "that the faithful may again take a more active part in the ecclesiastical offices, as they were wont to do in ancient times" (TLS, 3). The principle of active participation escalated in intensity during pre-Conciliar developments, culminating in the shaping of official attitudes and numerous articulations of Vatican II.

> Mother Church earnestly desires that all the faithful should be led to that full, conscious, and active participation in liturgical celebrations which is demanded by the very nature of the liturgy. Such participation by the Christian people as "a chosen race, a royal priesthood, a holy nation, a redeemed people" (1 Pet 2:9; 2:4–5), is their right and duty by reason of their baptism (SC, 14).

A fuller explanation of what constitutes actuosa participatio is given in various articles of the Constitution. The faithful present at the liturgy are to be "fully aware of what they are doing, actively engaged in the rite, and enriched by its effects" (11). Their participation is to be "full, conscious, and active" (14), carried out "internally and externally" (19), and does not exclude "at the proper times . . . a reverent silence" (30).

Great importance is placed upon the people's participation because it "is their right and duty" (14). It is "the aim to be considered before all else" in the restoration of the liturgy, "the primary and indispensable source from which the faithful are to derive the true Christian spirit" (14). Such a radical reorientation from mere attendance at the sacred rites to a sharing in their actualization imposes certain obligations. The faithful, "when present at this mystery of faith, should not be there as strangers or silent spectators," but should consciously participate "with devotion and full collaboration," eager to "give thanks to God" and to "learn also to offer themselves" as they offer the Divine Victim with the priest (48). So that the liturgy might produce its full effects, "it is necessary that the faithful come to it with proper dispositions, that their minds should be attuned to their voices, and that they should cooperate with divine grace . . . " (11). In this way, "they should be drawn day by day into ever more perfect union with God and with each other, so that finally God may be all in all" (48).

Priests also have responsibilities directly related to the *actuosa participatio* of the people. They are "to ensure that the faithful take part fully aware of what they are doing" (11) and "zealously strive to achieve [active participation], by means of the necessary instruction, in all their pastoral work" (14). They should make every effort to see that the faithful are instructed by God's word during the liturgy and "insistently teach them to take their part in the entire Mass" (56). By promoting "the liturgical instruction of the faithful and also their active participation in the liturgy," pastors will fulfill "one of the chief duties of a faithful dispenser of the mysteries of God" (19). To accomplish this, it is necessary that "the pastors themselves, in the first place, become thoroughly imbued with the spirit and power of the liturgy" (14).

To achieve the full implementation of *actuosa participatio*, the Church must see, "first of all, to the liturgical instruction of the clergy" (14), ensure the proper training of all "who are appointed to teach liturgy in seminaries, religious houses of study, and theological faculties" (15) and help Church leaders "to live the liturgical life and to share it with the faithful entrusted to their care" (18).

The principle of *actuosa participatio* is so deeply rooted in the decisions of Vatican II that it can be said to be constitutive of all post-Conciliar reform and renewal. Its effect on the shape of the liturgy, on liturgical elements, offices, and institutions, has been revolutionary. The rites have had to relinquish, not only superfluous accretions, but age-old, cherished practices long thought to be integral.

> In order that the Christian people may more certainly derive an abundance of graces from the sacred liturgy, holy Mother Church desires to undertake with great care a general restoration of the liturgy itself. . . . In this restoration, both texts and rites should be drawn up so that they express more clearly the holy things which they signify (21).

For this reason, "the rite of the Mass is to be revised in such a way that the intrinsic nature and purpose . . . may be more clearly manifested" so that active participation "may be more easily achieved" (50). In fact, all rites "should be distinguished by a noble simplicity; they should be short, clear, and unencumbered by useless repetitions" so that they might be "within the people's powers of comprehension" without need of extensive explanation (34).

This datum of liturgical theology underlies many of the directives concerning music in *Sacrosanctum concilium* and has radically altered music practice in the post-Conciliar Church. Without a doubt, the principle of *actuosa participatio* is the theological basis for much of what is sung today, and why.

> To promote active participation, the people should be encouraged to take part by means of acclamations, responses, psalmody, antiphons, and songs, as well as by actions, gestures, and bodily attitudes (30).

The singing itself has theological meaning as a dialogical response to God.

> For in the liturgy God speaks to his people and Christ is still proclaiming His gospel. And the people reply to God both by song and prayer (33).

Theologically, "the singing Church" is a *locus* of Christ's presence, as the Council itself confirmed.

> He is present, lastly, when the Church prays and sings, for he promised: "Where two or three are gathered together in my name, there am I in the midst of them" (Mt 18:20) (7).

The gathered community builds commitment and experiences grace through the sharing of prayer and song.

> When the Church prays or sings or acts, the faith of those taking part is nourished and their minds are raised to God, so that they may offer him their rational service and more abundantly receive his grace (33).

As a basic "right and duty," *actuosa participatio* means that whenever Christians celebrate, the people are to participate fully, and this directly affects their song.

> Bishops and other pastors of souls must be at pains to ensure that, whenever the sacred action is to be celebrated with song, the whole body of the faithful may be able to contribute that active participation which is rightly theirs (114).

To encourage participation, "religious singing by the people is to be skillfully fostered" so that "the voices of the faithful may ring out according to the norms and requirements of the rubrics" (118). In mission lands, or wherever "there are peoples who have their own musical traditions" that play a major role in their religious and social life, "a suitable place is to be given to it . . . in adapting worship to their native genius" (119). Composers are encouraged to provide "for the active participation of the entire assembly of the faithful" (121).

In articulating a theology of celebration, *Music in Catholic Worship* states:

> We are celebrating when we involve ourselves meaningfully in the thoughts, words, songs, and gestures of the worshiping community—when everything we do is wholehearted and authentic for us—when we mean the words and want to do what is done (3).

According to the *General Instruction of the Roman Missal,* "the pastoral effectiveness of a celebration depends in great measure on choosing readings, prayers, and songs which correspond to the needs, spiritual preparation, and attitude of the participants."[50] The Third Instruction on Liturgical Implementation says that "all means must be used to encourage singing by the people. New forms should be used which are adapted to various mentalities and to modern tastes."[51] It is clear that the vernacular has given rise to "a more pressing need for musical compositions in idioms that can be sung by the congregation and thus further communal participation" (*MCW*, 28; BCL *Newsletter*, 18 April, 1966). Such

50. April 3, 1969, art. 313.
51. CDW, *Liturgicae instaurationes*, September 5, 1970, art. 3c.

music "must be within its members' performance capability" for "the congregation must be comfortable and secure with what they are doing in order to celebrate well" (34). In implementing Conciliar directives regarding *actuosa participatio*, the Instruction *Musicam sacram* offers these lines toward a rationale for the singing Church:

> One cannot find anything more religious and more joyful in sacred celebrations than a whole congregation expressing its faith and devotion in song (16).

SENSUS COMMUNITATIS

The Council intended that *actuosa participatio* be far more than simply "active participation." Getting the congregation involved in the liturgy was conceived as the first step toward achieving a true *sensus communitatis* in the spirit of the early Church *koinonia*. The *plebs sancta* were to learn to participate "fully, actively, and as befits a community" (*SC*, 21). While "the preeminent manifestation of the Church consists in the full, active participation of all God's holy people" in the liturgy celebrated with the bishop, preferably in his cathedral Church (41), it was acknowledged that the real experience of community ordinarily happened at the lower level. Therefore, efforts should be made "to encourage a sense of community within the parish, above all in the common celebration of Sunday Mass" (42).

It is universally recognized that music has an innate capacity for creating community. For this reason, the Council suggested that "religious singing by the people is to be skillfully fostered" (118). Music "imparts a sense of unity to the congregation" and will often "assist the assembled believers to express and share the gift of faith" (*MCW*, 23). During the liturgy, "the two processional chants—the entrance song and the communion song—are very important for creating and sustaining an awareness of community" (60). The entrance song "helps people to become conscious of themselves as a worshiping community" (61). The communion song "should foster a sense of unity" as "it gives expression to the joy of unity in the body of Christ ... " (62). For many reasons, "singing, a natural sign of love, has an irreplaceable role in Christian worship," especially because:

The Community is formed in singing, assisting the blending of hearts with that of voices; eliminating differences of age, origin and social background; uniting everyone in a single aspiration of praise to God, Creator of the universe and Father of all.[52]

Realistically, not every worshiping community achieves that ideal of true *communitas*. Most struggle to overcome the differences arising from widespread diversity within the congregation. Pastoral planning "must consider the general makeup of the total community" and individuals "must keep in mind that to live and worship in community often demands a personal sacrifice. All must be willing to share likes and dislikes with others whose ideas and experiences may be quite unlike their own" (*MCW*, 17). Because faith experience varies, "greater liberty in the choice of music and style of celebration may be required as the participants are led toward that day when they can share their growing faith as members of the Christian community" (16). Supplementing Sunday worship with small group liturgies "in which the genuine sense of community is more readily experienced," because "music and other options may then be more easily suited to the particular group celebrating," ordinarily "can contribute significantly to growth in awareness of the parish as community" (18; BCL *Newsletter*, 17 February, 1967).

The distribution of roles within the assembly is a contributing factor in the building of a *sensus communitatis* (*SC*, 28, 29). The "genuine liturgical functions" restored by the Council have evolved to a variety of ministries in which the laity are involved in service to the local Church. Among these is the ministry of music. While "the entire worshiping assembly exercises a ministry of music," those particularly gifted are recognized as " the pastoral musicians, whose ministry is especially cherished by the Church" (*LMT*, 63). In addition to the officially constituted liturgical ministries, many parishes have "an organized 'planning team' or committee that meets regularly to achieve creative and coordinated worship and a good use of the liturgical and musical options of a flexible liturgy" (*MCW*, 10). In exercising its function, the team strives to maintain a sense of the community, so that its pastoral judgment will "enable these people to express their faith" here "in these concrete circumstances" (39).

52. Paul VI, Homily Addressed to St. Cecilia Association, September 24, 1972. Tr: *TPS* 17 (1972), p. 214.

The liturgical action is the action of an 'assembly' of people gathered together at a single time and in a single place. Every word, everything that is sung, all music that is played in the assembly is the concern of each and everyone. Whether a rite is carried out by one individual, or by a few people, or by everyone together, it is always a communal action.[53]

Local churches today are searching for music that "fosters unity of minds" and facilitates "communal celebration" (SC, 112, 27). The ideal articulated by Ambrose is the goal of the contemporary Church.

What a grand bond of unity becomes clearly evident when a multitude of diverse peoples sing in unison! Like a harp with many strings sounding a single melody! The fingers of a musician may strike wrong chords at times, but not here—for among God's people it is His Spirit who is the master-musician....[54]

THEOLOGICAL TENSIONS

Ecclesiastical legislation contains theological tensions that directly or indirectly affect Church music. Sometimes a basic dichotomy is implied in the legislation or a position is put forward that is at odds with the status quo. At other times, two diverse approaches are presented and legitimized, leading to polarization on the level of implementation. The following pages will consider briefly some of these underlying tensions of theological origin which have implications for music theology and practice.

One perennial area of tension is rooted in the Church's relationship to the world and the meaning it attributes to the "worldly" or "secular." The nil profanum of the Trent discussions on music has been echoed by all the popes of record right up to the present time. Some, like Trent, would only eliminate wanton elements that were improper or lascivious, while others would banish all secular or worldly "impurities" from the sacred rites. This latter stance reflects an attitude toward the world in which sacred and secular are clearly distinct. While Sacrosanctum concilium

---

53. Universa Laus, op. cit., art. 3/2.
54. Explanationes Psalmorum 1, 9: PL 14:925. Hayburn, PLSM, p. 571.

does not overtly maintain the sharp distinction between sacred and profane entities, the Constitution of this "sacred Council" does address the following as "sacred": liturgy, worship, rites, music, song, art, furnishings, images, buildings, vestments, signs. Leadership is to encourage and favor "art which is truly sacred" (124). Theoretically, all styles are now admissible, but not all is appropriate. While "there is hardly any proper use of material things which cannot thus be directed toward the sanctification of [people] and the praise of God" (61), instruments must be "suitable" or "made suitable for sacred use" and compositions must have "the qualities proper to genuine sacred music" (120–121).

What is the nature of the "sacred action" that calls for a "sacred song"? It is "the earthly liturgy" in which "we take part in a foretaste of that heavenly liturgy which is celebrated in the holy city of Jerusalem toward which we journey as pilgrims" (8). It is the action of "Christ Jesus, high priest of the new and eternal covenant" (83), of Jesus "the Immaculate Victim" (48), of Jesus "the Mediator," whose "humanity, united with the person of the Word, was the instrument of our salvation" (5). It is also the action of the Church, "present in this world and yet not at home in it" (2), coming together "to praise God in the midst of his Church" (10) while at the same time "standing before God's throne" (85). It is the reenactment of the "*mysterium fidei*" (48) which somehow must be "within the people's powers of comprehension" (34), both "sacrifice" and "supper" (10). It is made up of "immutable elements divinely instituted, and of elements subject to change" (21). These divergencies are difficult to reconcile.

A number of practical norms generate conflict or confusion. The principle states that "when the liturgy is celebrated something more is required than the mere observation of the laws governing valid and licit celebration" (11). Yet practically speaking, the laws must be kept, because "regulation of the sacred liturgy depends solely on the authority of the Church" and "therefore no other person, even if he be a priest, may add, remove, or change anything in the liturgy on his own authority" (22). The Tridentine understanding that the sacraments dispense grace *ex opere operato* is confronted by the insistence that through *actuosa participatio* the faithful may "more abundantly receive his grace" (33). The pastor is still referred to as a "faithful dispenser of the mysteries of God"

(19), even though the Council restored to the laity the right to share as "a royal priesthood" (14) by offering "not only through the hands of the priest, but also with him" (48). Eucharistic theology is expanded and enriched with an understanding of the Mass as the Lord's Supper, a paschal banquet, a sign of unity, a sacrament of love (47). At the same time, the Constitution confirms the canons of Trent (6, 7, 55), and the Mass remains the sacrifice of the Cross perpetuated throughout the centuries until Christ should come again (47). The church building is the "*domus Dei*" (126), yet the manner of assembling after the Council is more reflective of the *domus Ecclesiae*. The preeminent manifestation of the Church is in fact a cathedral liturgy (41), while parishes, derivative and "lesser groupings," are the *locus* of community life (42).

These and other tensions underlie the prescriptions on music. In several places the general principles speak of the purpose of the sacraments as "the sanctification of [people] and the glorification of God" (10, 59, 61). Chapter six reverses the order, stating that the purpose of sacred music "is the glory of God and the sanctification of the faithful" (112). On closer examination, chapter six seems at odds with the opening chapter. According to the general principles, rites and texts are to be completely revised to express what they really signify, yet the directives concerning music stress a preservation of the past. There is an "intimate connection between words and rites" (35) and music is valued "as sacred song united to the words" (112). Yet if the texts are to be rewritten and vernacular is to be permitted for "some of the prayers and chants" (36), how could Gregorian chant, so intimately associated with pre-Conciliar Latin texts, be awarded "pride of place" (116)? In chapter six the preference is for "true art having the needed qualities" (112), for compositions that are "genuine sacred music" (121). Yet earlier, the people's parts are emphasized: "acclamations, responses, psalmody, antiphons, and songs" (30), which call for simpler, more functional music. The chapter tilts toward a cathedral liturgy and the "more noble form" of worship celebrated "solemnly in song" (113). But the question remains: is solemnity the norm of celebration? Is it natural for a community assembled to keep a feast?

Chapter six is ambivalent in its reluctance to relinquish its past. Its reference to Pius X and the general tone of the chapter is indicative of its preference for a so-called golden age of music as normative. The new thrust is represented, but it is always in second place. The musical tradition should be preserved and fostered, but the people should also sing (114). Gregorian chant is especially suitable, but other kinds of music, particularly polyphony, "are by no means excluded" (116). The pipe organ as the traditional instrument "is to be held in high esteem," but other instruments "also may be admitted," provided they "accord with the dignity of the temple" and truly edify (120). Composers should increase the Church's "store of treasures," not confining themselves, however, only to works for large choirs, "but providing also for the needs of small choirs and for the active participation of the faithful" (121). The general principles and norms of *Sacrosanctum concilium* convey a sense of urgency about restoring to the people their participative rights along with the many changes such a radical shift requires. The directives on music make allowance for the new, but favor keeping things the way they were.

There is a tension between liturgy and music, between participation and performance, between ritual and repertoire. There is a deeper tension concerning music itself that stems from the music makers. The advent of amateur music has threatened artistic standards with "the cheap, the trite, the musical cliché often found in popular songs" (*MCW*, 26). The root of the opposition is not theological, writes Rembert Weakland, it is esthetical. There is tension because "we feel instinctively that only the very best . . . is worthy of God's house, and somehow we see our congregational singing as failing to achieve a satisfactory level of musical excellency."[55] Yet "we cannot go backward in time to find an artmusic that will satisfy the liturgy demands of today."[56] Indeed, "we are *from* the past, rather than simply *for* it . . . .Works of art are peaks of achievement. Each generation has to begin a new climb."[57]

Nostalgia for the past has tended to distort a perception of the facts. People forget that much church music has been so bad for so long that mediocrity is also inherited from tradition and not solely

55. "Congregational Malaise," *Catholic Choirmaster* 48 (1962), p. 147.

56. Weakland, "Music As Art in Liturgy," *op cit.,* p. 5.

57. John Michael East, "Praise Him With the Lyre," *The Way* 19 (1979), pp. 188–189.

the product of Conciliar change. Except in exceptional circumstances, neither Gregorian chant nor polyphony was performed very well in the decades before the Council. Written for basilicas and palace chapels, this treasury of Catholic Church music has been the heritage of larger choirs and never the parish ideal. That is not to disparage past treasures. It is simply to point out that our precious heritage must be approached selectively. That is true of all music, even popular forms. Art music stands on its own merits, not simply as part of a past that is missed or a present determined to achieve pride of place again. Its educational function should not be overlooked in the dialogue concerning liturgy. Making available the best of tradition is both inspiring and informative. There is much to be learned, not only aesthetically, but of the language of faith as well. It is easy to select the best of the past. Classics are always popular. The present, however, needs time to develop. Much can be lost if the selection process is too rigidly imposed too soon. In this, artistic and popular music both share a common ground.

One is tempted to ask if the artistic and the popular are really that far apart. If it is possible for true art to become popular, can the popular ever be considered art? Again a word from Rembert Weakland, who prefers to call the popular song "people's art or people's music."

> It must be a communal expression and a communal experience of faith and belief that finds its expression in music . . . It must be a product that everyone can claim as being true to who they are. Everyone has to "own"it; it is a shared art, it is art—work—that everyone feels and senses in their being.[58]

Joseph Gelineau adds this insight to the dialogue concerning aesthetics.

> The "aesthetics" of a liturgical song is thus not only to do with the quality of the text and the music, but with the whole ethos of the celebration of which this song is a part. Thus a very simple tune can be dismissed as worthless if taken in isolation but make a marvelous contribution to the spirit and beauty of the celebration. . . . The final question is, what aesthetics are we talking about in the liturgy . . .

58. "Claim Your Art," *Pastoral Music* 5 (June-July 1981), p. 36.

What value do we put on what is made manifest (the realities of faith), and what in that which manifests them?[59]

To harmonize the tensions between the artistic and the popular, Gelineau offers some practical suggestions concerning the *munus ministeriale* of music in the post-Concilar Church. "The first service that music and singing can offer the liturgy is to give it a 'tool for celebration.' " There are levels of complexity. One would naturally expect "something more sumptuous" for a feast. A hymn, however, is "primarily a shared means of praying rather than a literary or musical 'work.' . . . What would be 'faults' in a literary anthology or at a concert aren't necessarily so in a liturgical action." A second service would be to offer the kind of music "so suited to what it is celebrating that it would be an inexhaustible source of prayer, meaning, and feeling . . . a music that was not full of itself but the bearer of silence and worship," for "just as images ought to make us contemplate the invisible, so should music enable us to hear the unheard."[60] These suggestions are a valid effort to harmonize the tension between liturgy and its music, embracing both the artistic and the popular, the professional and the amateur song.

The purpose of the liturgy is the transfiguration of human souls. The idea of Christian transfiguration is the art-principle of the liturgy.[61]

Transfiguration, or transformation, is possible with both art and popular music. Each strives to achieve this liturgical goal in a somewhat different way. The masterpieces of antiquity and the present that anchor the soul in beauty offer a glimpse of transcendence in a momentary lift above the workaday world. The simpler songs that engage the heart in the act of making music alert one to the immanence of God's Word here and now. A theology of church music could do much to harmonize the unnecessary tensions between these two musical gifts of God. Liturgy and life would both benefit if a balance were restored.

59. *The Liturgy Today and Tomorrow* (New York: Paulist, 1978), p. 90.

60. *Ibid.* All citations in this paragraph taken from pp. 91–92.

61. Dom Ildefons Herwegen, *The Art-Principle of the Liturgy*, tr. by William Busch (Collegeville: Liturgical Press, 1931), p. 1.

DOMINANT THEOLOGICAL THEMES

Although they do not always proceed from the same set of assumptions, music, liturgy, and the Church share a common stock of symbols, since music is integral to the liturgy, which is the Church's ritual expression. Therefore, by way of summary, the following is an attempt to articulate a dominant and integrating theological theme underlying popular perceptions of the Church, the liturgy, and its music in each of the twentieth-century periods under consideration here.

PERFECT OFFERING

The pre-Conciliar Church as the *societas perfecta*, divinely instituted, hierarchically ordered, is theologically described as the *mysticum corpus*, with all of its members functioning in perfect coordination. Jesus, as Head of the Body, is High Priest of the eternal covenant, ordained by God to "perfect and lead to perfection as many as were to be sanctified,"[62] who presents at the heavenly altar the *offertorium* of his Church: the Mass, the sacrifice of Calvary, offered "in an unbloody manner. . . . the same now offering by the ministry of priests who then offered Himself on the cross."[63] The silent laity attend the Mass and join themselves to this perfect offering, so that along with the Divine Victim, their prayers will arise like incense as a sacrifice of praise. Song is part of this offering, "a foretaste of the heavenly liturgy" in which the Church "is united with the never-ending procession of the Blessed in heaven, who sing hymns in praise of the Spotless Lamb."[64] Song is an act of consecration. It is for God, not for people. Sacred chant, perfectly rendered, the Divine Office, sung precisely as prescribed by those duly appointed, is the Church's perfect prayer of praise. Among Church musicians, concern is for the song. Nothing must mar its flawless perfection, nothing profane, nothing banal. The song is the perfect offering. The song praises God.

62. "Doctrine Concerning the Sacrifice of the Mass," chap. 1, in Schroeder, *Canons and Decrees of the Council of Trent, op. cit.*, p. 144.

63. *Ibid.*, chap. 2, p. 145.

64. John XXIII, *Nel fervore di questa*, Address at Blessing of New Organ in St. Peter's, September 26, 1962. Tr: *TPS* 8 (1962/63), p. 362.

PASTORAL EXPERIENCE

The Conciliar Church is a Church on the move. The *populus Dei* joins with Jesus, *Pascha nostrum*, in his journey through death to life. The *ecclesia* is made manifest when, assembled at the sacrifical banquet, all actively participate in a communal experience, a personal experience, of Jesus as Redeemer and Lord. Liturgy is the source and summit of the activities of the Church, its celebration a pastoral experience of the priesthood of all believers. Singing creates the experience, for song is celebration. Singing serves the assembly, enabling *communitas*, uniting minds and hearts. Among liturgists, particularly, concern is for the singing. Texts are translated, rites are rewritten, songs are simplified, all in order to get the people singing. The goal is a singing assembly. Singing is a pastoral experience because it reaches out to people, connects them with each other, mediates the Word of Life to an assembly of believers, puts the power of the liturgical event in touch with human need. The singing praises God.

SIGN AND SYMBOL

The post-Conciliar Church is the *sacramentum mundi*, an eschato-logical sign, a symbol of hope and healing in the midst of a suffering world. Jesus, Lord of human history, love incarnate, chose to make this world the primary arena of grace in order to prepare the way for the world that is to come. Salvation is the kingdom of justice and the kingdom is in our midst. Prayer is a shared responsibility, the cultic expression of culture, where the signs and symbols of a commitment in faith are lifted up in praise. "People in love make signs of love, not only to express their love but also to deepen it. Love never expressed dies. Christians' love for Christ and for one another and Christians' faith in Christ and in one another must be expressed in the signs and symbols of celebration or they will die" (*MCW*, 4). And "among the many signs and symbols used by the Church to celebrate its faith, music is of preeminent importance" (23). Song is important, not for itself, but for what it can accomplish. It is a tool of transformation, capable of effecting a conversion of the heart. Song is for the singer. The singer praises God.

THEOLOGICAL BASES

Theological themes draw things together in a neatly ordered structure. Life is a lot less tidy, however, and while the facts attest to the validity of these assertions, care must be taken not to overstate their case. It is particularly important to understand that the themes emphasized in each of the pre-Conciliar, Conciliar, and post-Conciliar periods are not mutually exclusive, nor can they be. That has been part of the problem. What is needed is an integration of the theological orientations they express. A theology of church music can and must draw them together as three aspects of a single theme: the Church in praise of God. Such a theology must address with equal care the singer and the singing and the song, for the music of the post-Conciliar liturgy must be a perfect offering of the heart, a pastoral experience of a caring people, and a sign and symbol of love.

The value of such structuring is the light that is thrown on separate elements when examined in relation. Music, often treated in isolation, is seen to function within a liturgy that is the theological expression of the Church. When music is theologically in tune with the rite, it contributes to a meaningful worship. When it follows a different drummer, spiritual chaos ensues.

There is still much groundwork to be done to prepare a theology of church music. What may have to precede such a task is a theology of music that exists outside the restrictions of the church. The relationship of church music to music in general is not altogether clear. It is evident from the documents examined that the Church has had its own perspective, distinguishing the music prescribed for use in its rituals from that enjoyed by the general public. Such a stance is no longer acceptable in this post-Conciliar age. The validation of society and culture emanating from Vatican II is a definite mandate to investigate thoroughly the possibilities for a partnership here.

What is particularly germane to a theology of church music are assumptions about the meaning of music in general, for such meaning must be at the heart of a theology concerning music practice. The documents under consideration have indicated that different understandings of the meaning of music underlie the different ways the Church has defined, described, and categorized the music set apart exclusively for its use. A brief consideration of some of the more popular theories concerning the meaning of music might offer some clarity to the theological intentions of the legislation already examined and give some indication of the potential for fruitful exploration in this related field.

The phenomenon of music, a distinctively human activity, dates back to the dawn of civilization. Throughout history, ideas have differed as to precisely what it means.

In archaic societies, music was constitutive of reality when it functioned as mythic reenactment of a celestial archetype. It materialized the meaning attributed to it by association with the rite, a meaning established *in illo tempore* by tribal ancestors, heroes, or gods.[65] Similarly, primitive cultures still associate certain music with specific acts, each with a meaning of its own.

> No rite in religious services, no secular act can be performed without the appropriate songs; and as a vital part of social existence music is firmly integrated in primitive life and an indispensable part of it.[66]

In those situations where music is integral to life, "everyone in a tribe is part of this music; everyone sings, and many enrich the inherited stock with creations of their own."[67] Textual remnants in the Hebrew scriptures attest to a variety of cultural psalms related to the rhythm of life,[68] and the various genres of cultic Psalms imply a meaningful relationship to the celebration of liturgical events.[69] Deeper subtleties of meaning were undoubtedly known to the Levites, a professional guild responsible for Temple music. Unfortunately, they were reluctant to divulge "trade secrets" and their knowledge died with them.[70]

---

65. Mircea Eliade, *The Myth of the Eternal Return*, tr. by Willard R. Trask (Princeton: University Press, 1954), pp. 5–6.

66. Curt Sachs, *The Wellsprings of Music* (New York: McGraw-Hill, 1965), p. 222.

67. *Ibid.*

68. See Otto Eissfeldt, *The Old Testament: An Introduction* (New York: Harper and Row, 1965), pp. 87–124.

69. See Bernard W. Anderson, *Out of the Depths* (Philadelphia: Westminster, 1970).

70. Eric Werner, *The Sacred Bridge* (New York: Columbia University Press, 1959), p. 577.

Throughout the ancient Near East, belief in "the magical power of music" led to its use during cultic sacrifice to "drive away the demons"[71] and to its cultivation as an ethical force. An early association of musical modes with emotional moods and ethical qualities yielded a variety of "Ethos-doctrines," Oriental forerunners to Hellenistic theories that would influence the quality of Greek life and the musical traditions of the Christian Church.[72] In Athens, musical instruction was the basis of responsible citizenship, moral conduct, and general well-being, and its practice was a public affair.[73] The intimate correspondence believed to exist between combinations of sound, cosmic phenomena, and human temperament was a "conversion of magic into music" of a deeply meaningful nature capable of influencing the will.[74]

Anthropologically, music is patterned behavior predicated on concepts that shape its practice and performance in a given society that has already determined what it means. "Each culture decides what it will and will not call music," distinguishing music from non-music or noise.[75] "A rallying point" for activities that contribute to "the continuity and stability of culture," music is "an integral part of culture" and therefore bound to reflect those "principles and values which animate the culture as a whole."[76] Although music is a universal in human culture, it is not a "universal language," for its dialects are many, making communication unintelligible when communities do not know what one another's music means.[77] Music and language have this in common: both tones and words have meaning, yet they differ in a significant way. Words, independent of their meaning, are assigned arbitrarily by language to things, while "tones must

71. Johannes Quasten, *Music and Worship In Pagan and Christian Antiquity* (Washington: The Pastoral Press, 1983), pp. 15–16.

72. Curt Sachs, *The Rise of Music in the Ancient World* (New York: Norton, 1943), p. 248.

73. Paul Henry Lang, *Music in Western Civilization* (New York: W.W. Norton, 1941), p. 13.

74. *Ibid.*, p. 14.

75. Alan P. Merriam, *The Anthropology of Music* (Northwestern University, 1964), pp. 27, 63.

76. *Ibid.*, pp. 225, 227, 250.

77. *Ibid.*, p. 10.

themselves create what they mean."[78] Language is essentially discursive. Units of meaning are successively understood as they combine to form larger units through a process called discourse. Music, like all the arts, is non-discursive or presentational, and the meaning of its parts can only be understood through the meaning of the whole.[79] Music is said to be a language, perhaps because of its capacity to communicate meaning that is aesthetic or emotional or intellectual. There are strong, divided opinions about the nature of meaning in music. "Absolutists" insist that musical meaning lies within the work of art itself, while "referentialists" attribute its meaning to some association with the extramusical world. To the absolute "formalist" musical meaning is primarily intellectual. The absolute "expressionist" attributes to music the capability of stimulating an emotional response in the listener.[80]

Various writers have addressed the question of musical meaning and approached it in different ways. "A melody is a series of tones that makes sense. . . . It is the dynamic quality that permits tones to become conveyors of meaning." As each tone in a dynamic field points beyond itself to a common center, "we hear in it the promise of a whole that it bears within itself."[81] In this sense, tones have "embodied meaning," that is, "one musical event (be it a tone, a phrase, or a whole section) has meaning because it points to and makes us expect another musical event."[82] Tones discharge their meaning upon the hearer directly in their sound. "When meaning sounds in a musical tone, a nonphysical force intangibly radiates from its physical conveyor." Because this force that "transcends the material is immediately manifested in a material datum," musical tones can be called "dynamic symbols" and, in this transcendent quality, are similar to religious symbols.[83]

78. Victor Zuckerkandl, *Sound and Symbol*, tr. by Willard R. Trask (Princeton: University Press, 1956), p. 67.

79. Susanne K. Langer, *Philosophy in a New Key* (Cambridge: Harvard University Press, 1951), pp. 96–97.

80. Leonard B. Meyer, *Emotion and Meaning in Music* (Chicago: University Press, 1956), pp. 1, 3.

81. Zuckerkandl, *op. cit.*, pp. 15, 21, 37.

82. Meyer, *op. cit.*, p. 35.

83. Zuckerkandl, *op. cit.*, pp. 68–69.

Music is "significant form," and its significance is that of a symbol . . . which by virtue of its dynamic structure can express the forms of vital experience which language is peculiarly unfit to convey. Feeling, life, motion and emotion constitute its import.[84]

"A symbol must have ascribed meaning."[85] The meaning of music is related to time. Because "our hearing is concerned with the stream of time," a whole new symbol world is opened to us, "symbols of becoming, of motion, of change." Music has enabled us "to think temporally, in the image of time."[86] Spatial images condition us to changelessness, the eternal, a state of rest. Music is charged with dynamism, and its kinetic energy links us to temporality.

The moment music becomes the voice of the "other" world, musical experiences can no longer challenge our concept of reality.[87]

Although clearly a symbolic form, music is "an unconsummated symbol," because "the assignment of one rather than another possible meaning to each form is never explicitly made."[88] Such an ambivalence of content enables music to reveal the deeper meaning. Its particular gift is insight, and it has "fulfilled its mission whenever our hearts are satisfied."[89]

Two factors prevalent in Western aesthetics are the attribution of emotion-producing qualities to music and of beauty to the product or its process.[90] Some consider emotion to be the consequence of the music, others would have it the cause.[91] Emotional response differs in people. Those who would relate it to cognition suggest that "emotion is evoked when a tendency to respond is inhibited."[92] This interruption of an expected musical

84. Susanne K. Langer, *Feeling and Form* (New York: Charles Scribner's Sons, 1953), p. 32.

85. Merriam, *op. cit.*, p. 232.

86. Zuckerkandl, *op. cit.*, pp. 233, 262–263.

87. *Ibid.*, pp. 363–364.

88. Langer, *Philosophy*, *op. cit.*, p. 240.

89. *Ibid.*, pp. 243–244.

90. Merriam, *op. cit.*, pp. 265–266.

91. John B. Davies, *The Psychology of Music* (Stanford, CA: University Press, 1978), p. 65.

92. Meyer, *op. cit.*, p. 22; also Davies, *op. cit.*, p. 79.

progression is meaningful in relation to its subsequent resolution. There is a direct correlation here between intellectual knowledge, emotion, and meaning that presumes a level of training and a familiarity with the music.

> Because expectation is largely a product of stylistic experience, music in a style with which we are totally unfamiliar is meaningless.[93]

Less sophisticated music lovers, on the other hand, associate emotion and meaning in music with other, more personal, factors. Whatever one's orientation, the following seems an accurate observation:

> Traditions and meanings are kept alive only through the dispositions and habits which form the subjective contexts of countless individuals ... There can be no aesthetic response whatever apart from the responses of individual [people] which give it meaning.[94]

This excursus on musical meaning has a point. When placed in juxtaposition to the corpus of Church music legislation, the fact becomes painfully apparent that those who legislate music practice represent a different world. It is probably safe to assert that those who have set the standards for church music often knew very little about music, how it functions in society, what it means in the different cultures included under the aegis of the Church and its laws. If reform is to proceed to renewal, if Church music is to achieve *aggiornamento*, it cannot continue to be structured outside the context of the modern world.

Before Vatican II, there appears to be no anthropological basis to criteria governing practice. In this area, American documents have made a real contribution by helping the Church to understand the priority of pastoral considerations and the unique relationship of a culture to its song. While aesthetic factors have often been reflected in papal documents, even here the aesthetic of music seems to have been poorly understood. It is doubtful the popes would have agreed with musicologist Leonard Meyer who holds

93. Meyer, *op. cit.*, p. 35.
94. *Ibid.*, quoting Henry A. Aiken, p. 61.   95. *Ibid.*, p. 35.

that "music in a style with which we are totally unfamiliar is meaningless."[95]

Episcopal documents reflect an awareness of the dialogue on music as symbol which was spearheaded earlier in this century by Susanne Langer and Victor Zuckerkandl. It is here that legislators, liturgists, church musicians, and musicologists should be able to find some common ground. An understanding of music as symbol, enriched by the perspectives of philosophy and musicology, can provide a bridge to a theology of music firmly rooted in the symbols of faith.

It is clear from the foregoing pages that music used in the liturgy of the Church has theological bases, and practical criteria governing its use are undoubtedly influenced by these. Even though unarticulated, theological orientations shape praxis, with or without one's assent. It is essential to confront the task of formulating the theology that must inform today's liturgical music in order to integrate ritual expression with the principles governing the rite. Clues to these theological bases can be obtained by examining those theological indicators, factors, and tensions embedded in legislation concerning music, liturgy, and the Church, and by reflecting on the dominant theological themes that arise from their common ground. A theology of music which would pull all the threads together is the step to be taken next. It is hoped that these reflections will have made a small beginning toward such a critical task.

Conclusions of This Study

A perceived polarity among contemporary liturgists and Church musicians concerning the use of music in the Roman Catholic liturgy provided the impetus for this book. The tension sometimes surfaced with intensity on the issue of artistic songs, or compositions of professional quality, and the popular or people's song. Because proponents of both positions claim fidelity to Church teachings, to the received texts as well as to the spirit of Vatican II, it was felt that the root of the problem had to extend beyond stylistic preference, and that Vatican II must be a major factor in

the tensions that persist. Several assumptions held firm throughout the investigation. The focus of the problem is in the legislation.
The problem is one of interpretation. The problem is essentially
theological.

As no theology of Catholic Church music as yet exists, the book
began with a search for the proper theological media. Since Rome
has, for centuries, mandated music practice, setting standards and
promulgating criteria whereby those standards might be maintained, ecclesiastical legislation is a primary source of attitudes and
information. It was felt that the documents might transmit more
than rules and regulations, that beneath practical norms lay
theological emphases which affect music practice. It would be
necessary first to articulate present criteria for music use, showing
developmental trends and changes brought about by Vatican II,
before searching for the theological basis. Once accomplished, the
final step would involve determining how criteria for use were
related to theology, whether or not this underlying theology had
changed as a result of Vatican II, and whether it affected music
practice. It was also felt that if there were theological bases to
Catholic Church music, and there had to be, theological criteria
would not be confined to music legislation, but could also be
found in documentation on liturgy and the nature of the Church,
because music is integral to the liturgy which is the Church's ritual
expression.

An examination of a broad spectrum of legislation, a study of
Sacrosanctum concilium, and a comparative analysis of selected
documents representative of twentieth-century music legislation
have yielded the following conclusions.

Two theological orientations are present in the Conciliar
documents on liturgy and the Church. A Tridentine theology with
its other-world emphasis and a new incarnational theology
involving this world are both represented in *Sacrosanctum
concilium*. These find their counterparts in the two Conciliar
documents on the nature of the Church: *Lumen gentium*, which is
essentially dogmatic, and *Gaudium et spes*, the pastoral constitution
on the Church in the modern world. Because a new theology now
coexists alongside a traditional understanding, these documents
communicate a theological ambivalence and mediate mixed
signals. Consequently, they provide the basis for polarization
resulting from diverse interpretations.

Two liturgical foci emerge from *Sacrosanctum concilium*. Theological priority is given to a cathedral liturgy, celebrated with the bishop surrounded by priests and people, as the preeminent manifestation of the Church. The pastoral challenge, however, still lies with the parish, in its struggle to cultivate and communicate a sense of community as the visible Church constituted throughout the world. These two types of liturgy would seem to imply radically different expectations with regard to ambiance and style.

The shift to a new theology has led to radical change, not only in the liturgy, but in an understanding of the mission of the Church. A more pastoral, communally engaging ritual based on comprehensible signs and symbols, and the validation of culture, mean a whole new approach to what might be appropriate for prayer and praise. If the Church is the *sacramentum mundi*, and its ritual representative of the Church, then elements of ritual must also be drawn from the rhythms of this world.

Two streams of music, rooted in diverse theological orientations and validated by the legislation, now coexist in the Catholic Church. Both are affirmed by *Sacrosanctum concilium* and are clearly represented there. The first is promoted by chapter one in all those liturgical principles and norms that call for active participation and imply the value of pastoral song. The second is supported by chapter six and calls for a continuation of the Church's rich musical tradition, both in the preservation of its precious heritage and by transmitting its values through future compositions. Nobility and solemnity, celebrational modes more appropriate to a cathedral liturgy, and the kind of religious singing where the voices assembled ring out, are qualitative criteria that meet and clash in the average parish liturgy. Later legislation shows that these tensions surface in regard to music quality and style.

The music given priority in chapter six has vestiges of "only the best for God." Those who prefer this music are faithful to the Conciliar Constitution and to Rome's interpretations and instructions. *Musicam sacram*, while promoting pastoral criteria, is theologically oriented to the past. Legislative prescriptions guide implementation of the texts of Vatican II. The Council, as the culmination of a long process of reform, is the end point of an era. Experimentation ceases with the revision of the books. Emphasis now is on adjustment and accommodation to the rite.

The music promoted by chapter one is music of and for the people. It can be any style or genre and respects a culture's songs. Guidelines issued by the American episcopal conference, *Music in Catholic Worship* and *Liturgical Music Today*, are rooted in chapter one. These allow for a lot of flexibility as they struggle to implement the spirit of Vatican II. Proponents of the pastoral song are faithful to the liturgical agenda of *Sacrosanctum concilium* and to local interpretations. The Council is seen as a decisive turning point, the beginning of a radically new era in the Church. Emphasis is on accommodation to culture and enculturation of the rite.

The new shifts in emphases call for a new set of criteria for evaluating and promoting the new pastoral song.

Since the inception of legislation, Catholic Church music history has known only one kind of music in its officially recognized rite. Its single set of criteria, while constantly shifting and adjusting, is essentially oriented toward the one kind of music in continuity with its tradition, although it has rewritten its prescriptions to accommodate the new. It is not without some consequence that Church music legislation emerged coterminus in history with the silencing of the people's song. Evolution toward a single, uniform style that became the responsibility of the ecclesiastical choir, and the development of magnificent works of art in the large, music centers of Europe, are what the legislation has been all about: correcting artistic expression back to liturgical norms and protecting a sacred repertoire from contamination by the profane. Legislation legitimizing the new pastoral song reflects a deep ambivalence, is emphatically accommodating, cautious, and at times frankly worried about this new sound that has found its way into the sacred precincts of the Church. Even the more progressive statements, on closer analysis, reveal that the pastoral song is being evaluated by standards taken from the experience of the past. There is a new song in the Church arising from a new theological emphasis. This calls for a new set of standards with criteria clearly arising from this new theological base. But if there is no clearly articulated theology of music, how will one know when criteria for judgment, be they musical, liturgical, or pastoral, are open to the present or unconsciously conditioned by prejudice from the past? If a whole corpus of legislation has been historically biased against a particular kind of music, it will take more than a change in directives to turn attitudes around.

Divisions have resulted from interpreting music documents without a sound theological basis. From the perspective of legislation, music has, to a large extent, always been unreflected. Attention has focused on what should be sung and how to sing it, rarely on why sing at all. Yet criteria that shape practice have theological bases that influence attitudes far more than we realize.

What is needed is a new theology of music to provide a sound basis for the use of music in the liturgy today. Such a theology would strive to reconcile polarities by first distinguishing those tensions which arise out of theological divergence from those related to professional expectations or simply personal preference. It would be based on both scripture and tradition and, for the first time since Church music was controlled by ecclesiastical legislation, seek to find its origins in the apostolic Church. It would take seriously the findings of New Testament exegetes regarding Christological hymns, integrate the Corinthian model, and seek to draw some insights from the experience of the early church communities and their pluriformity of styles. It would question why the Old Testament psalm remains the essential Christian song, and it would develop the "new song" symbolism inherited by Christianity from Judaism and attributed to Christ.

Such a theology would find its basis for reconciliation both in scripture and in Vatican II's *Sacrosanctum concilium*. Interpretation need not lead to polarization, but to an appreciation of two emphases resulting in a pluriformity of styles. Instead of two conflicting theologies, Church music would embrace a single theology with two orientations, mediating its different viewpoints through different cultural expressions at the appropriate times: a paschal theology that validates and reconciles two worldviews in the person of Jesus Christ who embraces both this world and the world to come in his passage through death to life. *Sacrosanctum concilium* recognized this and opened with these lines:

> It is of the essence of the Church that she be both human and divine, visible and yet invisibly equipped, eager to act and yet intent on contemplation, present in this world and yet not at home in it. . . . While the liturgy daily builds up those who are within into a holy temple of the Lord, into a dwelling place for God in the Spirit, to the mature measure of the fullness of Christ, at the same time it

marvelously strengthens their power to preach Christ, and thus shows forth the Church to those who are outside as a sign lifted up among the nations under which the scattered children of God may be gathered together, until there is one sheepfold and one shepherd (2).

One of the early Christian communities conceived of an incarnational theology in terms of the Word-made-flesh and expressed it in a song. The Church of the present is probing more deeply into the richness of that imagery and its meaning for our times. Vatican II documents have their own hermeneutic requiring time and some lived experience before their implications are more fully revealed. It may be that the past twenty years were necessary for surfacing the proper questions to ask of the text. With the Spirit's intervention, these documents will reveal their meaning, all in the proper time.

Vatican II is both end and beginning. Its time-conditioned statements are now out of date, but principles abide. Those who look to *Sacrosanctum concilium* may wish that chapter six had been written another way. Nevertheless, timeless values are embedded in the text. Namely, now that the Church is finally singing, there must be equal emphasis on both the singer and the song. Care must be taken to preserve the precious heritage entrusted to the present so that it can be transmitted to the future intact. Artists deserve respect and support, for the genius with which they have been gifted opens avenues to the transcendent as an eschatological sign. Simple folk must also be encouraged to share the song of the heart, for if good can come out of Nazareth and God can inhabit human flesh, then grace can choose its song.

On closer examination one has to admit that the issue is not the song itself, but where and when to sing it. This is not a music problem, but until the issue is squarely faced, music will continue to bear the burden of some of the unfinished agenda of Vatican II. The problem is that the liturgy itself has been only partially renewed, for liturgical reform and renewal has focused almost exclusively on the Church's official rites. There is still far too much emphasis on the Eucharist. Even here, the carefully structured parochial ritual has been the center of concern. Little effort has been made to encourage less formal, non-territorial or house church communities, or base communities modeled after the successful Latin American prototype. Pastoral alternatives to the Eucharist have been limited to an attempt to revitalize the Liturgy of the Hours.

There is a deeply felt need in the American Church for a more inclusive liturgical spirituality honoring a variety of liturgies whereby intentional communities, under lay leadership, might gather informally for prayer and praise. Such non-Eucharistic options could more easily extend across denominational lines and seek to embrace those who, for whatever reason, are classified as "unchurched." This is the primary arena for developing the new people's song, for song can help create such communities and integrate prayer and life. Such liturgical options can also support the development of the artist's song. Both professionals and amateurs would benefit from an additional forum free of the more constricting ritual and aesthetic expectations of the traditional, more formal rites. The basis for such developments is clearly articulated in *Sacrosanctum concilium*, which reminds us that "Christ is always present in his Church, especially in her liturgical celebrations," not only in the Mass and the sacraments and the proclamation of his word, but also "when the Church prays and sings, for he promised: 'Where two or three are gathered together in my name, there am I in the midst of them' " (*SC*, 7).

Finally, Church music legislation shapes music practice by guidelines, rules, or norms. As we have seen, practical criteria do have underlying theological intentions, but such assumptions cannot be our sole theological guide. In the absence of a theology of music, practical criteria at times have assumed far too much importance, and laws have functioned, not as theological correctives, but as aesthetic imperatives. Aesthetic criteria are important, particularly to musicians, but in Church music legislation, they cannot be paramount. The use of music in the liturgy is best determined by the music itself, by theology, and by legislation, each fulfilling its role responsibly in relationship to the other two: music as artistic expression, theology as reasoned articulation, legislation as the guardian of the deposit of faith. In this way legislation will ensure, not the aesthetic of music, but its theological integrity.

Bibliography

Document Sources

Acta Apostolica Sedis. Commentarium Officiale. Vol. 1–74. Roma Typis Polyglottis Vaticanis, 1909–1982.

Acta Sanctae Sedis. Authenticae et Officiales Apostolicae Sedis Actis Publice Evulgandis Declaratae. Vol. 1–41. Roma, Propaganda Fide, 1865–1908.

Bishops' Committee On the Liturgy Newsletter. Vol. 1–19. National Conference of Catholic Bishops. Washington, DC: United States Catholic Conference, 1965–1983.

Canon Law Digest, Vol. 1–8.

Codex Iuris Canonici Auctoritate Ioannis Pauli Pp. II Promulgatus. January 25, 1983.

Collectio Canonum in V Libris. Turnholti, Typographi Brepols Editores Pontificii, 1970.

Council Daybook: Vatican II. Three volumes. Ed. by Floyd Anderson. Washington, DC: NCWC, 1965, 1966.

CRUX Special (documents and reprints). CRUX Information Service. Clarity Publishing, Inc. 75 Champlain Street. Albany, NY.

Decreta authentica congregationis sacrorum rituum. 1863–1867.

Encyclicals and Other Messages of John XXIII, The. Ed. by the Staff of *The Pope Speaks.* Washington, DC: TPS Press, 1964.

Flannery, Austin, ed. *Vatican Council II.* The Conciliar and Post-Conciliar Documents. Northport, NY: Costello Publishing Co., 1981.

Hayburn, Robert F. *Papal Legislation on Sacred Music.* 95 A.D. to 1977 A.D. Collegeville MN: The Liturgical Press, 1979.

Megivern, James J., ed. *Worship and Liturgy.* Official Catholic Teachings. Wilmington, NC: McGrath Publishing Co., 1978.

Monks of Solesmes, The Benedictine, ed. *Papal Teachings: The Liturgy*. Tr. by the Daughters of St. Paul. Boston: St. Paul Editions, 1962.

Origins. NC Documentary Service. Vol. 1–11 (1972–1982).

Pope Speaks, The. The American Quarterly of Papal Documents. Vol. 1–27 (1954–1982).

Rites of the Catholic Church, The. As Revised by Decree of the Second Vatican Council and Published By Authority of Pope Paul VI. Tr. by The International Commission On English in the Liturgy. New York: Pueblo Publishing Co., 1976.

Schroeder, H.J. *Canons and Decrees of the Council of Trent*. Original Text With English Translation. St. Louis: B. Herder, 1941.

_____. *Disciplinary Decrees of the General Councils*. Text, Translation, and Commentary. St. Louis: B. Herder, 1937.

Seasoltz, R. Kevin. *The New Liturgy*. A Documentation, 1903–1965. New York: Herder and Herder, 1966.

United States Catholic Conference. (National Catholic Welfare Conference) 1312 Massachusetts Avenue, Washington, DC 20005.

Primary Sources

Documents of the Second Vatican Council

Sacrosanctum concilium, Constitution on the Sacred Liturgy, December 4, 1963. *AAS* 56 (1964), pp. 97–134. Tr. by National Catholic Welfare Conference News Service, 44 pages.

Inter mirifica, Decree on the Means of Social Communication, December 4, 1963. *AAS* 56 (1964), pp. 145–153. Tr. in Flannery, *Vatican Council II*, pp. 283–292.

Lumen gentium, Dogmatic Constitution on the Church, November 21, 1964. *AAS* 57 (1965), pp. 5–67. Tr. in Flannery, *Vatican Council II*, pp. 350–426.

Orientalium Ecclesiarum, Decree on the Eastern Catholic Churches, November 21, 1964. *AAS* 57 (1965), pp. 76–85. Tr. in Flannery, *Vatican Council II*, pp. 441–451.

Unitatis redintegratio, Decree on Ecumenism, November 21, 1964. *AAS* 57 (1965), pp. 90–107. Tr. in Flannery, *Vatican Council II*, pp. 452–470.

Christus Dominus, Decree on the Pastoral Office of Bishops in the Church. October 28, 1965. *AAS* 58 (1966), pp. 673–696. Tr. in Flannery, *Vatican Council II*, pp. 564–590.

Perfectae caritatis, Decree on the Adaptation and Renewal of the Religious Life, October 28, 1965. *AAS* 58 (1966), pp. 702–712. Tr. in Flannery, *Vatican Council II*, pp. 611–623.

Optatam totius, Decree on Priestly Formation, October 28, 1965. *AAS* 58 (1966), pp. 713–727. Tr. in Flannery, *Vatican Council II*, pp. 707–724.

Gravissimum educationis, Declaration on Christian Education, October 28, 1965. *AAS* 58 (1966), pp. 728–739. Tr. in Flannery, *Vatican Council II*, pp. 725–737.

Nostra aetate, Declaration on the Relation of the Church to Non-Christian Religions, October 28, 1965. *AAS* 58 (1966), pp. 740–744. Tr. in Flannery, *Vatican Council II*, pp. 738–742.

Dei verbum, Dogmatic Constitution on Divine Revelation, November 18, 1965. *AAS* 58 (1966), pp. 817–835. Tr. in Flannery, *Vatican Council II*, pp. 750–765.

Apostolicam actuositatem, Decree on the Apostolate of the Laity, November 18, 1965. *AAS* 58 (1966), pp. 837–864. Tr. in Flannery, *Vatican Council II*, pp. 766–798.

Dignitatis humanae, Declaration on Religious Liberty, December 7, 1965. *AAS* 58 (1966), pp. 929–946. Tr. in Flannery, *Vatican Council II*, pp. 799–812.

Ad gentes divinitus, Decree on the Missionary Activity of the Church, December 7, 1965. *AAS* 58 (1966), pp. 947–990. Tr. in Flannery, *Vatican Council II*, pp. 813–862.

Presbyterorum ordinis, Decree on the Ministry and Life of Presbyters, December 7, 1965. *AAS* 58 (1966), pp. 991–1024. Tr. in Flannery, *Vatican Council II*, pp. 863–902.

Gaudium et spes, Pastoral Constitution on the Church in the Modern World, December 7, 1965. *AAS* 58 (1966), pp. 1025–1115. Tr. in Flannery, *Vatican Council II*, pp. 903–1001.

Music Legislation (From 850 A.D.–1901)

Leo IV, *Una Res*, Letter to Abbot Honoratus, c. 850. British Museum: Codex no. 8873, fol. 168. Tr. in Hayburn, *Papal Legislation*, pp. 8–9.

Gregory IX, *Decretals*, On Choral Psalmody, c. 1227. In Romita, *Ius musicae liturgicae*, p. 46. Tr. in Hayburn, *Papal Legislation*, p. 12.

Clement V, Council of Vienne (1311–1312), On the Divine Office. In Romita, *Ius musicae liturgicae*, P. 46. Tr. in Hayburn, *Papal Legislation*, p. 13.

John XXII, *Docta Sanctorum Patrum*, 1324. *Corpus iuris canonici*, ed. a. 1582 *cum glossa (in aedibus populi Romani, iussu Gregorii XIII)*. Leipzig: Ed. Aem. Friedberg, 1879–1881. Vol. 1: 1256–1257. Tr. in Hayburn, *Papal Legislation*, pp. 20–21.

Council of Trent, *Sessio* XXII, Decree Concerning the Things to be Observed and Avoided in the Celebration of Mass, September 17, 1562. Tr. in Schroeder, *Canons and Decrees*, p. 151.

Pius V, *Motu proprio* for Spain on the Chant Books, December 17, 1571. Tr. in Hayburn, *Papal Legislation*, pp. 34–35.

Gregory XIII, Letter to G.P. Palestrina and Annibale Zoilo, October 25, 1577. Tr. in Hayburn, *Papal Legislation*, p. 37.

Sixtus V, *Immensa aeterni Dei*, May 1, 1585. *Bollettino Ceciliano* 13 (December 31, 1918), col. 68. Tr. in Hayburn, *Papal Legislation*, 70–72.

Clement VIII, *Motu proprio*, Awarding Papal Patent to Valesius and Parasoli, September 16, 1593. Tr. in Hayburn, *Papal Legislation*, pp.44–45.

Congregation of Rites, Decree of Praise for the New Method of Printing Chant, January 21, 1594. Tr. in Hayburn, *Papal Legislation*, p. 46.

Congregation of Rites, Revised Decree of January 21, 1594 on Praise for New Method of Printing Chant, March 29, 1594. Tr. in Hayburn, *Papal Legislation*, p. 47.

Congregation of Rites, Decree Forbidding the Publication of the Chant Books, May 2, 1598. Tr. in Hayburn, *Papal Legislation*, p. 50.

Paul V. Bull Granting Privilege to Raimondi to Print Chant Books for Fifteen Years, May 31, 1608. Tr. in Hayburn, *Papal Legislation*, pp. 58–61.

Paul V, Letter for the Instruction of Cardinal del Monte's Commission, August 28, 1608. Tr. in Hayburn, *Papal Legislation*, p. 61.

Congregation of Rites, On Authorizing G.B. Raimondi to Receive the Books Prepared by Anerio and Soriano, March 6, 1611. Tr. in Hayburn, *Papal Legislation*, p. 62.

Paul V, On the Chant Books, February 22, 1612. Tr. in Hayburn, *Papal Legislation*, pp. 62–64.

Urban VIII, On the Confraternity of Music, November 20, 1624. Tr. in Hayburn, *Papal Legislation*, pp. 73–75.

Urban VIII, On the Confraternity of Music, December 9, 1626. Tr. in Hayburn, *Papal Legislation*, pp. 75–76.

Alexander VII, *Piae sollicitudinis*, April 23, 1657. *Bullarum diplomatum et privilegiorum Romanorum Pontificum*. Turin: Augustae, 1857–1872. Vol. 16: 275. Tr. in Hayburn, *Papal Legislation*, pp. 76–78.

Innocent XI, Edict Confirming Constitution of Alexander VII, September 3, 1678. Tr. in Hayburn, *Papal Legislation*, pp. 79–80.

Innocent XI, Concerning Music Books in the Pontifical Chapel, October 15, 1687. *Bullarium Romanum* 19: 772. Tr. in Hayburn, *Papal Legislation*, p. 79.

Clement XI, Concerning Roman Confraternity of Music, September 9, 1716. *Bullarium Romanum* 21: 714. Tr. in Hayburn, *Papal Legislation*, pp. 81–87.

Benedict XIII, Concerns of Roman Council at Lateran, 1725. Tr. in Hayburn, *Papal Legislation*, pp. 87–88.

Benedict XIII, Concerning Gregorian Chant and the Discalced Brothers, January 27, 1727. Tr. in Hayburn, *Papal Legislation*, p. 88.

Benedict XIII, Concerning Gregorian Chant and the Franciscan Friars Minor, June 20, 1727. Tr. in Hayburn, *Papal Legislation*, pp. 88–89.

Benedict XIII, To the Convent of St. Radegundis in Milan, September 19, 1728. Tr. in Hayburn, *Papal Legislation*, pp. 89–90.

Clement XII, To Franciscan Friars Minor, July 12, 1731. Tr. in Hayburn, *Papal Legislation*, pp. 90–91.

Clement XII, Concerning Musicians in Pagan Worship, September 9, 1733. *Bullarii Romani continuatio summorum pontificum*. Prati: Aldina, 1856. Vol. 1: 432. Tr. in Hayburn, *Papal Legislation*, p. 92.

Benedict XIV, *Annus Qui*, On Church Music, February 19, 1749. In *Bullarium Benedicti Papae XIV*. Vol. VII: 34–91. Mechliniae, 1827. Tr. in Hayburn, *Papal Legislation*, pp. 92–108.

Benedict XIV, Decree for the Order of Minims of St. Francis de Paul, January 22, 1753. Tr. in Hayburn, *Papal Legislation*, pp. 108–110.

Pius VI, Decree to the Augustinian Nuns of Valencia, November 16, 1776. Tr. in Hayburn, *Papal Legislation*, pp. 110–111.

Pius VI, Decree to the Hermits of St. Paul, November 16, 1781. Tr. in Hayburn, *Papal Legislation*, p. 111.

Pius VI, Decree to the Canons Regular of St. Augustine, July 17, 1783. Tr. in Hayburn, *Papal Legislation*, pp. 111–112.

Pius VI, Decree to the Discalced Carmelites, March 14, 1786. Tr. in Hayburn, *Papal Legislation*, p. 112.

Pius VI, Decree to the Congregation of the Oratory, February 19, 1788. Tr. in Hayburn, *Papal Legislation*, p. 112.

Pius VI, *Quod aliquantum*, Encyclical on Choral Functions, March 10, 1791. Tr. in Hayburn, *Papal Legislation*, p. 113.

Cardinal Zurla, Vicar-General, Concerning Music for Rome, December 20, 1824. Tr. in Hayburn, *Papal Legislation*, pp. 132–133.

Pius VIII, Statutes of the Society of St. Cecilia, August 14, 1830. *Bullarii Romani continuatio summorum pontificum*. Prati: Aldina, 1856. Vol. 9: 139. Tr. in Hayburn, *Papal Legislation*, pp. 115–121.

Cardinal Carlo Odescalchi, Notification Renewing Prescription of Cardinal Zurla, January 31, 1835. Tr. in Hayburn, *Papal Legislation*, p. 133.

Cardinal Ostini, Letter to Gaspare Spontini on Music Reform, February 2, 1839. Tr. in Hayburn, *Papal Legislation*, p. 127.

Cardinal Patrizi, Edict Concerning Musical Abuses, August 16, 1842. Tr. in Hayburn, *Papal Legislation*, pp. 133–134.

Cardinal Patrizi, Circular Letter, November 18, 1856. Tr. in Hayburn, *Papal Legislation*, 134–136.

Cardinal Patrizi, Decree Concerning Composers, November 20, 1856. Tr. in Hayburn, *Papal Legislation*, pp. 136–137.

Congregation of Rites, Decree Concerning Ratisbon Edition, October 1, 1868. Tr. in Hayburn, *Papal Legislation*, p. 152.

Congregation of Rites, Decree Concerning Ratisbon Edition, March 11, 1869. Tr. in Hayburn, *Papal Legislation*, p. 153.

Congregation of Rites, Decree Concerning Ratisbon Edition, January 31, 1870. Tr. in Hayburn, *Papal Legislation*, p. 153–154.

Pius IX, *Multum ad commovendos animos*, Brief Sanctioning German Society of St. Cecilia, December 16, 1870. Tr. in Hayburn, *Papal Legislation*, pp. 128–129.

Congregation of Rites, Decree Concerning Ratisbon Edition, January 12, 1871. Tr. in Hayburn, *Papal Legislation*, p. 154.

Congregation of Rites, Letter Concerning Ratisbon Editions, January 20, 1871. Preface to *Graduale*. Regensburg: F. Pustet, February 2, 1871. Tr. in Hayburn, *Papal Legislation*, p. 154.

Congregation of Rites, Decree Concerning Ratisbon Edition, August 14, 1871. Tr. in Hayburn, *Papal Legislation*, p. 154.

Congregation of Rites, Letter to Frederick Pustet, May 30, 1873. *Decreta authentica* 3: 266. Tr. in Hayburn, *Papal Legislation*, p. 155.

Congregation of Rites, Decree Concerning the Ratisbon Choir Directory, November 27, 1873. Tr. in Hayburn, *Papal Legislation*, p. 155.

Leo XIII, Letter to Abbot Guéranger, March 19, 1875. Tr. in Hayburn, *Papal Legislation*, pp. 170–171.

Congregation of Rites, Decree Concerning the Ratisbon Edition, April 14, 1877. *Decreta authentica* 3: 266. Tr. in Hayburn, *Papal Legislation*, p. 156.

Congregation of Rites, Letter to Frederick Pustet, November 15, 1878. *Decreta authentica* 3: 257. Tr. in Hayburn, *Papal Legislation*, p. 157.

Congregation of Rites, Approval of Ratisbon *Vesperale*, April 26, 1879. Tr. in Hayburn, *Papal Legislation*, p. 157.

Congregation of Rites, Approval of Ratisbon Antiphonary, April 26, 1879. Tr. in Hayburn, *Papal Legislation*, pp. 157–158.

Leo XIII, Letter to Cardinal Caverot of Lyons, 1879. Tr. in Hayburn, *Papal Legislation*, p. 158.

Congregation of Rites, *Romanorum pontificum*, Decree Concerning Congress of Arezzo and Ratisbon Editions, April 10 and 26, 1883. *ASS* 15 (1883), p. 507. Tr. in Hayburn, *Papal Legislation*, pp. 159–161.

Leo XIII, Letter to Dom Pothier, March 8, 1884. In Romita, *Ius musicae liturgicae*, p. 280. Tr. in Hayburn, *Papal Legislation*, p. 175.

Congregation of Rites, Decree Concerning Publication of the Roman Ritual, March 24, 1884. Tr. in Hayburn, *Papal Legislation*, p. 162.

Leo XIII, Letter to Dom Pothier, May 3, 1884. In Romita, *Ius musicae liturgicae*, p. 280. Tr. in Hayburn, *Papal Legislation*, pp. 175–176.

Congregation of Rites, Decree Concerning Publication of the Roman Missal, May 10, 1884. Tr. in Hayburn, *Papal Legislation*, p. 162.

Congregation of Rites, Decree Approving Masses for the Dead, May 16, 1884. Tr. in Hayburn, *Papal Legislation*, p. 162.

Congregation of Rites, *Ordinatio quoad sacram musicam*, September 25, 1884. *ASS* 17 (1884), p. 340. Tr. in Hayburn, *Papal Legislation*, pp. 137–140.

Leo XIII, Letter of Praise to Frederick Pustet, April 6, 1885. *Decreta authentica* 3: 268. Tr. in Hayburn, *Papal Legislation*, p. 162.

Congregation of Rites, Decree of Approbation of Ratisbon Gradual, August 24, 1885. Tr. in Hayburn, *Papal Legislation*, p. 162.

Congregation of Rites, Decree Concerning Ceremonial of Bishops Published by Ratisbon, August 17, 1886. Tr. in Hayburn, *Papal Legislation*, pp. 162–163.

Congregation of Rites, *Quod Sanctus Augustinus*, Decree Concerning Ratisbon Edition, July 7, 1894. *Decreta authentica* 3: 264. Tr. in Hayburn, *Papal Legislation*, pp. 163–165.

Congregation of Rites, *De musica sacra*, Encyclical On Church Music Regulation, July 21, 1894. *Decreta authentica* 3: 268. Tr. in Hayburn, *Papal Legislation*, pp. 140–142.

Leo XIII, *Nos quidem*, Letter to Dom Delatte, May 17, 1901. Tr. in Hayburn, *Papal Legislation*, pp. 190–191.

*MUSIC LEGISLATION/Liturgy Legislation (Pre-Conciliar)

*MUSIC LEGISLATION will be written in CAPITAL LETTERS to distinguish it from liturgy legislation.

PIUS X, *TRA LE SOLLECITUDINI, MOTU PROPRIO* ON THE RESTORATION OF CHURCH MUSIC, NOVEMBER 22, 1903. *ASS* 36 (1903), PP. 329–339. TR IN SEASOLTZ, *THE NEW LITURGY*, PP. 3–10.

CARDINAL MERRY DEL VAL, LETTER TO DUTCH SOCIETY OF ST. GREGORY, DECEMBER 1, 1903. TR. IN HAYBURN, *PAPAL LEGISLATION*, PP. 236–237.

PIUS X, LETTER TO CARDINAL FISCHER, DECEMBER 1, 1903. TR. IN HAYBURN, *PAPAL LEGISLATION*, P. 237.

PIUS X, LETTER TO CARDINAL RESPIGHI, DECEMBER 8, 1903. *ASS* 36 (1904), PP. 325–329. TR. IN HAYBURN, *PAPAL LEGISLATION*, PP. 232–34.

CONGREGATION OF RITES, CIRCULAR LETTER ON MUSIC LEGISLATION, DECEMBER 29, 1903. *CONGREGATION OF SACRED RITES.* ROME: EX TYPOGRAPHIA POLYGLOTTA, 1903. TR. IN HAYBURN, *PAPAL LEGISLATION*, PP. 234–235.

CONGREGATION OF RITES, DECREE ON THE *MOTU PROPRIO* ON SACRED MUSIC, JANUARY 8, 1904. *DECRETA AUTHENTICA* 6 (AP. 1): 48. TR. IN HAYBURN, *PAPAL LEGISLATION*, PP. 253–254.

PIUS X, LETTER TO PETER WAGNER, JANUARY 10, 1904. ROMITA, *IUS MUSICAE LITURGICAE*, P. 133. TR. IN HAYBURN, *PAPAL LEGISLATION*, P. 237.

PIUX X, LETTER TO THE BISHOP OF LANGRES, FEBRUARY 10, 1904. ROMITA, *IUS MUSICAE LITURGICAE*, P. 133. TR. IN HAYBURN, *PAPAL LEGISLATION*, P. 237.

PIUS X, LETTER TO THE BISHOP OF LANGRES, FEBRUARY 10, 1904. HAYBURN, *PAPAL LEGISLATION*, P. 255.

CONGREGATION OF RITES, DECREE ON THE *LIBER USUALIS*, FEBRUARY 24, 1904. TR. IN HAYBURN, *PAPAL LEGISLATION*, P. 254.

PIUS X, LETTER TO FATHERS JOHANN WEISS AND MICHAEL HORN, MARCH 1, 1904. TR. IN HAYBURN, *PAPAL LEGISLATION*, P. 238.

PIUS X, *COL NOSTRO*, *MOTU PROPRIO* ON VATICAN EDITION OF THE CHANT, APRIL 25, 1904. *ASS* 36 (1904), PP. 586–588. TR. IN HAYBURN, *PAPAL LEGISLATION*, PP. 256–257.

PIUS X, LETTER TO DOM DELATTE, MAY 22, 1904. TR. IN HAYBURN, *PAPAL LEGISLATION*, PP. 257–258.

PIUS X, LETTER TO CHARLES BORDES, JULY 11, 1904. TR. IN HAYBURN, *PAPAL LEGISLATION*, P. 238.

CARDINAL RESPIGHI, LETTER TO ABBOT POTHIER, SEPTEMBER 4, 1904. TR. IN HAYBURN, *PAPAL LEGISLATION*, P. 260.

PIUS X, LETTER TO ABBESS OF STANBROOK, DECEMBER 29, 1904. IN HAYBURN, *PAPAL LEGISLATION*, PP. 238–239.

PIUS X, LETTER TO PETER WAGNER AND CONGRESS AT STRASBURG, JANUARY 23, 1905. TR. IN HAYBURN, *PAPAL LEGISLATION*, P. 239.

CARDINAL MERRY DEL VAL, LETTER TO DOM POTHIER, APRIL 3, 1905. TR. IN HAYBURN, *PAPAL LEGISLATION*, PP. 263–264.

CARDINAL MERRY DEL VAL, LETTER TO DOM POTHIER, JUNE 24, 1905. TR. IN HAYBURN, *PAPAL LEGISLATION*, PP. 264–265.

CONGREGATION OF RITES, DECREE CONCERNING DIRECTIONS TO PRINTERS, AUGUST 11, 1905. *DECRETA AUTHENTICA* 6 (AP. 1): 74. TR. IN HAYBURN, *PAPAL LEGISLATION*, PP. 286–287.

CONGREGATION OF RITES, DECREE ON THE *KYRIALE*, AUGUST 14,

1905. *DECRETA AUTHENTICA* 6 (AP. 1): 75. TR. IN HAYBURN, *PAPAL LEGISLATION*, P. 266.

CONGREGATION OF RITES, DECREE ON SOLESMES *KYRIALE* AND RHYTHMIC SIGNS, NOVEMBER 16, 1905. TR. IN HAYBURN, *PAPAL LEGISLATION*, PP. 275–276.

Congregation of the Council, *Sacra Tridentina Synodus*, Decree on the Daily Reception of Holy Communion, December 20, 1905. *ASS* 38 (1905), pp. 400–406. Tr. in Seasoltz, *The New Liturgy*, pp. 11–15.

CARDINAL MERRY DEL VAL, LETTER TO THE CARDINAL OF COLOGNE, JANUARY 26, 1906. TR. IN HAYBURN, *PAPAL LEGISLATION*, PP. 266–267.

CONGREGATION OF RITES, DECREE ON THE FORM OF THE CHANT NOTES, FEBRUARY 14, 1906. *DECRETA AUTHENTICA* 6 (AP. 1): 78. TR. IN HAYBURN, *PAPAL LEGISLATION*, P. 277.

CONGREGATION OF RITES, LETTER TO PRINTERS, MAY 2, 1906. TR. IN HAYBURN, *PAPAL LEGISLATION*, PP. 277–278.

Congregation of Rites, *De usu linguae Slavonicae*, Decree on the Use of the Slavonic Language in the Liturgy, December 18, 1906. *Decreta Authentica Congregationis Sacrorum Rituum* VI, p. 4196. Tr. in Seasoltz, *The New Liturgy*, pp. 15–17.

CONGREGATION OF RITES, ON THE PUBLICATION OF THE *CANTUS MISSAE*, JUNE 8, 1907. TR. IN HAYBURN, *PAPAL LEGISLATION*, P. 267.

CONGREGATION OF RITES, ON THE PUBLICATION OF THE *GRADUALE*, AUGUST 7, 1907. *DECRETA AUTHENTICA* 6 (AP. 1): 94. TR. IN HAYBURN, *PAPAL LEGISLATION*, PP. 267–268.

CONGREGATION OF BISHOPS AND REGULARS, ON MUSIC IN SEMINARIES, JANUARY 1, 1908. *ASS* 41 (1908), P. 229. TR. IN HAYBURN, *PAPAL LEGISLATION*, P. 240.

CONGREGATION OF RITES, DECREE CONCERNING PRINTING OF CHANTS, APRIL 8, 1908. *DECRETA AUTHENTICA* 6 (AP. 1): 98. TR. IN HAYBURN, *PAPAL LEGISLATION*, PP. 288–289.

CONGREGATION OF RITES, CONCERNING THE PRINTING OF PROPERS, NOVEMBER 27, 1908. *DECRETA AUTHENTICA* 6 (AP. 1): 103. TR. IN HAYBURN, *PAPAL LEGISLATION*, P. 289.

CONGREGATION OF RITES, CONCERNING PROPER OFFICES, MARCH 24, 1909. *DECRETA AUTHENTICA* 6 (AP. 1): 104. TR. IN HAYBURN, *PAPAL LEGISLATION*, PP. 289–290.

CONGREGATION OF RITES, ON THE *OFFICIUM DEFUNCTORUM*, MAY 12, 1909. *AAS* 1 (1909), P. 469. TR. IN HAYBURN, *PAPAL LEGISLATION*, P. 270.

PIUS X, BRIEF TO *LA MANECANTERIE DES PETITS CHANTEURS*, AUGUST 1, 1909. TR. IN HAYBURN, *PAPAL LEGISLATION*, P. 240.

CARDINAL MERRY DEL VAL, LETTER TO ANGELO DE SANTI, DECEMBER 25, 1909. *AAS* 2 (1910), P. 2. TR. IN HAYBURN, *PAPAL LEGISLATION*, PP. 296–297.

Congregation of the Sacraments, *Quam singulari*, Decree on the Age for Admission to First Communion, August 8, 1910. *AAS* 2 (1910), pp. 577–583. Tr. in Seasoltz, *The New Liturgy*, pp. 17–22.

CONGREGATION OF RITES, DECREE ON RHYTHMICAL SIGNS, JANUARY 25, 1911. *DECRETA AUTHENTICA* 6 (AP. 1): 116. TR. IN HAYBURN, *PAPAL LEGISLATION*, P. 283.

CONGREGATION OF RITES, ON THE COMMON TONES OF THE CHANT, APRIL 3, 1911. *CANTORINUS*. ROME: TYPIS POLYGLOTTIS VATICANIS, 1911—P. 1. TR. IN HAYBURN, *PAPAL LEGISLATION*, P. 270.

CONGREGATION OF RITES, DECREE ON RHYTHMICAL SIGNS, APRIL 11, 1911. *DECRETA AUTHENTICA* 6 (AP. 1): 116. TR. IN HAYBURN, *PAPAL LEGISLATION*, P. 284.

CONGREGATION OF RITES, ON OWNERSHIP OF *CANTORINUS*, APRIL 12, 1911. *CANTORINUS*. ROME: TYPIS POLYGLOTTIS VATI-CANIS, 1911—P. 1. TR. IN HAYBURN, *PAPAL LEGISLATION*, P. 270.

CONGREGATION OF RITES, CLARIFICATION CONCERNING *TYP-ICA* OR *JUXTA-TYPICA*, MAY 17, 1911. *DECRETA AUTHENTICA* 6 (AP. 2): 120. TR. IN HAYBURN, *PAPAL LEGISLATION*, PP. 290–291.

PIUS X, BRIEF APPROVING THE SCHOOL OF SACRED MUSIC AT ROME, NOVEMBER 4, 1911. TR. IN HAYBURN, *PAPAL LEGISLATION*, P. 296.

Pius X, *Divino afflatu*, Apostolic Constitution on the New Arrangement of the Psalter in the Roman Breviary, November 1, 1911. *AAS* 3 (1911), pp. 633–638. Tr. in Seasoltz, *The New Liturgy*, pp. 22–26.

CARDINAL RESPIGHI, REGULATIONS FOR SACRED MUSIC IN ROME, FEBRUARY 2, 1912. TR. IN HAYBURN, *PAPAL LEGISLATION*, PP. 241–247.

CONGREGATION OF RITES, CONCERNING THE ANTIPHONARY, DECEMBER 8, 1912. *DECRETA AUTHENTICA* 6 (AP. 2): 5. TR. IN HAYBURN, *PAPAL LEGISLATION*, P. 271.

Pius X, *Abhinc duos annos, Motu proprio*, Towards A Liturgical Reform, October 23, 1913. *AAS* 5 (1913), pp. 449–451. Tr. in Megivern, *Worship and Liturgy*, pp. 41–42.

CONGREGATION OF RITES, CONCERNING THE *"IMPRIMATUR,"* JUNE 3, 1914. *DECRETA AUTHENTICA* 6 (AP. 2): 16. TR. IN HAYBURN, *PAPAL LEGISLATION*, P. 291.

CARDINAL MERRY DEL VAL, RESCRIPT CONCERNING THE "PON-

TIFICAL" SCHOOL OF SACRED MUSIC, JULY 10, 1914. TR. IN HAYBURN, *PAPAL LEGISLATION*, P. 297.

CARDINAL MERRY DEL VAI, RESCRIPT TO THE ST. GREGORY SOCIETY OF AMERICA, MAY 15, 1915. *CATHOLIC CHOIRMASTER* 1 (OCTOBER 1915), P. 2. IN HAYBURN, *PAPAL LEGISLATION*, P. 322.

BENEDICT XV, *QUUM IAMPRIDEM*, APOSTOLIC CONSTITUTION ON CHORAL CHAPEL SINGERS, JULY 11, 1915. *AAS* 7 (1915), P. 319. TR. IN HAYBURN, *PAPAL LEGISLATION*, PP. 320–322.

BENEDICT XV, LETTER ON TENTH ANNIVERSARY OF PONTIFICAL SCHOOL, JULY 16, 1919. TR. IN HAYBURN, *PAPAL LEGISLATION*, P. 297.

BENEDICT XV, LETTER CONCERNING HONORS FOR PALESTRINA, SEPTEMBER 19, 1921. *AAS* 13 (1921), PP. 473–474. TR. IN HAYBURN, *PAPAL LEGISLATION*, PP. 322–323.

CONGREGATION OF RITES, CONCERNING PUBLICATION OF OFFICE FOR HOLY WEEK, FEBRUARY 22, 1922. TR. IN HAYBURN, *PAPAL LEGISLATION*, PP. 271–272.

PIUS XI, LETTER TO CARDINAL DUBOIS, MARCH 12, 1922. TR. IN HAYBURN, *PAPAL LEGISLATION*, P. 320.

PIUS XI, *AD MUSICAE SACRAE, MOTU PROPRIO* ON THE PONTIFICAL SCHOOL OF MUSIC, NOVEMBER 22, 1922. *AAS* 14 (1922), pp. 623–626. TR. IN HAYBURN, *PAPAL LEGISLATION*, PP. 298–299.

PIUS XI, *INSTITUTUM NOVUM*, LETTER TO CARDINAL DUBOIS ON THE FOUNDING OF THE GREGORIAN INSTITUTE OF PARIS, APRIL 10, 1924. *AAS* 16 (1924), PP. 185–186. TR. IN HAYBURN, *PAPAL LEGISLATION*, PP. 323–324.

PIUS XI, LETTER TO CARDINAL DUBOIS ON THE CHANT OF CARMELITE NUNS, OCTOBER 12, 1924. TR. IN HAYBURN, *PAPAL LEGISLATION*, PP. 324–325.

Congregation of Rites, Decree on the Form of Liturgical Vestments, December 9, 1925. *AAS* 18 (1926), pp. 58–59. Tr. in Seasoltz, *The New Liturgy*, pp. 35–36.

Pius XI, *Quas primas*, Encyclical Letter on the Kingship of Christ, December 11, 1925. *AAS* 17 (1925), pp. 593–610. Tr. in Seasoltz, *The New Liturgy*, pp. 36–46.

PIUS XI, LETTER TO THE ITALIAN ASSOCIATION OF ST. CAECELIA, FEBRUARY 6, 1927. TR. IN HAYBURN, *PAPAL LEGISLATION*, P. 325.

CONGREGATION OF RELIGIOUS, LETTER TO THE ITALIAN ASSOCIATION OF ST. CAECELIA, FEBRUARY 18, 1927. TR. IN HAYBURN, *PAPAL LEGISLATION*, P. 325.

CARDINAL BISLETI, LETTER TO THE ST. GREGORY SOCIETY OF

AMERICA, JULY 8, 1927. TR. IN *CATHOLIC CHOIRMASTER* 12 (1927), P. 75.

CARDINAL BISLETI, LETTER TO ARCHBISHOP McNICHOLAS, JULY 11, 1927. TR. IN *CATHOLIC CHOIRMASTER* 12 (1927), P. 74.

PIUS XI, LETTER TO CARDINAL BISLETI ON CONVENTION HONORING GUIDO OF AREZZO, APRIL 17, 1928. *AAS* 20 (1928), PP. 138–139. TR. IN HAYBURN, *PAPAL LEGISLATION*, PP. 332–334.

PIUS XI, LETTER TO THE ARCHBISHOP OF TOLEDO, OCTOBER 19, 1928. *AAS* 20 (1928), PP. 383–384. TR. IN HAYBURN, *PAPAL LEGISLATION, PP. 334.*

Pius XI, *Miserentissimus Redemptor,* Encyclical Letter on the Sacred Heart, May 8, 1928. *AAS* 20 (1928), pp. 165–178. Tr. in Seasoltz, *The New Liturgy,* pp. 47–57.

PIUS XI, LETTER TO CARDINAL DUBOIS ON LATIN PRONUNCIATION, NOVEMBER 30, 1928. TR. IN HAYBURN, *PAPAL LEGISLATION,* P. 327.

PIUS XI, *DIVINI CULTUS,* APOSTOLIC CONSTITUTION ON THE LITURGY AND GREGORIAN CHANT, DECEMBER 20, 1928. *AAS* 21 (1929), PP. 33–41. TR. IN SEASOLTZ, *THE NEW LITURGY,* PP. 58–63.

CARDINAL GASPARRI, LETTER IN PRAISE OF ITALIAN ASSOCIATION OF ST. CAECELIA, FEBRUARY 6, 1929. TR. IN HAYBURN, *PAPAL LEGISLATION,* P. 335.

PIUS XI, LETTER CONGRATULATING MECHLIN INSTITUTE OF SACRED MUSIC, MAY 8, 1929. *AAS* 21 (1929), PP. 654–655. TR. IN HAYBURN, *PAPAL LEGISLATION,* PP. 334–335.

CONGREGATION OF CEREMONIES, CONCERNING MUSIC AT CEREMONIES IN ROME, DECEMBER 2, 1930. *AAS* 23 (1931), PP. 57–59. TR. IN HAYBURN, *PAPAL LEGISLATION,* PP. 335–336.

PIUS XI, *DEUS SCIENTIARUM DOMINUS,* APOSTOLIC CONSTITUTION ON SEMINARY CURRICULUM WITH SECTIONS ON MUSIC, MAY 24, 1931. *AAS* 23 (1931), PP. 241–262. TR. IN HAYBURN, *PAPAL LEGISLATION,* PP. 301–302.

CONGREGATION OF THE COUNCIL, ON COPYRIGHT PRIVILEGES, FEBRUARY 25, 1932. *AAS* 24 (1933), PP. 72–73. TR. IN HAYBURN, *PAPAL LEGISLATION,* P. 303.

CARDINAL BISLETI, LETTER TO THE BISHOP OF REGENSBURG ON THE CONGRESS OF THE SOCIETY OF ST. CAECELIA, FEBRUARY 18, 1933. TR. IN HAYBURN, *PAPAL LEGISLATION,* P. 336.

CONGREGATION OF SEMINARIES AND UNIVERSITIES, DECREE ON THE MASTER'S DEGREE FROM THE PONTIFICAL SCHOOL, MARCH 12, 1936. *AAS* 28 (1936), P. 417. TR. IN HAYBURN, *PAPAL LEGISLATION,* P. 303.

Pius XII, *Mystici Corporis Christi*, Encyclical Letter on the Mystical Body of Christ, June 29, 1943. *AAS* 35 (1943), pp. 193–248. Tr. by NCWC, 1943.

Pius XII, *Divino afflante Spiritu*, Encyclical Letter on the Promotion of Biblical Studies, September 30, 1943. *AAS* 35 (1943), pp. 297–325. Tr. by NCWC.

Pius XII, *In cotidianis precibus*, Motu proprio on the New Latin Version of the Psalms in the Divine Office, March 24, 1945. *AAS* 37 (1945), pp. 65–67. Tr. in Seasoltz, *The New Liturgy*, pp. 104–107.

Pius XII, *Mediator Dei*, Encyclical Letter on the Sacred Liturgy, November 20, 1947. *AAS* 39 (1947), pp. 521–595. Tr. by NCWC.

Congregation of the Sacraments, Rescript on the Confirmation of Children in Danger of Death, November 18, 1948. Tr. in *The Jurist* 9 (1949), pp. 261–262.

Holy Office, Decree on the Use of Chinese in the Mass, April 12, 1949. Tr. in *Canon Law Digest* 5, p. 429.

CARDINAL PIZZARDO, LETTER ON THE PONTIFICAL INSTITUTE OF SACRED MUSIC, AUGUST 15, 1949. TR. IN HAYBURN, *PAPAL LEGISLATION*, P. 304.

CARDINAL PIZZARDO, CIRCULAR LETTER ON MUSIC IN SEMINARIES, AUGUST 15, 1949. *AAS* 41 (1949), PP. 618–619. TR. IN HAYBURN, *PAPAL LEGISLATION*, PP. 304–305.

MSGR. G.B. MONTINI, LETTER TO ARCHBISHOP MIRANDA OF MEXICO CITY, NOVEMBER 7, 1949. TR. IN HAYBURN, *PAPAL LEGISLATION*, PP. 342–343.

CONGREGATION OF RITES, DECREE APPROVING VERNACULAR FOR GERMANY, MARCH 21, 1950. *DOCUMENTA PONTIFICIA* 1: 178. TR. IN HAYBURN, *PAPAL LEGISLATION*, P. 477.

PIUS XII, LETTER CONCERNING HONORS FOR GUIDO OF AREZZO, MAY 25, 1950. *AAS* 42 (1950), PP. 477–479. TR. IN HAYBURN, *PAPAL LEGISLATION*, PP. 343–344.

Pius XII, *Menti Nostrae*, Apostolic Exhortation on the Development of Holiness in the Priestly Life, September 23, 1950. *AAS* 42 (1950), pp. 657–702. Tr. in Seasoltz, *The New Liturgy*, pp. 161–170.

SACRED CONGREGATION OF RELIGIOUS, ON MUSIC IN RELIGIOUS ORDERS, APRIL 11, 1951. TR. IN HAYBURN, *PAPAL LEGISLATION*, PP. 305–306.

PIUS XII, CONCERNING PONTIFICAL INSTITUTE OF SACRED MUSIC, MAY 7, 1951. TR. IN HAYBURN, *PAPAL LEGISLATION*, P. 306.

Holy Office, *Sacrae artis*, Instruction on Sacred Art, June 30, 1952. *AAS* 44 (1952), pp. 542–546. Tr. in Seasoltz, *The New Liturgy*, pp. 174–178.

Pius XII, *Christus Dominus*, Apostolic Constitution on the New Discipline for the Eucharistic Fast, January 6, 1953. *AAS* 45 (1953), pp. 15–24. Tr. in Seasoltz, *The New Liturgy*, pp. 178–185.

Holy Office, *Constitutio Apostolica*, Instruction on the New Discipline for the Eucharistic Fast, January 6, 1953. *AAS* 45 (1953), pp. 47–51. Tr. in Seasoltz, *The New Liturgy*, pp. 185–189.

Holy Office, *Quaesitum est*, Decree on Evening Mass Aboard Ship, May 31, 1953. *AAS* 45 (1953), p. 426. Tr. in Seasoltz, *The New Liturgy*, pp. 189–190.

Congregation of the Council, *Circa nuove formule*, Circular Letter on Changes to be made in the Catechism of Blessed Pius X, November 14, 1953. *AAS* 45 (1953), pp. 809–810. Tr. in Seasoltz, *The New Liturgy*, pp. 190–191.

MSGR. G.B. MONTINI, LETTER TO CARDINAL PIZZARDO ON FIFTIETH ANNIVERSARY OF *MOTU PROPRIO*, NOVEMBER 22, 1953. TR. IN HAYBURN, *PAPAL LEGISLATION*, PP. 306–308.

Holy Office, *Viene chiesto*, Response On Privileges Regarding First Christmas Mass in the Evening of the Vigil, December 12, 1953. *AAS* 45 (1953), p. 806. Tr. in Seasoltz, *The New Liturgy*, p. 191.

Holy Office, *Cum Sacra Rituum Congregatio*, Decree on the Eucharistic Fast in the Celebration of the Paschal Vigil, April 7, 1954. *AAS* 46 (1954), p. 142. Tr. in Seasoltz, *The New Liturgy*, pp. 191–192.

Congregation of Rites, Private Response, On the Use of English in the Celebration of Certain Sacraments, June 3, 1954. *Dioecesium Americae Septentrionalis, Collectio Rituum* (1954), v–vi. Tr. in Seasoltz, *The New Liturgy*, pp. 192–193.

PIUS XII, *MIT WOHLWOLLEN*, LETTER TO CARDINAL INNITZER ON THE INTERNATIONAL CONGRESS OF SACRED MUSIC IN VIENNA, OCTOBER, 1954. TR. IN *THE POPE SPEAKS* 2 (1955), PP. 79–80.

Pius XII, *Magnificate Dominum mecum*, Allocution on Various Liturgical Problems, November 2, 1954. *AAS* 46 (1954), pp. 666–677. Tr. in Seasoltz, *The New Liturgy*, pp. 194–203.

Congregation of Rites, *Cum nostra hac aetate*, Decree on the Simplification of the Rubrics, March 23, 1955. *AAS* 47 (1955), pp. 218–224. Tr. in Seasoltz, *The New Liturgy*, pp. 203–209.

HOLY OFFICE, NORMS FOR SUNG MASS IN VERNACULAR IN GERMANY, JUNE 1, 1955. *DOCUMENTA PONTIFICIA* 2: 18. TR. IN HAYBURN, *PAPAL LEGISLATION*, PP. 477–478.

Congregation of Rites, *Maxima redemptionis nostrae*, Decree on the Restoration of the Liturgy of Holy Week, November 16, 1955. *AAS* 47 (1955), pp. 838–847. Tr. in Seasoltz, *The New Liturgy*, pp. 209–218.

PIUS XII, *MUSICAE SACRAE DISCIPLINA*, ENCYCLICAL LETTER ON THE DISCIPLINE OF SACRED MUSIC, DECEMBER 25, 1955. *AAS* 48

(1956), PP. 5–25. TR. IN *THE POPE SPEAKS* 3 (1956), PP. 7–23 or SEASOLTZ, THE NEW LITURGY, pp. 218–233.

PIUS XII, ADDRESS TO THE POLYPHONIC CHOIR OF THE MEDICAL SOCIETY OF BARCELONA, JULY 29, 1956. TR. IN *THE POPE SPEAKS* 3 (1956), P. 270.

Pius XII, *Vous Nous avez demande*, Allocution to the International Congress of Liturgy Meeting in Assisi, September 22, 1956. *AAS* 48 (1956), pp. 711–725. Tr. in *The Assisi Papers: Proceedings of the First International Congress of Pastoral Liturgy*. Collegeville MN: The Liturgical Press, 1957—pp. 223–236.

Pius XII, *Sacram Communionem, Motu proprio* on Extension of Provisions for Evening Mass and the Eucharistic Fast, March 19, 1957. *AAS* 49 (1957), pp. 177–178. Tr. in Seasoltz, *The New Liturgy*, pp. 249–250.

Holy Office, *De valida concelebratione*, Response on the Validity of Concelebration, May 23, 1957. *AAS* 49 (1957), p. 370. Tr. in Seasoltz, *The New Liturgy*, p. 250.

Congregation of Rites, *Sanctissimam Eucharisticam*, Response on Custody of the Blessed Sacrament, June 1, 1957. *AAS* 49 (1957), pp. 425–426. Tr. in Seasoltz, *The New Liturgy*, p. 253.

CARDINAL PIZZARDO, LETTER TO BISHOP BLANCHET ON MUSIC CONGRESS IN PARIS, JUNE 25, 1957. TR. IN HAYBURN, *PAPAL LEGISLATION*, PP. 309–310.

CARDINAL PIZZARDO, CIRCULAR LETTER ON MUSIC IN SEMINARIES, NOVEMBER 22, 1957. TR. IN HAYBURN, *PAPAL LEGISLATION*, PP. 310–311.

Congregation for the Propagation of the Faith, Private Response on Permission for Vernacular in Various Parts of the Mass, February 24, 1958. Tr. in Seasoltz, *The New Liturgy*, p. 254.

CONGREGATION OF RITES, *DE MUSICA SACRA ET SACRA LITURGIA*, INSTRUCTION ON SACRED MUSIC, SEPTEMBER 3, 1958. *AAS* 50 (1958), PP. 630–663. TR. IN *THE POPE SPEAKS* 5 (1959), PP. 223–250, OR NCWC NEWS SERVICE, 34 PAGES.

Congregation of Rites, Private Response on the Dialogue Mass and the Rosary During Mass, February 6, 1960. Tr. in Seasoltz, *The New Liturgy*, p. 294.

John XXIII, *Il Signore*, Allocution to Lenten Preachers and Parish Priests of Rome, February 10, 1959. *AAS* 51 (1959), pp. 190–195. Tr. in Seasoltz, *The New Liturgy*, pp. 286–290.

John XXIII, Amendment of the Good Friday Prayers Regarding the Jews, March 17, 1959. Tr. in Seasoltz, *The New Liturgy*, pp. 292–293.

Congregation of Rites, *A nonnullis locorum*, Decree on Omission of Leonine Prayers After Mass, March 9, 1960. *AAS* 52 (1960), p. 360. Tr. in Seasoltz, *The New Liturgy*, pp. 296–297.

John XXIII, *Venerabiles Fratres*, Apostolic Letter on Worship of the Most Precious Blood, June 30, 1960. *AAS* 52 (1960), pp. 545–550. Tr. in Seasoltz, *The New Liturgy*, pp. 300–304.

Congregation of Rites, Declaration on Revision of Particular Calendars, July 20, 1960. Tr. in Seasoltz, *The New Liturgy*, p. 424.

John XXIII, *Rubricarum instructum*, *Motu proprio* on Reform of the Rubrics, July 25, 1960. *AAS* 52 (1960), pp. 593–595. Tr. in Seasoltz, *The New Liturgy*, pp. 305–307.

Congregation of Rites, *Novum rubricarum Breviarii*, Decree on the New Rubrics for the Breviary and Missal, July 26, 1960. *AAS* 52 (1960), p. 596. Tr. in Seasoltz, *The New Liturgy*, p. 307.

Congregation of Rites, *Sanctissimus Dominus Noster*, Decree on Regulations for Publishers of Liturgical Books, July 26, 1960. *AAS* 52 (1960), pp. 732–734. Tr. in Seasoltz, *The New Liturgy*, pp. 425–427.

John XXIII, *Animo praesentes*, Radio Message to the International Eucharistic Congress at Munich, August 7, 1960. *AAS* 52 (1960), pp. 774–776. Tr. in Seasoltz, *The New Liturgy*, pp. 427–430.

JOHN XXIII, ADDRESS TO THE CHOIR BOYS OF THE *PUERI CANTORES*, JANUARY 1, 1961. TR. IN *THE POPE SPEAKS* 6 (1961), PP. 60–63.

John XXIII, *L'incontro*, Allocution to Lenten Preachers and Parish Priests of Rome, February 13, 1961. *AAS* 53 (1961), pp. 154–158. Tr. in Seasoltz, *The New Liturgy*, pp. 437–442.

Congregation of Rites, *Ad rubricarum Codicem*, Instruction on Local Calendars and the Revised Code of Rubrics, February 14, 1961. *AAS* 53 (1961), pp. 168–180. Tr. in Seasoltz, *The New Liturgy*, pp. 443–453.

Congregation for the Propagation of the Faith, Indult on the Use of Vernacular in Certain Parts of the Mass, July 12, 1961. Tr. in Seasoltz, *The New Liturgy*, p. 453–454.

John XXIII, *Accogliere una cosi*, Allocution on Sacred Art, October 28, 1961. Tr. in Seasoltz, *The New Liturgy*, pp. 456–460.

JOHN XXIII, ON THE FIFTIETH ANNIVERSARY OF THE PONTIFICAL INSTITUTE OF SACRED MUSIC, DECEMBER 8, 1961. TR. IN HAYBURN, *PAPAL LEGISLATION*, PP. 314–316.

Congregation for the Propagation of the Faith, Private Response on Permission for A Female to Read the Epistle and Gospel in the Vernacular at Mass, December 16, 1961. Tr. in Seasoltz, *The New Liturgy*, p. 455.

John XXIII, *Veterum sapientia*, Apostolic Constitution on Latin as the Official Language of the Church, February 22, 1962. *AAS* 54 (1962), pp. 129–135. Tr. in *The Pope Speaks* 8 (1962), pp. 31–37.

Congregation of Rites, *Ordo Baptismi adultorum*, Decree on Changes in the Roman Ritual for the Baptism of Adults, April 16, 1962. *AAS* 54 (1962), pp. 310–311. Tr. in Seasoltz, *The New Liturgy*, pp. 462–466.

JOHN XXIII, ADDRESS TO THE INTERNATIONAL CONFEDERATION OF COMPOSERS, JUNE 23, 1962. TR. IN HAYBURN, *PAPAL LEGISLATION,* PP. 381–382.

JOHN XXIII, DEDICATION OF NEW ORGAN AT ST. PETER'S, SEPTEMBER 26, 1962. TR. IN *THE POPE SPEAKS* 8 (1962), PP. 359–362.

JOHN XXIII, *IL NOUS EST,* ADDRESS TO THE DELEGATES OF UNESCO, SEPTEMBER 29, 1962. *AAS* 54 (1962), PP. 721–723. TR. IN *THE POPE SPEAKS* 8 (1962), PP. 362–363.

PAUL VI, *NOBILE SUBSIDIUM LITURGIAE,* INSTITUTION OF *CONSOCIATIO INTERNATIONALIS MUSICAE SACRAE,* NOVEMBER 22, 1963. *AAS* 56 (1965), PP. 231–234. TR. IN *CAECILIA* 90 (1964), PP. 10–12.

MUSIC LEGISLATION   /   Liturgy Legislation (Post-Conciliar)

*Major Reform Legislation (Universal)
   Supplementary Documentation (Universal)
      Episcopal Statements (United States)

Holy Office, *In Apostolica Constitutione,* Decree on Reducing the Communion Fast For Priests Celebrating Mass, January 10, 1964. *AAS* 56 (1964), p. 212. Tr. in Seasoltz, *The New Liturgy,* p. 501.

Paul VI, *Sacram Liturgiam, Motu proprio* on Implementing the Constitution on the Liturgy, January 29, 1964. *AAS* 56 (1964), pp. 139–144. Tr. in *The Pope Speaks* 9 (1964), pp. 299–302.

Consilium, Decree on the Approval of English in the Liturgy, April 2, 1964. Tr. in Seasoltz, *The New Liturgy,* pp. 506–507.

> Decree Adopted by the American Hierarchy on the Use of English in Accordance with the Constitution on the Sacred Liturgy, April 2, 1964. In Seasoltz, *The New Liturgy,* pp. 504–506.

Congregation of Rites, *Quo actuosius,* Decree on the New Formula for Distributing Holy Communion, April 25, 1964. *AAS* 56 (1964), pp. 337–338. Tr. in Seasoltz, *The New Liturgy,* p. 508.

> Congregation of Rites, On the Invocation of the Holy Spirit, April 25, 1964. *AAS* 56 (1964), p. 338. Tr. in *American Ecclesiastical Review* 151 (1964), p. 55.

Consilium, Decree on the Execution of the Approved English Texts,

---

**Major reform legislation is listed in the first column, supplementary legislation in the second, and local legislation pertaining only to the United States is listed in the third.

May 1, 1964. Tr. in Seasoltz, *The New Liturgy*, pp. 508–510.

Paul VI, *Ci premerebbe*, Allocution on Sacred Art, May 7, 1964. *AAS* 56 (1964), pp. 438–444. Tr. in Seasoltz, *The New Liturgy*, pp. 510–515.

Congregation of the Council, Fulfillment of Sunday Mass Obligation on Saturday, June 12, 1964. Tr. in *Canon Law Digest* 6, pp. 670–672.

Congregation of Rites and *Consilium, Inter Oecumenici*, The First Instruction on the Proper Implementation of the Constitution on the Liturgy, September 26, 1964. *AAS* 56 (1964), pp. 877–900. Tr. in *The Pope Speaks* 10 (1965), pp. 186–200.

Consilium, Letter on Using Only One Vernacular Version, October 16, 1964. *Notitiae* 1 (1965), pp. 194–196.

Paul IV, *Haud mediocre Nobis*, Allocution to the *Consilium* on Revising the Liturgy, October 29, 1964. *AAS* 56 (1964), pp. 993–996.

U.S. Bishops' Commission on the Liturgical Apostolate, Directives for the Use of the Vernacular at Mass, October 29, 1964. In Seasoltz, *The New Liturgy*, pp. 534–543.

Paul VI, *Attentis multarum regionum*, On Reducing the Time of the Communion Fast, November 21, 1964. *AAS* 57 (1965), p. 186.

Holy Office, *Sul digiuno eucharistico*, Clarification on Shortening of Communion Fast, December 4, 1964. Tr. in Seasoltz, *The New Liturgy*, p. 544.

Congregation of Rites, *Quum Constitutio*, Decree Promulgating A *Kyriale Simplex*, December 14, 1964. *AAS* 57 (1965), p. 407. Tr. in *Canon Law Digest* 6, p. 102.

Congregation of Rites, *Edita instructione*, Decree Concerning Chants for the Roman Missal and for Concelebration, December 14, 1964. *AAS* 57 (1965), p. 408. Tr. in *Canon Law Digest* 6.

Congregation of Rites, On Vernacular in the Divine Office, January 9, 1965. *Commentarium pro Religiosis* 44 (1965), pp. 206–207. Tr. in *Canon Law Digest* 6, p. 501.

Consilium, On the Prayer of the Faithful or Common Prayer, January 13, 1965.

Congregation of Rites and *Consilium, Nuper edita Instructio*, On Revisions for the Order of Mass, January 27, 1965. *AAS* 57 (1965), pp. 408–409. Tr. in Seasoltz, *The New Liturgy*, pp. 574–614.

Paul VI, *Investigabiles Divitias Christi*, Apostolic Letter, On Veneration of the Sacred Heart, February 6, 1965. *AAS* 57 (1965), pp. 298–301.

Paul VI, *Non possiamo tacere*, Address to Pastors and Lenten Preachers on the Preacher and the New Liturgy, March 1, 1965. Tr. in *The Pope Speaks* 10 (1965), pp. 228–233.

Congregation of Rites, *Pientissima Mater Ecclesia*, Decree on Permission for Priests to Carry the Oil of the Sick When Traveling, March

4, 1965. *AAS* 57 (1965), p. 409. Tr. in *Canon Law Digest* 8, pp. 475–476.

Congregation of Rites, *Ecclesiae semper,* Decree on Concelebration and Communion Under Both Kinds, March 7, 1965. *AAS* 57 (1965), pp. 410–412. Tr. in Seasoltz, *The New Liturgy,* pp. 544–547.

Congregation of Rites, *Quamplures Episcopi,* Decree on Changes in the Order of Holy Week, March 7, 1965. *AAS* 57 (1965), pp. 412–413.

Paul VI, *La Nostra conversazione,* Address on Two Reactions to the New Liturgy, March 17, 1965. Tr. in *The Pope Speaks* 10 (1965), pp. 343–345.

Congregation of Rites, *Plures locorum Ordinarii,* Decree on Permission for the Passion to be Read by A Non-Deacon, March 25, 1965. *AAS* 57 (1965), pp. 413–414.

Congregation for Extraordinary Ecclesiastical Affairs, On Lay Religious Distributing Communion, April 24, 1965. *Commentarium pro Religiosis* 45 (1966), p. 337. Tr. in *Canon Law Digest* 6, pp. 560–561.

Congregation of Rites, Instruction on Proper Masses and Offices, June 1, 1965. *Notitiae* 1 (1965), pp. 197–198.

Consilium, Passim quandoque, Statement on Unauthorized Experiments, June 15, 1965. *Notitiae* 1 (1965), p. 145.

Consilium, Le renouveau liturgique, First Letter to Presidents of Conferences of Bishops, June 30, 1965. *Notitiae* 1 (1965), pp. 257–264. Tr. in BCL *Newsletter* 2 (1966), pp. 17–19.

Congregation of Rites, *Partes quae,* On the Use of the Vernacular in the Ordination Rite, July 17, 1965. *Notitiae* 1 (1965), pp. 277–279. Tr. in *Canon Law Digest* 6, pp. 587–588.

Paul VI, *Dilecti Fili Noster,* Letter on the Blessed Sacrament, July 19, 1965. *AAS* 57 (1965), p. 857.

Consilium, On A Dispensation From the Hour of Prime, August 22, 1965. *Commentarium pro Religiosis* 44 (1965), p. 297. Tr. in *Canon Law Digest* 6, p. 114.

Paul VI, *Mysterium Fidei,* Encyclical Letter on the Holy Eucharist, September 3, 1965. *AAS* 57 (1965), pp. 753–774. Tr. in *The Pope Speaks* 10 (1965), pp. 309–328.

Paul VI, *Vos omnes qui,* Address to Congress of Liturgical Translators, November 10, 1965. *AAS* 57 (1965), pp. 967–970. Tr. in *The Pope Speaks* 11 (1966), pp. 70–71.

Congregation of Rites and *Consilium, In edicendis normis,* Instruction on the Language to be used in the Recitation of the Divine Office and the Celebration of the 'Conventual' or 'Community' Mass Among Religious, November 23, 1965. *AAS* 57 (1965), pp. 1010–1013. Tr. in *The Pope Speaks* 11 (1966), pp. 70–71.

BISHOPS' COMMISSION ON THE LITURGICAL APOSTO-

LATE, "MUSICAL TONES FOR ENGLISH LITURGICAL TEXTS," BCL *NEWSLETTER* 1 (DECEMBER 1965), PP. 14–15.

Consilium, On the Use of Sign Language at Mass, December 10, 1965. Tr. in *Canon Law Digest* 6, pp. 552–553.

Consilium, On Supplementary Weekday Biblical Readings, January, 1966. *Notitiae* 2 (1966), pp. 6–7.

Consilium, *L'heureux development*, Letter on Guidelines for Liturgical Reform, January 25, 1966. *Notitiae* 2 (1966), pp. 157–161.

Congregation of Rites and *Consilium*, *Cum nostra aetate*, Decree on the Printing of Liturgical Books, January 27, 1966. *AAS* 58 (1966), pp. 169–171. Tr. in *The Pope Speaks* 12 (1967), pp. 30–31.

Paul VI, *Peculiare ius*, Apostolic Letter on Pontifical Altars in Roman Patriarchal Basilicas, February 8, 1966. *AAS* 58 (1966), pp. 119–122. Tr. in *Canon Law Digest* 6, pp. 555–557.

Congregation of Rites, *Cum hac nostra aetate*, On Giving Communion in Hospitals, February 14, 1966. *Notitiae* 2 (1966), p. 328. Tr. in Flannery, *Vatican Council II*, p. 61.

Paul VI, *Paenitemini*, Apostolic Constitution on Penance, February 17, 1966. *AAS* 58 (1966), pp. 177–198. Tr. in *The Pope Speaks* 11 (1966), pp. 362–371.

Congregation for the Doctrine of the Faith, *Matrimonii sacramentum*, Instruction on Mixed Marriages, March 18, 1966. *AAS* 58 (1966), pp. 235–239. Tr. in *The Pope Speaks* 11 (1966), pp. 114–118.

Congregation of the Council, On Masses for Tourists, March 19, 1966. *Notitiae* 2 (1966), pp. 185–189.

BISHOPS' COMMISSION ON THE LITURGICAL APOSTOLATE, "STATEMENTS ON CHURCH MUSIC," BCL *NEWSLETTER* 2 (APRIL 1966), PP. 29–30.

CARDINAL DELL'ACQUA, LETTER TO *UNIVERSA LAUS*, MAY 11, 1966. *NOTITIAE* 2 (1966), P. 199. TR. IN HAYBURN, *PAPAL LEGISLATION*, P. 545.

Congregation of Rites, *Cum proximo anno*, Change in the Date for the Feast of St. Joseph, May 13, 1966. *AAS* 58 (1966), p. 529.

Congregation for the Propagation of the Faith, On Lay Religious As Distributors of Holy Communion, May 31, 1966. Tr. in *Canon Law Digest* 6, pp. 560–561.

Congregation for the Doctrine of the Faith, On Funeral Services At A Crematory Chapel, July 9, 1966. Tr. in *Canon Law Digest* 8, p. 851.

Paul VI, *Sacrificium laudis*, Apostolic Letter to Clerical Institutes Bound By Choir, August 15, 1966. *Notitiae* 2 (1966), pp. 252–255.

CARDINAL CICOGNANI, LETTER TO INTERNATIONAL MUSIC CONVENTION IN MILWAUKEE, AUGUST 12, 1966. *NOTITIAE* 2

(1966), PP. 292–293. TR. IN HAYBURN, *PAPAL LEGISLATION,* PP. 558–559.

Paul VI, *Christi Matri Rosarii,* Encyclical Letter on the Rosary, September 15, 1966. *AAS* 58 (1966), pp. 745–749.

Paul VI, *Ecce adstat Concilium,* Address to *Consilium* on Guidelines for Liturgical Renewal, October 13, 1966. *AAS* 58 (1966), pp. 1145–1150. Tr. in *The Pope Speaks* 12 (1967), pp. 9–14.

Congregation of Rites and *Consilium, Da qualche tempo,* Declaration on Liturgical Changes Being Taken by Private Individuals, December 29, 1966. *AAS* 59 (1967), pp. 85–86. Tr. in *The Pope Speaks* 12 (1967), pp. 30–33.

Paul VI, *Indulgentiarum doctrina,* Apostolic Constitution on Indulgences, January 1, 1967. *AAS* 59 (1967), pp. 5–24. Tr. in *The Pope Speaks* 12 (1967), pp. 124–135.

Congregation for the Oriental Churches, *Crescens matrimoniorum mixtorum,* On Marriages Between Catholics and Baptized Oriental Non-Catholics, February 22, 1967. *AAS* 59 (1967), pp. 165–166. Tr. in *The Pope Speaks* 12 (1967), pp. 122–24.

Congregation of the Council, *Quaesitum est,* On Days of Penance, February 24, 1967. *AAS* 59 (1967), p. 229.

BISHOPS' COMMISSION ON THE LITURGICAL APOSTO-LATE, "STATEMENT ON MASSES IN HOMES AND ON MUSIC," BCL *NEWSLETTER* 3 (FEBRUARY 1967), PP. 69–70.

CONGREGATION OF RITES AND *CONSILIUM, MUSICAM SACRAM,* INSTRUCTION ON MUSIC IN THE LITURGY, March 5, 1967. *AAS* 59 (1967), PP. 300–320. TR. IN *THE POPE SPEAKS* 12 (1967), PP. 173–186 or USCC.

Paul VI, *Iuvat Nos,* Address to *Consilium* on Obstacles to Liturgical Renewal, April 19, 1967. *AAS* 59 (1967), pp. 418–421. Tr. in *The Pope Speaks* 12 (1967), pp. 110–113.

Congregation of Rites and *Consilium, Tres abhinc annos,* A Further Instruction on the Correct Implementation of the Constitution on the Liturgy, May 4, 1967. *AAS* 59 (1967), pp. 442–448. Tr. in *The Pope Speaks* 12 (1967), pp. 244–249.

Paul VI, *Signum magnum,* Apostolic Address on Our Lady, May 13, 1967. *AAS* 59 (1967), pp. 465–475.

Congregation of Rites, On Changes in the Order of Mass, May 18, 1967. *Notitiae* 3 (1967), pp. 195–211.

Congregation of Rites and *Consilium, Eucharisticum mysterium,* Instruction on Eucharistic Worship, May 25, 1967. *AAS* 59 (1967), pp. 539–573. Tr. in *The Pope Speaks* 12 (1967), pp. 211–236.

Paul VI, *Sacrum Diaconatus Ordinem,* Apostolic Letter on General Norms For Restoring the Permanent Diaconate, June 18, 1967. *AAS* 59 (1967), pp. 697–704. Tr. in *The Pope Speaks* 12 (1967), pp. 237–243.

Consilium, On Translations of the Roman Canon, August 10, 1967. *Notitiae* 3 (1967), pp. 326–327.

Congregation for Religious, On the Divine Office in the Vernacular, September 20, 1967. *Commentarium pro Religiosis* 49 (1968), p. 64. Tr. in *Canon Law Digest* 7, pp. 101–102.

BISHOPS' COMMISSION ON THE LITURGICAL APOSTO-LATE, "STATEMENT ON COPYRIGHT VIOLATIONS," BCL *NEWSLETTER* 3 (DECEMBER 1967), PP. 109–110.

BISHOPS' COMMISSION ON THE LITURGICAL APOSTO-LATE, "DEVELOPMENT OF EFFECTIVE LITURGICAL MUSIC," BCL *NEWSLETTER* 3 (DECEMBER 1967), P. 110.

PAUL VI, *SIAMO LIETI*, ADDRESS TO THE EIGHTH INTERNATIONAL CONVENTION OF CHOIR SINGERS IN ITALY, APRIL 22, 1968. *AAS* 60 (1968), PP. 265–267. TR. IN HAYBURN, *PAPAL LEGISLATION*, PP. 559–560.

Paul VI, *Pontificalis domus*, Apostolic Letter on the Papal Household, May 28, 1968. *AAS* 60 (1968), pp. 305–315. Tr. in *Canon Law Digest* 7, pp. 314–322.

Congregation of Rites, On New Eucharistic Prayers and Prefaces, May 23, 1968. *Notitiae* 4 (1968), p. 156.

Consilium, On the Catechesis of the New Eucharistic Prayers, June 2, 1968. *Notitiae* 4 (1968), pp. 148–155.

Consilium, Letter Concerning New Eucharistic Prayers, June 2, 1968. *Notitiae* 4 (1968), pp. 146–148. Tr. in BCL *Newsletter* 4 (1968), pp. 146–147.

Congregation of Rites, *Domus Dei decorem*, On Minor Basilicas, June 6, 1968. *AAS* 60 (1968), pp. 536–539. Tr. in *Canon Law Digest* 7, pp. 28–33.

Paul VI, *Pontificalis Romani*, Apostolic Constitution on the New Rite of Ordination, June 18, 1968. *AAS* 60 (1968), pp. 369–373.

Paul VI, *Pontificalia insignia*, Apostolic Letter on Revision of Pontifical Insignia, June 21, 1968. *AAS* 60 (1968), pp. 374–377. Tr. in *Canon Law Digest* 7, pp. 373–376.

Congregation of Rites, *Pontificales ritus*, On Pontifical Insignia and Rites, June 21, 1968. *AAS* 60 (1968), pp. 406–412. Tr. in *Canon Law Digest* 7, pp. 376–382.

Sacred Penitentiary, *In Constitutione Apostolica*, On New Edition of Treasury of Indulgences, June 29, 1968. *AAS* 60 (1968), pp. 413–414.

Sacred Penitentiary, *Indulgentia est remissio*, On Norms For Granting Indulgences, n.d. *AAS* 60 (1968), pp. 414–419.

Congregation for the Doctrine of the Faith, On Mixed Marriage In A Catholic Church Before A Minister, September 3, 1968. Tr. in *Canon Law Digest* 7, pp. 764–765.

Congregation of Rites, *Ad solemnia*, On Celebrations For the Recently Canonized or Beatified, September 12, 1968. *AAS* 60 (1968), p. 602. Tr. in *Canon Law Digest* 7, pp. 32–33.

PAUL VI, ADDRESS TO THE ITALIAN ASSOCIATION OF ST. CAECILIA, SEPTEMBER 18, 1968. TR. IN HAYBURN, *PAPAL LEGISLATION*, PP. 561–563.

Paul VI, *Facile conicere potestis*, Allocution to the *Consilium* on Control of the Liturgy, October 14, 1968. *AAS* 60 (1968), pp. 732–737. Tr. in *The Pope Speaks* 13 (1968/69), pp. 351–355.

Consilium, On Translations of the New Eucharistic Prayers, November 6, 1968. *Notitiae* 4 (1968), p. 356.

Consilium, Instruction on Translations for Celebrations With the People, January 25, 1969. *Notitiae* 5 (1969), pp. 3–12. Tr. in Megivern, *Worship and Liturgy*, pp. 352–358.

Congregation of Rites, Decree on the Publication of Liturgical Books, January 27, 1969.

Paul VI, *Mysterii paschalis*, Apostolic Letter on General Norms for the Liturgical Year and the New Roman Calendar, February 14, 1969. *AAS* 61 (1969), pp. 222–226. Tr. in *The Pope Speaks* 14 (1969), pp. 181–184.

Congregation of Rites, On New Order of Marriage, March 19, 1969. *Notitiae* 5 (1969), p. 203. Tr. in *Rites*, p. 253.

Congregation of Rites, *Anni liturgici*, Decree on the Revision of the Roman Calendar, March 21, 1969. *Notitiae* 5 (1969), pp. 163–164.

Congregation for Religious, On the Divine Office in the Vernacular, March 21, 1969. *Commentarium pro Religiosi* 51 (1970), pp. 182–183. Tr. in *Canon Law Digest* 7, pp. 546–547.

Secretariat of State, *Ut sive sollicite*, On Dress, Titles and Coats of Arms, March 31, 1969. *AAS* 61 (1969), pp. 334–340. Tr. in *Canon Law Digest* 7, pp. 137–143.

Paul VI, *Missale Romanum*, Apostolic Constitution on the New Roman Missal, April 3, 1969. *AAS* 61 (1969), pp. 217–222. Tr. in *The Pope Speaks* 14 (1969), pp. 165–169.

Congregation of Sacred Rites, General Instruction of the Roman Missal, April 3, 1969.

Congregation of Sacred Rites, On the Promulgation of the New Roman Missal, April 6, 1969. *Notitiae* 5 (1969), p. 147.

Consilium, On the Adaptation of the Liturgy to India, April 25, 1969. *Notitiae* 5 (1969), p. 365–366.

Paul VI, *Nostrum hoc Consistorium,* Address on Further Steps in Church Renewal, April 28, 1969. Tr. in *The Pope Speaks* 14 (1969), pp. 158–164.

BISHOPS' COMMITTEE ON THE LITURGY, "STATEMENT ON COPYRIGHT VIOLATIONS," BCL *NEWSLETTER* 5 (MAY 1969), P. 177.

Paul VI, *Sacra Rituum Congregatio,* Apostolic Constitution on Dividing the Congregation of Sacred Rites into Two Congregations and Integrating *Consilium* into the Congregation for Divine Worship, May 8, 1969. *AAS* 61 (1969), pp. 297–305. Tr. in *The Pope Speaks* 14 (1969), pp. 174–180.

Congregation for Divine Worship, *Actio pastoralis Ecclesiae,* Instruction on Masses for Special Gatherings, May 15, 1969. *AAS* 61 (1969), pp. 806–811. Tr. in *CRUX Special,* July 18, 1969.

Congregation for Divine Worship, *Ordinem Baptismi parvulorum,* Decree On the Order of Baptism of Infants, May 15, 1969. *AAS* 61 (1969), p. 548. Tr. in *Rites,* p. 187.

Congregation for Divine Worship, *Ordinem lectionum Scripturae,* Decree on the Promulgation of the New Mass Lectionary, May 25, 1969. *AAS* 61 (1969), pp. 548–549.

Congregation for Divine Worship, General Introduction to the New Mass Lectionary, May 25, 1969. *Notitiae* 5 (1969), pp. 240–255.

Congregation for Divine Worship, *Memoriale Domini,* Instruction on the Manner of Administering Holy Communion, May 29, 1969. *AAS* 61 (1969), pp. 541–545. Tr. in *CRUX Special,* July 18, 1969.

Congregation for Divine Worship, *En réponse,* Letter on Distributing Holy Communion in the Hand, May 29, 1969. *AAS* 61 (1969), pp. 546–547.

Congregation for Divine Worship, On Lay Persons Distributing Holy Communion, June 25, 1969. Tr. in *Canon Law Digest* 7, pp. 650–651.

Congregation for Divine Worship, *Decreto Sacrae Congregationis,* Decree On Norms for Particular Calendars, June 29, 1969. *Notitiae* 5 (1969), p. 283.

Congregation for Divine Worship, *Petentibus nonnullis,* On the Revised Order of Baptism of Infants, July 10, 1969. *AAS* 61 (1969), pp. 549–550.

Congregation for Divine Worship, Instruction on the New Mass Lectionary, July 25, 1969. *Notitiae* 5 (1969), pp. 238–239.

Congregation for Divine Worship, On the Revised Order for Funerals, August 15, 1969. *Notitiae* 5 (1969), pp. 423–424. Tr. in *Rites,* p. 651.

Congregation for Divine Worship, Statement on the Integrity of

Vernacular Texts, September 15, 1969. *Notitiae* 5 (1969), pp. 333–334.

Paul VI, *Antiquae nobilitatis*, Apostolic Address on the Rosary, October 7, 1969. *AAS* 61 (1969), pp. 137–149. Tr. in *The Pope Speaks* 14 (1969/70), pp. 247–251.

Congregation for Divine Worship, *Constitutione Apostolica*, Instruction on the Gradual Application of *Missale Romanum*, October 20, 1969. *AAS* 61 (1969), pp. 749–753. Tr. in *The Pope Speaks* 14 (1970), pp. 375–379.

Paul VI, *Vogliamo richiamare*, Address on the New Order of Mass, November 19, 1969. *AAS* 61 (1969), pp. 777–780. Tr. in *The Pope Speaks* 14 (1969), pp. 326–332.

Secretariat for Christian Unity, *Dans ces derniers temps*, Declaration On Common Celebration of the Eucharist, January 7, 1970. *AAS* 62 (1970), pp. 184–188. Tr. in *Canon Law Digest* 7, pp. 796–801.

Congregation for Divine Worship, *Professionis ritus*, On A New Order for Religious Profession, February 2, 1970. *AAS* 62 (1970), p. 553. Tr. in *Canon Law Digest* 7, pp. 515–516.

Congregation for Divine Worship, Clarification on Using Only One Vernacular Version, February 6, 1970. *Notitiae* 6 (1970), pp. 84–85.

Congregation for Divine Worship, Letter on Liturgical Book Royalties, February 25, 1970.

Congregation for Divine Worship, On Renewal of Priestly Promises at the Chrism Mass, March 6, 1970. *Notitiae* 6 (1970), pp. 87–89.

Congregation for Divine Worship, *Celebrationis eucharisticae*, On the New Edition of the Roman Missal, March 26, 1970. *AAS* 62 (1970), p. 554. Tr. in *Canon Law Digest* 7, p. 632.

Paul VI, *Matrimonia mixta, Motu proprio* on Mixed Marriages, March 31, 1970. *AAS* 62 (1970), pp. 257–263. Tr. in *The Pope Speaks* 15 (1970), pp. 134–139.

PAUL VI, ADDRESS ON CHOIRS AND LITURGICAL RENEWAL, APRIL 6, 1970. TR. IN *THE POPE SPEAKS* 16 (1970), PP. 27–28.

Paul VI, *Gaudemus sane vos,* Address to the *Consilium* at the Completion of Its Work, April 10, 1970. *AAS* 62 (1970), pp. 272–274.

Congregation for Divine Worship, Statement on Authorship and Copyright, May 15, 1970. *Notitiae* 6 (1970), p. 153.

Vicariate of Rome, Instruction on Forty Hours, May 28, 1970. *Notitiae* 6 (1970), pp. 257–262.

Congregation for Divine Worship, *Consecrationis virginum ritus*, On the New Rite of Consecration for Virgins, May 31, 1970. *AAS* 62 (1970), p. 650.

Congregation for Divine Worship, *Calendaria particularia*, Instruction on

Local Calendars and Mass Propers, June 24, 1970. *AAS* 62 (1970), pp. 651–663.

Congregation for Divine Worship, *Sacramentali Communione*, Instruction on Extension of the Faculty to Distribute Holy Communion Under Both Kinds, June 29, 1970. *AAS* 62 (1970), pp. 664–666. Tr. in *The Pope Speaks* 15 (1970), pp. 245–248.

Congregation for Divine Worship, Norms for Religious Profession, July 15, 1970. *Notitiae* 6 (1970), pp. 114–117. Tr. in *Canon Law Digest* 7, pp. 516–520.

Congregation for Divine Worship, On Vernacular Translation of the New Order for Religious Profession, July 15, 1970. *Notitiae* 6 (1970), pp. 317–318. Tr. in *Canon Law Digest* 7, pp. 521–522.

Congregation for Divine Worship, On Adaptations of the New Order for Religious Profession, July 15, 1970. *Notitiae* 6 (1970), pp. 318–322. Tr. in *Canon Law Digest* 7, pp. 522–526.

Pontifical Commission for Interpreting Decrees of the Council, *Patres Pontificiae Commissionis*, On General Delegation for Parochial Deacon, July 19, 1970. *AAS* 62 (1970), p. 571. Tr. in *Canon Law Digest* 7, p. 752.

Congregation for the Clergy, *Litteris Apostolicis*, Decree On Mass for the People, July 25, 1970. *AAS* 63 (1971), pp. 943–944.

Congregation for Divine Worship, *Liturgicae instaurationes*, Third Instruction on the Correct Implementation of the Constitution on the Sacred Liturgy, September 5, 1970. *AAS* 62 (1970), pp. 692–704. Tr. in *The Pope Speaks* 15 (1971), pp. 402–411.

Congregation for Divine Worship, *Ordine lectionum Missae*, Decree On the New Latin Lectionary, September 30, 1970. *AAS* 63 (1971), p. 710.

Congregation for the Clergy, On Reform of Choir Vesture, October 30, 1970. *Notitiae* 8 (1972), pp. 36–37. Tr. in *Canon Law Digest* 7, pp. 382–383.

Paul VI, *Laudis canticum*, Apostolic Constitution Promulgating the New Liturgy of the Hours, November 1, 1970. *AAS* 63 (1971), pp. 527–535. Tr. in *The Pope Speaks* 16 (1971), pp. 129–135.

Congregation for Divine Worship, *Abbatem et Abbatissam*, Decree On the Order of Blessing An Abbot and Abbess, November 9, 1970. *AAS* 63 (1971), pp. 710–711.

Congregation for Divine Worship, *Ritibus Hebdomodae sanctae*, Decree On Blessing of Oils and Consecration of Chrism, December 3, 1970. *AAS* 63 (1971), p. 711. Tr. in *Rites*, p. 517.

Secretariat for Christian Unity, On Non-Catholic Christian Sponsors, December 3, 1970. *Notitiae* 7 (1971), pp. 92–93. Tr. in *Canon Law Digest* 7, pp. 597–599.

Congregation for Divine Worship, General Instruction on the Liturgy of the Hours, February 2, 1971.

Congregation for Divine Worship, *Horarum Liturgia*, Decree On the Publication of the Liturgy of the Hours, April 11, 1971. *AAS* 63 (1971), p. 712.

Congregation for the Clergy, *Opera artis*, Letter on the Historico-Artistic Patrimony of the Church, April 11, 1971. *AAS* 63 (1971), pp. 315–317.

Congregation for Divine Worship, *Instructione de Constitutione*, Notification About the Roman Missal, Liturgy of the Hours, and Calendar, June 14, 1971. *AAS* 63 (1971), pp. 712–715. Tr. in *Canon Law Digest* 7, pp. 54–57.

Paul VI, *Divinae consortium naturae*, Apostolic Constitution on the Rite of Confirmation, August 15, 1971. *AAS* 63 (1971), pp. 657–664. Tr. in *The Pope Speaks* 16 (1971), pp. 223–228.

Congregation for Divine Worship, *Peculiare Spiritus Sancti*, Decree on the New Order for Confirmation, August 22, 1971. *AAS* 64 (1972), p. 77. Tr. in *Rites*, p. 289.

Congregation for Divine Worship, Statement on *ad interim* Texts, November 11, 1971. *Notitiae* 7 (1971), pp. 379–383.

Paul VI, *Ultimis temporibus*, Declaration on the Ministerial Priesthood, November 30, 1971. *AAS* 63 (1971), pp. 898–922. Tr. in *The Pope Speaks* 16 (1971), pp. 359–376.

Congregation for Divine Worship, *Ordinis Baptismi adultorum*, Decree On the Order for Christian Initiation of Adults, January 6, 1972. *AAS* 64 (1972), p. 252. Tr. in *Rites*, p. 19.

Congregation for Divine Worship, Norms for Thursday, Friday, and Saturday of Holy Week and Easter Octave, March 3, 1972. *Notitiae* 8 (1972), pp. 96–99.

Congregation for the Doctrine of the Faith, On Fragments of the Host, May 2, 1972. *Notitiae* 8 (1972), p. 227. Tr. in *Canon Law Digest* 7, p. 635.

Secretariat for Promoting Christian Unity, *In quibus rerum circumstantis*, Instruction Concerning Cases When Other Christians May Be Admitted to Eucharistic Communion in the Catholic Church, June 1, 1972. *AAS* 64 (1972), pp. 518–525. Tr. in *Canon Law Digest* 7, pp. 583–590.

Pontifical Commission for Interpreting Decrees of the Council, *Patres Pontificiae Commissionis*, Response On the Imposition of Hands in Confirmation, June 9, 1972. *AAS* 64 (1972), p. 526. Tr. in *Canon Law Digest* 7, p. 611.

BISHOPS' COMMITTEE ON THE LITURGY, *MUSIC IN CATHOLIC WORSHIP*, 1972. UNITED STATES CATHOLIC CONFERENCE, WASHINGTON, DC.

Congregation for the Doctrine of the Faith, *Sacramentum paenitentiae,* Pastoral Norms Concerning General Sacramental Absolution, June 16, 1972. *AAS* 64 (1972), pp. 510–514. Tr. in *The Pope Speaks* 17 (1972), pp. 280–284.

   Congregation for the Doctrine of the Faith, On An Optional Patristic Lectionary, July 9, 1972. Tr. in *Canon Law Digest* 7, pp. 108–109.

Congregation for Divine Worship, *In celebratione Missae,* Declaration on Concelebration, August 7, 1972. *AAS* 64 (1972), pp. 561–563. Tr. in BCL *Newsletter* 9 (1973), pp. 363–364.

Paul VI, *Ministeria quaedam, Motu proprio* on the Diaconate, August 15, 1972. *AAS* 64 (1972), pp. 529–534. Tr. in *The Pope Speaks* 17 (1972), pp. 257–261.

Paul VI, *Ad pascendum, Motu proprio* on Reform of First Tonsure, Minor Orders and Subdiaconate, August 15, 1972. *AAS* 64 (1972), pp. 534–540. Tr. in *The Pope Speaks* 17 (1972), pp. 234–240.

PAUL VI, ADDRESS TO THE ITALIAN ASSOCIATION OF ST. CAECILIA, SEPTEMBER 24, 1972. TR. IN *THE POPE SPEAKS* 18 (1972), PP. 212–215.

   Congregation for Divine Worship, On An Optional Patristic Lectionary, October, 1972. *Notitiae* 8 (1972), pp. 249–250.

   Congregation for Divine Worship, *Cum de nomine Episcopi,* On Naming the Bishop in the Eucharistic Prayer, October 9, 1972. *AAS* 64 (1972), pp. 692–694. Tr. in *Canon Law Digest* 7, pp. 59–60.

Paul VI, *Sacram Unctionem infirmorum,* Apostolic Constitution on the Rite of Anointing and Pastoral Care of the Sick, November 30, 1972. *AAS* 65 (1973), pp. 5–9. Tr. in *The Pope Speaks* 17 (1973), pp. 378–381.

Congregation for Divine Worship, *Ministeriorum disciplina,* Decree On Rites for Lector and Acolyte, and Admission to Diaconate and Priesthood, December 3, 1972. *AAS* 65 (1973), pp. 274–275. Tr. in *Rites,* p. 725.

Congregation for Divine Worship, *Infirmis cum Ecclesia,* Decree on Anointing and Pastoral Care of the Sick, December 7, 1972. *AAS* 65 (1973), pp. 275–276. Tr. in *Rites,* p. 577.

   Congregation for Divine Worship, On Changes in the General Instruction for the Roman Missal, December 23, 1972. *Notitiae* 9 (1973), pp. 34–38.

Congregation for the Discipline of the Sacraments, *Immense caritatis,* Instruction on Facilitating Sacramental Communion in Particular Circumstances, January 29, 1973. *AAS* 65 (1973), pp. 264–271. Tr. in *The Pope Speaks* 18 (1973), pp. 45–51.

   Congregation for Divine Worship, On New Vestment for Mass, March 15, 1973. *Notitiae* 8 (1973), pp. 96–98.

   Congregation for Divine Worship, *Patronus, liturgica,* On Norms for Patron Saints and Images of Mary, March 19, 1973. *AAS* 65 (1973), pp. 276–279. Tr. in *Canon Law Digest* 8, pp. 912–916.

Congregation for the Doctrine of the Faith, *Sacra Congregatio*, Declaration On the Sacrament of Penance, March 23, 1973. *AAS* 65 (1973), p. 678. Tr. in *Canon Law Digest* 8, p. 1214.

Congregation for Divine Worship, *Pluries decursu temporis*, On Coronation of An Image of Mary, March 25, 1973. *AAS* 65 (1973), pp. 280–281. Tr. in *Canon Law Digest* 8, pp. 908–909.

Congregation for Divine Worship, *Eucharistiae participationem*, Letter to the Presidents of Episcopal Conferences Concerning Eucharistic Prayers, April 27, 1973. *AAS* 65 (1973), pp. 340–347. Tr. in *The Pope Speaks* 18 (1973), pp. 132–139.

Congregation for the Discipline of the Sacraments, *Sanctus Pontifex*, Declaration on the Sacrament of Penance Before First Communion, May 24, 1973. *AAS* 65 (1973), p. 410. Tr. in *Canon Law Digest* 8, pp. 563–564.

PAUL VI, ADDRESS TO THE *CONSOCIATIO INTERNATIONALIS MUSICAE SACRAE*, JUNE 12, 1973. TR. IN HAYBURN, *PAPAL LEGISLATION*, PP. 567–568.

Congregation for the Clergy, On Ending the Experimentation Concerning First Communion and First Confession, June 20, 1973. Tr. in *Canon Law Digest* 8, pp. 565–570.

Congregation for Divine Worship, *Eucharistiae sacramentum*, Decree On Holy Communion and Worship of the Eucharist Outside of Mass, June 21, 1973. *AAS* 65 (1973), p. 610. Tr. in *Rites*, pp. 453–454.

Paul VI, Address on Prayer, August 22, 1973. Tr. in *The Pope Speaks* 18 (1973), pp. 207–210.

Congregation for Divine Worship, On A New Edition for the Baptism of Infants, August 29, 1973. *Notitiae* 9 (1973), pp. 268–272.

CARDINAL VILLOT, TO THE NATIONAL CONGRESS ON SACRED MUSIC IN GENOA, SEPTEMBER 26, 1973. TR. IN HAYBURN, *PAPAL LEGISLATION*, PP. 568–569.

Secretariat for Christian Unity, *Nota su alcune*, Declaration on Intercommunion, October 17, 1973. *AAS* 65 (1973), pp. 616–619.

Congregation for Divine Worship, *Dum toto terrarum*, Letter on Norms for Translating Liturgical Books, October 25, 1973. *AAS* 66 (1974), pp. 98–99. Tr. in *Canon Law Digest* 8, pp. 67–69.

Congregation for Divine Worship, *Pueros baptizatos*, Directory for Masses With Children, November 1, 1973. *AAS* 66 (1974), pp. 30–46. Tr. in *The Pope Speaks* 18 (1974), pp. 317–331.

Congregation for the Clergy, Letter on Preaching By Lay Persons, November 20, 1973. Tr. in *Canon Law Digest* 8, pp. 941–944.

Congregation for Divine Worship, *Reconciliationem inter Deum*, Decree On the Rite of Penance, December 2, 1973. *AAS* 66 (1974), pp. 172–173. Tr. in *Rites*, pp. 339–340.

Congregation for the Doctrine of the Faith, *Instauratio liturgica*, Declaration on Sacramental Forms and Their Approbation, January 25, 1974. *AAS* 66 (1974), p. 661. Tr. in *Canon Law Digest* 8, pp. 72–73.

BISHOPS' COMMITTEE ON THE LITURGY, "MINISTERS OF CHURCH MUSIC AND CATECHISTS," BCL *NEWSLETTER* 10 (FEBRUARY 1974), PP. 411–412.

Paul VI, *Marialtus cultus*, Apostolic Exhortation on Devotion to Mary, February 11, 1974. *Notitiae* 10 (1974), pp. 153–157.

Bishops' Committee On the Liturgy, "Ten Years of Liturgical Renewal," BCL *Newsletter* 10 (March 1974), pp. 411–412.

Paul VI, Address on the New Order of Penance, April 3, 1974. *Notitiae* 10 (1974), pp. 225–227.

Paul VI, *Firma in Traditione*, Apostolic Letter on Faculties Concerning Mass Stipends, June 13, 1974. *AAS* 66 (1974), pp. 308–311. Tr. in *Canon Law Digest* 8, pp. 530–533.

Bishops' Committee On the Liturgy, *Ministries in the Church*, 1974.

Congregation for Divine Worship, *Conferentiarum episcopalium*, On Preparation of Liturgical Books, October 28, 1974. Tr. In Flannery, *Vatican Council II*, pp. 281–282.

Congregation for Divine Worship, On Eucharistic Prayers for Masses With Children and for Masses of Reconciliation, November 1, 1974. *Notitiae* 11 (1975), pp. 4–6. Tr. in BCL *Newsletter* 11 (1975), pp. 453–456.

Commission for the Interpretation of the Decrees of the Second Vatican Council, On Faculties of Deacons Relative to Sacramentals and Blessings, November 13, 1974. *AAS* 66 (1974), p. 667. Tr. in *Canon Law Digest* 8, p. 849.

Commission for Jewish-Catholic Dialogue, On Christian and Jewish Liturgies, December 1, 1974. *AAS* 67 (1975) pp. 73–79. Tr. in *The Pope Speaks* 19 (1974), pp. 352–357.

Paul VI, Letter to Solesmes on the Centenary of the Death of Dom Guéranger, January 20, 1975. *Notitiae* 11 (1975), pp. 170–172.

Congregation for the Doctrine of the Faith, *Ecclesiae pastorum*, Decree on New Norms for Publication of Liturgical Books, March 19, 1975. *AAS* 67 (1975), pp. 281–284. Tr. in *Canon Law Digest* 8, pp. 991–996.

Paul VI, Homily on the Eucharist and the Ministerial Priesthood, March 27, 1975. Tr. in *The Pope Speaks* 20 (1975), pp. 62–65.

Pontifical Commission for Interpretation of Decrees of the Council, On the Minister of Confirmation, April 25, 1975. *AAS* 67 (1975), p. 348.

Congregation for Divine Worship, On the English Formula for Confirmation, May 5, 1975. *Notitiae* 11 (1975), p. 172. Tr. in *Canon Law Digest* 8, pp. 474–475.

Congregation for the Sacraments, On the Delegation of the Minister of Confirmation, May 9, 1975. Tr. in *Canon Law Digest* 8, pp. 475–478.

Paul VI, *Constans Nobis studium*, Apostolic Constitution on the Suppression of the Congregation for the Discipline of the Sacraments and the Congregation for Divine Worship and the Formation of the New Congregation for the Sacraments and Divine Worship, July 11, 1975. *AAS* 67 (1975), pp. 417–420. Tr. in *Canon Law Digest* 8, pp. 224–227.

Congregation for the Sacraments and Divine Worship, Essay on Dance in the Liturgy, *Notitiae* 11 (1975), pp. 202–205. Tr. in *Canon Law Digest* 8, pp. 78–82 and BCL *Newsletter* 18 (April/May 1982), pp. 14–16.

Paul VI, *Ex quo die*, Address to the Consistory on Fidelity to the Council, May 24, 1976. *AAS* 68 (1976), pp. 369–382. Tr. in *The Pope Speaks* 21 (1976), pp. 204–212.

Congregation for Divine Worship, Letter on Vernacular in the Liturgy, June 5, 1976. *Notitiae* 12 (1976), pp. 300–302. Tr. in BCL *Newsletter* 13 (1977), pp. 49–50.

Congregation for the Doctrine of the Faith, *Accidit in diversis*, Decree On Celebration of Public Masses for Deceased Non-Catholics, June 11, 1976. *AAS* 68 (1976), pp. 621–622. Tr. in *Canon Law Digest* 8, pp. 864–866.

Paul VI, *Venerabilis Frater Noster*, Letter to Cardinal Knox On the Eucharist and the Hungers of the Human Family, July 7, 1976. *AAS* 68 (1976), pp. 454–456. Tr. in *The Pope Speaks* 21 (1976), pp. 269–271.

CARDINAL VILLOT, TO THE TWENTY-SECOND CONGRESS OF THE ITALIAN ASSOCIATION OF ST. CAECELIA, SEPTEMBER 22, 1976. TR. IN *THE POPE SPEAKS* 23 (1976), PP. 4–8.

Paul VI, Letter to Archbishop Lefebvre, October 11, 1976. *Origins* 6 (1976/77), pp. 416–420.

Congregation for the Doctrine of the Faith, *Inter insigniores aetatis*, Declaration On the Admission of Women to the Priesthood, October 15, 1976. *AAS* 69 (1977), pp. 98–116. Tr. in *The Pope Speaks* 22 (1977), pp. 108–122.

Congregation for the Sacraments and Divine Worship and the Congregation for the Clergy, Letter on Confession and First Communion, March 31, 1977. Tr. in *The Pope Speaks* 22 (1977), pp. 200–203.

Paul VI, Six Addresses on the Paschal Mystery, April 13–May 18,

1977. Tr. in *The Pope Speaks* 22 (1977), pp. 204–216.

Paul VI, Address on the Dimensions of Communion, April 18, 1977. Tr. in *The Pope Speaks* 22 (1977), pp. 235–240.

Congregation for the Sacraments and Divine Worship, On the New Order of Dedication of A Church and Altar, May 29, 1977. *Notitiae* 13 (1977), pp. 364–390.

PAUL VI, *A VOI*, HOMILY AT MASS WITH MEMBERS OF ITALIAN ASSOCIATION OF ST. CAECELIA, SEPTEMBER 25, 1977. *AAS* 69 (1977), PP. 647–649. TR. IN HAYBURN, *PAPAL LEGISLATION*, PP. 577–578.

Secretariat of State, Letter on the Influence of the Liturgical Movement on the Life of the Church in Latin America, July 21, 1977. Tr. in *The Pope Speaks* 22 (1977), pp. 320–328.

Secretariat of State, Letter to National Italian Liturgical Week (August 29–September 2, 1977) on Mass and the Lord's Day. Tr. in *The Pope Speaks* 22 (1977), pp. 369–372.

Congregation for the Sacraments and Divine Worship, *Celebratio Baptismatis Domini*, Decree on the Transfer of the Feast of the Baptism of the Lord, October 7, 1977. *AAS* 69 (1977), p. 682. Tr. in *Canon Law Digest* 8, pp. 93–94.

Congregation for the Sacraments and Divine Worship, Norms for Revised Local Calendars, December, 1977. *Notitiae* 13 (1977), pp. 557–558.

Congregation for the Doctrine of the Faith, On General Absolution, January 20, 1978. *Notitiae* 14 (1978), pp. 6–7.

Paul VI, *Inter eximia episcopalis*, Apostolic Letter on Concession of the Pallium, May 11, 1978. *AAS* 70 (1978), pp. 441–442.

Paul VI, *We Welcome You*, Address to American Bishops on the Eucharist and the Church's Life, June 15, 1978. *AAS* 70 (1978), pp. 419–423. Also in *The Pope Speaks* 23 (1978), pp. 215–219.

National Conference of Catholic Bishops, *Environment and Art in Catholic Worship*, 1978. United States Catholic Conference, Wash., DC.

National Conference of Catholic Bishops, Pastoral Statement of the U.S. Catholic Bishops On Handicapped People, 1978. USCC, Wash., DC.

John Paul II, *Scripturarum thesaurus*, Apostolic Constitution Promulgating the New Typical Vulgate Edition of the Bible, April 25, 1979. *AAS* 71 (1979), pp. 557–559.

Congregation for Catholic Education, *La Sacra Congregazione*, Instruction on Liturgical Education and Formation of Seminaries, June 3, 1979. *Notitiae* 15 (1979), pp. 526–565. Tr. in *The Pope Speaks* 25 (1980), pp. 321–341.

John Paul II, *A vou la paix*, Homily on Eucharistic Unity, November

29, 1979. Tr. in *The Pope Speaks* 25 (1980), pp. 16–20.

John Paul II, *Dominicae Cenae*, Apostolic Letter on the Mystery and Worship of the Eucharist, February 24, 1980. *AAS* 72 (1980), pp. 113–148. Tr. in *Origins* 9 (March 7, 1980), pp. 653–666.

Congregation for the Sacraments and Divine Worship, *Inaestimabile donum*, Instruction Concerning Abuses in Worship, April 3, 1980. *AAS* 72 (1980), pp. 331–343. Tr. in *The Pope Speaks* 25 (1980), pp. 197–206.

National Conference of Catholic Bishops, "Called and Gifted: Catholic Laity 1980," Pastoral Reflections On the Laity, November 1980. In *Origins* 10 (November 27, 1980), pp. 370–373.

BISHOPS' COMMITTEE ON THE LITURGY, "LETTER TO COMPOSERS OF LITURGICAL MUSIC," BCL *NEWSLETTER* 16 (DECEMBER 1980), PP. 237–239.

JOHN PAUL II, HOMILY ON SACRED MUSIC, SEPTEMBER, 1980. TR. IN *SACRED MUSIC* 108 (WINTER 1981), PP. 7–8.

Congregation for the Doctrine of the Faith, *Pastoralis actio*, Instruction on Infant Baptism, October 20, 1980. *AAS* 72 (1980), pp. 1137–1156. Tr. in *The Pope Speaks* 26 (1981), pp. 6–19.

JOHN PAUL II, ADDRESS AT THE BLESSING OF A MOBILE PIPE ORGAN IN ST. PETER'S, APRIL 11, 1981. TR. IN *SACRED MUSIC* 108 (WINTER 1981), PP. 8–9.

JOHN PAUL VI, ADDRESS ON THE SISTINE CHOIR, APRIL 18, 1981. TR. IN *SACRED MUSIC* 108 (WINTER 1981), pp. 9–10.

John Paul II, *Nel rivolgerri*, Address on the Artist As Mediator Between the Gospel and Life, April 27, 1981. Tr. in *The Pope Speaks* 26 (1981), pp. 223–226.

BISHOPS' COMMITTEE ON THE LITURGY, "NEW DIRECTIONS FOR LITURGICAL MUSIC," BCL *NEWSLETTER* 17 (MAY–JUNE 1981), PP. 20–21.

Holy Office, Letter Approving NCCB Proposal to Delete "men" From the Institution Narrative, November 17, 1981 (Prot. N. 2016/81/6.) BCL *Newsletter* 17 (December 1981), p. 45.

National Conference of Catholic Bishops, A Pastoral Letter on Health and Healing, November, 1981. In *Origins* 11, No. 25 (December 3, 1981), pp. 396–402.

NATIONAL CONFERENCE OF CATHOLIC BISHOPS, *LITURGICAL MUSIC TODAY*, 1982. UNITED STATES CATHOLIC CONFERENCE, WASHINGTON, DC.

Related Legislation

John XXIII, Address to the College of Cardinals on the Day of His Election, October 28, 1958. Tr. in *The Encyclicals and Other Messages of*

John XXIII, pp. 9–10.

John XXIII, *Questa festiva*, Address to the Roman Cardinals Announcing An Ecumenical Council, January 25, 1959. *AAS* 51 (1959), pp. 65–69. Tr. in *The Pope Speaks* 5 (1959), pp. 398–401.

John XXIII, *Ad Petri Cathedram*, Encyclical Letter on the Advance of Truth, Unity and Peace, June 29, 1959. *AAS* 51 (1959), pp. 497–531. Tr. in *The Pope Speaks* 5 (1959), pp. 359–383.

John XXIII, *Princeps Pastorum*, Encyclical Letter on the Catholic Missions, November 28, 1959. *AAS* 51 (1959), pp. 833–864. Tr. in *The Pope Speaks* 6 (1960), pp. 123–145.

John XXIII, *La Nostra prima*, Address on the Ecumenical Council, June 5, 1960. *AAS* 52 (1960), pp. 517–526. Tr. in *The Pope Speaks* 6 (1960), pp. 231–239.

John XXIII, *Superno Dei nutu*, Motu proprio on Establishing the Preparatory Commissions, June 5, 1960. *AAS* 52 (1960), pp. 433–437. Tr. in *The Pope Speaks* 6 (1960), pp. 240–243.

John XXIII, *Ad aprire questo*, Address to the Preparatory Commissions, November 14, 1960. Tr. in *The Pope Speaks* 6 (1960), pp. 376–385.

John XXIII, *Mater et Magistra*, Encyclical Letter on Christianity and Social Progress, May 15, 1961. *AAS* 53 (1961), pp. 401–464. Tr. in *The Pope Speaks* 7 (1961/62), pp. 295–343.

John XXIII, *Congregatos Vos*, Address to the Central Preparatory Commission, June 12, 1961. *AAS* 53 (1961), pp. 495–499. Tr. in *The Pope Speaks* 7 (1961), pp. 241–245.

John XXIII, *Progredientes leniter dies*, Address to the Central Preparatory Commission, June 20, 1961. *AAS* 53 (1961), pp. 499–503. Tr. in *The Pope Speaks* 7 (1961), pp. 246–250.

John XXIII, *Humanae salutis*, Apostolic Constitution Proclaiming the Second Ecumenical Council of the Vatican, December 25, 1961. *AAS* 54 (1962), pp. 5–13. Tr. in *The Pope Speaks* 7 (1961), pp. 353–361.

John XXIII, *Sacrae laudis*, Apostolic Exhortation on the Divine Office for the Council, January 6, 1962. Tr. in *The Pope Speaks* 8 (1962), pp. 63–69.

John XXIII, *Iam octo mensium*, Address on Preparing for the Council, January 23, 1962. *AAS* 54 (1962), pp. 97–101. Tr. in *The Pope Speaks* 8 (1962), pp. 70–74.

John XXIII, *Septimo hoc conventu*, Address At the Conclusion of the Preparatory Stage of the Ecumenical Council, June 20, 1962. *AAS* 54 (1962), pp. 461–466. Tr. in *The Pope Speaks* 8 (1962), pp. 182–187.

John XXIII, *Paenitentiam Agere*, Encyclical on Penance for the Success of the Council, July 1, 1962. *AAS* 54 (1962), pp. 481–491. Tr. in *Encyclicals and Other Messages of John XXIII*, pp. 397–408.

John XXIII, *Appropinquante Concilio*, Motu proprio Establishing Regulations for the Council, August 6, 1962. *AAS* 54 (1962), pp. 609–611. Tr. in *The Pope Speaks* 8 (1963), pp. 282–288.

John XXIII, *Gaudet Mater Ecclesia,* Address At the Opening of the Council, October 11, 1962. *AAS* 54 (1962), pp. 786–796. Tr. in *The Pope Speaks* 8 (1962), pp. 207–216.

John XXIII, *Notre rencontre,* Address to the Observer Delegates, October 13, 1962. *AAS* 54 (1962), pp. 814–816. Tr. in *Encyclicals and Other Messages of John XXIII,* pp. 436–438.

John XXIII, *Prima Sessio,* Address At the Close of the Council's First Session, December 8, 1962. *AAS* 55 (1963), pp. 35–41. Tr. in *Encyclicals and Other Messages of John XXIII,* pp. 439–446.

John XXIII, *Mirabilis ille,* Letter to Each of the Council Fathers On Thoughts for the Council's Recess, January 6, 1963. *AAS* 55 (1963), pp. 149–159. Tr. in *Encyclicals and Other Messages of John XXIII,* pp. 447–458.

John XXIII, *Pacem in Terris,* Encyclical Letter on Peace on Earth, April 11, 1963. *AAS* 55 (1963), pp. 257–304. Tr. in *The Pope Speaks* 9 (1961), pp. 13–48.

Paul VI, *Salvete, Fratres,* Address At the Opening of the Second Session of the Council, September 29, 1963. *AAS* 55 (1963), pp. 841–859. Tr. in *The Pope Speaks* 9 (1964), pp. 125–141.

Paul VI, *Pastorale munus, Motu proprio* on Faculties of Local Ordinaries, November 30, 1963. *AAS* 56 (1964), pp. 5–12. Tr. in *Canon Law Digest* 6, pp. 370–378.

Paul VI, *Tempus iam advenit,* Address on the Progress of the Council, December 4, 1963. *AAS* 56 (1964), pp. 31–40. Tr. in *The Pope Speaks* 9 (1964), pp. 221–229.

Pontifical Biblical Commission, *Sancta Mater Ecclesia,* Instruction on the Historical Truth of the Gospels, April 21, 1964. *AAS* 56 (1964), pp. 712–718. Tr. in *Canon Law Digest* 6, pp. 789–797.

Paul VI, *Ecclesiam Suam,* Encyclical Letter on the Church, August 6, 1964. *AAS* 56 (1964), pp. 609–659. Tr. in *The Pope Speaks* 10 (1965), pp. 253–292.

Secretariat of State, *Cum admotae,* Rescript On Faculties of Religious Superiors of Clerical Exempt Institutes, November 6, 1964. *AAS* 59 (1967), pp. 374–378.

Paul VI, *Ecclesiae sanctae, Motu proprio* on Norms Implementing Four Decrees of Vatican II, August 6, 1966. *AAS* 58 (1966), pp. 757–787. Tr. in *The Pope Speaks* 11 (1966), pp. 376–400.

Paul VI, *Libentissimo sane animo,* Address on Theology As Bridge Between Faith and Authority, October 1, 1966. *AAS* 58 (1966), pp. 889–896. Tr. in *The Pope Speaks* 11 (1966), pp. 348–354.

Secretariat for Christian Unity, *Ad totam Ecclesiam,* An Ecumenical

Directory—Part One, May 14, 1967. *AAS* 59 (1967), pp. 574–592. Tr. in *The Pope Speaks* 12 (1967), pp. 250–263.

Paul VI, *Ancora una volta*, Address on Post-Conciliar Activities, June 24, 1967. *AAS* 59 (1967), pp. 786–794. Tr. in *The Pope Speaks* 12 (1967), pp. 203–210.

Paul VI, *Regimini Ecclesiae Universae*, Apostolic Constitution on Re-organizing the Roman Curia, August 15, 1967. *AAS* 59 (1967), pp. 885–928. Tr. in *The Pope Speaks* 13 (1968/69), pp. 393–420.

Paul VI and Patriarch Athenagoras I, Statement, October 28, 1967. *AAS* 59 (1967), pp. 1054–1055.

Congregation for Bishops, *Peregrinans in terra*, General Directory for Ministry to Tourists, April 30, 1969. *AAS* 61 (1969), pp. 361–384. Tr. in *The Pope Speaks* 14 (1969), pp. 380–397.

Congregation for Bishops, *Nemo est*, Instruction on Pastoral Care of Migrants, August 22, 1969. *AAS* 61 (1969), pp. 614–643.

Congregation for the Clergy, *Inter ea*, Circular Letter on the Education and Formation of the Clergy, November 4, 1969. *AAS* 62 (1970), pp. 123–134. Tr. in *The Pope Speaks* 15 (1970), pp. 75–83.

Paul VI, *Apostolicae caritatis*, Apostolic Letter, On Pontifical Commission for Migrants and Travelers, March 19, 1970. *AAS* 62 (1970), pp. 193–197.

Secretariat for Christian Unity, *Spiritus Domini*, Ecumenical Directory—Part Two, April 16, 1970. *AAS* 62 (1970), pp. 705–724. Tr. by NCCB.

Paul VI and Patriarch Vaskin I, Statement, May 12, 1970. *AAS* 62 (1970), pp. 416–417. Tr. in *The Pope Speaks* 15 (1970), pp. 155–156.

Congregation for the Clergy, *Ad normam Decreti*, General Catechetical Directory, April 11, 1971. *AAS* 64 (1972), pp. 97–176.

Paul VI, Address on the Importance of Belonging to the "People of God," September 1, 1971. Tr. in *Teachings of Pope Paul VI: 1971*, pp. 134–138.

Paul VI and Patriarch Mar Ignatius Jacobus III, Statement, October 27, 1971. *AAS* 63 (1971), pp. 814–815.

Paul VI, Address on the Church's Future Path, June 22, 1973. Tr. in *The Pope Speaks* 18 (1973), pp. 93–102.

Secretariat for Christian Unity, On Ecumenical Collaboration, February 22, 1975. Tr. in *Canon Law Digest* 8, pp. 870–872.

Paul VI, Four Addresses on Prayer, June 2–23, 1976. Tr. in *The Pope Speaks* 21 (1976), pp. 272–280.

Paul VI, Address At the Secret Consistory on the Sign of Unity, June 27, 1977. Tr. in *The Pope Speaks* 22 (1977), pp. 273–280.

John Paul II, *Redemptor hominis*, Encyclical Letter on the Redeemer of Man, March 4, 1979. *AAS* 71 (1979), pp. 257–324. Tr. in *Origins* 8 (1979), pp. 625–644.

John Paul II, *Dives et misericordia*, Encyclical on the Mercy of God,

November 30, 1980. *AAS* 72 (1980), pp. 1177–1232. Tr. in *The Pope Speaks* 26 (1981), pp. 20–58.

Secondary Sources

Music

Books

Apel, Willi. *Gregorian Chant*. Bloomington: Indiana Univ. Press, 1958.

Augustine. *De Musica*. Tr. by Robert Catesby Taliaferro. In *The Fathers of the Church*. Vol. 4. New York: Cima, 1947.

Backman, E. Louis. *Religious Dances in the Christian Church and in Popular Medicine*. Tr. by E. Classen, London: George Allen, 1952.

Baumen William A. *The Ministry of Music*. A Guide For the Practicing Church Musician. Second Edition. Ed. by Thomas Fuller and Elaine Rendler. Washington, DC: Liturgical Conference, 1979.

Bowra, C.M. *Primitive Song*. New York: Mentor, 1962.

Brehm, Leon Gerard. *The Liturgical Aim of the "Motu Proprio" in the Music of the Mass*. Thesis. Boston University, 1940.

Chambers, G.B. *Folksong-Plainsong: A Study in Origins and Musical Relationships*. London: Merlin Press, 1956.

Davies, John Booth. *The Psychology of Music*. Stanford, CA: Stanford University Press, 1978.

Davison, Archibald T. *Church Music*. Illusion and Reality. Cambridge: Harvard University Press, 1952.

Deiss, Lucien. *Spirit and Song of the New Liturgy*. Cincinnati: World Library Publications, 1976.

Earley, Frances. *The Musical Mass of the Roman Catholic Church Before, During and Since the Time of Palestrina: His Influence On Same*. Thesis. Wayne University, 1940.

Fellerer, Karl Gustav. *The History of Catholic Church Music*. Tr. by Francis A. Brunner. Baltimore: Helicon, 1961.

Funk, Virgil C., ed. *Music In Catholic Worship*. The NPM Commentary. Washington, DC: National Association of Pastoral Musicians, 1982.

Funk, Virgil C. and Huck, Gabe, ed. *Pastoral Music in Practice*. Washington, DC: National Association of Pastoral Musicians, 1981.

Gelineau, Joseph. *Voices and Instruments in Christian Worship*. Tr. by Clifford Howell. Collegeville: The Liturgical Press, 1964.

Green, Sidney and Ogilvie, Gordon. *Music For the Parish*. Grove Booklet on Ministry and Worship 26. Bramcote: Grove Books, 1974.

Grout, Donald Jay. *A History of Western Music*. New York: W.W. Norton, 1960.

Hannum, Harold B. *Music and Worship*. Nashville: Southern Publishing Association, 1969.

Hartley, Kenneth R. *Bibliography of Theses and Dissertations in Sacred Music*. Detroit: Information Coordinators, Inc., 1966.

Hayburn, Robert F. *Papal Legislation on Sacred Music*. 95 A.D. to 1977 A.D. Collegeville: The Liturgical Press, 1979.

————. *Pope Saint Pius X and the Vatican Edition of the Chant Books*. Dissertation. University of California, 1964.

Huijbers, Bernard. *The Performing Audience*. Six and a Half Essays on Music and Song in Liturgy. Tr. by Ray Noll *et al*. Phoenix: North American Liturgy Resources, 1980.

Hume, Paul. *Catholic Church Music*. New York: Dodd, Mead and Company, 1960.

Johnson, Lawrence J. *The Mystery of Faith: The Ministries of Music*. Washington, DC: National Association of Pastoral Musicians, 1983.

Kroll, Josef. *Die Christliche Hymnodik*. Bis Zu Klemens von Alexandreia. Darmstadt: Wissenschaftliche Buchgesellschaft, 1968.

Leaver, Robin. *The Liturgy and Music*. A Study of the Use of the Hymn in Two Liturgical Traditions. Grove Liturgical Study 6. Bramcote: Grove Books, 1976.

Liturgical Conference, ed. *A Manual For Church Musicians*. Washington, DC: The Liturgical Conference, 1964.

Liturgical Conference and The Church Music Association of America, ed. *Harmony and Discord*. An Open Forum. Washington, DC: The Liturgical Conference, 1966.

McDonald, Alex. *A Study of Contemporary Musical Settings of the Roman Catholic Mass In Light of Their Conformity With the Motu Proprio of Pius X and Subsequent Papal Pronouncements Concerning Sacred Music*. Thesis. Wayne State University, 1958.

McKinnon, James William. *The Church Fathers and Musical Instruments*. Dissertation. Columbia University, 1965.

Majeske, Edward J. *Church Music in Canon Law*. Thesis. Wayne University, 1945.

Marietta, Sister. *Singing the Liturgy*. Milwaukee: Bruce, 1956.

Maryosip, Michael, ed. *The Oldest Christian Hymn-Book, A.D. 100*. (Odes of Solomon). Temple, Texas: Gresham's, 1948.

Matonti, Charles J. *Discovering Principles for the Composition and Use of Contemporary Liturgical Music Through the Study of Selected Requiem Masses*. Dissertation. Columbia University Teacher's College, 1972.

Mead, G.R.S. *The Hymn of Jesus*. London: John M. Watkins, 1963.

Merriam, Alan P. *The Anthropology of Music*. Northwestern University Press, 1964.

Meyer, Leonard B. *Emotion and Meaning in Music*. Chicago: University Press, 1956.

_____. *Music, The Arts, and Ideas*. Patterns and Predictions in Twentieth-Century Culture. Chicago: University Press, 1967.

Middlecamp, Ralph. *Introduction to Catholic Music Ministry*. Glendale, Arizona: Pastoral Arts Associates, 1978.

Murray, Joseph Bernard. *The Influence of Plainchant and Polyphony On the Music of the Roman Catholic Church*. Thesis. Boston University, 1937.

Nemmers, Erwin Esser. *Twenty Centuries of Catholic Church Music*. Milwaukee: Bruce, 1949.

Nettl, Paul. *Luther and Music*. Tr. by Frida Best and Ralph Wood. Philadelphia: Muhlenberg, 1948.

O'Connor, Mary Alice. *The Role of Music in the English Vernacular of the Roman Catholic Church: 1963–1974*. Dissertation. Catholic University, 1974.

Overath, Johannes, ed. *Sacred Music and Liturgy Reform*. After Vatican II. Proceedings of the Fifth International Church Music Congress, Chicago-Milwaukee, August 21–28, 1966. Rome: *Consociatio Internationalis Musicae Sacrae*, 1969.

Patrick, Millar. *The Story of the Church's Song*. Richmond: John Knox Press, 1962.

Peterson, Robert Douglas. *The Folk Idiom in the Music of Contemporary Protestant Worship in America*. Dissertation. Columbia University, 1972.

Phillips, C. Henry. *The Singing Church*. London: Faber & Faber, 1968.

Phillips, C.S. *Hymnody, Past and Present*. New York: MacMillan, 1937.

Pierik, Marie. *When the People Sang*. Boston: McLaughlin & Reilly, 1949.

Pike, Alfred. *A Theology of Music*. Toledo, Ohio: Gregorian Institute of America, 1953.

Pons, André. *Droit ecclesiastique et Musique sacrée*. Tome I-IV. St.-Maurice (Suisse): Editions de l'Oeuvre St-Augustin, 1958–1961.

Pottie, Charles S. *The Theological Meaning of Music in Christian Worship: Two Views: Joseph Gelineau and Erik Routley*. Thesis. Graduate Theological Union, Berkeley, California, 1980.

Pratt, Carroll C. *The Meaning of Music*. New York: McGraw, 1931.

Predmore, George V. *Church Music in the Light of the Motu Proprio*. A Guide for the Catholic Choirmaster and Organist. Rochester, NY: The Seminary Press, 1924.

_____. *Sacred Music and the Catholic Church*. Boston: McLaughlin and Reilly, 1950.

Quasten, Johannes. *Music and Worship in Pagan and Christian Antiquity*. Tr. by Boniface Ramsey. Washington, DC: National Association of Pastoral Musicians, 1983.

Robertson, Alec. *Music of the Catholic Church*. London: Burns & Oates, 1961.

Romita, Florentius. *Ius Musicae Liturgicae*. Rome: Edizioni Liturgiche, 1947.

Routley, Erik. *Church Music and the Christian Faith*. Carol Stream, Illinois: Agape, 1978.

———. *Church Music and Theology*. London: SCM, 1959.

———. *Music Leadership in the Church*. A Conversation Chiefly With My Friends. Nashville: Abingdon, 1967.

———. *Music, Sacred and Profane*. London: Independent Press Ltd., 1960.

———. *Twentieth Century Church Music*. London: Herbert Jenkins, 1964.

Sachs, Curt. *The Wellsprings of Music*. Ed. by Jaap Kunst. New York: McGraw-Hill, 1965.

Sanders, Jack T. *The New Testament Christological Hymns*. Cambridge: University Press, 1971.

Schille, Gottfried. *Frühchristliche Hymnen*. Berlin: Evangelische Verlagsanstalt, 1965.

Schmitt, Francis P. *Church Music Transgressed*. Reflections On "Reform." New York: Seabury Press, 1977.

Schoenbachler, Timothy. *Folk Music In Transition: The Pastoral Challenge*. Phoenix: Pastoral Arts Associates, 1979.

Skeris, Robert A. *Chroma Theou*. On the Origins and Theological Interpretation of the Musical Imagery Used By the Ecclesiastical Writers of the First Three Centuries, With Special Reference to the Image of Orpheus. Altötting: Verlag Alfred Coppenrath, 1976.

Smith, William Sheppard. *Musical Aspects of the New Testament*. Amsterdam: Uitgeverij W. Ten Have N.Y., 1962.

Sparksman, Brian Joseph. *The Minister of Music in the Western Church: A Canonical-Historical Study*. Dissertation. Catholic U., 1981.

Squire, Russell N. *Church Music* St. Louis: Bethany Press, 1962.

Stravinsky, Igor. *Poetics of Music*. Tr. by Arthur Knodel and Ingolf Dahl. Cambridge, MA: Harvard Univ. Press, 1970.

Taylor, Margaret Fisk. *A Time To Dance*. Symbolic Movement in Worship. Philadelphia: United Church Press, 1967.

Universa Laus, ed. *Growing In Church Music*. Proceedings of A Meeting On "Why Church Music?" Conducted by The Society of St. Gregory and *Universa Laus*. Washington, DC: *Universa Laus*, 1979.

Walton, Janet Roland. *The Contributions of Aesthetics to Liturgical Renewal*. Dissertation. Columbia U. Teachers College, 1979.

Weiler, William Joseph. *An Investigation of Qualities of Music Essential to the Roman Catholic Liturgy*. Dissertation. Northwestern University, 1960.

Zuckerkandl, Victor. *Sound and Symbol*. Music and the External World. Tr. by William R. Trask. Princeton: Princeton U. Press, 1969.

Articles

Ainslie, John. "English Liturgical Music Before Vatican II." In *English Catholic Worship*. Liturgical Renewal In England Since 1900. Ed. by J.D. Crichton *et al*. London: Geoffrey Chapman (1979), pp. 47–59.

_____. "English Liturgical Music Since the Council." In *English Catholic Worship*. Liturgical Renewal In England Since 1900. Ed. by J.D. Crichton *et al*. London: Geoffrey Chapman (1979), pp. 93–109.

_____. "Tradition Means Development. The Liturgy: What Are We Composing For?" *Music and Liturgy* 3 (1977), pp. 42–46.

Antcliffe, Herbert. "Hymn Tunes: A Catholic Heritage." *Caecilia* 78 (1951), pp. 205–207.

Antonelli, Fernando. "Commentary." *Worship* 32 (1957/58), pp. 626–637.

Aymans, Winfried. "Continuity and Development in Ecclesiastical Legislation Concerning Gregorian Chant in the Light of Vatican II." *Sacred Music* 106 (Fall 1979), pp. 3–10.

Bagnell, Mary. "Missalette: Can It Work?" *Pastoral Music* 6 (Dec.-Jan., 1982), pp. 39–41.

Bauman, William A. "Church Music in America: Vatican II to '82." Paper given at Symposium for Church Composers. Milwaukee, July 7, 1982.

_____. "Music for Prayer." *NCMEA Overtones* 7 (June, 1972).

_____. "Musical, Liturgical, Pastoral Judgements: New Songs, New Judgements?" In *Pastoral Music in Practice*. Ed. by Virgil C. Funk and Gabe Huck. Washington, DC: National Association of Pastoral Musicians (1981), pp. 107–115.

_____. "The New Mass—Challenge to the Creative Musician." *NCMEA Overtones* 5 (December, 1969).

_____. "Parish Song and the Struggle for Quality." *North American Liturgical Week* 27 (1966), pp. 182–186.

Becker, Bruno. "Singing For An English Liturgy." *Sacred Music* 97 (Summer 1970), pp. 8–18.

Bender, Harold S. "The Hymnology of the Anabaptists." *Mennonite Quarterly Review* 31 (1957), pp. 5–10.

Bernier, Alfred. "St. Robert Bellarmine, S.J., and Liturgical Music." *Caecilia* 79 (1952), pp. 241–244; 80 (1952/53), pp. 36–43, 77–81, 117–122, 177–182, 226–231.

Bevenot, Laurence. "Words, Words, Words. . . ." *Music and Liturgy* 5 (1979), pp. 94–97.

Bilotti, Domenico. "Prayer and Song in the Human Family Today (Italy)." Tr. by James Langdale. *Concilium* 52 (1970), pp. 119–123.

Blanchard, Robert I. "Church Music Today: The Center Position." In

Harmony and Discord. An Open Forum on Church Music. Washington, DC: The Liturgical Conference (1966), pp. 27–35.

———. "Let's Be Practical." *Sacred Music* 92 (1965), pp. 14–16.

Bly, Joseph J. "Contemporary Musical Settings of the Liturgy." *Orate Fratres* 23 (1947/48), pp. 517–523.

Bomm, Urbanus. "Gregorian Chant and Liturgical Singing in the Vernacular." In *Sacred Music and Liturgy Reform.* Ed. by Johannes Overath. Rome: *Consociatio Internationalis Musicae Sacrae* (1969), pp. 163–168.

Borello, Luciano. "Liturgical Reform and Sacred Music in Italy." Tr. by Anthony M. Buono. *Concilium* 22 (1967), pp. 110–116.

Botz, Paschal. "Alleluia: Our Easter Song." *Orate Fratres* 20 (1945/46), pp. 241–250.

Bragers, Achille. "Chant—The Handmaid of the Liturgy." *Caecilia* 75 (1948), pp. 178–183.

Braun, H. Myron. "In Pursuit of Excellence." *Sacred Music* 98 (Fall 1971), pp. 3–5.

———. "Sunday the Musician Was A Theologian." *The Christian Ministry* (1977), pp. 12–16.

Breig, James. "The Hit-and-Miss Parade of Catholic Hymns." *U.S. Catholic* 45 (July 1980), pp. 28–30.

Bronson, Bertrand H. "Folksong and the Modes." *Musical Quarterly* 32 (1946), pp. 37–49.

Brownstead, Frank. "The Catholic Liturgy and Hymns." *Pastoral Liturgy* 5 (June-July, 1981), pp. 39–43.

Brunner, Francis A. "A Primer of Laws of Church Music." *Caecilia* 73 (1945/46), pp. 45–46ff; 74 (1946/47), pp. 14–15ff; 79 (1951/52), pp. 48–49ff.

———. "The New Instruction on Sacred Music and Liturgy." *Caecilia* 85 (1958), pp. 378–381.

Bularzik, Rembert. "Gregorian Chant In Its Liturgical Setting." *Catholic Choirmaster* 20 (1934), pp. 115–119.

Bultmann, Rudolph. "*Bekenntnis- und Liedfragmente im ersten Petrusbrief.*" *Exegetica* (1967), pp. 285–297.

Burke, Eileen C. "When Is Music Pastoral?" *Pastoral Music* 4 (April-May 1980), pp. 22–23.

Burkley, Francis. "Contemporary Church Music: A Few Asides." *Sacred Music* 92 (1966), pp. 104–106.

———. "Contemporary Trends in Church Music Composition." *North American Liturgical Week* 20 (1959), pp. 108–111.

Burne, Martin. "Quality: Musical and Religious." *Pastoral Music* 4 (June-July 1980), pp. 16–19.

Butler, Richard. "The Church Musician In History." *Pastoral Music* 3 (Feb.-March 1979), pp. 12–13.

Caglio, Ernest Moneta. "Sacred Music." In *The Commentary On the Constitution and On the Instruction on the Sacred Liturgy*. Ed. by A. Bugnini. New York: Benziger Brothers (1965), pp. 244–267.

Carducci-Agustini, Mo. Edgardo. "Can the 'Exclusive' Systems of Contemporary Music Be Applied to Sacred Art?" Tr. by Paul Hotin. *Caecilia* 78 (1951), pp. 224–225.

Carley, James R. "The Theology of Music In Worship." *Encounter* 24 (1963), pp. 365–378.

Carlin, Ramon. "A Diocese Sings." *Orate Fratres* 24 (1949/50), pp. 456–460.

Carter, Sydney. "Context." *Modern Liturgy* 7 (1980), pp. 8–9.

Chute, James. "Musical Grace." *Modern Liturgy* 7 (1980), pp. 6–7.

Collins, Patrick W. "Music and Worship: Thoughts On An Anniversary." *Musart* 26 (Winter 1974), pp. 3–9.

Cols, Domingo. "Sacred Music in the Perspective of Liturgical Renewal." Tr. by Paul Burns. *Concilium* 22 (1967), pp. 117–121.

Conley, Charles. "Describing the Pastoral Musicians' Role." *Pastoral Music* 5 (Oct.-Nov. 1981), pp. 31–36.

Conley, Thomas P. "I Hear Whole Congregations Singing." *National Liturgical Week* (1953), pp. 49–56.

Connare, William G. "Exploring the Musical Dimensions of the New Order of the Mass." *Sacred Music* 97 (Spring 1970), pp. 5–10.

Conry, Tom. "Toward A Revisionist Theology of Liturgical Music and Text." *Pastoral Music* 5 (April-May 1981), pp. 26–31.

Consociatio Internationalis Musicae Sacrae. "Memorandum on Sacred Music." *Sacred Music* 98 (Winter 1971), pp. 3–10.

Corry, Andrew. "Towards Plainsong," *Orate Fratres* 7 (1932/1933), pp. 499–504.

Costa, Eugenio. "The European Scene: Some Lessons From the Last 15 Years (1963–1978)." In *Growing In Church Music*. Proceedings of A Meeting On "Why Church Music?" Washington, DC: *Universa Laus* (1979), pp. 31–38.

Crickmore, Leon. "Music, Liturgy and Contemplation." *The Clergy Review* 52 (1967), pp. 705–712.

Culbreth, Charles D. "Seeking A Balance: Spirituality and Technicalities." *Modern Liturgy* 7 (1980), p. 34.

Cunningham, Joseph. "Does It Fit? The Liturgical Judgement." In *Music In Catholic Worship*. Ed. by Virgil C. Funk. Washington, DC: NPM (1982), pp. 73–77.

Cunningham, W. Patrick. "Money and Music." *Worship* 49 (1975), pp. 411–418.

_____. "Toward An Aesthetic of Liturgical Music." *Communio* 5 (1978), pp. 363–381.

Cyr, Louis. "The Church Musician." Tr. by David Smith. *Concilium* 72 (1972), pp. 91–103.

Day, Thomas. "A Syllabus of Musical Errors." *Commonweal* 103 (August 27, 1976), pp. 553–557.

_____. "Thoughts on Church Music." *Sacred Music* 101 (Summer 1974), pp. 16–22.

_____. "Twentieth-Century Church Music: An Elusive Modernity." *Communio* 6 (1979), pp. 236–256.

Dean, Aldheim. "The New Instruction On Sacred Music." *The Clergy Review* 44 (1959), pp. 145–160.

de Albuquerque, Amaro Cavalcanti. "Sacred Music in the Liturgical Renewal in Brazil." Tr. by Ronald Weeks. *Concilium* 22 (1967), pp. 132–135.

De Brant, Cyr. "Forerunners of the *Motu Proprio*." *Catholic Choirmaster* 29 (1943), pp. 6–9.

_____. "Pius X's *Motu Proprio*—Fifty Years Ago." *Catholic Choirmaster* 39 (1953), pp. 102–106.

_____. "The 'Secret' of 1903." *Catholic Choirmaster* 46 (1960), pp. 58–60.

Deiss, Lucien. "Liturgical Chant According to the Constitution of Vatican II." *Sacred Music* 93 (1966), pp. 44–52.

_____. "Liturgical Principles for Today's Music." *Pastoral Music* 2 (1978), pp. 20–26.

De Pinto, Basil. "Gregorian Music and Vernacular Liturgy." *Sacred Music* 92 (1965), pp. 38–46.

DeSola, Carla and Deitering, Carolyn. "Dance: A Liturgical Art." *Pastoral Music* 5 (Aug.-Sept. 1981), pp. 17–21.

Donovan, Kevin. "The Assembly and Its Music." *Music and Liturgy* 2 (1976), pp. 5–12.

Donovan, Vincent C. "The Law of Liturgical Music." *Liturgical Arts* 1 (1932), pp. 130–137.

Dowdey, Landon G. "Music to Enter the World By: A View From the Far Left." In *Harmony and Discord*. An Open Forum on Church Music. Washington, DC: The Liturgical Conference (1966), pp. 43–49.

Dreisoerner, Charles. "Report on the Liturgical Side of the N.C.M.E.A." *Worship* 29 (1954/55), pp. 409–414.

Dubay, William H. "Who's Got the Hymns?" *America* 109 (Aug. 17, 1963), pp. 158–159.

Ducey, W. Michael. "Blessed Pius and the Praise of God." *Orate Fratres* 25 (1950/51), pp. 509–514.

Duffy, Sister Mary Philip. "Correlation of Music and Liturgy: The Teacher's Challenge to Creativity." *Musart* 26 (1974), pp. 17–23.

Duffy, Regis. "Pastoral Music—Its Own Art Form." *Pastoral Music* 5 (June-July 1981), pp. 27–30.

Durst, Luanne. "From 'Musical Liturgy Is Normative' to 'Prayer: Performance and Participation.'" *Pastoral Music* 3 (Dec.-Jan. 1979), pp. 54–55.

East, John Michael. "The Challenge of Vatican II to the English Tradition." *Music and Liturgy* 4 (1978), pp. 144–152.

_____. "Praise Him With the Lyre." *The Way* 19 (1979), pp. 180–189.

Ehmann, Benedict. "Music in the Liturgy." *Catholic Choirmaster* 33 (1947), pp. 51–54, 81.

Eissfeldt, Otto. "Songs." In *The Old Testament: An Introduction.* New York: Harper & Row (1965), pp. 87–124.

Ellard, Gerald. "But Song and Dialog Mass Combine!" *Catholic Choirmaster* 29 (1943), p. 99–101, 153–155.

_____. "'Liturgical Movement' Four Centuries Old." *Orate Fratres* 20 (1945), pp. 49–58.

Emmais, Esteban. "The Law Regarding Church Music." *Catholic Choirmaster* 21 (1935), pp. 36–38.

Eskrew, Harry and McElrath, Hugh T. "The Hymn and Theology." In *Sing With Understanding.* An Introduction to Christian Hymnology. Nashville: Broadman Press (1980), pp. 59–71.

Faulkner, Quentin. "Teaching Music to Future Priests." *Liturgy* 24 (1979), pp. 34–38.

_____. "What is 'Sacred Music'?" *The AGO-RCCO Magazine* (1978), pp. 55–57.

Fellerer, Karl Gustav. "Church Music and the Council of Trent." *Musical Quarterly* 39 (1953), pp. 576–594.

_____. "Liturgy and Music." In *Sacred Music and Liturgy Reform.* Ed. by Johannes Overath. Rome: *Consociatio Internationalis Musicae Sacrae* (1969), pp. 71–88.

_____. "Palestrina." *Sacred Music* 92 (1965), pp. 66–77.

Fernandez, Juan Carlos. "Gregorian Chant and the People." *Orate Fratres* 15 (1940/41), pp. 368–370.

Fitzer, Joseph. "Instrumental Music in the Liturgy." *Worship* 45 (1971), pp. 539–553.

_____. "Psalms, Hymns, and Troubled Waters." *Sacred Music* 99 (Summer 1972), pp. 3–8.

Fleming, Austin. "Are We Ministers of Music or Directors of the Ministry of Music?" *Pastoral Music* 5 (Feb.-March 1981), pp. 39–42.

Foley, Edward. "On the 'Breath of Dawn' and Other Metaphors." *Pastoral Music* 5 (Apr.-May 1981), pp. 23–25.

_____. "Toward A Working Definition of Music in Ritual: A Pre-Theological Investigation." Paper presented to North American Academy of Liturgy Music Group, January 4, 1983. Unpublished.

Foley, John. "Guidelines For Composing (and Judging) Pastoral Music." *Pastoral Music* 4 (Apr.-May 1980), pp. 27–31; (June-July 1980), pp. 45–49; (Aug.-Sept. 1980), pp. 49–51.

Fox, Matthew. "The Art of Ministering Pastoral Music." *Pastoral Music* 5 (June-July 1981), pp. 16–19.

Funk, Virgil C. "Will It Work? The Pastoral Judgement." In *Music In Catholic Worship*. Ed. by Virgil C. Funk. Washington, DC: National Association of Pastoral Musicians (1982), pp. 79–81.

Gajard, Dom Joseph. "Music and Prayer." *Sacred Music* 100 (Summer 1973), pp. 3–7.

Gelineau, Joseph. "The Animator." *Pastoral Music* 3 (Oct.-Nov. 1979), pp. 19–22.

_____. "Are New Forms of Liturgical Singing and Music Developing?" Tr. by Lancelot Sheppard. *Concilium* 52 (1970), pp. 37–46.

_____. "Balancing Performance and Participation." *Pastoral Music* 3 (June-July 1979), pp. 22–24.

_____. "The Chants of the Baptismal Liturgy." Tr. by John Rogers. *Concilium* 22 (1967), p. 69–87.

_____. "*Dum supplicat et psallit Ecclesia.*" Tr. by Theodore Westow. *Concilium* 1 (1964), pp. 31–34.

_____. "The Importance of Prayer For the Musician." *Pastoral Music* 3 (June-July 1979), pp. 51–53.

_____. "Music and Singing in the Liturgy." In *The Study of Liturgy*. Ed. by Cheslyn Jones, Geoffrey Wainwright, Edward Yarnold. New York: Oxford Press (1978), pp. 440–449.

_____. "The Renewal of Liturgical Chant." In *The Liturgy and Vatican II*. Ed. by William Barauna. English edition by Jovian Lang. Chicago: Franciscan Herald Press (1966), pp. 231–247.

_____. "The Role of Sacred Music." Tr. by Theodore L. Westow. *Concilium* 2 (1965), pp. 59–65.

_____. "What No Ear Has Heard . . ." *Music and Liturgy* 5 (1979), pp. 86–93.

George, Justus. "Splendor of the Chant." *Orate Fratres* 21 (1946/47), pp. 541–545.

Godfrey, Aaron W. "These Were Our Mantras." *Liturgy* 23 (1978), p. 33.

Gomez, Miguel Dario Miranda. "Function of Sacred Music and *Actuosa Participatio.*" *Sacred Music and Liturgy Reform*. Ed. by Johannes Overath. Rome: *Consociatio Internationalis Musicae Sacrae* (1969), pp. 111–116.

Grabert, Colman. "Toward the Development of An Authentic English Sung Mass." *Worship* 40 (1966), pp. 80–90.

Green, F. Pratt. "Poet and Hymn Writer." *Worship* 49 (1975), pp. 190–201.

Grindal, Gracia. "The Language of Worship and Hymnody: Tone." *Worship* 52 (1978), pp. 509–517.

Guentner, Francis J. "The Mass and the Moderns." *Caecilia* 80 (1953), pp. 194–196, 247–250.

_____. "The Use of Religious Music." *North American Liturgical Week* 20 (1959), pp. 111–114.

Gundry, Robert H. "The Form, Meaning and Background of the Hymn Quoted in 1 Tim 3:16." *Apostolic History and the Gospel (Festschrift für F.F. Bruce)*. Exeter Devon (1970), pp. 203–222.

Gutfreund, Edward. "Is It Any Good? The Musical Judgement." In *Music In Catholic Worship*. Ed. by Virgil C. Funk. Wash. DC: National Association of Pastoral Musicians (1982), pp. 67–71.

Hacker, John G. "Does the Church Allow Women to Sing in Our Church Choirs Or Does She Not?" *Catholic Choirmaster* 20 (1934), pp. 204–206.

Hall, Martin. "Music and Pastoral Liturgy." In *Pastoral Liturgy*. A Symposium. Ed. by Harold Winstone. London: Collins (1965), pp. 55–65.

Halmo, Joan. "Hymns for the Paschal Triduum." *Worship* 55 (1981), pp. 137–159.

Hanson, Donald. "What Kind of Church Music Should There Be?" *Pastoral Music* 5 (Oct.-Nov. 1981), pp. 25–30.

Hayburn, Robert. "The Liturgical Spirit and Liturgical Singing." *Caecilia* 79 (1952), pp. 133–135, 160.

Hellriegel, Martin B. "Singers and Servers." *Worship* 29 (1954/55), pp. 83–89.

_____. "Why Song Surpasses Silence At Mass." *National Liturgical Week* (1953), pp. 26–29.

Helmbold, Andrew K. "Redeemer Hymns—Gnostic and Christian." *New Dimensions in New Testament Study*. Ed. by R.N. Longenecker & M.C. Tenney. Grand Rapids: Zondervan (1974), pp. 71–78.

Henchal, Michael. "Integrity: Musician, God, Parish." *Pastoral Music* 4 (Aug.-Sept. 1980), pp. 22–26.

Henkes, Lea and Ford, Paul. "Pastoral Music in the U.S.: A Grassroots Survey." *Pastoral Music* 6 (Dec.-Jan. 1982), pp. 42–45.

Herman, Maurice C. "Organist and Congregation." *Orate Fratres* 24 (1949/50), pp. 565–568.

Heywood, Robert B. "Let My People Sing!" *Worship* 40 (1966), pp. 349–360.

Higginson, J. Vincent. "Brief History of the Society of St. Gregory." *Catholic Choirmaster* 50 (1964), pp. 159–160, 180.

_____. "The Choir Director As Arbiter of Music." *Catholic Choirmaster* 31 (1945), p. 108–111.

_____. "Essentially Vocal." *Catholic Choirmaster* 35 (1949), pp. 56–58.

————. "Forerunners of the *Motu Proprio* (II)." *Catholic Choirmaster* 29 (1943), pp. 53–55, 88.

————. "History of the Saint Gregory Society." *Catholic Choirmaster* 26 (1940), pp. 57–59, 160–163.

————. "The Revival of Gregorian Chant." *Catholic Choirmaster* 35 (1949), pp. 113–128.

Hodgetts, Michael. "Recusant Liturgical Music." *The Clergy Review* 61 (1976), pp. 151–157.

————. "Rhythm and Meaning in Liturgical Translation." *Music and Liturgy* 2 (1976), pp. 19–24.

Hoelty-Nickel, Theodore. "Luther and Music." In *Luther and Culture*. Decorah, Iowa: Luther College Press (1960), pp. 145–211.

Holleman, A.W.J. "Early Christian Liturgical Music." *Studia Liturgica* 8 (1972), pp. 185–192.

————. "The Oxyrhynchus Papyrus 1786 and the Relationship Between Ancient Greek and Early Christian Music." *Vigiliae Christianae* 26 (1972), pp. 1–17.

Hotin, Paul J. "The Role of the Choir in the Restoration of Sacred Music." *North American Liturgical Week* 20 (1959), pp. 114–119.

Howell, Clifford. "A New Approach to Vernacular Psalm-Singing." *Worship* 30 (1955/56), pp. 25–31.

————. "The *Betsingmesse*." *Caecilia* 81 (1954), pp. 226–231.

————. "But What About the Chant?" In *Liturgy For the People*. Essays in Honor of Gerald Ellard, S.J. Ed. by William Leonard. Milwaukee: Bruce Pub. Co. (1963), pp. 120–131.

————. "Completing the Dialog Mass With Song." *Worship* 32 (1957/58), pp. 66–71.

————. "Let the People Sing At Mass." *Catholic Choirmaster* 36 (1950), pp. 131–144.

————. "Vernacular Hymns At Low Mass." *The Clergy Review* 44 (1959), pp. 394–407.

Hovda, Robert W. "Sacred Music in the Teaching of the Church." In *Harmony and Discord*. An Open Forum on Church Music. Washington, DC: The Liturgical Conference (1966), pp. 2–7.

Hucke, Helmut. "Changing Concepts of Church Music." In *Growing In Church Music*. Proceedings of A Meeting On "Why Church Music?" Washington, DC: *Universa Laus* (1979), pp. 17–29.

————. "Church Music." Tr. by Theodore L. Westow. *Concilium* 2 (1965), pp. 111–133.

————. "Introduction: New Church Music in the Vernacular." Tr. by Eileen O'Gorman. *Concilium* 12 (1966), pp. 93–94.

————. "Jazz and Folk Music in the Liturgy." Tr. by John Drury. *Concilium* 42 (1969), pp. 138–172.

————. "Musical Requirements of Liturgical Reform." Tr. by Eileen

O'Gorman. *Concilium* 12 (1966), pp. 45–73.

_____. "The Roman Instruction on Music in the Liturgy." Tr. by Theodore L. Westow. *Concilium* 32 (1968), pp. 119–136.

_____. "Towards A New Kind of Church Music." Tr. by N.D. Smith. *Concilium* 62 (1971), pp. 87–97.

Huegle, Gregory. "Church Compositions Without Liturgical Foundation." *Orate Fratres* 7 (1932/33), pp. 211–215, 402–407; 8 (1933/34), pp. 24–29.

_____. "Liturgy and the 'Big Tone'." *Orate Fratres* 9 (1934/35), pp. 467–470.

_____. "May We Look For A Simplified Edition of the Vatican Gradual?" *Orate Fratres* 6 (1932), pp. 115–120.

_____. "One Hundred Years Ago." *Caecilia* 65 (1938), p. 88.

_____. "Why Is Liturgical Music So Austere?" *Orate Fratres* 6 (1931/32), pp. 56–60.

Hughesdon, Harold and Hughesdon, Helen Mary. "*In Unitate*: Ceremonies and Music." *Sacred Music* 104 (1977), pp. 21–22.

Huijbers, Bernard. "Is Music the Catalyst?" *Music and Liturgy* 5 (1979), pp. 76–86.

_____. "The Nature of Liturgical Music." *Music and Liturgy* 4 (1978), pp. 50–54.

Hume, Paul. "Music in Church." *Catholic Choirmaster* 42 (1956), pp. 134–137, 168.

_____. "Music in the Seminary." *Worship* 31 (1956/57), pp. 405–408.

_____. "Yes, But Why Do We Have to Sing?" *North American Liturgical Week* 26 (1965), pp. 131–136.

Hunkins, Arthur B. "Problems of American Church Music." *Sacred Music* 97 (Summer 1970), pp. 3–7.

_____. "The Serious Contemporary Composer and the Church Today." *Sacred Music* 95 (Winter 1968), pp. 3–6.

Hustad, Donald P. "Music and the Church's Outreach." *Review and Expositor* 69 (1972), pp. 177–185.

Inwood, Paul. "Adapting the Liturgy." *Music and Liturgy* 4 (1978), pp. 103–114.

Jabusch, Willard F. "Priestly Ministry of Music." *Chicago Studies* 14 (1975), pp. 37–47.

Johnson, David N. "What is Sacred Music?" *Musart* 23 (1971), pp. 12, 20–21.

Johnson, Earl. "Sacred Music and the Funeral Rites." *North American Liturgical Week* 23 (1962), pp. 195–199.

Johnson, Lawrence J. "How Far Have We Come?" *Pastoral Music* 6 (Feb.-March 1982), pp. 13–16.

Joncas, Michael. "Prayer and Music: Singing the Meaning of the Words." In *Pastoral Music in Practice*. Ed. by Virgil C. Funk and Gabe Huck.

Washington, DC: NPM (1981), pp. 135–140.

Jungmann, Josef. "Sacred Music." In *Commentary On the Documents of Vatican II*. Vol. I. Ed. by Herbert Vorgrimler. New York: Herder (1967), pp. 76–80.

Kalb, Marie Therese. "Directives To A Pastoral Musician." *Pastoral Music* 6 (Oct.-Nov. 1981), pp. 37–41.

Kavanagh, Aidan. "Theology of Celebration." *Pastoral Music* 4 (Dec.-Jan. 1980), pp. 16–17.

Kearney, Moira. "Sacred Music in South Africa." *Concilium* 22 (1967), pp. 128–131.

Keifer, Ralph A. "The Noise In Our Solemn Assemblies." *Worship* 45 (1971), pp. 13–21.

Kellenbenz, Eugene. "Musical Settings For the Psalms in Languages Ancient and Modern." *North American Liturgical Week* 23 (1962), pp. 188–192.

Kellner, Joseph. "Hymns Adapted to the Mass." *Worship* 32 (1957/58), pp. 239–244.

Kelly, F. Joseph. "Beauty In the Art of Music Is Its Religious Element." *Catholic Choirmaster* 20 (1934), pp. 172–174.

_____. "The Chief Ends of Sacred Music." *Catholic Choirmaster* 21 (1935), pp. 8–9.

_____. "Music An Art, Not An Accomplishment!" *Caecilia* 65 (1938), pp. 10–11.

Kister, Daniel A. "Dance and Theater in Christian Worship." *Worship* 45 (1971), pp. 588–598.

_____. "Musical-Liturgical Artistry in the Mass." *Worship* 41 (1967), pp. 450–464.

Kremer, Marie. "The Professional Pastoral Musician." *Pastoral Music* 4 (April-May 1980), pp. 24–26.

Kremer, Joseph C. "The Questions of Song." *Worship* 54 (1980), pp. 411–417.

Lang, Paul Henry. "*Aggiornamento* in Sacred Music." *Sacred Music* 92 (1965), pp. 11–14.

_____. "The *Patrimonium Musicae Sacrae* and The Task of Sacred Music Today." In *Sacred Music and Liturgy Reform*. Ed. by Johannes Overath. Rome: CIMS (1969), pp. 238–250.

Leddy, Margaret. "Orientation of Church Musicians to Chant." *North American Liturgical Week* 20 (1959), pp. 119–122.

Ledogar, Robert J. "Faith, Feeling, Music and the Spirit." *Worship* 43 (1969), pp. 13–23.

Lee, Patrick. "The Text Writer's Problem." *Music and Liturgy* 5 (1979), pp. 40–44.

Lennards, Joseph. "Possibilities and Limitations of Congregational

Singing." In *Sacred Music and Liturgy Reform*. Ed. by Joseph Overath. Rome: CIMS (1969), pp. 148–162.

Lercaro, James Cardinal. "Active Participation: The Basic Principle of the Pastoral-Liturgical Reforms of Pius X." *Worship* 28 (1953/54), pp. 120–128.

Lieberson, S.A. "The Problem of Modernization of Liturgical Music." *Caecilia* 75 (1948), pp. 122–125.

Loew, Josef. "The New Instruction." *Worship* 33 (1958/59), pp. 2–13.

Lord, Albert B. "Songs and the Song" and "Writing and Oral Tradition." In *The Singer of Tales*. Cambridge: Harvard University Press, 1964— pp. 99–123, 124–138.

Lowinsky, Edward E. "Musical Genius—Evolution and Origins of A Concept." *Musical Quarterly* (1966), pp. 321–495.

Luecke, Sister Jane Marie. "Adapting the Psalm Tones to English." *Liturgical Arts* 34 (1965), pp. 7–12.

Lyonnet, Stanislas. "*L'hymne christologique de l'épitre aux Colossiens et la fête juive du nouvel an*." *Recherches de Science Religieuse* 48 (1960), pp. 93–100.

McBride, Alfred. "Psalms Are Songs of Faith." *Worship* 38 (1963/64), pp. 427–429.

McKenna, Edward J. "Crisis in Liturgical Music." *America* 127 (December 5, 1981), pp. 360–361.

_____. "Liturgical Music in Ireland." *Worship* 51 (1977), pp. 420–433.

McLaughlin, Thomas H. "A Bishop Speaks On the *Vox Populi*." *Catholic Choirmaster* 31 (1945), pp. 102–104f.

_____. "Pastoral Letter On Sacred Music." *Catholic Choirmaster* 24 (1938), pp. 168–171.

McManus, Frederick R. "Chant in the Vernacular." *Worship* 34 (1959/60), pp. 227–230.

_____. "Commentaries On the SRC Instruction." *Worship* 34 (1959/60), pp. 107–110.

_____. "Hymns At Low Mass." *Worship* (1960/61), pp. 398–403.

_____. "The New Instruction." *Worship* 33 (1958/59), pp. 188–192.

_____. "Sacred Music and the Choir." *North American Liturgical Week* 24 (1963), pp. 172–176.

McNaspy, Clement J. "*Aggiornamento* and Liturgical Music." *North American Liturgical Week* 24 (1963), pp. 165–171.

_____. "Expression of Faith and Religion Through Art and Music." *North American Liturgical Week* 23 (1962), pp. 192–194.

_____. "Helping Your Congregation to Participate." *Pastoral Music* 3 (Dec.-Jan. 1979), pp. 31–34.

_____. "Liturgical Music For Today." *America* 116 (November 14, 1970), pp. 401–404.

———. "Liturgy and the Arts." In his *Our Changing Liturgy*. New York: Hawthorn Books (1966), pp. 127–154.

———. "Men of Sacred Music: St. Augustine." *Caecilia* 72 (1945), pp. 89–91, 116.

———. "Music of the People in Sacred Worship." *North American Liturgical Week* 25 (1964), pp. 198–204.

———. "Our Daily Musical Bread." *Caecilia* 79 (1951), pp. 8–9.

———. "Singing With the Church." *Caecilia* 71 (1944), pp. 205–208.

———. "Vacuum Or Opportunity." *Sacred Music* 92 (Winter 1966), pp. 98–100.

———. "Yes, But Why Do We Have To Sing?" *North American Liturgical Week* 26 (1965), pp. 136–140.

Madsen, Cletus P. "The Dialogue Mass and Hymns." *North American Liturgical Week* 20 (1959), pp. 105–108.

———. "Participating Musically in the Small Parish." *North American Liturgical Week* 23 (1962), pp. 184–188.

Maginty, Edward A. "Liturgical Music and England." *Orate Fratres* 8 (1933/34), pp. 549–555.

Mahrt, William Peter. "The Musical Shape of the Liturgy. Part I: The Gregorian Mass in General." *Sacred Music* 102 (Fall 1975), pp. 5–13.

———. "Part II: The Interpolation of Polyphonic Music." *Sacred Music* 102 (Winter 1975), pp. 16–26.

———. "Part III: The Service of the Readings." *Sacred Music* 103 (Summer 1976), pp. 3–17.

———. "Part IV: The Function of the Organ." *Sacred Music* 104 (Winter 1977), pp. 3–18.

Mannion, John B. "A Word From the Non-Musician: The Left Position." In *Harmony and Discord. An Open Forum On Church Music*. Washington, DC: Liturgical Conference (1966), pp. 36–42.

March, Ralph S. "Are You A True Minister of Music?" *Sacred Music* 99 (Winter 1972), pp. 3–13.

Marian, Sister M. "Holy Mother Church, My Music Teacher." *Catholic Choirmaster* 35 (1949), pp. 101–103.

Marier, Theodore. "The Choir and Congregational Participation." *North American Liturgical Week* 22 (1961), pp. 142–146.

———. "Contemporary Church Music and the *Motu Proprio*." *Caecilia* 73 (1946), pp. 127–129, 160.

———. "Music As Communicative Art." *Caecilia* 83 (1956), pp. 118–123, 149.

———. "The *Schola Cantorum* and the Parish School." In *Liturgy For the People*. Essays in Honor of Gerald Ellard, S.J. Ed. by William Leonard. Milwaukee: Bruce (1963), pp. 104–119.

Martin, Ralph P. "An Early Christian Hymn (Col 1:15–20)." *Evangelical Quarterly* 36 (1964), pp. 195–205.

Masson, Charles. "*L'hymne christologique de l'épitre aux Colossiens* I, 15–30." *Revue de Théologie et de Philosophie* 36, n.s. (1948), pp. 138–142.

Mauch, Diane Farrell. "Music As A Ministry to Individual Creativity." *Liturgy* 23 (1978), pp. 28–30.

Mawby, Colin. "Church Music Since Vatican II." *Sacred Music* 103 (1976), pp. 3–9.

May, Georg. "Ecclesiastical Legislation On Liturgy and Church Music After the Second Vatican Council." *Sacred Music* 106 (Spring 1979), pp. 9–21; (Fall), pp. 11–21; (Winter), pp. 7–14.

Mbunga, Stephen. "Church Music in Tanzania." *Concilium* 12 (1966), pp. 111–117.

Melloh, John. "The Dilemma of Pastoral Music." *Pastoral Music* 4 (Aug.-Sept. 1980), pp. 42–46.

_____. "Feel the Music." *Pastoral Music* 4 (Dec.-Jan. 1980), pp. 22–25.

Meltz, Ken. "Interpreting the Atonement in Music." *Liturgy* 1, n.s. (1980), pp. 69–72.

Michel, Virgil. "The Chant of the Church." *Orate Fratres* 11 (1936/37), pp. 363–365.

_____. "Modernism and the Chant." *Orate Fratres* 11 (1936/37), pp. 463–465.

Milner, Anthony. "A Composer's Problems: I." *Caecilia* 81 (1954), pp. 77–78.

_____. "The Instruction On Sacred Music." *Worship* 41 (1967), pp. 322–333

Mitchell, Nathan. "A God Who Hears." *Pastoral Music* 3 (Oct.-Nov. 1979), pp. 29–35.

_____. "The Changing Role of the Pastoral Musician." *Pastoral Music* 2 (1978), pp. 12–19.

_____. "The Musician As Minister." *Pastoral Music* 4 (Aug.-Sept. 1980), pp. 27–31, 39–41.

Montini, Giovanni B. "The Restoration of Liturgical Music." *Catholic Choirmaster* 40 (1954), pp. 3–4, 36.

Morgan, Maureen M. "The Economics of Church Music." *Pastoral Music* 4 (Aug.-Sept. 1980), pp. 12–13.

Morriss, Frank. "The Folk-Art Myth and Liturgical Debasement." *Sacred Music* 100 (Winter 1973), pp. 10–16.

Murphy, Joseph A. "Church Music Standards." *Catholic Choirmaster* 46 (1960), pp. 5–9, 16.

_____. "The Law On Sacred Music." *Catholic Choirmaster* 46 (1960), pp. 129–130.

Murray, Dom Gregory. "The Authentic Rhythm of Gregorian Chant." *Caecilia* 86 (1959), pp. 57–71.

_____. "Congregational Singing At Mass." *Catholic Choirmaster* 34 (1948), pp. 155–157.

Navarro, Juan. "Is the *Motu Proprio* of Blessed Pius Tenth On Sacred Music Binding In Conscience?" *Caecilia* 81 (1954), pp. 140–145.

Nemmers, Erwin Esser. "Early American Catholic Church Music." *Catholic Choirmaster* 40 (1954), pp. 158–159, 190.

———. "The History of American Catholic Church Music." *Catholic Choirmaster* 32 (1946), pp. 6–9, 43–46, 54–56, 88, 133–139.

Nettl, Bruno. "Notes On Musical Composition In Primitive Culture." *Anthropological Quarterly* 27 (1954), pp. 81–90.

Niceta of Remesiana. "Liturgical Singing." Tr. of *De utilitate hymnorum* by Gerard Walsh. *Caecilia* 78 (1951), pp. 135–138, 167.

Nicholson, David. "Contemporary Church Music and the Singing Congregation." *Caecilia* 83 (1956), pp. 78–80.

———. "Plainchant and the Vernacular." *Sacred Music* 100 (Summer 1973), pp. 15–18.

Nugent, Peter. "The Sacredness of Liturgical Music." *Sacred Music* 95 (Spring 1968), pp. 20–24.

Oates, John M. "Pastoral Liturgy and Music." *Sacred Music* 103 (1976), pp. 7–10.

O'Connell, J.B. "The New Instruction of the Sacred Congregation of Rites." *The Clergy Review* 44 (1959), pp. 90–99.

O'Donohoe, Joseph. "Catholic Hymns and Hymn Singing." *Caecilia* 64 (1937), pp. 155–158.

O'Laoghaire, Diarmuid. "Prayer and Song in the Human Family Today (Ireland)." *Concilium* 52 (1970), pp. 124–127.

Onofrey, Robert E. and Froehlich, James E. "Instrumental Music: Sacred Communication." *Pastoral Music* 3 (Feb.-March 1979), pp. 15–17.

Overath, Johannes. "Church Music in the Light of the Constitution of the Liturgy." *Sacred Music* 92 (1965), pp. 3–11.

———. "The Council." *Sacred Music* 105 (1978), pp. 3–8.

———. "Sacred Music Since the Council." *Sacred Music* 99 (Fall 1972), pp. 7–14.

Paine, John G. "The Copyright Law." *Caecilia* 63, (1936), pp. 429–431.

Parker, Alice. "Hymns in History." *Pastoral Music* 3 (June-July 1979), pp. 25–28.

Peeters, Flor. "Choirmasters and Organists—Vatican Council II." Tr. by E. Leemans. *Sacred Music* 92 (Winter 1966), pp. 100–104.

Peloquin, C. Alexander. "A New Song For A New Liturgy." *Liturgical Arts* 39 (1970), pp. 7–9.

Petit, Leo. "The Sacramentality of Chant." *Caecilia* 79 (1951/52), pp. 2–4, 46–47, 86.

Pfeil, Elmer. "Catholic Music Since Vatican II: Overcoming Inertia." *The Christian Ministry* (1977), pp. 18–19.

Philibert, Paul. "Two Become One: Performance and Participation." In

Pastoral Music in Practice. Ed. by Virgil C. Funk and Gabe Huck. Washington, DC: NPM (1981), pp. 75–80.

Phillips, Gerald. "Church Music Today—Where Are We?" *Liturgical Arts* 39 (1971), pp. 49–53.

_____. "Music In Our Worship." *Sacred Music* 93 (1966), pp. 36–43.

Pike, Alfred. "Religious and Secular Music." *Catholic Choirmaster* 49 (1963), pp. 83–84, 86.

Pirner, Reuben G. "Hymns of the Day and Season." *Liturgy* 1, n.s. (1980), pp. 79–84.

Purney, Wilfred. "Church Music—Retrospect and Prospect." *The Clergy Review* 53 (1968), pp. 971–977.

Quack, Erhard. "Contemporary Church Music." Tr. by Simon King. *Concilium* 52 (1970), pp. 147–149.

_____. "Music For Divine Worship in the German Language." Tr. by Eileen O'Gorman. *Concilium* 12 (1966), pp. 103–109.

Quinn, Patrick J. "The Architectural Implications of the Choir in the Worshiping Community." *Liturgical Arts* 34 (1966), pp. 38–46.

Quinn, Frank C. "Music and the Prayer of Praise." *Worship* 46 (1972), pp. 214–219.

Reboud, Réné. "Sacred Music For the People: France Since World War II." Tr. by David H. Connor. *Concilium* 12 (1966), pp. 95–101.

Rees, Elizabeth. "Liturgy and the Composer." *Music and Liturgy* 3 (1977), pp. 39–42.

Reinhold, H.A. "About Music and Other Things." *Orate Fratres* 18 (1943/44), pp. 514–520.

_____. "Choir and/or People." *Orate Fratres* 18 (1943/44), pp. 73–76.

_____. "Liturgical Discernment." *Catholic Choirmaster* 31 (1945), pp. 51–53.

_____. "Praying Wisely—in Latin and English." *Orate Fratres* 21 (1946/47), pp. 75–79.

Rendler, Elaine. "Claim Your Art!" *Pastoral Music* 4 (April-May 1980), pp. 19–21.

_____. "Give Them Songs to Remember." *Liturgy* 24 (July-Aug. 1979), pp. 31–32.

_____. "Ministering Pastoral Music in Practice." *Pastoral Music* 5 (June-July 1981), pp. 20–23.

Rennings, Heinrich. "Spotlight on the Reform of the Funeral Rite." Tr. by Theodore L. Westow. *Concilium* 32 (1968), pp. 109–116.

Repp, Ray. "Folk Music: Secular or Sacred?" *Liturgical Arts* 35 (1966), pp. 18–20.

Reuter, Paul. "The Folk Tradition in Liturgical Music." *Sacred Music* 93 (1966), pp. 8–17.

Richens, R.H. "The Role of Music in An English High Mass." *The Clergy Review* 50 (1965), pp. 432–438.

Riedel, Johannes. "Folk, Rock and Black Music in the Church of Today." *Worship* 44 (1970), pp. 514–527.

Rivers, Clarence Joseph. "Music and the Dramatic Structure of the Mass." *Liturgy* 23 (1978), pp. 26–27.

_____. "Music and the Liberation of Black Catholics." *Freeing the Spirit* 1 (1971), pp. 26–28.

_____. "Yes, But Why Do We Have to Sing?" *North American Liturgical Week* 26 (1965), pp. 141–148.

Robinson, James M. "Primitive Christian 'Hodayoth.' " Drew University Theological School, 1965. Unpublished translation.

Rocchus, Father. "Worldly Music in Church: A Demon." *Orate Fratres* 7 (1932/33), pp. 227–230.

Roff, Joseph. "Music During A Low Mass." *Catholic Choirmaster* 39 (1953), pp. 51–52, 59.

Rossini, Carlo. "Women in Church Choirs." *Caecilia* 61 (1935), pp. 162–164, 322–326.

Routley, Erik. "A National Hymnal?" *Worship* 49 (1975), pp. 263–271.

_____. "Christian Hymnody and Christian Maturity." *Worship* 51 (1977), pp. 505–523.

_____. "Church Music and Hymnody: Browsing Among Recent Books." *Worship* 53 (1979), pp. 404–413.

_____. "Church Music: The Dilemma of Excellence." *Pastoral Music* 3 (June-July 1979), pp. 29–33.

_____. "Contemporary Catholic Hymnody: An Afterword." *Worship* 47 (1973), pp. 417–423.

_____. "Contemporary Catholic Hymnody In Its Wider Setting: Foreign Books and Liturgical Music." *Worship* 47 (1973), pp. 322–337.

_____. "Contemporary Catholic Hymnody In Its Wider Setting: The Larger Hymnals." *Worship* 47 (1973), pp. 194–211.

_____. "Contemporary Catholic Hymnody In Its Wider Setting: The Smaller Hymnals." *Worship* 47 (1973), pp. 258–273.

_____. "The Eucharistic Hymns of Isaac Watts." *Worship* 48 (1974), pp. 526–535.

_____. "Hymnody: Our Annual Roundup." *Worship* 54 (1980), pp. 446–455.

_____. "Hymns: A Roundup for 1977." *Worship* 52 (1978), pp. 108–120.

_____. "The New Lutheran Book of Worship: A Preview of the Hymns." *Worship* 52 (1978), pp. 403–408.

_____. "1976: A Vigorous Year in Hymnology." *Worship* 51 (1977), pp. 120–126.

_____. "Prayers We Have In Common: The Musical Implications." *Worship* 47 (1973), pp. 137–143.

_____. "Progress Report in Hymnody." *Worship* 49 (1975), pp. 393–399.

_____. "Sexist Language: A View From A Distance." *Worship* 53 (1979), pp. 2–11.

_____. "Theology For Church Musicians." *Theology Today* 34 (1977), pp. 20–28.

_____. "Things Are Looking Better." *Worship* 50 (1976), pp. 43–49.

Rowthorn, Jeffery. "Phoenix *Resurgens*: The Yale Institute of Sacred Music." *Worship* 48 (1974), pp. 480–489.

Ryan, Kenneth. "The Church and the Musician." *Orate Fratres* 7 (1932/33), pp. 304–306.

Ryan, William F. "John's Hymn to the Word." *Worship* 37 (1962/63), pp. 285–292.

Saliers, Don E. "Hymns From Yesterday ... For Tomorrow." *Pastoral Music* 5 (April-May 1981), pp. 32–34.

_____. "The Integrity of Sung Prayer." *Worship* 55 (1981), pp. 290–303.

Sanders, Jack T. "Hymnic Elements in Ephesians 1–3." *Zeitschrift für die neutestamentliche Wissenshaft* 56 (1965), pp. 214–232.

Schalk, Carl. "Church Music Today: The Change in Change." *Perkins Journal* 27 (Winter 1973), pp. 15–21.

_____. "Theology of Church Music." In *Key Words In Church Music*. St. Louis: Concordia, 1978.

_____. "Thoughts On Smashing Idols: Church Music in the '80s." *The Christian Century* (September 20, 1981), pp. 960–963.

Schalz, Nicolas. "*La Notion de 'Musique Sacrée.' Une tradition recente.*" *La Maison-Dieu* 108 (1971), pp. 32–57.

Schirmann, Jefim. "Hebrew Liturgical Poetry and Christian Hymnology." *Jewish Quarterly Review* 44 (1953), pp. 123–161.

Schmidt, Herman. "Political Symbols, Poems and Songs." Tr. by Hubert Hoskins. *Concilium* 92 (1974), pp. 123–152.

Schmidt, Joseph. "A Parish Sings." *Orate Fratres* 24 (1949/50), pp. 26–28.

Schmitt, Francis P. "A Commentary On the Statement of the Bishops' Committee On the Liturgy." *Liturgical Arts* 36 (1968), pp. 79–81.

_____. "Leaning Right?" In *Harmony and Discord*. An Open Forum On Church Music. Washington, DC: Liturgical Conference (1966), pp. 17–26.

Schuler, Richard J. "An Impoverishment?" *Sacred Music* 108 (Spring 1981), pp. 3–4.

_____. "The Battle." *Sacred Music* 107 (Winter 1980), p. 25.

_____. "Church Music After Vatican II." *Sacred Music* 103 (1976), pp. 15–18.

————. "The Congregation: Its Possibilities and Limitations in Singing." *Sacred Music* 94 (Winter 1967), pp. 12–43.

————. "Education in Music, The Answer to Our Liturgical Problems." *Sacred Music* 93 (1966), pp. 29–36.

————. "Encyclical *Musicae Sacrae Disciplina.*" *Caecilia* 84 (1957), pp. 90–94.

————. "Humanism and the Sacred." *Sacred Music* 96 (Winter 1969), pp. 3–6.

————. "*Motu Proprio* (1903–1978)." *Sacred Music* 105 (Winter 1978), pp. 21–23.

————. "The *Motu Proprio* and the Progress of Church Music." *Catholic Choirmaster* 39 (1953), pp. 99–101.

————. "Native Music for the Missions." *Sacred Music* 102 (1975), pp. 27–30.

————. "1967 Instruction—Ten Years Later." *Sacred Music* 104 (1977), pp. 3–12.

————. "Sacred Music and Contemplation."*Sacred Music* 106 (Spring 1979), pp. 23–26.

————. "The Sacred and the Secular in Music." *Sacred Music* 93 (1966), pp. 85–92.

————. "True and Sacred." *Sacred Music* 105 (Spring 1978), pp. 31–32.

Seguy, Jean. "St. Augustine and the Vernacular." *Caecilia* 81 (1954), pp. 257–258, 260.

Selner, John C. "Golden Years." *Catholic Choirmaster* 50 (1964), pp. 147–148.

————. "*Mediator Dei*: The New Letter On the Liturgy." *Catholic Choirmaster* 35 (1949), pp. 5–7, 51–53, 82, 99–100, 103.

————. "Sacred Chant and the Liturgy." *Catholic Choirmaster* 42 (1956), pp. 130, 161–166.

————. "Singing the New Songs." *Sacred Music* 92 (1965), pp. 61–63.

Senchur, Becket G. "Toward A Spirituality of Liturgical Music." *Pastoral Music* 4 (June–July 1980), pp. 20–24.

Sessions, Kyle C. "The Sources of Luther's Hymns and the Spread of the Reformation." *Lutheran Quarterly* 17 (1965), pp. 206–223.

Sheehan, Shawn G. "Distribution of Roles." *North American Liturgical Week* 22 (1961), pp. 131–135.

Sheldon, Sister Gertrude Marie. "The Benedictine Heritage of Sacred Music." *Caecilia* 83 (1956), pp. 161–167, 209–211, 267–273.

Sherry, Robert J. "Song in the Liturgy." *Catholic Choirmaster* 45 (1959), pp. 143–146, 176.

Smith, Fidelis. "Hymnology and the Encyclical '*Musicae sacrae disciplina.*'" *Catholic Choirmaster* 42 (1956), pp. 91–100.

————. "Modern Music: Let's Face It!" *Caecilia* 84 (1957), pp. 32–44.

_____. "Music, Sanity, and Spirituality." *Catholic Choirmaster* 43 (1957), pp. 3–7, 41.

_____. *"Musicae Sacrae Disciplina:* Pius XII's Encyclical On Sacred Music." *Musical Quarterly* 43 (1957), pp. 461–479.

_____. "Musical Instruments in Church." *Caecilia* 84 (1957), pp. 237–254.

_____. "Towards An Aesthetics of Sacred Music." *Caecilia* 85 (1958), pp. 107–117.

Smith, Henry Augustine. "The Expression of Religion in Music." In *The Arts and Religion*. The Ayer Lectures of the Colgate-Rochester Divinity School, 1943. New York: MacMillan (1944), pp. 93–132.

Snow, Robert, J. "Reactions On the Recent Music Congress." *Sacred Music* 93 (1966), pp. 97–109.

Söhngen, Oskar. "What Is the Position of Church Music in Germany Today?" In *Cantors At the Crossroads*. Ed. by Johannes Riedel. St. Louis: Concordia, 1967.

Somerville, Stephen. "Sacred Music in Canada and the United States." *Concilium* 22 (1967), pp. 122–127.

Stanley, David M. *"Carmenque Christo Quasi Deo Dicere. . . . "* *Catholic Biblical Quarterly* 20 (1958), pp. 173–191.

Stefani, Gino. "Does the Liturgy Still Need Music?" Tr. by Anthony M. Buono. *Concilium* 42 (1969), pp. 71–86.

Stevenson, Robert. "Luther's Musical Achievement." *Lutheran Quarterly* 3 (1951), pp. 255–262.

Stohr, Albert. "The Encyclical 'On Sacred Music' and Its Significance for the Care of Souls." In *The Assisi Papers*. Collegeville: Liturgical Press (1957), pp. 186–200.

Sullivan, Kathryn. "Blessed Be the God and Father of Our Lord Jesus Christ." In *Liturgy For the People*. Ed. by William Leonard. Milwaukee: Bruce (1963), pp. 29–37.

Thibodeau, Ralph. "Fiasco in Church Music." *Commonweal* 84 (April 8, 1966), pp. 73–75, 78.

Thurston, Ethel. "Ethos in Music." *Catholic Art Quarterly* 16 (1953), pp. 110–122.

Tipton, Julius R. "The Composer and the Liturgy." *Musart* 26 (1974), pp. 11–14.

Tompkins, Haldan D. "Crossroads In Church Music." *Worship* 38 (1963/64), pp. 48–52.

_____. "Music, Bricks and Mortar," *Worship* 38 (1963/64), pp. 644–651.

_____. "Sacred Music and the Constitution." *Worship* 38 (1963/64), pp. 289–296.

Tortolano, William. "Rhythm in the Twentieth Century Mass." *Sacred Music* 95 (Summer 1968), pp. 5–15.

Trotter, F. Thomas. "A Theology of Church Music." *The Choral Journal* 14 (1974), p. 15.

Udulutsch, Irvin. "Musical Instruments in Church Use." *North American Liturgical Week* 20 (1959), pp. 128–131.

Ulanov, Barry. "Music in the Church: A Declaration of Dependence." In *Harmony and Discord. An Open Forum On Church Music*. Washington, DC: The Liturgical Conference (1966), pp. 50–58.

Universa Laus. "Music In Christian Celebration." Document On Points of Reference and Beliefs Held in Common—1980. In *Music and Liturgy* 6 (1980), pp. 151–161.

Vail, James H. "Values in Church Music: A Reassessment." *Sacred Music* 99 (1972), pp. 9–17.

Vallerand, Jean. "Church Polyphony, Gregorian Chant and the Modern Ear." *Caecilia* 79 (1952), pp. 92–95.

Vawter, Bruce. "The Colossians Hymn and the Principle of Redaction." *Catholic Biblical Quarterly* 33 (1971), pp. 62–81.

———. "The Development of the Expression of Faith in the Worshipping Community: In the New Testament." *Concilium* 82 (1973), pp. 22–29.

Vellek, Ita. "Selection of Liturgical Music." *Sacred Music* 101 (Spring 1974), pp. 17–21.

Verrilli, William. "Ministry of Music vs. Minister of Music." *Pastoral Music* 5 (Feb.–March 1981), pp. 24–26.

Veuthey, Michel. "Liturgical Singing—The Condemned Man Awaiting His Pardon." *Music and Liturgy* 3 (1977), pp. 66–68.

Vitry, Dom Ermin. "A Crisis From the Beginning." *Caecilia* 85 (1958), pp. 160–165.

———. "An Answer to An Inquiry." *Orate Fratres* 10 (1935/36), pp. 439–445.

———. "Dom Pothier and the Gregorian Restoration." *Orate Fratres* 10 (1935/36), pp. 575–584.

———. "Examination of Conscience." *Caecilia* 83 (1956), pp. 86, 124–126.

———. "Liturgical Apostolate and Musical Restoration." *Orate Fratres* 10 (1935/36), pp. 54–58.

———. "Liturgical Inspiration of Musical Methods." *Orate Fratres* 10 (1935/36), pp. 248–256.

———. "The Mission of Sacred Polyphony." *Caecilia* 65 (1938), pp. 137–138.

———. "Music and Prayer." *Orate Fratres* 25 (1950/51), pp. 549–558.

———. "Priestly Leadership in Sacred Music." *Orate Fratres* 10 (1935/36), pp. 343–349.

———. "What About Our Children Choirs?" *Orate Fratres* 14 (1939/40), pp. 57–62.

_____. "Why People Do Not Like Gregorian Chant." *Orate Fratres* 10 (1935/36), pp. 151–155.

Wagner, Lavern J. "Moving Toward A Golden Era: American Catholic Liturgical Music, 1947–1964." *Sacred Music* 106 (Summer 1979), pp. 7–10.

Wagner, Laverne. "Polyphony Today?" *Sacred Music* 94 (Winter 1967), pp. 3–11.

Walker, Mary Lu. "Where Have All the Lilies Gone?" *Modern Liturgy* 7 (1980), pp. 36–37.

Walsh, Eugene. "The Plan of the Community Low Mass." *North American Liturgical Week* 22 (1961), pp. 136–142.

Walsh, Thomas Joseph. "The True Purpose of Sacred Music." *Catholic Choirmaster* 22 (1936), pp. 78–81.

Ward, Justine B. "Father J.B. Young, S.J." *Catholic Choirmaster* 10 (1924), pp. 120–124.

_____. "The Reform in Church Music." *The Atlantic Monthly* 97 (1906), p. 455–463.

Watkins, Keith. "Congregational Song for Folk-Protestant Worship." *Worship* 46 (1972), pp. 86–97.

Weakland, Rembert. "The Church Composer and the Liturgical Challenge." In *Liturgy For the People*. Ed. by William Leonard. Milwaukee: Bruce (1963), pp. 132–146.

_____. "Claim Your Art." *Pastoral Music* 5 (June–July 1981), pp. 34–38.

_____. "Comments: The State of the Question." *Sacred Music* 92 (1965), pp. 27–29.

_____. "Congregational Malaise." *Catholic Choirmaster* 48 (1962), pp. 147–149.

_____. "Music and Liturgy in Evolution." *Liturgical Arts* 35 (1967), pp. 114–117.

_____. "Music and the Constitution." *North American Liturgical Week* 25 (1964), pp. 204–209.

_____. "Music As Art in Liturgy." *Worship* 41 (1967), pp. 5–15.

_____. "Music Ministry, Today and Tomorrow." In *Pastoral Music in Practice*. Ed. by Virgil C. Funk and Gabe Huck. Washington, DC: NPM (1981), pp. 1–9.

_____. "Recent Trends in Catholic Church Music." *Liturgical Arts* 33 (1965), pp. 32–33.

_____. "The Sung Mass and Its Problems." *North American Liturgical Week* 26 (1965), pp. 238–244.

_____. "The Task of A Liturgical Musician." *Origins* 7 (1978), pp. 685–688.

Weind, Teresita. "What Makes Pastoral Music Pastoral?" *Pastoral Music* 5 (June–July 1981), pp. 24–26.

Wilkey, Jay W. "Music As Religious Expression in Contemporary Society." *Review and Expositor* 69 (1972), pp. 199–216.

———. "Prolegomena to A Theology of Music." *Review and Expositor* 69 (1972), pp. 507–517.

Winnen, J.A. "It Must Be Done—It Can Be Done." *Orate Fratres* 11 (1936/37), pp. 337–345.

Winter, Paul. "*Magnificat* and *Benedictus*—Maccabean Psalms?" *Bulletin of the John Rylands Library* 37 (1954), pp. 328–347.

Wojcik, Richard J. "The New Design of Liturgical Music." *Chicago Studies* 6 (1967), pp. 139–154.

Woodworth, G. Wallace. "Latin and the Vernacular in Catholic and Protestant Churches, Sixteenth and Twentieth Centuries: A Parallel." *Sacred Music* 94 (Fall 1967), pp. 3–15.

Wurm, Robert. "Possible: A Gregorian–English Psalter." *Sacred Music* 92 (Winter 1966), pp. 107–115.

Wyton, Alec. "What's Happening in Church Music Today?" *Sacred Music* 98 (Fall 1971), pp. 6–10.

Young, Alfred. "An American Prelude to Pius X: On Congregational Singing." *Orate Fratres* 21 (1946/47), pp. 356–362.

Young, Guilford C. "Church Music in Australia." *Concilium* 12 (1966), pp. 127–130.

Liturgy and Worship

Books

Avila, Rafael. *Worship and Politics*. Maryknoll, NY: Orbis, 1981.

Bacchiocchi, Samuele. *From Sabbath to Sunday*. Rome: Pontifical Gregorian University Press, 1977.

Balasuriya, Tissa. *The Eucharist and Human Liberation*. Maryknoll, NY: Orbis, 1979.

Baumstark, A. *Comparative Liturgy*. Westminster: Newman, 1958.

Becker, Charles Joseph. *Iteration of Mass: A Study of the Liturgical Regulations From the Thirteenth Century to the Present*. Dissertation. Washington, D.C.: Catholic University, 1962.

Benz, Ernst. *The Eastern Orthodox Church: Its Thought and Life*. Tr. by Richard and Clara Winston. Chicago: Aldine Pub. Co., 1963.

Bishops' Committee On the Liturgy. *The Cathedral. A Reader*. Washington, DC: USCC, 1979.

———. *The Environment for Worship*. Washington, DC: USCC, 1980.

Bouyer, Louis. *Eucharist*. Tr. by Charles Underhill Quinn. Notre Dame: University Press, 1968.

_____. *Liturgical Piety*. Notre Dame: University Press, 1955.

_____. *The Liturgy Revived*. A Doctrinal Commentary on the Conciliar Constitution on the Liturgy. Notre Dame: University Press, 1964.

_____. *Rite and Man*. Natural Sacredness and Christian Liturgy. Tr. by M. Joseph Costelloe. Notre Dame: University Press, 1963.

Brightman, F.E. *Liturgies Eastern and Western*. Vol. 1. *Eastern Liturgies*. Oxford: Clarendon, 1896.

Brilioth, Yngve. *Eucharistic Faith and Practice*. Tr. by A.G. Hebert. London & New York: MacMillan, 1930.

Calian, Carnegie Samuel. *Icon and Pulpit*. Philadelphia: Westminster, 1968.

Casel, Odo. *The Mystery of Christian Worship*. Tr. by I.T. Hale. Westminster: Newman, 1962.

Champlin, Joseph. *Christ Present and Yet to Come*. The Priest and God's People at Prayer. Maryknoll, NY: Orbis, 1971.

_____. *The Mass In A World of Change*. Notre Dame: Ave Maria Press, 1973.

Charley, Julian W. *The Anglican-Roman Catholic Agreement on the Eucharist*. With An Historical Introduction and Theological Commentary. Grove Booklet on Ministry and Worship 1. Bramcote: Grove Books, 1971.

Crichton, J.D. *The Once and the Future Liturgy*. Dublin: Veritas Publications, 1977.

Cullmann, Oscar. *Baptism in the New Testament*. Tr. by J.K.S. Reid. London: SCM, 1950.

_____. *Early Christian Worship*. Tr. by A. Stewart Todd and James B. Torrance. London: SCM Press, 1953.

Cully, Iris V. *Christian Worship and Church Education*. Philadelphia: Westminster, 1967.

Danielou, Jean. *The Bible and the Liturgy*. Notre Dame: University Press, 1956.

Davies, Horton. *Worship and Theology in England*. The Ecumenical Century, 1900–1965. Vol. 5. Princeton: Princeton University Press, 1965.

Davis, Charles. *Liturgy and Doctrine*. The Doctrinal Basis of the Liturgical Movement. New York: Sheed and Ward, 1960.

_____. *Sacraments of Initiation*. New York: Sheed and Ward, 1964.

Deiss, Lucien. *The Christian Celebration*. Tr. by Gerald J.E. Sullivan. Chicago: World Library Publications, 1977.

_____. *Persons in Liturgical Celebrations*. Tr. by Diane Karampas. Chicago: World Library Publications, 1978.

Deiss, Lucien, ed. *Early Sources of the Liturgy*. Tr. by Benet Weatherhead. New York: Alba House, 1967.

Delling, Gerhard. *Worship in the New Testament*. Tr. by Percy Scott. Philadelphia: Westminster, 1962.

Delorme, J. *et al. The Eucharist in the New Testament.* A Symposium. Tr. by E.M. Stewart. Baltimore: Helicon, 1964.

Devine, George. *Liturgical Renewal.* An Agonizing Reappraisal. New York: Alba House, 1973.

Diekmann, Godfrey. *Come, Let Us Worship.* New York: Image Books, 1966.

_____. *Personal Prayer and the Liturgy.* London: Geoffrey Chapman, 1969.

Dix, Gregory. *The Shape of the Liturgy.* London: Adam and Charles Black, 1975.

Duffy, Regis. *Real Presence.* Worship, Sacraments and Commitment. New York: Harper and Row, 1982.

Dugmore, C.W. *The Influence of the Synagogue Upon the Divine Office.* London: Oxford, 1944.

Egeria's Travels. Tr. by John Wilkinson. London: SPCK, 1971.

Eller, Vernard. *In Place of Sacraments.* A Study of Baptism and the Lord's Supper. Grand Rapids: Eerdmans, 1972.

Every, George. *The Mass.* Dublin: Gill and MacMillan, 1978.

Gallen, John, ed. *Christians At Prayer.* Notre Dame: University Press, 1977.

Garside, Charles. *Zwingli and the Arts.* New Haven: Yale Press, 1966.

Gelineau, Joseph. *The Liturgy Today and Tomorrow.* New York: Paulist Press, 1978.

Gerhard, H.P. *The World of Icons.* New York: Harper and Row, 1971.

Guardini, Romano. *The Spirit of the Liturgy.* Tr. by Ada Lane. New York: Benziger, 1931.

Guzie, Tad. *The Book of Sacramental Basics.* New York: Paulist, 1981.

_____. *Jesus and the Eucharist.* New York: Paulist Press, 1974.

Hageman, Howard G. *Pulpit and Table.* Richmond: John Knox Press, 1962.

Hahn, Ferdinand. *The Worship of the Early Church.* Tr. by David E. Green. Philadelphia: Fortress Press, 1973.

Hall, Sister Jeremy. *The Full Stature of Christ.* The Ecclesiology of Virgil Michel, O.S.B. Collegeville: Liturgical Press, 1976.

Hammond, C.E. *Liturgies Eastern and Western.* Oxford: Clarendon, 1878.

Hardison, O.B. *Christian Rite and Christian Drama in the Middle Ages.* Baltimore: Johns Hopkins, 1965.

Harrelson, Walter. *From Fertility Cult to Worship.* New York: Doubleday, 1970.

Hatchett, Marion J. *Sanctifying Life, Time and Space.* An Introduction to Liturgical Study. New York: Seabury Press, 1976.

Hearne, Brian and Lucas, Denys, ed. *Celebration.* Gaba Institute Pastoral Papers 39. Kampala, Uganda: Gaba Publications, 1975.

Hellwig, Monika. *The Eucharist and the Hunger of the World*. Paramus: Paulist Press, 1976.

_____. *The Meaning of the Sacraments*. Dayton: Pflaum, 1972.

Herwegen, Dom Ildefons. *The Art-Principle of the Liturgy*. Tr. by William Busch. Collegeville: Liturgical Press, 1931.

Hildebrand, Dietrich von. *Liturgy and Personality*. New York: Longmans, Green and Co., 1943.

Hofinger, Johannes, ed. *Liturgy and the Missions*. The Nijmegen Papers. New York: P.J. Kenedy and Sons, 1960.

Hofinger, Johannes *et al. Worship: The Life of the Missions*. Tr. by Mary Perkins Ryan. Notre Dame: University Press, 1958.

Hovda, Robert W. *Strong, Loving and Wise*. Presiding in Liturgy. Washington, D.C.: Liturgical Conference, 1976.

Hovda, Robert W. and Huck, Gabe. *There's No Place Like People*. Chicago: Argus Communications, 1971.

Howell, Clifford. *Of Sacraments and Sacrifice*. Collegeville: Liturgical Press, 1952.

Idelsohn, Abraham Z. *Jewish Liturgy and Its Development*. New York: Schocken Books, 1975.

International Congress of Pastoral Liturgy, First. *The Assisi Papers*. Proceedings: September 18–22, 1956. Collegeville, MN: Liturgical Press, 1957.

Jenson, Robert W. *Visible Words*. The Interpretation and Practice of Christian Sacraments. Philadelphia: Fortress Press, 1978.

Jeremias, Joachim. *The Eucharistic Words of Jesus*. Tr. by Norman Perrin. London: SCM, 1974.

Jones, Cheslyn; Wainwright, Geoffrey; and Yarnold, Edward. *The Study of Liturgy*. New York: Oxford, 1978.

Jones, Paul D. *Rediscovering Ritual*. New York: Newman, 1973.

Jungmann, Josef A. *The Early Liturgy*. Tr. by Francis A. Brunner. Notre Dame: University Press, 1959.

_____. *Liturgical Worship*. New York: Frederick Pustet Co., 1941.

_____. *The Mass*. An Historical, Theological and Pastoral Survey. Tr. by Julian Fernandes, S.J. Collegeville: Liturgical Press, 1976.

_____. *The Mass of the Roman Rite*. Its Origins and Development. Vol. 2. Tr. by Francis A. Brunner. New York: Benziger, 1951.

_____. *The Masses of the Roman Rite*. Its Origins and Development. Vol. 2. Tr. by Francis A. Brunner. New York: Benziger, 1955.

_____. *Public Worship*. A Survey. Tr. by Clifford Howell. Collegeville: Liturgical Press, 1957.

Kavanagh, Aidan. *The Shape of Baptism*. The Rite of Christian Initiation. New York: Pueblo, 1978.

Keifer, Ralph A. *To Give Thanks and Praise*. Washington, DC: National

Association of Pastoral Musicians, 1980.

Kilmartin, Edward J. *Church, Eucharist, and Priesthood.* A Theological Commentary On "The Mystery and Worship of the Most Holy Eucharist." New York: Paulist, 1981.

Klauser, Theodore. *A Short History of the Western Liturgy.* Tr. by John Halliburton. New York: Oxford, 1979.

Kraus, Hans-Joachim. *Worship in Israel.* Tr. by Geoffrey Buswell. Richmond: John Knox Press, 1965.

Krause, Fred. *Liturgy in Parish Life.* A Study of Worship and the Celebrating Community. New York: Alba House, 1979.

Kucharek, Casimir. *The Byzantine-Slav Liturgy of St. John Chrysostom.* Its Origin and Development. Allendale, NJ: Alleluia Press, 1971.

Lampe, G.W.H. *The Seal of the Spirit.* London: SPCK, 1967.

Leeming, Bernard. *Principles of Sacramental Theology.* New York: Longmans, Green and Co., 1956.

Lietzmann, Hans. *Mass and the Lord's Supper.* Four Fascicles. Tr. by Dorothea H.G. Reeve. Leiden: E.J. Brill, 1953, 1954, 1955.

Luther, Martin. "The Blessed Sacrament of the Holy and True Body of Christ, and the Brotherhoods." 1519. Tr. by Jeremiah J. Schindel. In *Luther's Works.* Vol. 35. pp. 49–73.

_____. "A Treatise on the New Testament, that is, the Holy Mass." 1520. Tr. by Jeremiah J. Schindel. In *Luther's Works.* Vol. 35. pp. 79–111.

_____. "The Babylonian Captivity and the Church." 1520. Tr. by A.T.W. Steinhauser. In *Luther's Works.* Vol. 36. pp. 11–126.

_____. "A Treatise On Christian Liberty." 1520. Tr. by W.A. Lambert. In *Three Treatises.*

_____. "The Misuse of the Mass." 1521. Tr. by Frederick C. Ahrens. In *Luther's Works.* Vol. 36. pp. 133–235.

_____. "Concerning the Order of Public Worship." 1523. Tr. by Paul Z. Strodach. In *Luther's Works.* Vol. 53. pp. 11–14.

_____. "An Order of Mass and Communion For the Church At Wittenberg." 1523. Tr. by Paul Z. Strodach. In *Luther's Works.* Vol. 53. pp. 18–40.

_____. "A Christian Exhortation to the Livonians Concerning Public Worship and Concord." 1525. Tr. by Paul Z. Strodach. In *Luther's Works.* Vol. 53. pp. 45–50.

_____. "The German Mass and Order of Service." 1526. Tr. by Augustus Steimle. In *Luther's Works.* Vol. 53. pp. 53–90.

_____. "That These Words of Christ, 'This Is My Body,' etc., Still Stand Firm Against the Fanatics." 1527. Tr. by Robert H. Fischer. In *Luther's Works.* Vol. 37. pp. 5–150.

_____. "Confession Concerning Christ's Supper." 1528. Tr. by Robert H. Fischer. In *Luther's Works.* Vol. 37. pp. 161–372.

_____. "The Marburg Colloquoy and the Marburg Articles." 1529. Tr. by Martin Lehmann. In *Luther's Works*. Vol. 38. pp. 15–89.

_____. "Brief Confession Concerning the Holy Sacrament." 1544. Tr. by Martin Lehmann. In *Luther's Works*. Vol. 38. pp. 287–319.

MacDonald, Alexander B. *Christian Worship in the Primitive Church*. Edinburgh: T and T Clark, 1934.

McDonnell, Kilian. *John Calvin, the Church and the Eucharist*. Princeton: University Press, 1967.

MacGregor, Geddes. *The Rhythm of God*. A Philosophy of Worship. New York: Seabury, 1974.

Maritain, Jacques and Raissa. *Liturgy and Contemplation*. Tr. by Joseph W. Evans. New York: P.J. Kenedy and Sons, 1960.

Martimort, A.G. *et al. The Liturgy and the Word of God*. Collegeville: Liturgical Press, 1959.

Martin, Ralph P. *Worship in the Early Church*. Westwood, NJ: Fleming H. Revell, 1964.

Martos, Joseph. *Doors to the Sacred*. A Historical Introduction to Sacraments in the Catholic Church. Garden City: Doubleday, 1981.

Marx, Paul B. *Virgil Michel and the Liturgical Movement*. Collegeville: Liturgical Press, 1957.

Maxwell, William D. *An Outline of Christian Worship*. London: Oxford, 1936.

Michel, Dom Virgil. *The Liturgy of the Church*. According to the Roman Rite. New York: MacMillan, 1937.

Micklem, Nathaniel. *Christian Worship*. London: Oxford, 1936.

Micks, Marianne H. *The Future Present*. New York: Seabury, 1970.

Mitchell, Leonel L. *Liturgical Change: How Much Do We Need?* New York: Seabury, 1975.

_____. *The Meaning of Ritual*. New York: Paulist, 1977.

Mitchell, Nathan. *Cult and Controversy*. The Worship of the Eucharist Outside Mass. New York: Pueblo, 1982.

Mossi, John P., ed. *Modern Liturgy Handbook*. A Study and Planning Guide for Worship. New York: Paulist, 1976.

Moule, C.F.D. *Worship in the New Testament*. Richmond: John Knox Press, 1961.

Murphy Center for Liturgical Research. *Made, Not Born*. New Perspectives On Christian Initiation and the Catechumenate. Notre Dame: University Press, 1976.

National Office For Black Catholics. *This Far By Faith*. American Black Worship and Its African Roots. Washington, DC: NOBC and the Liturgical Conference, 1977.

Neville, Gwen Kennedy and Westerhoff, John H. *Learning Through Liturgy*. New York: Seabury Press, 1978.

Nichols, James Hastings. *Corporate Worship in the Reformed Tradition.* Philadelphia: Westminster, 1968.

Oesterley, W.O.E. *The Jewish Background of the Christian Liturgy.* Gloucester, Mass: Peter Smith, 1965.

Old, Hughes Oliphant. *The Patristic Roots of Reformed Worship.* Zürich: Theologischer Verlag, 1975.

Padovano, Anthony T. *Presence and Structure.* A Reflection On Celebration, Worship, and Faith. New York: Paulist Press, 1976.

Panikkar, Raimundo. *Worship and Secular Man.* London: Darton, Longman and Todd, 1973.

Pacquier, Richard. *Dynamics of Worship.* Tr. by Donald MacLeod. Philadelphia: Fortress Press, 1967.

Powers, David N. *Gifts That Differ.* Lay Ministries Established and Unestablished. New York: Pueblo, 1980.

Powers, Joseph M. *Eucharistic Theology.* New York: Herder, 1967.

––––––. *Spirit and Sacrament.* New York: Seabury, 1973.

Rahner, Karl. *The Church and the Sacraments.* New York: Herder, 1963.

Read, Herbert. *Icon and Idea.* New York: Schocken Books, 1965.

Reinhold, H.A. *The American Parish and the Roman Liturgy.* New York: MacMillan, 1958.

––––––. *The Dynamics of Liturgy.* New York: Macmillan, 1961.

Richardson, Cyril C. *Zwingli and Cranmer On the Eucharist.* Evanston, Ill: Seabury-Western Theological Seminary, 1949.

Richardson, R.D. *Supplementary Essay: A Further Inquiry Into Eucharistic Origins With Special Reference to New Testament Problems.* Seven Fascicles. Leiden: E.J. Brill, 1955–1976.

Richstatter, Thomas. *Liturgical Law Today.* New Style, New Spirit. Chicago: Franciscan Herald Press, 1977.

Rivers, Clarence Joseph. *Soulfull Worship.* Cincinnati: Stimuli, 1974.

––––––. *The Spirit in Worship.* Cincinnati: Stimuli, 1978.

Roguet, A.-M. *Christ Acts Through the Sacraments.* Tr. by Carisbrooke Dominicans. Collegeville, MN: Liturgical Press, 1954.

Sacerdotal Communities of Saint-Severin of Paris and Saint-Joseph of Nice. *The Liturgical Movement.* Tr. by Lancelot Sheppard. *Twentieth-Century Encyclopedia of Catholicism.* Vol. 115. New York: Hawthorn Books, 1964.

Sagovsky, Nicholas. *Modern Roman Catholic Worship: The Mass.* Grove Booklet On Ministry and Worship 34. Bramcote: Grove Books, 1975.

Schillebeeckx, E. *Christ the Sacrament of Encounter With God.* Tr. by Paul Barrett. New York: Sheed and Ward, 1963.

––––––. *The Eucharist.* Tr. by N.D. Smith. New York: Sheed and Ward, 1968.

Schmemann, Alexander. *For the Life of the World: Sacraments and Orthodoxy.* St. Vladimir's Seminary Press, 1973.

_____. *Introduction to Liturgical Theology.* Tr. by Asheleigh E. Moorehouse. London: Faith Press Ltd., 1966.

_____. *Of Water and the Spirit.* A Liturgical Study of Baptism. St. Vladimir Press, 1974.

Searle, Mark, ed. *Liturgy and Social Justice.* Collegeville: Liturgical Press, 1980.

Seasoltz, R. Kevin. *New Liturgy, New Laws.* Collegeville: The Liturgical Press, 1980.

Segundo, Juan Luis. *The Sacraments Today.* New York: Maryknoll, 1974.

Shepherd, Massey Hamilton, ed. *The Liturgical Renewal of the Church.* New York: Oxford, 1960.

_____. *Liturgy and Education.* New York: Seabury, 1965.

_____. *The Reform of Liturgical Worship.* New York: Oxford, 1961.

Skrobucha, Heinz. *Icons.* Tr. by M.V. Herzfeld and R. Gaze. Philadelphia: Dufour Editions, 1965.

Sloyan, Gerard S. *Liturgy In Focus.* Glen Rock, NJ: Paulist, 1964.

_____. *Worship In A New Key.* What the Council Teaches On the Liturgy. New York: Doubleday/Echo, 1966.

Sloyan, Virginia, ed. *Signs, Songs and Stories.* Another Look At Children's Liturgies. Washington, D.C.: The Liturgical Conference, 1974.

Snyder, Ross. *Contemporary Celebration.* Nashville: Abingdon, 1971.

Southern Baptist-Roman Catholic Midwestern Regional Conference. *The Theology and Experience of Worship.* Kansas City, Missouri. November 28–30, 1977. Washington, DC: USCC, 1978.

Srawley, J.H. *The Early History of the Liturgy.* Cambridge: University Press, 1947.

Taylor, Michael J., ed. *Liturgical Renewal in the Christian Churches.* Baltimore: Helicon, 1967.

_____. *The Protestant Liturgical Renewal.* A Catholic Viewpoint. Westminster: Newman, 1963.

Thompson, Bard. *Liturgies of the Western Church.* New York: Collins World, 1961.

Thurian, Max. *The Eucharistic Memorial.* Part One. The Old Testament. Tr. by J.G. Davies. Richmond: John Knox Press, 1960.

_____. *The Eucharistic Memorial.* Part Two. The New Testament. Tr. by J.G. Davies. Richmond: John Knox Press, 1961.

Tiller, John. *A Modern Liturgical Bibliography.* Grove Booklet On Ministry and Worship 23. Bramcote: Grove Books, 1974.

Underhill, Evelyn. *Worship.* New York: Harper, 1957.

Vajta, Vilmos. *Luther On Worship.* Philadelphia: Muhlenberg, 1958.

Van De Poll, G.J. *Martin Bucer's Liturgical Ideas.* Van Gorcum & Comp. N.V.: 1954.

Verghese, Paul. *The Joy of Freedom.* Eastern Worship and Modern Man. London: Lutterworth Press, 1967.

Verheul, A. *Introduction to the Liturgy.* Towards A Theology of Worship. London: Burns and Oates, 1968.

von Allmen, Jean-Jacques. *The Lord's Supper.* London: Lutterworth Press, 1969.

_____. *Worship: Its Theology and Practice.* New York: Oxford Press, 1965.

Vööbus, Arthur. *Liturgical Traditions in the Didache.* Stockholm: ETSE, 1968.

Werner, Eric. *The Sacred Bridge.* Liturgical Parallels in Synagogue and Early Church. New York: Schocken Books, 1970.

White, James F. *Christian Worship in Transition.* Nashville: Abingdon, 1976.

_____. *Introduction to Christian Worship.* Nashville: Abingdon, 1980.

_____. *New Forms of Worship.* Nashville: Abingdon, 1971.

Willimon, William H. *Word, Water, Wine and Bread.* Valley Forge: Judson Press, 1980.

_____. *Worship As Pastoral Care.* Nashville: Abingdon, 1979.

Winter, Miriam Therese. *Preparing the Way of the Lord.* Nashville: Abingdon, 1978.

Worgul, George S. *From Magic to Metaphor.* A Validation of the Christian Sacraments. New York: Paulist, 1980.

Wright, John H. *A Theology of Christian Prayer.* New York: Pueblo, 1979.

Articles

Adam, Karl. "The Dogmatic Bases of the Liturgy." *Orate Fratres* 11 (1936/37), pp. 481–487, 529–536; (1937/38), pp. 8–14, 56–59, 97–104, 145–151.

Aghiorgoussis, Maximos. "The Holy Eucharist in Ecumenical Dialogue: An Orthodox View." *Journal of Ecumenical Studies* 3 (1976), pp. 204–222.

Althaus, Paul. "The Sacrament," "Baptism," and "The Lord's Supper." In *The Theology of Martin Luther.* Tr. by R.C. Schultz. Philadelphia: Fortress (1966), pp. 345–403.

Annabring, Joseph J. "A Bishop's Program." *Worship* 30 (1955/56), pp. 50–59.

_____. "The Constitution *Christus Dominus* in Action." *Worship* 30 (1955/56), pp. 390–394.

Antonelli, Ferdinando. "The Liturgical Reform of Holy Week: Importance, Realizations, Perspectives." In *The Assisi Papers*. Collegeville: Liturgical Press (1957), pp. 149–166.

"Apostolic Constitutions." In *Early Sources of the Liturgy*. Ed. by Lucien Deiss. New York: Alba House (1967), pp. 151–183.

"Apostolic Tradition of Hippolytus of Rome." In *Early Sources of the Liturgy*. Ed. by Lucien Deiss. New York: Alba House (1967), pp. 27–73.

Attwater, Donald. "A Layman Looks At Liturgy." *Orate Fratres* 10 (1935/36), pp. 532–537.

_____. "The Aesthetic Appeal." *Orate Fratres* 7 (1932/33), pp. 485–491.

Baier, David. "Liturgy the Incarnation of Dogma," *Orate Fratres* 9 (1934/35), pp. 444–448.

Barauna, William. "Active Participation, the Inspiring and Directive Principle of the Constitution." In *The Liturgy of Vatican II*. Ed. by William Barauna. Chicago: Franciscan Herald Press (1966), pp. 131–193.

Barberena, Tomás Garcia. "The Canonical Ordering of the Sacraments." *Concilium* 38 (1968), pp. 6–15.

Baumgarten, J.M. "Sacrifice and Worship Among the Jewish Sectarians of the Dead Sea (Qumran) Scrolls." *Harvard Theological Review* 46 (1953), pp. 154–157.

Bea, Augustine. "The Pastoral Value of the Word of God in the Sacred Liturgy." In *The Assisi Papers*. Collegeville: Liturgical Press (1957), pp. 74–90.

Beachy, Alvin J. "The Theology and Practice of Anabaptist Worship." *Mennonite Quarterly Review* 40 (1966), pp. 163–178.

Beauduin, Lambert. "Abbot Marmion and the Liturgy." *Orate Fratres* 22 (1947/48), pp. 303–314.

Becker, Sister Johanna. "The Christian Potential of the Secular." *Worship* 32 (1957/58), pp. 189–192.

Bishop, Edmund. "The Genius of the Roman Rite." In his *Liturgica Historica*. Oxford: Clarendon Press (1962), pp. 1–19.

Bishop, Joseph. "Liturgy As Subversive Activity." *Commonweal* 93 (December 25, 1970), pp. 324–327.

Borobio, Dionisio. "The 'Four Sacraments' of Popular Religiosity: A Critique." Tr. by Paul Burns. *Concilium* 112 (1979), pp. 85–99.

Botte, Dom Bernard *et al.* "The Teaching of Tradition Concerning the Priesthood of the Faithful." *Orate Fratres* 9 (1934/35), pp. 410–416.

Bottorff, J.F. "Toward A Theology of Liturgical Language." *Liturgy* 23 (1978), pp. 20–26.

Botz, Paschal. "Creed and Cult." *Orate Fratres* 10 (1935/36), pp. 491–498.

Bro, Bernard. "Man and the Sacraments: The Anthropological Substructure of the Christian Sacraments." *Concilium* 31 (1968), pp. 33–50.

Bromily, G.W., ed. "Of Baptism" and "On the Lord's Supper." In *Zwingli and Bullinger*. Library of Christian Classics 24—pp. 119–238.

Buchanan, John. "Liturgy and Sociology." *Orate Fratres* 10 (1935/36), pp. 357–412.

Buckley, J.C. "A People Prepared To Celebrate." In *Pastoral Liturgy*. A Symposium. Ed. by Harold Winstone. London: Collins (1965), pp. 30–44.

Bugnini, Annibale. "Why A Liturgy Reform?" *Worship* 29 (1954/55), pp. 562–569.

Bularzik, Rembert. "The Liturgy In Relation to Life." *Orate Fratres* 6 (1932), pp. 248–254, 299–307.

_____. "Renewal of the Social Order in Christ." *Orate Fratres* 9 (1934/35), pp. 262–275.

Burghardt, Walter J. "A Theologian's Challenge to Liturgy." *Theological Studies* 35 (1974), pp. 233–248.

Busch, William. "About the Encyclical *Mediator Dei*." *Orate Fratres* 22 (1947/48), pp. 153–156.

_____. "The Liturgy A School of Catholic Action." *Orate Fratres* 7 (1932/33), pp. 6–12.

_____. "On Liturgical Reforms." *Orate Fratres* 11 (1936/37), pp. 352–357.

Butler, J.F. "Presuppositions in Modern Theologies of the Place of Worship." *Studia Liturgica* 3 (1964), pp. 210–226.

Capelle, Abbot Bernard. "The Holy See and the Liturgical Movement." *Orate Fratres* 11 (1936/37), pp. 1–8, 50–61.

_____. "The Pastoral Theology of the Encyclicals *Mystici Corporis* and *Mediator Dei*." In *The Assisi Papers*. Collegeville: The Liturgical Press (1957), pp. 32–43.

Carroll, Thomas J. "Pius XII Envisions the Future." *National Liturgical Week* (1953), pp. 163–180.

Casel, Dom Odo. "On the Idea of the Liturgical Festival." *Orate Fratres* 11 (1936/37), pp. 407–411, 445–449.

Centre de Pastorale Liturgique. "First Principles For Church Architecture." Conclusions of Session at Versailles, August 30–September 1, 1960. In *Worship* 35 (1960/61), pp. 509–515.

Cicognani, Gaetano Cardinal. "Opening Address: First International Congress of Pastoral Liturgy." In *The Assisi Papers*. Collegeville: The Liturgical Press (1957), pp. 1–17.

Clarine, Sister M. "A Report On Four Years of Praying With Understanding." *Worship* 29 (1954/55), pp. 279–287.

Clement of Rome. "First Letter to the Corinthians." In *Early Christian Fathers*. Tr. and ed. by Cyril C. Richardson. Philadelphia: Westminster (1953), pp. 33–73.

Collins, Mary. "Critical Questions for Liturgical Theology." *Worship* 53 (1979), pp. 302–317.

_____. "Local Liturgical Legislation: United States of America." *Concilium* 72 (1972), pp. 148–151.

_____. "Who Are the Hearers of the Word?" *Liturgy* 25 (January–February 1980), pp. 5–8, 42–44.

Confrey, Burton. "Reactions to Basing Catholic Action on the Liturgy." *Orate Fratres* 7 (1932/33), pp. 66–72.

Crabtree, Arthur B. "The Eucharist in Baptist Life and Thought." *Journal of Ecumenical Studies* 13 (1976), pp. 296–305.

Crichton, J.D. "The Holy Spirit in Eucharistic Celebration." In *Pastoral Liturgy. A Symposium*. Ed. by Harold Winstone. London: Collins (1965), pp. 15–29.

Cullmann, Oscar. "The Meaning of the Lord's Supper in Primitive Christianity." Tr. by J.G. Davies. In *Essays on the Lord's Supper*. London: Lutterworth Press, 1958.

Curran, Sister Mary Antonina. "Liturgy: the Summit and Source of Christian Life." *North American Liturgical Week* 26 (1965), pp. 168–174.

Cyril of Jerusalem. "Catechetical Lectures 1–18." Tr. by Leo P. McCauley. In *The Fathers of the Church*. Vol. 61 (1969) and Vol. 64 (1970). Washington, DC: Catholic University Press.

_____. "Mystagogical Lectures." I-V. Tr. by Leo P. McCauley. In *The Fathers of the Church*. Vol. 64. Washington, DC: Catholic University Press, 1970.

Dahl, Nils. "*Anamnesis: Mémoire et Commemoration dans le christianisme primitif.*" *Studia Liturgica* 1 (1947), pp. 69–95.

Danneels, Godfried. "Communion Under Both Kinds." Tr. by Theodore L. Westow. *Concilium* 2 (1965), pp. 153–158.

Davies, Horton. "Reshaping the Worship of the United Church of Christ." *Worship* 41 (1967), pp. 542–551.

Davis, Charles. "Episcopate and Eucharist." *Worship* 38 (1963/64), pp. 502–515.

_____. "Odo Casel and the Theology of Mysteries." *Worship* 34 (1959/60), pp. 428–438.

_____. "The Theology of Transubstantiation." *Sophia* 3 (1964), pp. 12–24.

Davis, H.F. *et al*. "A Definite Plan About the Vernacular." *Orate Fratres* 17 (1942/43), pp. 310–312.

de la Bedoyere, Michael. "Introducing the Vernacular." *Orate Fratres* 17 (1942/43), pp. 209–212.

"Didache, The." In *Early Christian Fathers.* Tr. and ed. by Cyril C. Richardson. Phildelphia: Westminster (1953), pp. 161–179.

"Didascalia of the Apostles, The." In *Early Sources of the Liturgy.* Ed. by Lucien Deiss. New York: Alba House (1967), pp. 77–96.

Diekmann, Godfrey. "Liturgical Practice in the United States and Canada." *Concilium* 12 (1966), pp. 157–166.

———. "Mass Commentary." *Worship* 33 (1958/59), pp. 56–66.

———. "Michael A. Mathis, R.I.P." *Worship* 34 (1959/60), pp. 276–278.

———. "The Place of Liturgical Worship." *Concilium* 2 (1965), pp. 67–107.

———. "The Reform of Catholic Liturgy: Are We Too Late?" *Worship* 41 (1967), pp. 142–151.

———. "Two Approaches to Understanding the Sacraments." *Worship* 31 (1956/57), pp. 504–520.

———. "Worship." In *Theology of Renewal.* Vol. 2. Ed. by L.K. Shook. New York: Herder and Herder (1968), pp. 88–99.

Dolan, John P. "The Sixteenth Century." *Worship* 33 (1958/59), pp. 515–523.

Doncoeur, Paul. "The Problem of Community Worship." *Orate Fratres* 21 (1946/47), pp. 217–228.

Ducey, Michael. "Maria Laach and the Liturgy." *Orate Fratres* 9 (1934/35), pp. 108–113.

Dulles, Avery. "Intercommunion Between Lutherans and Roman Catholics." *Journal of Ecumenical Studies* 13 (1976), pp. 250–257.

Dwyer, Robert J. "The Artist and the Church." *Worship* 32 (1957/58), pp. 121–131.

Ediger, Elmer M. "The Mennonite Approach to Worship." *Mennonite Quarterly Review* 29 (1955), pp. 197–211.

Ellard, Gerald. "The American Scene, 1926–51." *Orate Fratres* 25 (1950/51), pp. 500–508.

———. "Liturgical Formation: The End and the Means." *Orate Fratres* 7 (1932/33), pp. 255–260.

———. "Liturgical Formation vs. Information." *Orate Fratres* 7 (1932/33), pp. 101–104.

———. "People Need A Simpler Mass." *Worship* 34 (1959/60), pp. 131–137.

Ellard, Gerald, ed. "Pope Pius XI On Corporate Worship." *Orate Fratres* 10 (1935/36), pp. 553–561.

———. "Progress of the Dialog Mass in Chicago." *Orate Fratres* 14 (1939/40), pp. 19–25.

———. "Thanks For 'Liturgical' 1957." *Worship* 32 (1957/58), pp. 71–76.

———. "Thy Kingdom Come, In the Liturgy, Today and Tomorrow." *North American Liturgical Week* 23 (1962), pp. 100–106.

Elliott, John H. "The Rehabilitation of An Exegetical Step-Child: 1 Peter in Recent Research." *Journal of Biblical Literature* 95 (1976), pp. 243–254.

Ellis, John Tracy. "Archbishop Carroll and the Liturgy in the Vernacular." In his *Perspectives in American Catholicism*. Baltimore: Helicon (1963), pp. 127–133.

Empereur, Jake. "The Liturgy That Does Justice." *Modern Liturgy* 7 (August 1980), p. 2f.

"Euchology of Serapion of Thmuis, The." In *Early Sources of the Liturgy*. Ed. by Lucien Deiss. New York: Alba House (1967), pp. 97–134.

Fink, Peter. "Liturgy and Pluriformity." *The Way* 20 (1980), pp. 97–107.

_____. "Three Languages of Christian Sacraments." *Worship* 52 (1978), pp. 561–575.

_____. "Towards A Liturgical Theology." *Worship* 47 (1973), pp. 601–609.

Fischer, Balthasar. "Catholic Liturgy in the Light of the Vatican Council and the Post-Conciliar Reform of the Liturgy." *One In Christ* 13 (1977), pp. 23–32.

Florenskii, Archpriest Pavel. "On the Icon." Tr. by John Lindsay Opie. *Eastern Churches Review* 7 (1976), pp. 11–37.

Floristan, Casiano. "The Assembly and Its Pastoral Implications." Tr. by Paul Burns. *Concilium* 12 (1966), pp. 33–44.

Florovsky, Georges. "The Iconoclastic Controversy." In his *Christianity and Culture*. Vol. 2. Collected Works. Belmont, Mass: Nordland (1974), pp. 101–119.

Franklin, R.W. "Guéranger: A View On the Centenary of His Death." *Worship* 49 (1975), pp. 318–328.

_____. "Guéranger and Pastoral Liturgy: A Nineteenth-Century Context." *Worship* 50 (1976), pp. 146–162.

_____. "The Nineteenth-Century Liturgical Movement." *Worship* 53 (1979), pp. 12–39.

Gallen, John. "American Liturgy: A Theological Locus." *Theological Studies* 35 (1974), pp. 302–311.

Ganss, George E. "The Function of Liturgy In Establishing the Christian Social Order." *Orate Fratres* 11 (1936/37), pp. 163–168, 358–362, 499–505.

Garrone, Gabriel. "The Pastoral Import of *Christus Dominus*." In *The Assisi Papers*. Collegeville: The Liturgical Press (1957), pp. 139–148.

Gärtner, Bertil. "John 6 and the Jewish Passover." In *Coniectanea Neotestamentica* 17 (1959), pp. 5–52.

Gelineau, Joseph. "Celebrating the Paschal Liberation." Tr. by V. Green. *Concilium* 92 (1974), pp. 107–119.

_____. "L'Église Répond A Dieu par la parole de Dieu." In *Parole de Dieu et liturgie*. Le Congrès de Strasbourg. Paris: Les éditions du Cerf (1958), pp. 155–179.

Gerlier, Pierre Cardinal. "Bilingual Rituals and the Pastoral Efficacy of the Sacraments." In *The Assisi Papers*. Collegeville: Liturgical Press (1957), pp. 44–56.

Giese, Vincent J. "Virgil Michel and the Congress of the Lay Apostolate." *Worship* 32 (1957/58), pp. 58–66.

Gilkey, Langdon. "Symbols, Meaning, and the Divine Presence." *Theological Studies* 35 (1974), pp. 250–267.

Gillan, Garth. "Expression, Discourse, and Symbol." *Worship* 41 (1967), pp. 16–31.

Greeley, Andrew. "Mass Culture Milieu." *Worship* 33 (1958/59), pp. 19–26.

———. "Religious Symbolism, Liturgy and Community." *Concilium* 62 (1971), pp. 59–69.

Griffin, John J. "Catholic Action and the Liturgical Life." *Orate Fratres* 9 (1934/35), pp. 362–371.

———. "The Liturgical Economy and Social Reconstruction." *Orate Fratres* 11 (1936/37), pp. 69–74, 200–205.

———. "The Spiritual Foundations of Catholic Action." *Orate Fratres* 9 (1934/35), pp. 455–464.

Gritsch, Eric W. and Jenson, Robert W. "Sacraments—the Visible Word." In *Lutheranism. The Theological Movement and Its Confessional Writings*. Philadelphia: Fortress Press (1976), pp. 70–90.

Guzie, Tad. "The Vernacular Isn't Everything." *America* 109 (August 17, 1963), pp. 164–165.

Gy, Pierre-Marie. "Pastoral Liturgy." *Worship* 37 (1962/63), pp. 559–562.

Häring, Bernard. "Liturgical Piety and Christian Perfection." *Worship* 34 (1959/60), pp. 523–535.

Hageman, Howard G. "Coming of Age of the Liturgical Movement." *Studia Liturgica* 2 (1963), pp. 256–265.

———. "The Liturgical Revival." *Theology Today* 6 (1950), pp. 490–505.

Hall, Jeremy. "American Liturgical Movement: The Early Years." *Worship* 50 (1976), pp. 472–487.

Hallinan, Paul. "The Church's Liturgy: Growth and Development." *North American Liturgical Week* 25 (1964), pp. 94–100.

———. "How to Understand Changes in the Liturgy." Atlanta: GB Publications, 1964.

———. "Toward A People's Liturgy." *Worship* 42 (1968), pp. 258–263.

Hasel, Gerhard F. "Basic Proposals for Doing Old Testament Theology" and "The Question of History, History of Tradition, and Salvation History." In his *Old Testament Theology*. Grand Rapids: Eerdmans (1972), pp. 57–75, 129–143.

Hellriegel, Martin B. "Merely Suggesting." *Orate Fratres* 15 (1940/41). pp. 390–397, 442–448.

_____. "Towards A Living Parish." *Worship* 30 (1955/56), pp. 16–25.

Henkey, Charles H. "Liturgical Theology." *Yearbook of Liturgical Studies* 4 (1963), pp. 77–107.

Herwegen, Ildefons. "Liturgy and Preaching." *Orate Fratres* 6 (1931/32), pp. 556–562; 7 (1932/33), pp. 20–26.

Hitchcock, James. "The Decline of the Sacred." *Sacred Music* 100 (1973), pp. 3–9.

Hofinger, John. "Liturgical Training in Seminaries." *Worship* 30 (1955/56), pp. 424–437.

_____. "Missionary Values of the Liturgy." *Worship* 32 (1957/58), pp. 207–218.

Holmes, Urban T. "Liminality and Liturgy." *Worship* 47 (1973), pp. 386–396.

_____. "Ritual and Social Drama." *Worship* 51 (1977), pp. 197–213.

Houtart, Francois. "Sociological Aspects of the Liturgy." *Worship* 42 (1968), pp. 342–363.

Hovda, Robert. "Liturgy Is More Than Mass." *U.S. Catholic* 44 (June 1979), pp. 33–37.

_____. "The Underground Experiment in Liturgy." *Catholic Mind* 66 (1968), pp. 15–27.

Howell, Clifford. "No Parrots in Church." *Worship* 36 (1961/62), pp. 327–335.

_____. "Problems of Participation." *Worship* 26 (1952), pp. 161–173.

_____. "What Form Dialog Mass?" *Worship* 31 (1956/57), pp. 566–570.

Huels, John M. "The Interpretation of Liturgical Law." *Worship* 55 (1981), pp. 218–237.

Jackman, Arthur. "Reflections On the Liturgical Movement." *Orate Fratres* 13 (1938/39), pp. 400–402.

Jacobs, Osmund. "The Liturgy and Catholic Action." *Orate Fratres* 10 (1935/36), pp. 517–521.

Jenson, Robert W. "Eucharist: Its Relative Necessity, Specific Warrant and Traditional Order." *Dialog* 14 (1975), pp. 122–133.

Jones, Bayard H. "The History of the Nestorian Liturgies." *Anglican Theological Review* 46 (1964), pp. 155–176.

_____. "The Quest for the Origins of the Christian Liturgies." *Anglican Theological Review* 46 (1964), pp. 5–21.

Jungmann, Josef A. "A Great Gift of God to the Church." In *The Liturgy of Vatican II.* Vol. 1. Ed. by William Barauna. Eng. ed. by Jovian Lang. Chicago: Franciscan Herald Press (1966), pp. 65–70.

_____. "Church Art." *Worship* 29 (1954/55), pp. 68–82.

_____. "Constitution on the Sacred Liturgy." Tr. by Lalit Adolphus. In *Commentary on the Documents of Vatican II.* Ed. by Herbert Vorgrimler. New York: Herder and Herder (1967), pp. 1–87.

————. "The Eucharist and Pastoral Practice." *Worship* 35 (1960/61), pp. 83–90.

————. "Eucharistic Piety." *Worship* 35 (1960/61), pp. 410–420.

————. "Holy Church." *Worship* 30 (1955/56), pp. 3–12.

————. "Liturgy, Devotions and the Bishop." Tr. by Theodore L. Westow. *Concilium* 2 (1965), pp. 51–58.

————. "The Liturgy In the Parish." *Worship* 31 (1956/57), pp. 62–67.

————. "Liturgy On the Eve of the Reformation." *Worship* 33 (1958/59), pp. 505–515.

————. "The Pastoral Effect of the Liturgy." *Orate Fratres* 23 (1948/49), pp. 481–491.

————. "The Pastoral Idea in the History of the Liturgy." In *The Assisi Papers*. Collegeville: Liturgical Press (1957), pp. 18–31.

————. "*Pia Exercitia* and Liturgy." *Worship* 33 (1958/59), pp. 616–622.

————. "The Sense For the Sacred." *Worship* 30 (1955/56), pp. 354–360.

————. "What the Sunday Mass Could Mean." *Worship* 37 (1962/63), pp. 21–30.

Justin. "Apology I." In *Early Christian Fathers*. Tr. and ed. by Cyril C. Richardson. Philadelphia: Westminster (1953), pp. 242–289.

Kalokyris, Constantine D. "The Essence of Orthodox Iconography." *Greek Orthodox Theological Review* 14 (1969), pp. 42–64.

Käsemann, Ernst. "A Primitive Christian Baptismal Liturgy." In *Essays On New Testament Themes*. Tr. by W.J. Montague. London: SCM (1964), pp. 149–168.

————. "*Das Formular einer neutestamentlichen Ordinationsparänese.*" *Neutestamentliche Studien für Rudolf Bultmann*. Berlin: Alfred Töpelmann (1954), pp. 261–268.

————. "*Liturgie im Neutestament.*" *Religion in Geschichte und Gegenwart*. Band 4. pp. 402–403.

————. "The Pauline Doctrine of the Lord's Supper." In *Essays on New Testament Themes*. Tr. by W.J. Montague. London: SCM (1964), pp. 108–135.

————. "Worship and Everyday Life." *New Testament Questions of Today*. London: SCM (1969), pp. 188–195.

Kavanagh, Aidan. "Life-Cycle Events, Civil Ritual and the Christian." *Concilium* 112 (1979), pp. 14–24.

————. "Liturgical Business Unfinished and Unbegun." *Worship* 50 (1976), pp. 354–364.

————. "Ministries in the Community and in the Liturgy." *Concilium* 72 (1972), pp. 55–67.

————. "Relevance and Change in the Liturgy." *Worship* 45 (1971), pp. 58–72.

Keifer, Ralph A. "Preparation of the Altar and the Gifts Or Offertory?"

Worship 48 (1974), pp. 595–600.

———. "Rite or Wrong." *Commonweal* 102 (August 15, 1975), pp. 328–330.

Kelly, Walter J. "The Authority of Liturgical Laws." *The Jurist* 28 (1968), pp. 397–424.

Kennedy, Eugene C. "The Contribution of Religious Ritual to Psychological Balance." *Concilium* 62 (1971), pp. 53–58.

Kiesling, Christopher. "Liturgy: Call to Social Justice." *Modern Liturgy* 7 (August 1980), pp. 4–5f.

———. "Roman Catholic and Reformed Understandings of the Eucharist." *Journal of Ecumenical Studies* 13 (1976), pp. 268–276.

Kilmartin, Edward J. "Liturgical Theology II." *Worship* 50 (1976), pp. 312–315.

———. "The Orthodox-Roman Catholic Dialogue on the Eucharist." *Journal of Ecumenical Studies* 13 (1976), pp. 213–221.

Klauser, Theodore. "Directives For the Building of A Church." *Orate Fratres* 24 (1949/50), pp. 9–18.

Kloppenburg, Bonaventura. "Chronicle of Amendments of the Constitution." In *The Liturgy of Vatican II*. Vol. 1. Ed. by William Barauna. Chicago: Franciscan Herald Press (1966), pp. 71–94.

Krueger, J.F. "Liturgical Development in Wittenberg from 1520 to 1530." *Lutheran Church Quarterly* 4 (1931), pp. 292–303.

Ladrière, Jean. "The Performativity of Liturgical Language." Tr. by John Griffiths. *Concilium* 82 (1973), pp. 50–62.

Lajeunie, Etienne. "The Spiritual Doctrine of Pius XI." *Orate Fratres* 14 (1939/40), pp. 26–31, 73–76.

Larkin, Christopher. "The Artist As Prophet." *Worship* 32 (1957/58), pp. 175–181.

Larsen, Kenneth J. "Language As Aural." *Worship* 54 (1980), pp. 18–35.

Lavanoux, Maurice. "A Practical Aspect of Liturgical Art." *Orate Fratres* 10 (1935/36), pp. 570–574.

Lawler, Justus George. "The Dawn of the Sacred." *Worship* 32 (1957/58), pp. 137–149.

Lécuyer, Joseph. "The Liturgical Assembly: Biblical and Patristic Foundations." Tr. by Charles McGrath. *Concilium* 12 (1966), pp. 3–18.

Leeming, Bernard. "Liturgy and Mystery." *America* 109 (August 17, 1963), pp. 153–155.

Leenhardt, F.J. "This Is My Body." In *Essays On the Lord's Supper*. Tr. by J.G. Davies. London: Lutterworth Press, (1958), pp. 24–85.

Leonard, William J. "Pius X and the Restoration of Liturgical Life." *National Liturgical Week* (1953), pp. 153–162.

Lercaro, James Cardinal. "The Christian Church." *Worship* 31 (1956/57), pp. 434–443.

———. "Directives For Mass." *Worship* 30 (1955/56), pp. 581–595.

————. "The Simplification of the Rubrics and the Breviary Reform." In *The Assisi Papers*. Collegeville: Liturgical Press (1957), pp. 203–219.

Lindbeck, George A. "A Lutheran View of Intercommunion With Roman Catholics." *Journal of Ecumenical Studies* 13 (1976), pp. 242–249.

"Liturgies of St. John Chrysostom and St. Basil." *The Byzantine Liturgy*. Tr. by Clement C. Englert. New York: Fordham, 1952.

Llopis, Joan. "The Message of Liberation in the Liturgy." Tr. by J.P. Donnelly. *Concilium* 92 (1974), pp. 65–73.

Loew, Josef. "The New Holy Week Liturgy A Pastoral Opportunity." *Worship* 30 (1955/56), pp. 94–113.

————. "Official Diocesan Liturgical Commissions." *Worship* 29 (1954/55), pp. 439–448.

Louden, R. Stuart. "Recent Developments in Ecumenical Liturgical Studies." *Studia Liturgica* 4 (1965), pp. 114–120.

Lukken, Gerard. "The Unique Expression of Faith in the Liturgy." Tr. by David Smith. *Concilium* 82 (1973), pp. 11–21.

McCormack, H. "The Act of Christ in the Mass." *Worship* 37 (1962/63), pp. 630–639.

McDonnell, Kilian. "Calvin's Conception of the Liturgy and the Future of the Roman Catholic Liturgy." *Concilium* 42 (1969), pp. 87–97.

————. "The Constitution on the Liturgy As An Ecumenical Document." *Worship* 41 (1967), pp. 486–497.

————. "Liturgy and the Perils of Experience." *America* 121 (August 16, 1969), pp. 93–95.

————. "The Meaning of Tradition." *Worship* 32 (1957/58), pp. 149–158.

————. "Themes in Ecclesiology and Liturgy From Vatican II." *Worship* 41 (1967), pp. 66–84.

McKenna, Norman. "The Liturgy and Reconstruction." *Orate Fratres* 12 (1937/38), pp. 337–342.

Mackenzie, Ross. "Reformed and Roman Catholic Understandings of the Eucharist." *Journal of Ecumenical Studies* 13 (1976), pp. 260–267.

McLuhan, Marshall. "Liturgy and Media." *The Critic* 31 (January–February 1973), pp. 15–23.

McMahon, L.M. "Towards A Theology of the Liturgy: Dom Odo Casel and the 'Mysterientheorie.'" *Studia Liturgica* 3 (1964), pp. 129–154.

McManus, Frederick R. "The Berakah Award For 1980." *Worship* 54 (1980), pp. 360–378.

————. "The Constitution on Liturgy Commentary." *Worship* 38 (1963/64), pp. 314–374, 450–496, 515–565.

————. "The Council, Renewal, and the Tasks Before Us." *North American Liturgical Week* 24 (1963), pp. 55–60.

————. "Ecumenical Import of the Constitution on the Liturgy." *Studia Liturgica* 4 (1965), pp. 1–8.

_____. "The Juridical Power of the Bishop in the Constitution on the Sacred Liturgy." *Concilium* 2 (1965), pp. 33–49.

_____. "The Law, the Liturgy, and Participation." *North American Liturgical Week* 20 (1959), pp. 43–51.

_____. "Liturgical Law and Difficult Cases." *Worship* 48 (1974), pp. 347–366.

_____. "The Restored Liturgical Catechumenate." *Worship* 36 (1961/62), pp. 536–549.

_____. "Seminary Training." *Worship* 33 (1958/59), pp. 39–41.

_____. "Vatican Council II." *Worship* 37 (1962/63), pp. 2–11, 140–153.

_____. "Woman Commentator Or Lector." *Worship* 34 (1959/60), pp. 353–356.

McNally, Robert E. "The Word of God and the Mystery of Christ." *Worship* 38 (1963/64), pp. 392–402.

McNamara, Martin. "The Liturgical Assemblies and Religious Worship of the Early Christians." *Concilium* 42 (1969), pp. 20–36.

McNaspy, Clement J. "Jesuits and Liturgy." *Worship* 35 (1960/61), pp. 298–301.

_____. "The Language of Prayer." In *Liturgy For the People.* Essays in Honor of Gerald Ellard, S.J. Ed. by William Leonard. Milwaukee: Bruce (1963), pp. 91–103.

_____. "The Vernacular Re-Viewed." *Worship* 35 (1960/61), pp. 241–250.

Macquarrie, John. "Subjectivity and Objectivity." *Worship* 41 (1967) pp. 152–160.

Mahon, Leo T. "What Is To Be Done?" *Commonweal* 82 (August 20, 1965), pp. 590–597.

Maldonado, Luis. "Further Liturgical Reform." Tr. by John H. Stevenson. *Concilium* 32 (1968), pp. 87–97.

Maly, Eugene H. "The Interplay of World and Worship in the Scripture." *Concilium* 62 (1971), pp. 30–39.

Manders, Hendrik. "Concelebration." Tr. by Theodore L. Westow. *Concilium* 2 (1965), pp. 135–151.

Manigne, Jean-Pierre. "The Poetics of Faith in the Liturgy." Tr. by Francis McDonagh. *Concilium* 82 (1973), pp. 40–50.

Marsili, Salvatore. "Liturgical Texts For Modern Man." Tr. by Anthony M. Buono. *Concilium* 42 (1969), pp. 49–70.

Martin, Ralph P. "The Composition of I Peter in Recent Study." *Vox Evangelica.* London: Epworth Press (1962), pp. 29–41.

Meinberg, Cloud H. "A Matter of Love." *Worship* 32 (1957/58), pp. 132–136.

Merkle, John C. "Worship, Insight and Faith in the Theology of Abraham Joshua Heschel." *Worship* 49 (1975), pp. 583–596.

Merton, Thomas. "Liturgy and Spiritual Personalism." *Worship* 34 (1959/60), pp. 494–507.

Meyer, Hans. "How Much Change Is Permissible in the Liturgy?" Tr. by John Drury. *Concilium* 42 (1969), pp. 37–48.

———. "The Social Significance of the Liturgy." Tr. by Francis McDonagh. *Concilium* 92 (1974), pp. 34–50.

Micara, Clement Cardinal. "The Sacred Congregation of Rites On the Vernacular in the Liturgy." *Orate Fratres* 22 (1947/48), pp. 320–322.

Michel, Virgil. "A Cardinal Speaks." *Orate Fratres* 12 (1937/38), pp. 167–171, 208–211, 250–254.

———. "Art and the Christ-Life." *Orate Fratres* 11 (1936/37), pp. 488–492.

———. "Back to the Liturgy." *Orate Fratres* 11 (1936/37), pp. 9–14.

———. "Christian Culture." *Orate Fratres* 13 (1938/39), pp. 296–304.

———. "The Cooperative Movement and the Liturgical Movement." *Orate Fratres* 14 (1939/40), pp. 152–160.

———. "The Liturgy and Modern Thought." *Orate Fratres* 13 (1938/39), pp. 205–212.

———. "Liturgy and the Changing World." *Orate Fratres* 12 (1937), pp. 1–7.

———. "Liturgy and the Psychology of Education. *Orate Fratres* 14 (1939/40), pp. 529–532.

———. "The Liturgy the Basis of Social Regeneration. *Orate Fratres* 9 (1934/35), pp. 536–545.

———. "Personality and Liturgy." *Orate Fratres* 13 (1938/39), pp. 156–159.

———. "The Sacramental System." *Orate Fratres* 9 (1934/35), pp. 114–119.

———. "The Scope of the Liturgical Movement." *Orate Fratres* 10 (1935/36), pp. 485–490.

———. "Why Not Evening Mass?" *Orate Fratres* 12 (1937/38), pp. 29–31.

Miller, Charles E. "Lay Participation in the Mass: Theological Basis." *Worship* 33 (1958/59), pp. 285–289, 347–353.

Miller, John H. "Altar Facing the People: Fact Or Fable?" *Worship* 33 (1958/59), pp. 83–91.

———. "The Distribution of Liturgical Roles According to the Constitution." *Yearbook of Liturgical Studies* 5 (1964), pp. 47–56.

Miller, Paul M. "Worship Among the Early Anabaptists." *Mennonite Quarterly Review* 30 (1956), pp. 235–246.

Milner, Paulinus. "A Commentary On the Liturgical Constitution." In *The People Worship*. Ed. by Lancelot Sheppard. New York: Hawthorn Books (1967), pp. 198–227.

Mitchell, Leonel L. "The Episcopal Church and Liturgical Renewal." *Worship* 48 (1974), pp. 490–499.

Mitchell, Nathan. "L'Zikkaron." *Liturgy* 24 (March–April 1979), pp. 9–10.

Moltmann, Jürgen. "The Liberating Feast." Tr. by Francis McDonagh. *Concilium* 92 (1974), pp. 74–84.

Montini, John Baptist Cardinal. "Liturgical Formation." Tr. by Leonard Doyle. *Worship* 33 (1958/59), pp. 136–164.

Moran, Gabriel. "The Theology of Secularity: What Happens to Worship?" *Worship in The City of Man*. North American Liturgical Week (1966), pp. 80–90.

Moran, Robert E. "Theology of the Parish." *Worship* 38 (1963/64), pp. 421–426.

Moule, C.F.D. "A Reconsideration of the Context of Maranatha." *Journal of New Testament Studies* 6 (1960), pp. 307–310.

_____. "The Nature and Purpose of I Peter." *Journal of New Testament Studies* 3 (1956), pp. 1–11.

Narsai. "Liturgical Homilies." Tr. by R.H. Connolly. *Text and Studies* 8. Ed. by J.A.T. Robinson. Cambridge: University Press (1909), pp. 1–75.

Nelson, J. Robert. "Methodist Eucharistic Usage: From Constant Communion to Benign Neglect to Sacramental Recovery." *Journal of Ecumenical Studies* 13 (1976), pp. 278–285.

Neunheuser, Burkhard. "Mystery Presence." *Worship* 34 (1959/60), pp. 120–127.

Nichols, James Hastings. "The Liturgical Tradition of the Reformed Churches." *Theology Today* 11 (1954), pp. 210–224.

Niesel, Wilhelm. "The Order of Public Worship in the Reformed Churches." *Scottish Journal of Theology* 2 (1949), pp. 381–390.

Noirot, Marcel. "Legitimate Liturgical Customs Contrary to Rubrics." *Worship* 29 (1954/55), pp. 16–22.

O'Connell, John P. "Liturgical Translation." *Worship* 32 (1957/58), pp. 101–103.

O'Hara, Edwin V. "The Observance of Holy Week in the United States in 1956." In *The Assisi Papers*. Collegeville: Liturgical Press (1957), pp. 167–175.

O'Hanlon, Daniel. "The Secularity of Christian Worship." In *Worship in the City of Man*. North American Liturgical Week (1966), pp. 16–28.

Olson, Oliver K. "Contemporary Trends in Liturgy Viewed From the Perspective of Classical Lutheran Theology." *Lutheran Quarterly* 26 (1974), pp. 110–157.

_____. "Liturgy As 'Action'." *Dialog* 14 (1975), pp. 108–113.

O'Mahony, James E. "Liturgy and Religious Experience." *Orate Fratres* 10 (1935/36), pp. 446–451.

L'Osservatore Romano. "The Approved Chapter One." *Worship* 38 (1963/64), pp. 153–164.

O'Toole, Christopher J. "Circular Letter." *Worship* 34 (1959/60), pp. 101–106.

Pascher, Joseph. "Relation Between Bishop and Priests According to the Liturgy Constitution." Tr. by Theodore L. Westow. *Concilium* 2 (1965), pp. 25–32.

Pelikan, J. "Luther and the Liturgy." In *More About Luther.* Decorah, Iowa: Luther College Press (1958), pp. 3–42.

Pichard, Joseph. "The Situation Today." *Worship* 32 (1957/58), pp. 181–189.

Pillai, C.A. Joachim. "Acceptable Worship." *Worship* 38 (1963/64), pp. 402–408.

Power, David N. "Cult To Culture: The Liturgical Foundation of Theology." *Worship* 54 (1980), pp. 482–495.

_____. "Liturgical Ministry: The Christian People's *Poesis* of Time and Place." *Worship* 52 (1978), pp. 211–222.

_____. "Sacramental Celebration and Liturgical Ministry." *Concilium* 72 (1972), pp. 26–42.

_____. "The Song of the Lord in An Alien Land." *Concilium* 92 (1974), pp. 85–106.

_____. "Two Expressions of Faith: Worship and Theology." *Concilium* 82 (1973), pp. 95–103.

_____. "Unripe Grapes: The Critical Function of Liturgical Theology." *Worship* 52 (1978), pp. 386–399.

_____. "Words That Crack: The Uses of 'Sacrifice' in Eucharistic Discourse." *Worship* 53 (1979), pp. 386–402.

Powers, Joseph M. "Liturgical Theology I." *Worship* 50 (1976), pp. 307–312.

Quasten, Johannes. "The Conflict of Early Christianity With the Jewish Temple Worship." *Theological Studies* 2 (1941), pp. 481–487.

Quinn, James. "Ecumenics and the Eucharist." *The Month* 33 (1965), pp. 210–216, 272–281; 34 (1965), pp. 170–176.

Rahner, Karl. "The Presence of the Lord in the Christian Community At Worship." *Theological Investigations* X. New York: Herder and Herder (1973), pp. 71–83.

_____. "What Is A Sacrament?" *Worship* 47 (1973), pp. 274–284.

Rankin, O.S. "The Extent of the Influence of the Synagogue Service Upon Christian Worship." *Journal of Jewish Studies* 1 (1948), pp. 27–32.

Ratcliff, E.C. "The English Usage of Eucharistic Consecration, 1548–1662." In *Liturgical Studies.* London: SPCK (1976), pp. 203–221.

_____. "The Liturgical Work of Archbishop Cranmer." In *Liturgical Studies.* London: SPCK (1976), pp. 184–202.

Ratzinger, Joseph. "The First Session." *Worship* 37 (1962/63), pp. 529–535.

Reed, Luther D. "The Liturgical Movement." In his *Worship*. Philadelphia: Muhlenberg (1959), pp. 372–384.

Regan, Patrick. "Liturgy and the Experience of Celebration." *Worship* 47 (1973), pp. 592–600.

Reinhardt, Kurt F. "Art and the Liturgy." *Orate Fratres* 8 (1933/34), pp. 442–448.

Reinhold, H.A. "A Radical Social Transformation Is Inevitable." *Orate Fratres* 19 (1944/45), pp. 362–368.

_____. "Desiderata To Be Prayed For." *Orate Fratres* 20 (1945/46), pp. 230–235.

_____. "The Discussion Continues." *Orate Fratres* 18 (1943/44), pp. 314–321.

_____. "From the Vernacular Front." *Orate Fratres* 21 (1946/47), pp. 459–466.

_____. "The German Lesson." *Orate Fratres* 19 (1944/45), pp. 411–416.

_____. "The Liturgical Movement to Date." *National Liturgical Week* (1947), pp. 9–20.

_____. "The Mother Tongue: Pro's and Foes." *Orate Fratres* 25 (1950/51), pp. 121–127.

_____. "No Time to Stop." *Commonweal* 82 (August 20, 1965), pp. 583–585.

_____. "To Recite With Fuller Understanding." *Orate Fratres* 19 (1944/45), pp. 385–390.

_____. "The Vernacular Again." *Orate Fratres* 18 (1943/44), pp. 127–132.

Rennings, Heinrich. "What Is the Liturgy Supposed To Do?" Tr. by Theodore L. Westow. *Concilium* 42 (1969), pp. 120–137.

Richardson, R.D. "*Berakah* and *Eucharistia*." *Church Quarterly Review* 148 (1945), pp. 194–220.

_____. "Eastern and Western Liturgies: the Primitive Basis of Their Later Differences." *Harvard Theological Review* 42 (1949), pp. 125–148.

Richstatter, Thomas. "Changing Styles of Liturgical Law." *The Jurist* 38 (1978), pp. 415–425.

Robinson, J.A.T. "Traces of A Liturgical Sequence in 1 Co 16:20–24." *Journal of Theological Studies*, n.s., 4 (1953), pp. 38–41.

Roguet, A.M. "Liturgical Renewal and the Renewal of Preaching." In *The Assisi Papers*. Collegeville: Liturgical Press (1957), pp. 91–94.

Rordorf, W. "*La Confession de Foi et son 'Sitz im Leben' dans L'Eglise Ancienne*." *Novum Testamentum* 9 (1967), pp. 225–238.

Russell, Ralph. "Liturgical Spirituality Is Scriptural." *Worship* 34 (1959/60), pp. 567–573.

Ryan, John J. "Post-Tribal Worship." *Commonweal* 82 (August 20, 1965), pp. 586–589.

Savarimuthu, A. "A Report On the Indian Rite Mass." *Worship* 44 (1970), pp. 238–247.

Schexnayder, Maurice. "Things Blessed Pius X Would Wish to Have Seen." *National Liturgical Week* (1953), pp. 137–146.

Schillebeeckx, E. "Transubstantiation, Transfinalization, Transfiguration." Tr. by David J. Rock. *Worship* 40 (1966), pp. 324–338.

Schmemann, Alexander. "The Liturgical Revival and the Orthodox Church." In *Eucharist and Liturgical Renewal*. Ed. by M.H. Shepherd. New York: Oxford (1960), pp. 115–132.

_____. "Liturgical Theology, Theology of Liturgy, and Liturgical Reform." *St. Vladimir Theological Quarterly* 13 (1969), pp. 217–224.

_____. "Sacrament and Symbol." In *For the Life of the World*. St. Vladimir Press (1973), pp. 135–151.

_____. "Theology and Liturgical Tradition." In *Worship in Scripture and Tradition*. Ed. by Massey Shepherd. New York: Oxford (1963), pp. 165–178.

Schmidt, Gail Ramshaw. "*De Divinis Nominibus*: The Gender of God." *Worship* 56 (1982), pp. 117–131.

Schmidt, Herman. "A General View." Tr. by Theodore L. Westow. *Concilium* 52 (1970), pp. 128–140.

_____. "Lines of Political Action in Contemporary Liturgy." Tr. by Hubert Hoskins. *Concilium* 92 (1974), pp. 13–33.

_____. Liturgy and Modern Society—Analysis of the Current Situation." Tr. by Hubert Hoskins. *Concilium* 62 (1971), pp. 14–29.

_____. "The Liturgy and the Modern World." *Worship* 37 (1962/63), pp. 509–513.

_____. "The Problem of Language In Liturgy." *Worship* 26 (1951/52), pp. 276–292, 342–349.

Schoenbechler, Roger. "The *Missa Recitata.*" *Orate Fratres* 7 (1932/33), pp. 77–84.

Schoonenberg, Piet. "Christ's Eucharistic Presence." *Chicago Studies* 5 (1966), pp. 135–152.

_____. "Presence and the Eucharistic Presence." *Cross Currents* 17 (1967), pp. 39–54.

_____. "The Real Presence in Contemporary Discussion." *Theological Digest* 15 (1967), pp. 3–11.

Searle, Mark. "Liturgy As Metaphor." *Worship* 55 (1981), pp. 98–120.

Seasoltz, Kevin. "Anthropology and Liturgical Theology: Searching For A Compatible Methodology." *Concilium* 112 (1979), pp. 3–13.

Sheets, John R. "The Mystery of the Church and the Liturgy." *Worship* 38 (1963/64), pp. 612–620.

Sheppard, Lancelot C. "How Much Is the Vernacular Allowed Now?" *Orate Fratres* 14 (1939/40), pp. 212–219.

_____. "The Liturgy and Language." *Orate Fratres* 11 (1936/37), pp. 62–68.

Sloyan, Gerard. "The Liturgical Proclamation of the Word of God." *North American Liturgical Week* 22 (1961), pp. 7–15.

Smits, Kenneth. "Augustine and Liturgical Pluriformity." *Worship* 44 (1970), pp. 386–398.

_____. "Liturgical Reform in Cultural Perspective." *Worship* 50 (1976), pp. 98–110.

Sorg, Rembert. "In Defense of Latin." *Orate Fratres* 19 (1944/45), pp. 113–119.

Stanley, David M. "Liturgical Influences On the Formation of the Four Gospels." *Catholic Biblical Quarterly* 21 (1959), pp. 24–38.

Stegmann, Basil. "The Liturgy and the Scriptures." *Orate Fratres* 10 (1935/36), pp. 511–516.

Stevick, Daniel B. "The Language of Prayer." *Worship* 52 (1978), pp. 542–560.

_____. "Responsibility for Liturgy." *Worship* 50 (1976), pp. 291–306.

Stuhlmueller, Carroll. "The Holy Eucharist: Symbol of Christ's Glory." *Worship* 34 (1959/60), pp. 258–269.

_____. "The Holy Eucharist: Symbol of the Passion." *Worship* 34 (1959/60), pp. 195–205.

Talley, Thomas J. "The Sacredness of Contemporary Worship." In *Worship in the City of Man*. North American Liturgical Week (1966), pp. 28–38.

Tegels, Aelred. "Liturgy and Culture: Adaptation or Symbiosis?" *Worship* 41 (1967), pp. 364–372.

_____. "Relevance: The Present Liturgical Reform." *Proceedings of North American Liturgical Week* 26 (1965), pp. 14–21.

Tena, Pedro. "The Liturgical Assembly and Its President." Tr. by Paul Burns. *Concilium* 72 (1972), pp. 43–54.

Theissen, Canon J. "The Parish, the Setting of the Liturgical Life." *Orate Fratres* 8 (1933/34), pp. 30–33, 76–82.

Theodore of Mopsuestia. "On the Lord's Prayer and On the Sacraments of Baptism and the Eucharist." *Woodbrooke Studies*. Vol. VI. Cambridge: W. Heffer and Sons, 1933.

Thompson, Harold Joseph. "For A Revival of the Liturgical Arts In Our Day." *Orate Fratres* 6 (1932), pp. 352–358, 395–403, 443–450.

Thornton, T.C.G. "I Peter, A Paschal Liturgy?" *Journal of Theological Studies* 12 (1961), pp. 14–26.

Thurian, Max. "Present Aims of the Liturgical Movement." *Studia Liturgica* 3 (1964), pp. 107–114.

Tinsley, John. "Liturgy and Art." *Concilium* 62 (1971), pp. 70–77.

Toporoski, Richard. "The Language of Worship." *Worship* 52 (1978), pp. 489–508.

Tracy, George E. "Limit Language: A Deeper Heritage." *Worship* 50 (1976), pp. 206–213.

Tseng-Tsiang, Pierre-Celestine Lou. "The Case For A Chinese Liturgy." *Orate Fratres* 20 (1945/46), pp. 227–229.

Tucker, Dunstan. "The Council of Trent, Guéranger and Pius X." *Orate Fratres* 10 (1935/36), pp. 538–544.

Vagaggini, Cipriano. "The Bishop and the Liturgy." Tr. by Philip Perfetti. *Concilium* 2 (1965), pp. 7–24.

————. "Fundamental Ideas of the Constitution." In *The Liturgy of Vatican II*. Ed. by William Barauna. Chicago: Franciscan Herald Press (1966), pp. 95–129.

————. "General Norms For the Reform and Fostering of the Liturgy." In *Commentary On the Constitution and On the Instruction On the Sacred Liturgy*. Ed. by A. Bugnini and C. Braga. Tr. by Vincent P. Mallon. New York: Benziger (1965), pp. 62–79.

————. "Liturgy and Contemplation." *Worship* 34 (1959/60), pp. 507–523.

van Bekkum, Wilhelm. "Liturgical Development in Indonesia." Tr. by Theodore L. Westow. *Concilium* 12 (1966), pp. 119–125.

————. "The Liturgical Revival in the Service of the Missions." In *The Assisi Papers*. Collegeville: Liturgical Press (1957), pp. 95–112.

————. "Liturgy: A Celebration of Our Existence." *Worldmission* 22 (Fall 1971), pp. 38–45.

Vandenbrouke, Francis. "At the Roots of Our Liturgical Malaise." *Theology Digest* 9 (1961), pp. 131–136.

van de Walle, Ambroos-Remi. "How We Meet Christ in the Liturgical Community." Tr. by Theodore L. Westow. *Concilium* 12 (1966), pp. 19–31.

van Eyden, Réné. "The Place of Women in Liturgical Functions." Tr. by David Smith. *Concilium* 72 (1972), pp. 68–81.

van Iersel, Bastiaan. "Some Biblical Roots of the Christian Sacrament." *Concilium* 31 (1968), pp. 5–20.

van Unnik, W.C.. "I Clement 34 and the 'Sanctus'." *Vigiliae Christianae* 5 (1951), pp. 204–248.

Vann, Gerald. "Returning Symbols." *Worship* 34 (1959/60), pp. 588–596.

Vergote, Antoine. "Symbolic Gestures and Actions in the Liturgy." Tr. by Barbara Wall. *Concilium* 62 (1971), pp. 40–52.

Vilanova, Evangelista. "The Development of the Expression of Faith in the Worshipping Community: In the Post-Apostolic Age." Tr. by Dinah Livingstone. *Concilium* 82 (1973), pp. 29–39.

————. "The Liturgical Crisis and Criticism of Religion." Tr. by Paul

Burns. *Concilium* 42 (1969), pp. 6–19.

Vincente, Francisco Miranda. "The Theological Significance of the Constitution on the Sacrament of Orders." In *The Assisi Papers*. Collegeville: Liturgical Press (1957), pp. 128–138.

Vismans, Thomas. "Liturgy Or Rubrics?" Tr. by Theodore L. Westow. *Concilium* 12 (1966), pp. 83–91.

Vogel, Cyrille. "An Alienated Liturgy." Tr. by John Griffiths. *Concilium* 72 (1972), pp. 11–25.

von Allmen, J.J.. "A Short Theology of the Place of Worship." *Studia Liturgica* 3 (1964), pp. 155–171.

von Hildebrand, Dietrich. "Liturgy Is Personal." *Orate Fratres* 16 (1941/42), pp. 386–392.

Vosko, Richard S. "American Culture Vs. American Worship." *Pastoral Music* 6 (Dec.-Jan. 1982), pp. 24–26.

Wagner, Johannes. "Liturgical Art and the Care of Souls." In *The Assisi Papers*. Collegeville: Liturgical Press (1957), pp. 57–73.

Wainwright, Geoffrey. "Risks and Possibilities of Liturgical Reform." *Studia Liturgica* 8 (1971–72), pp. 65–80.

Walsh, David W. "Social Justice and Liturgy in Contemporary Spirituality." *Modern Liturgy* 7 (August 1980), pp. 30–31.

Walsh, Eugene A. "The Gelineau Psalms." *Worship* 34 (1959/60), pp. 356–358.

Weakland, Rembert G. "The 'Sacred' and Liturgical Renewal." *Worship* 49 (1975), pp. 512–529.

Weaver, Bertrand. "Joy In the Liturgy." *Worship* 38 (1963/64), pp. 254–259.

Wenninger, William. "A Diocese Directs." *Worship* 32 (1957/58), pp. 192–196.

Werner, Eric. "The Doxology in Synagogue and Church." *Hebrew Union College Annual* 19 (1945/46), pp. 275–351.

Wesseling, Theodore. "The Encyclical 'Mystici Corporis Christi': Summary and Commentary." *Orate Fratres* 17 (1942/43), pp. 529–537.

White, James F. "The New American Methodist Communion Order." *Worship* 41 (1967), pp. 552–560.

Wilkinson, John. "Liturgy in the Twentieth Century." In *Eucharistic Theology Then and Now*. London: SPCK (1968), pp. 90–105.

Winzen, Damasus. "Maria Laach: Fifty Years." *Orate Fratres* 17 (1942/43), pp. 111–116.

_____. "Some Observations On the Revised Psalter." *Orate Fratres* 20 (1945/46), pp. 540–551.

Zarri, Adriana. "Woman's Prayer and Man's Liturgy." Tr. by James Langdale. *Concilium* 52 (1970), pp. 73–86.

Related Readings

Books

Anderson, Bernard W. *Out of the Depths*. Philadelphia: Westminster, 1970.

Augustine. *Confessions*. Tr. by Vernon J. Bourke. *Fathers of the Church*. Vol. 5. New York: 1953.

Bainton, Roland H. *Christendom*. Vol. 1 and 2. New York: Harper & Row, 1964.

_____. *Here I Stand*. The Life of Martin Luther. New York: 1950.

Bonner, Gerald. *St. Augustine of Hippo*. Philadelphia: Westminster, 1963.

Bouyer, Louis. *Christian Initiation*. New York: MacMillan, 1960.

Brown, Raymond E. *The Gospel According to John, I–XII. The Anchor Bible*. Vol. 29. New York: Doubleday, 1966.

Brown, Peter. *Augustine of Hippo*. London: Faber and Faber, 1967.

Campbell, Joseph, ed. *Myths, Dreams, and Religion*. New York: Dutton, 1970.

Chadwick, Henry. *The Early Church*. Grand Rapids: Eerdmans, 1967.

Childs, Brevard S. *Biblical Theology in Crisis*. Philadelphia: Westminster, 1970.

Corwin, Virginia. *St. Ignatius and Christianity in Antioch*. New Haven: Yale University Press, 1960—pp. 1–30.

Cox, Harvey. *The Feast of Fools*. A Theological Essay On Festivity and Fantasy. Cambridge: Harvard Univ. Press, 1969.

_____. *The Secular City*. New York: MacMillan, 1965.

Danielou, Jean. *Gospel Message and Hellenistic Culture*. Tr. by John Austin Baker. London: Darton, Longman and Todd, 1973.

_____. *The Origins of Latin Christianity*. Tr. by David Smith and John Austin Baker. London: Darton, Longman and Todd, 1977.

_____. *The Theology of Jewish Christianity*. Tr. by John A. Baker. London: Darton, Longman and Todd, 1964.

Daniel-Rops, Henri. *The Catholic Reformation*. Tr. by J. Warrington. London, 1961.

Dentan, Robert C. *Preface To Old Testament Theology*. New Haven: Yale, 1950.

Dickens, A.C. *The English Reformation*. Fontana/Collins, 1964.

Doty, William G. *Letters in Primitive Christianity*. Philadelphia: Fortress, 1973.

Eliade, Mircea. *Images and Symbols*. New York: Sheed and Ward, 1961.

_____. *Myth and Reality*. New York: Harper and Row, 1963.

_____. *The Myth of the Eternal Return*. Tr. by Willard R. Trask. New York: Pantheon, 1954.

_____. *Myths, Dreams and Mysteries*. Tr. by Philip Mairet. New York: Harper Torchbooks, 1960.

_____. *Myths, Rites and Symbols*. Vol 1 and 2. Ed. by Wendell Beane and William G. Doty. New York: Harper and Row, 1975.

_____. *Rites and Symbols of Initiation*. The Mysteries of Birth and Rebirth. Tr. by Willard R. Trask. New York: Harper Torchbooks, 1958.

_____. *The Sacred and the Profane*. Tr. by Willard R. Trask. New York: Harcourt, Brace, 1959.

Ellis, John Tracy, ed. *Documents of American Catholic History*. Milwaukee: Bruce, 1962.

Farrer, Austin. *The Glass of Vision*. Westminster: Dacre Press, 1948.

Fawcett, Thomas. *The Symbolic Language of Religion*. Minneapolis: Augsburg, 1971.

Fox, Matthew. *On Becoming A Musical, Mystical Bear*. Spirituality American Style. New York: Harper and Row, 1972.

Frei, Hans. *The Eclipse of Biblical Narrative*. New Haven: Yale, 1974.

Gospel According to Thomas, The. Tr. by A. Guillaumont. New York: Harper and Brothers, 1959.

Grant, Robert M., ed. *Gnosticism*. A Source Book of Heretical Writings From the Early Christian Period. New York: Harper and Brothers, 1961.

_____. *Gnosticism and Early Christianity*. New York: Columbia Univ., 1959.

Grimm, Harold J. *The Reformation Era, 1500–1650*. New York: Macmillan, 1965.

Guardini, Romano. *The Church and the Catholic*. Tr. by Ada Lane. New York: Sheed and Ward, 1953.

Guilday, Peter. *A History of the Councils of Baltimore* (1791–1884). New York: MacMillan, 1932.

Hahn, Herbert F. *Old Testament in Modern Research*. Philadelphia: Muhlenberg Press, 1954.

Häring, Bernard. *The Johannine Council*. Witness To Unity. Tr. by Edwin G. Kaiser. New York: Herder and Herder, 1963.

_____. *Road to Renewal*. Perspectives of Vatican II. New York: Alba House, 1966.

Harned, David Baily. *Theology and the Arts*. Philadelphia: Westminster, 1966.

Heschel, Abraham. *Man's Quest For God*. Studies in Prayer and Symbolism. New York: Scribner's, 1954.

Huizinga, J. *Homo Ludens*. A Study of the Play-Element in Culture. Boston: Beacon Press, 1950.

Jaeger, Lorenz. *The Ecumenical Council, The Church and Christendom.* Tr. by A.V. Littledale. New York: P.J. Kenedy and Sons, 1961.

Jedin, Hubert. *A History of the Council of Trent.* Tr. by Dom Ernest Graf. Vol. 1 and 2. St. Louis: B. Herder, 1957.

Keen, Sam. *To A Dancing God.* New York: Harper and Row, 1970.

Kelly, J.N.D. *Jerome.* London: Duckworth, 1975.

Kraft, H. *Early Christian Thinkers.* An Introduction to Clement of Alexandria and Origen. New York: Association Press, 1963.

Küng, Hans. *Art and the Question of Meaning.* Tr. by Edward Quinn. New York: Crossroad, 1981.

_____. *The Church.* New York: Image Books, 1976.

_____. *The Council in Action.* Theological Reflections on the Second Vatican Council. Tr. by Cecily Hastings. New York: Sheed & Ward, 1963.

_____. *The Council, Reform and Reunion.* Tr. by Cecily Hastings. New York: Sheed and Ward, 1961.

_____. *Why Priests?* New York: Doubleday, 1972.

Langer, Susanne K. *Feeling and Form.* A Theory of Art. New York: Charles Scribner's, 1953.

_____. *Philosophy In A New Key.* A Study in the Symbolism of Reason, Rite, and Art. Cambridge: Harvard Univ. Press, 1951.

Littel, Franklin Hamlin. *The Origins of Sectarian Protestantism.* New York: MacMillan, 1964.

Lohmuller, Rev. Martin Nicholas. *The Promulgation of Law.* A Dissertation. Canon Law Studies, No. 241. Washington, DC: Catholic University, 1947.

McKenzie, John L. *Mastering the Meaning of the Bible.* Wilkes-Barre, PA: Dimension Books, 1966.

Maier, Gerhard. *The End of the Historical-Critical Method.* Tr. by Edwin W. Leverenz and Rudolph F. Norden. St. Louis: Concordia, 1977.

Manschreck, Clyde L., ed. *A History of Christianity.* Readings in the History of the Church From the Reformation to the Present. Englewood Cliffs, NJ: Prentice-Hall, 1964.

Maritain, Jacques. *The Responsibility of the Artist.* New York: Charles Scribner's Sons, 1960.

Marrou, Henri. *St. Augustine and His Influence Through the Ages.* Tr. by Patrick Hepburne-Scott. New York: Harper Torchbooks, 1957.

Martin, F. David. *Art and the Religious Experience.* The Language of the Sacred. Lewisburg: Bucknell University Press, 1972.

May, Rollo, ed. *Symbolism in Religion and Literature.* New York: George Braziller, 1960.

Mohler, James A. *The Origin and Evolution of the Priesthood.* New York: Alba House, 1970.

Moore, George Foot. *Judaism. In the First Centuries of the Christian Era.* Vol. 1. Cambridge: Harvard Press, 1927.

Moule, C.F.D. *The Birth of the New Testament.* London: Adam & Charles Black, 1962.

Murphy, John L. *The General Councils of the Church.* Milwaukee: Bruce, 1960.

Neale, Robert E. *In Praise of Play. Toward A Psychology of Religion.* New York: Harper and Row, 1969.

Newman, Jeremiah. *Change and the Catholic Church. An Essay in Sociological Ecclesiology.* Baltimore: Helicon, 1965.

Niebuhr, H. Richard. *The Meaning of Revelation.* New York: MacMillan, 1941.

Nouwen, Henri J.M. *Creative Ministry.* New York: Doubleday, 1971.

Novak, Michael. *Ascent of the Mountain, Flight of the Dove.* New York: Harper and Row, 1971.

O'Connor, Elizabeth. *Eighth Day of Creation. Gifts and Creativity.* Waco, Texas: Word, 1971.

Otto, Rudolf. *The Idea of the Holy.* Tr. by John W. Harvey. New York: Oxford, 1972.

Parker, T.H.L. *John Calvin: A Biography.* Philadelphia: Westminster Press, 1975.

Pelikan, Jaroslav. *Luther the Expositor.* Introduction to the Reformer's Exegetical Writings. *Luther's Works.* Companion Volume.

Petry, Ray C., ed. *A History of Christianity.* Readings in the History of the Early and Medieval Church. Englewood Cliffs, NJ: Prentice-Hall, 1962.

Philo. *De Vita Contemplativa.* Tr. by F.H. Colson. Loeb Classical Library. Vol. 9. Cambridge: Harvard, 1941.

Raab, Clement. *The Twenty Ecumenical Councils of the Catholic Church.* Westminster: Newman, 1959.

Rahner, Hugo, ed. *The Parish: From Theology to Practice.* Tr. by Robert Kress. Westminster, MD: Newman, 1958.

Rahner, Karl. *The Church After the Council.* New York: Herder and Herder, 1966.

_____. *The Shape of the Church To Come.* Tr. by Edward Quinn. New York: Seabury Press, 1974.

Sanders, James. *Torah and Canon.* Philadelphia: Fortress, 1972.

Schillebeeckx, Edward. *God the Future of Man.* Tr. by N.D. Smith. New York: Sheed and Ward, 1968.

_____. *Ministry.* Leadership in the Community of Jesus Christ. New York: Crossroad, 1981.

_____. *Vatican II: A Struggle of Minds.* Tr. by M.H. Gill and Son. Dublin: Gill and Son, 1963.

_____. *Vatican II: The Real Achievement*. Tr. by H.J.J. Vaughan. London: Sheed and Ward, 1967.

Schweizer, Eduard. *Church Order in the New Testament*. London: SCM, 1961.

Simon, Ulrich. *Story and Faith in the Biblical Narrative*. London: SPCK, 1975.

Tardini, Domenico Cardinal. *Memories of Pius XII*. Tr. by Rosemary Goldie. Westminster, MD: The Newman Press, 1961.

Tavard, George H. *The Church Tomorrow*. New York: Herder and Herder, 1965.

Tillich, Paul. *Dynamics of Faith*. New York: Harper, 1957.

_____. *Theology of Culture*. New York: Oxford, 1964.

van Bilsen, Bertrand. *The Changing Church*. Adapted by Henry J. Koren. Pittsburgh: Duquesne, 1966.

van der Leeuw, Gerardus. *Sacred and Profane Beauty. The Holy in Art*. Tr. by David E. Green. New York: Holt, Rinehart and Winston, 1963.

van der Meer, F. *Augustine the Bishop*. Tr. by Brian Battershaw and G.R. Lamb. New York: Sheed and Ward, 1961.

Vermes, Geza. *The Dead Sea Scrolls in English*. Baltimore: Penguin, 1972.

von Campenhausen, Hans. "Jerome." In *The Fathers of the Latin Church*. Tr. by Manfred Hoffman. London: Adam and Charles Black, 1964.

Wellhausen, Julius. *Prolegomena to the History of Ancient Israel*. New York: Meridian, 1957.

Wild, Doris. *Holy Icons*. Switzerland: Hallwag Berne, 1961.

Wilder, Amos N. *The Language of the Gospel*. New York: Harper and Row, 1964.

_____. *Theopoetic*. Theology and the Religious Imagination. Philadelphia: Fortress, 1976.

Wilken, Robert L. *The Myth of Christian Beginnings*. New York: Doubleday, 1971.

Wright, G. Ernest. *God Who Acts*. Biblical Theology As Recital. London: SCM Press, 1952.

Articles

Alberigo, Giuseppe. "The Council of Trent." *Concilium* 7 (1965), pp. 69–87.

Alexander, S. "The Historicity of Things." In *Philosophy and History*. Ed. by Raymond Klibansky and H.J. Paton. New York: Harper and Row (1963), pp. 11–25.

Anderson, Bernhard W. "Confrontation With the Bible." *Theology Today* 30 (1973), pp. 267–271.

_____. "The Contemporaneity of the Bible." *Princeton Seminary Bulletin* 42 (1969), pp. 38–50.

_____. "The Crisis in Biblical Theology." *Theology Today* 28 (1971), pp. 321–327.

Barnard, L.W. "Origen's Christology and Eschatology." *Anglican Theological Review* 46 (1964), pp. 314–319.

Barr, James. "The Problem of Old Testament Theology and the History of Religion." *Canadian Journal of Theology* 3 (1957), pp. 141–149.

_____. "Story and History in Biblical Theology." *Journal of Religion* 56 (1976), pp. 1–17.

Barrett, C.K. "The Prologue of St. John's Gospel." In *New Testament Essays.* London: SPCK (1972), pp. 27–48.

Barrett, Cyril. "Culture and the Sacred." *The Way* 19 (1979), pp. 173–179.

Baumgärtel, Friedrich. "The Hermeneutical Problem of the Old Testament." In *Essays on Old Testament Hermeneutics.* Ed. by Claus Westermann. Tr. by James Luther Mays. Richmond: John Knox Press (1963), pp. 134–159.

Benko, Stephen. "The Magnificat. A History of the Controversy." *Journal of Biblical Literature* 86 (1967), pp. 263–275.

Betz, O. "Biblical Theology." *Interpreter's Dictionary of the Bible* I, pp. 432–437.

Boyle, Paul. "The Renewal of Canon Law and the Resolutions of the Canon Law Society of America, 1965." *Concilium* 28 (1967), pp. 69–77.

Brown, Raymond E. "The Magnificat." In *The Birth of the Messiah.* Garden City, NY: Doubleday (1977), pp. 355–366.

Brown, Robert McAfee. "My Story and 'The Story'." *Theology Today* 32 (1975), pp. 167–173.

Bulgakov, S. "Religion and Art." In *The Church of God.* Ed. by E.L. Mascall. London: SPCK (1934), pp. 175–191.

Burghardt, Walter J. "Did Saint Ignatius of Antioch Know the Fourth Gospel?" *Theological Studies* 1 (1940), pp. 1–26.

Butler, Christopher. "Institution Versus Charismata." In *Theology of Renewal.* Vol. 2. Ed. by L.K. Shook. New York: Herder and Heder (1968), pp. 42–54.

Campbell, Joseph. "The Secularization of the Sacred." In *The Religious Situation: 1968.* Ed. by Donald R. Cutler. Boston: Beacon (1968), pp. 601–637.

Chenu, M.-D. "The History of Salvation and the Historicity of Man in the Renewal of Theology." In *Theology of Renewal.* Vol. 1. Ed. by L.K. Shook. New York: Herder and Herder (1968), pp. 153–165.

Clements, R.E. "Interpreting Old Testament Theology." In *A Century of Old Testament Study.* London: Lutterworth Press (1976), pp. 118–138.

Comblin, Joseph. "Secularization: Myths and Real Issues." *Concilium* 47 (1969), pp. 121–133.

Concilium General Secretariat. "Toward A Renewal Of Religious Language." Tr. by Theodore L. Westow. *Concilium* 42 (1969), pp. 174–180.

Congar, Yves. "The Sacralization of Western Society in the Middle Ages." *Concilium* 47 (1969), pp. 55–71.

———. "Theology's Tasks After Vatican II." In *Theology of Renewal.* Vol. 1. Ed. by L.K. Shook. New York: Herder and Herder (1968), pp. 47–65.

Conzelmann, Hans. "Hellenistic Christianity Before Paul" and "Paul and His Communities." In *History of Primitive Christianity.* Tr. by John E. Steely. Nashville: Abingdon (1973), pp. 68–77, 91–109.

Copleston, Frederick. "The Patristic Period." In his *A History of Philosophy.* Vol. 2. Westminster: Newman (1957), pp. 13–39.

Craddock, Fred B. "All Things in Him: A Critical Note on Col 1:15–20." *New Testament Studies* 12 (1965/66), pp. 78–80.

Craig, Clarence T. "Biblical Theology and the Rise of Historicism." *Journal of Biblical Literature* 62 (1943), pp. 281–294.

Crites, Stephen. "The Narrative Quality of Experience." *Journal of the American Academy of Religion* 34 (1971), pp. 291–311.

Culley, R.C. "An Approach to the Problem of Oral Tradition." *Vetus Testamentum* 13 (1963), pp. 115–125.

Daube, David. "The Earliest Structure of the Gospels." *New Testament Studies* 5 (1958/59), pp. 174–187.

de Echevarria, Lamberto. "The Theology of Canon Law." *Concilium* 28 (1967), pp. 7–15.

Dibelius, Martin. "Mythology." In *From Tradition to Gospel.* Tr. by Bertram Lee Woolf. London: James Clarke (1971), pp. 266–286.

Dombois, Hans. "The Basic Structure of Church Law." *Concilium* 48 (1969), pp. 42–50.

Ebeling, Gerhard. "The Meaning of Biblical Theology." *Journal of Theological Studies* 6 (1955), pp. 210–225.

Erikson, Erik H. "The Development of Ritualization." In *The Religious Situation: 1968.* Ed. by Donald R. Cutler. Boston: Beacon (1968), pp. 711–733.

Every, George. "Sacralization and Secularization in East and West in the First Millenium After Christ." *Concilium* 47 (1969), pp. 27–38.

Fairweather, Eugene R. "Some Philosophical Contributions to Theological Renewal." In *Theology of Renewal.* Vol. 1. Ed. by L.K. Shook. New York: Herder and Herder (1968), pp. 356–375.

Fink, Karl August. "An Historical Note On the Constitution of the Church." *Concilium* 58 (1970), pp. 13–25.

Frankel, Charles. "Explanation and Interpretation in History." In *Theories of History*. Ed. by Patrick Gardiner. Glencoe, IL: The Free Press (1959), pp. 408–427.

Gabler, Johann Philipp. "A Discourse on the Proper Distinction Between Biblical and Dogmatic Theology and the Boundaries To Be Drawn for Each." (1787) Tr. by Karlfried Froehlich. In *Oratio de iusto discrimine theologiae biblicae et dogmaticae regundisque finibus*.

Geertz, Clifford. "Ethos, World View, and the Analysis of Sacred Symbols." In his *The Interpretation of Cultures*. New York: Basic Books (1973), pp. 126–141.

_____. "Religion As A Cultural System." In *The Religious Situation: 1968*. Ed. by Donald R. Cutler. Boston: Beacon (1968), pp. 639–688.

Gellner, Ernest. "Holism Versus Individualism In History and Sociology." In *Theories of History*. Ed. by Patrick Gardiner. Glencoe, IL: The Free Press (1959), pp. 489–503.

Gentile, Giovanni. "The Transcending of Time in History." Tr. by E.F. Carritt. In *Philosophy and History*. Ed. by Raymond Klibansky and H.J. Paton. New York: Harper and Row (1963), pp. 91–105.

Gilkey, Langdon. "Addressing God in Faith." *Concilium* 82 (1973), pp. 62–76.

_____. "Cosmology, Ontology, and the Travail of Biblical Language." *Journal of Religion* 41 (1961), pp. 194–205.

_____. "Modern Myth-Making and the Possibilities of Twentieth-Century Theology." In *Theology of Renewal*. Vol. 1. New York: Herder (1968), pp. 283–312.

_____. "The Theological Background of the Present Crisis." In his *Naming the Whirlwind: The Renewal of God-Language*. Indianapolis: Bobbs-Merrill (1969), pp. 73–106.

Gillespie, Thomas W. "The Laity in Biblical Perspective." In *The New Laity*. Ed. by Ralph D. Bucy. Waco, Texas: Word (1978), pp. 13–33.

Grillmeier, Aloys. "The Mystery of the Church." Tr. by Kevin Smyth. In *Commentary On the Documents of Vatican II*. Vol. 1. New York: Herder and Herder (1967), pp. 138–152.

Groethuysen, Bernard. "Towards An Anthropological Philosophy." Tr. by Sheila A. Kerr. In *Philosophy and History*. Ed. by Raymond Klibansky and H.J. Paton. New York: Harper and Row (1963), pp. 77–89.

Groot, Jan. "The Church As Sacrament of the World." *Concilium* 31 (1968), pp. 51–66.

Gunkel, Hermann. "The History of Religion and Old Testament Criticism." In *Fifth International Congress of Free Christianity and Religious Progress: Proceedings and Papers*. (Berlin, 1910) Ed. by Charles W. Wendte. London: Williams and Norgate (1911), pp. 114–125.

Hauerwas, Stanley. "Story and Theology." *Religion in Life* 45 (1976), pp. 339–350.

Hazelton, Roger. "Theology and Metaphor." *Religion in Life* 46 (1977), pp. 7–21.

Hegel, Georg Wilhelm. "Philosophical History." Tr. by J. Sibree. In *Theories of History*. Ed. by Patrick Gardiner. Glencoe, IL: The Free Press (1959), pp. 60–73.

Herberg, Will. "Biblical Faith As *Heilsgeschichte*." In *Faith Enacted As History*. Ed. by Bernhard W. Anderson. Philadelphia: Westminster (1976), pp. 32–42.

_____. "Judaism and Christianity: Their Unity and Difference." In *Faith Enacted in History*. Ed. by Bernhard W. Anderson. Philadelphia: Westminster (1976), pp. 44–64.

Hoffman, Ernst. "Platonism In Augustine's Philosophy of History." In *Philosophy and History*. Ed. by Raymond Klibansky and H.J. Paton. New York: Harper and Row (1963), pp. 173–190.

Hooke, S.H. "Christianity and the Mystery Religions." In *Judaism and Christianity*. Vol. 1. *The Age of Transition*. New York: MacMillan (1937), pp. 237–250.

_____. "The Emergence of Christianity From Judaism." In *Judaism and Christianity*. Vol. 1. The Age of Transition. New York: MacMillan (1937), pp. 253–281.

_____. "The Way of the Initiate." In *Judaism and Christianity*. Vol. 1. The Age of Transition. New York: MacMillan (1937), pp. 213–233.

Houtart, Francois. "The Church and the Developing Nations: Some Questions for the Theologians." In *Theology of Renewal*. Vol. 2. Ed. by L.K. Shook. New York: Herder and Herder (1968), pp. 358–383.

Huizing, Petrus. "The New Codification of the Church Order: Nature and Limits." *Concilium* 28 (1967), pp. 27–36.

_____. "The Reform of Canon Law." *Concilium* 8 (1965), pp. 95–128.

Huizinga, Johan. "A Definition of the Concept of History." Tr. by D.R. Cousin. In *Philosophy and History*. Ed. by Raymond Klibansky and H.J. Paton. New York: Harper and Row (1963), pp. 1–10.

James, E.O. "Religion in the Graeco-Roman World." In *Judaism and Christianity*. Vol. 1. The Age of Transition. New York: MacMillan (1937), pp. 29–56.

Jimenez-Urresti, Teodoro. "Canon Law and Theology: Two Different Sciences." *Concilium* 28 (1967), pp. 17–26.

Jones, Douglas. "The Background and Character of the Lukan Psalms." *Journal of Theological Studies* 19 (1968), pp. 19–50.

Käsemann, Ernst. "Ministry and Community in the New Testament." In *Essays On New Testament Themes*. Tr. by W.J. Montague. London: SCM (1964), pp. 63–94.

Kelly, J.N.D. "Credal Elements in the New Testament" and "Creeds and Baptism." In his *Early Christian Creeds*. New York: David McKay (1960), pp. 1–61.

Kelsey, David H. "Appeals To Scripture In Theology." *Journal of Religion* 48 (1968), pp. 1–21.

_____. "Recital and Presence." In his *The Uses of Scripture in Recent Theology*. London: SCM, 1975—pp. 32–55.

Koenig, Franz Cardinal. "Theology of Communications and the Renewal of the Church." In *Theology of Renewal*. Vol. 2. Ed. by L.K. Shook. New York: Herder and Herder (1968), pp. 285–306.

Leger, Paul-Emile Cardinal. "Theology of the Renewal of the Church." In *Theology of Renewal*. Vol. 1. Ed. by L.K. Shook. New York: Herder and Herder (1968), pp. 19–33.

Lohse, Eduard. "Pauline Theology in the Letter to the Colossians." *New Testament Studies* 15 (1969), pp. 211–220.

Lonergan, Bernard. "Theology in Its New Context." In *Theology of Renewal*. Vol. 1. Ed. by L.K. Shook. New York: Herder (1968), pp. 34–46.

Long, Burke O. "Recent Field Studies in Oral Literature and their Bearing On Old Testament Criticism." *Vetus Testamentum* 26 (1976), pp. 187–198.

Lossky, Vladimir. "The Theology of the Image." In *The Image and Likeness of God*. Ed. by John Erikson and Thomas Bird. St. Vladimir's Seminary Press (1974), pp. 125–139.

McBrien, Richard. "The Church: Sign and Instrument of Unity." *Concilium* 58 (1970), pp. 45–52.

McClendon, James Wm. "Biography As Theology." *Cross Currents* 21 (1971), pp. 415–431.

McKenzie, John L. "The Word of God in Church and World." In *Worship in the City of Man*. North American Liturgical Week (1966), pp. 72–80.

Martin, Ralph P. "The Form Analysis of Philippians 2, 5–11." *Texte und Untersuchungen* 87 (*Studia Evangelica*, 2). Ed. by F.L. Cross. Berlin: Academie-Verlag (1964), pp. 611–620.

Metz, Johann Baptist. "A Short Apology of Narrative." *Concilium* 85 (1973), pp. 84–96.

Meyer, Paul. "The This-Worldliness of the New Testament." Inaugural Address. Princeton Theological Seminary. February 28, 1979. Unpublished paper.

Meyvaert, Paul. "Bede and Gregory the Great." Mount Holyoke College, MA: Jarrow Lecture, 1964. Reprinted 1976. 26 pages.

Moeller, Charles. "Renewal of the Doctrine of Man." In *Theology of Renewal*. Vol. 2. Ed. by L.K. Shook. New York: Herder (1968), pp. 420–463.

Moffatt, James. "An Approach to Ignatius." *Harvard Theological Review* 29 (1936), pp. 1–38.

Mohrmann, Christine. "The Ever-Recurring Problem of Language in the

Church." In *Theology of Renewal*. Vol. 2. Ed. by L.K. Shook. New York: Herder and Herder (1968), pp. 204–221.

Moule, C.F.D. "The Influence of Circumstances on the Use of Christological Terms." *Journal of Theological Studies* 10 n.s. (1959), pp. 247–263.

Muilenburg, James. "Form Criticism and Beyond." *Journal of Biblical Literature* 88 (1969), pp. 1–18.

Neumann, Johannes. "The Social Nature of the Church and Its Consequences for Canon Law." *Concilium* 48 (1969), pp. 11–24.

O'Dea, Thomas. "The Church as *Sacramentum Mundi.*" *Concilium* 58 (1970), pp. 36–44.

Oesterley, W.O.E. "The General Historical Background." In *Judaism and Christianity*. Vol. 1. The Age of Transition. New York: MacMillan (1937), pp. 3–25.

Orsy, Ladislas. "The Canons On Ecclesiastical Laws Revisited: *Glossae* On Canons 8–24." *The Jurist* 37 (1977), pp. 112–425.

———. "The Interpreter and His Art." *The Jurist* 40 (1980), pp. 27–56.

Papajohn, John. "Philosophical and Metaphysical Basis of Icon Veneration in the Eastern Orthodox Church." *Greek Orthodox Theological Review* 2 (1956), pp. 83–89.

Pegis, Anton. "The Notion of Man in the Context of Renewal." In *Theology of Renewal*. Vol. 1. Ed. by L.K. Shook. New York: Herder (1968), pp. 250–264.

Philips, Gerard. "Dogmatic Constitution On the Church: History of the Constitution." Tr. By Kevin Smyth. In *Commentary On the Documents of Vatican II*. Vol. 1. New York: Herder and Herder (1967), pp. 105–137.

Power, David. "Cultural Encounter and Religious Expression." *Concilium* 102 (1977), pp. 100–112.

———. "The Odyssey of Man in Christ." *Concilium* 112 (1979), pp. 100–111.

Rahner, Karl. "Theological Reflections on the Problem of Secularization." In *Theology of Renewal*. Vol. 1. Ed. by L.K. Shook. New York: Herder and Herder (1968), pp. 167–192.

Reegen, Otto Ter. "The Rights of the Laity." *Concilium* 38 (1968), pp. 16–27.

Richardson, Cyril C. "The Church in Ignatius of Antioch." *Journal of Religion* 17 (1937), pp. 428–443.

Ricoeur, Paul. "Biblical Hermeneutics." *Semeia* 4. Ed. by John Dominic Crossan. Society of Biblical Literature (1975), pp. 29–73.

———. "Tasks of the Ecclesial Community in the Modern World." In *Theology of Renewal*. Vol. 2. Ed. by L.K. Shook. New York: Herder and Herder (1968), pp. 242–254.

Ridderbos, Herman. "The Structure and Scope of the Prologue to the Gospel of John." *Novum Testamentum* 8 (1966), pp. 180–201.

Robinson, James M. "A Formal Analysis of Colossians 1: 15–20." *Journal of Biblical Literature* 76 (1957), pp. 270–287.

Robinson, J.A.T. "The Relation of the Prologue to the Gospel of John." *New Testament Studies* 9 (1962/63), pp. 120–129.

Sanders, James. "Hermeneutics." *Interpreter's Dictionary of the Bible.* Supplementary Volume. pp. 402–407.

Schillebeeckx, Edward. "The Crisis in the Language of Faith As A Hermeneutical Problem." *Concilium* 85 (1973), pp. 31–45.

_____. "The Layman in the Church." Tr. by Colman O'Neill. In *Vatican II: The Theological Dimension.* Ed. by Anthony D. Lee. The Thomist Press (1963), pp. 262–283.

_____. "Theology of Renewal Talks About God." In *Theology of Renewal.* Vol. 1. Ed by L.K. Shook. New York: Herder and Herder (1968), pp. 83–104.

Schweizer, Eduard. "Two New Testament Creeds Compared: 1 Corinthians 15:3–5 and 1 Timothy 3:16." *Neotestimentica.* Stuttgart: Verlag (1963), pp. 122–135.

Setién, José. "Tensions In the Church." *Concilium* 48 (1969), pp. 66–80.

Shannon, Peter. "The Code of Canon Law: 1918–1967." *Concilium* 28 (1967), pp. 49–57.

Shepherd, Massey Hamilton. "Smyrna in the Ignatian Letters: A Study in Church Order." *Journal of Religion* 20 (1940), pp. 141–159.

Smith, Huston. "Secularization and the Sacred: The Contemporary Scene." In *The Religious Situation: 1968.* Ed. by Donald R. Cutler. Boston: Beacon (1968), pp. 583–600.

Spicq, Ceslaus. "The Pastoral Church in the New Testament." Tr. by Franis J. Turpin. In *Vatican II: The Theological Dimension.* Ed. by Anthony D. Lee. The Thomist Press, 1963.

Stendahl, Krister. "Biblical Theology." *Interpreter's Dictionary of the Bible.* Vol. 1. pp. 418–432.

Suenens, Léon-Joseph Cardinal. "Co-responsibility: Dominating Idea of the Council and Its Pastoral Consequences." In *Theology of Renewal.* Vol. 2. Ed. by L.K. Shook. New York: Herder (1968), pp. 7–18.

Swift, Thomas P. "The Pastoral Office of Episcopal Vicar: Changing Role and Powers." *The Jurist* 40 (1980), pp. 225–256.

Timko, Philip. "Orthodox Ecclesiology and Ecumenical Practice." *Worship* 50 (1976), pp. 137–145.

Trudinger, L. Paul. "The Prologue of John's Gospel: Its Extent, Content and Intent." *Reformed Theological Review* 33 (1974), pp. 11–17.

Turner, Victor. "Passages, Margins, and Poverty: Religious Symbols of Communitas." *Worship* 46 (1972), pp. 390–412, 482–494.

_____. "Ritual, Tribal and Catholic." *Worship* 50 (1976), pp. 504–526.

Wallace, D.H. "Historicism and Biblical Theology." *Texte und Untersuchungen* 88 (*Studia Evangelica*, 3), (1964), pp. 223–227.

Walsh, W.H. " 'Meaning' in History." In *Theories of History*. Ed. by Patrick Gardiner. Glencoe, IL: The Free Press (1959), pp. 296–307.

Ware, Kallistos. "The Theology of the Icon: A Short Anthology." *Eastern Churches Review* 8 (1976), pp. 3–10.

Watson, Philip S. "The Doctrine of the Word." In *Let God Be God!* An Interpretation of the Theology of Martin Luther. London: Epworth Press (1958), pp. 149–189.

Weinrich, Harald. "Narrative Theology." *Concilium* 85 (1973), pp. 46–56.

Wicker, Brian. "Metaphor and Analogy" and "Metaphor and God." In his *The Story-Shaped World*. Notre Dame: University Press, 1975.

Willis, David. "The Material Assumptions of Integrative Theology: the Conditions of Experiential Church Dogmatics." Inaugural Address. Princeton Theological Seminary. April 18, 1979. Unpublished paper.

Wilson, R. McL. "Gnosis, Gnosticism and the New Testament." *Studies in the History of Religions* (Supplements to *Numen*) 12. Leiden: E.J. Brill (1967), pp. 511–527.

Winninger, Paul. "A Pastoral Canon Law." *Concilium* 48 (1969), pp. 51–65.

Winquist, Charles E. "The Act of Storytelling and the Self's Homecoming." *Journal of the American Academy of Religion* 42 (1974), pp. 101–113.

Wolff, Hans Walter. "The Hermeneutics of the Old Testament." Tr. by Keith Crim. In *Essays on Old Testament Hermeneutics*. Ed. by Claus Westermann. Richmond: John Knox Press (1963), pp. 160–199.

To:

_____

From:

_____

Date:

_____

Message:

_____

_____

_____

_____

_____

_____

Published by Christian Art Publishers
PO Box 1599, Vereeniging, 1930, RSA

© 2016
First edition 2016

Cover designed by Christian Art Publishers

Images used under license from Shutterstock.com

Printed in China

ISBN 978-1-4321-1652-1

16 17 18 19 20 21 22 23 24 25 – 11 10 9 8 7 6 5 4 3 2

Illustrated
PRAYERS from
the Bible

**CHRISTIAN ART
PUBLISHERS**

Rejoice ALWAYS, *pray* continually, GIVE *thanks* in all circumstances; for this is *God's* will for you IN CHRIST JESUS.

1 Thessalonians 5:16-18 NIV

1

I Will Follow You

How sweet are Your words to my taste,

sweeter than honey to my mouth!

I gain understanding from Your precepts;

therefore I hate every wrong path.

Your word is a lamp for my feet,

a light on my path.

I have taken an oath and confirmed it,

that I will follow Your righteous laws.

Preserve my life, LORD, according to Your word.

Accept, LORD, the willing praise of my mouth,

and teach me Your laws.

PSALM 119:103-108 NIV

Reflection

Your *word* is a **LAMP** for my **FEET,** a light on *my path.*

2

Your Unfailing Love

I have not kept the good news of
Your justice hidden in my heart;
I have talked about Your faithfulness and saving power.
I have told everyone in the great assembly
of Your unfailing love and faithfulness.
Lord, don't hold back Your tender mercies from me.
Let Your unfailing love and faithfulness always protect me.

Psalm 40:10-11 NLT

Reflection

_____
_____
_____
_____
_____
_____
_____
_____
_____
_____
_____
_____
_____
_____
_____
_____
_____
_____
_____
_____
_____

Let Your *unfailing love* & faithfulness always protect me.

3

You Alone Are God

You are great and do marvelous deeds;

You alone are God.

Teach me Your way, L<small>ORD</small>,

that I may rely on Your faithfulness;

give me an undivided heart,

that I may fear Your name.

You, Lord, are a compassionate and gracious God,

slow to anger, abounding in love and faithfulness.

P<small>SALM</small> 86:10-11, 15 <small>NIV</small>

Reflection

You *alone* ARE GOD.

4

Your Priceless Love

Your love, LORD, reaches to the heavens,
Your faithfulness to the skies.
Your righteousness is like the highest mountains,
Your justice like the great deep.
You, LORD, preserve both people and animals.
How priceless is Your unfailing love, O God!
People take refuge in the shadow of Your wings.

PSALM 36:5-7 NIV

Reflection

People take

REFUGE

in the *shadow*

of *Your* WINGS.

5

Teach Me to Do Your Will

I desire to do Your will, my God;

Your law is within my heart.

I proclaim Your saving acts in the great assembly;

I do not seal my lips, LORD, as You know.

I do not hide Your righteousness in my heart;

I speak of Your faithfulness and Your saving help.

PSALM 40:8-10 NIV

Reflection

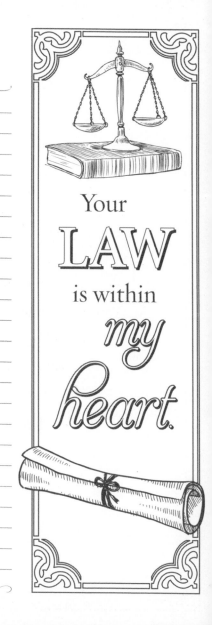

Your
LAW
is within
my
heart.

6

You Are a Mighty God

The heavens praise Your wonders, LORD,

Your faithfulness too, in the assembly of the holy ones.

For who in the skies above can compare with the LORD?

Who is like You, LORD God Almighty?

You, LORD, are mighty,

and Your faithfulness surrounds You.

PSALM 89:5-6, 8 NIV

Reflection

I *praise* You, LORD, *for* You are MIGHTY.

7

A Blessing of Peace

The L ORD bless you and keep you;

the L ORD make His face shine upon you,

and be gracious to you;

the L ORD lift up His countenance upon you

and give you peace.

N UMBERS 6:24-26 NKJV

Reflection

The LORD BLESS you & KEEP you.

8

Be with Me, Lord

Oh, that You would bless me
and enlarge my territory!
Let Your hand be with me,
and keep me from harm
so that I will be free from pain.

1 Chronicles 4:10 niv

Reflection

Let Your HAND be WITH ME.

9

All I Need

The eyes of all look expectantly to You,
and You give them their food in due season.
You open Your hand and satisfy
the desire of every living thing.
The LORD is righteous in all His ways,
gracious in all His works.
The LORD is near to all who
call upon Him in truth.

PSALM 145:15-18 NKJV

Reflection

You satisfy the DESIRE of every living thing.

10

You Are Over All Things

O LORD, the God of our ancestor Israel,

may You be praised forever and ever!

Yours, O LORD, is the greatness, the power,

the glory, the victory, and the majesty.

Everything in the heavens and on earth is Yours, O LORD,

and this is Your kingdom.

We adore You as the One who is over all things.

Wealth and honor come from You alone,

for You rule over everything.

Power and might are in Your hand,

and at Your discretion

people are made great and given strength.

1 CHRONICLES 29:10-12 NLT

Reflection

We *adore You* as the One who is over ALL THINGS.

11

Everything Comes from You

O our God, we thank You and praise Your glorious name!
Everything we have has come from You,
and we give You only what You first gave us!
We are here for only a moment, visitors and
strangers in the land as our ancestors were before us.
Our days on earth are like a passing shadow,
gone so soon without a trace.
O LORD our God, it all belongs to You!

1 CHRONICLES 29:13-16 NLT

Reflection

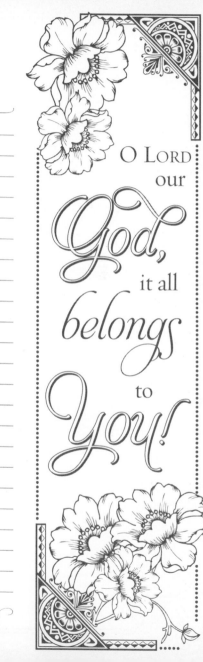

O Lord our *God,* it all *belongs* to *You!*

12

I Entrust My Life to You

Show me the way I should go,

for to You I entrust my life.

Teach me to do Your will,

for You are my God;

may Your good Spirit

lead me on level ground.

For Your name's sake, LORD,

preserve my life; in Your righteousness,

bring me out of trouble.

PSALM 143:8, 10-11 NIV

Reflection

Show
me
the way
I should go.

13

Guard My Life

Guard my life and rescue me;

do not let me be put to shame,

for I take refuge in You.

May integrity and uprightness protect me,

because my hope, LORD, is in You.

PSALM 25:20-21 NIV

Reflection

I take REFUGE in YOU.

14

You Are My Help

I lift up my eyes to the hills.

From where does my help come?

My help comes from the LORD,

who made heaven and earth.

He will not let your foot be moved;

He who keeps you will not slumber.

The LORD is your keeper;

the LORD is your shade on your right hand.

The LORD will keep you from all evil;

He will keep your life.

The LORD will keep

your going out and your coming in

from this time forth and forevermore.

PSALM 121: 1-3, 5, 7-8 ESV

Reflection

My HELP comes *from* the LORD.

15

I Will Fear No Evil

Even though I walk
through the darkest valley,
I will fear no evil,
for You are with me;
Your rod and Your staff,
they comfort me.
You prepare a table before me
in the presence of my enemies.
You anoint my head with oil;
my cup overflows.
Surely Your goodness and love
will follow me all the days of my life,
and I will dwell in the house
of the LORD forever.

PSALM 23:4-6 NIV

Reflection

Surely Your
goodness &
love
will follow me.

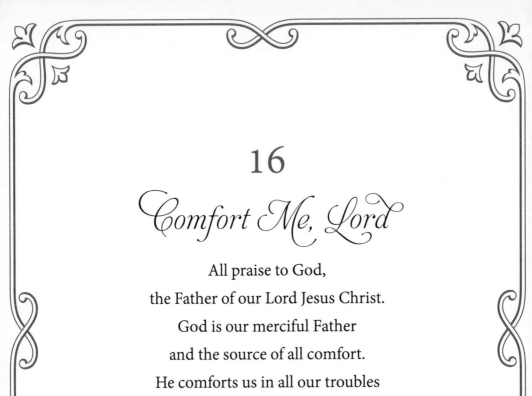

16

Comfort Me, Lord

All praise to God,
the Father of our Lord Jesus Christ.
God is our merciful Father
and the source of all comfort.
He comforts us in all our troubles
so that we can comfort others.
When they are troubled,
we will be able to give them
the same comfort God has given us.

2 CORINTHIANS 1:3-4 NLT

Reflection

God is our
MERCIFUL
Father &
the source of all comfort.

17

A Pure Heart

Hide Your face from my sins
and blot out all my iniquity.
Create in me a pure heart, O God,
and renew a steadfast spirit within me.
Do not cast me from Your presence
or take Your Holy Spirit from me.
Restore to me the joy of Your salvation
and grant me a willing spirit, to sustain me.

PSALM 51:9-12 NIV

Reflection

Create in me a PURE HEART, O God.

18

I Trust in You

When I am afraid,

I will put my trust in You.

I praise God for what He has promised.

I trust in God, so why should I be afraid?

What can mere mortals do to me?

You keep track of all my sorrows.

You have collected all my tears in Your bottle.

You have recorded each one in Your book.

PSALM 56:3-4, 8 NLT

Reflection

I PRAISE GOD
for what He has
PROMISED.

19

You Are My Shelter

Hear my cry, O God;

attend to my prayer.

From the end of the earth I will cry to You,

when my heart is overwhelmed;

lead me to the rock that is higher than I.

For You have been a shelter for me,

a strong tower from the enemy.

I will abide in Your tabernacle forever;

I will trust in the shelter of Your wings.

PSALM 61:1-4 NKJV

Reflection

You
have
been a
SHELTER
FOR ME.

20

Save Me from the Storm

Be merciful to me, O God, be merciful to me,

for in You my soul takes refuge;

in the shadow of Your wings I will take refuge,

till the storms of destruction pass by.

I cry out to God Most High,

to God who fulfills His purpose for me.

He will send from heaven and save me.

God will send out His steadfast love and His faithfulness!

PSALM 57:1-3 ESV

Reflection

_____
_____
_____
_____
_____
_____
_____
_____
_____
_____
_____
_____
_____
_____
_____
_____
_____
_____
_____

He will send *from* *heaven* and save me.

21

I Love the Lord My Savior

I love You, Lord God,

and You make me strong.

You are my mighty rock,

my fortress, my protector,

the rock where I am safe,

my shield,

my powerful weapon,

and my place of shelter.

I praise You, Lord!

I prayed, and You rescued me.

When I was fenced in,

You freed and rescued me

because You love me.

Psalm 18:1-3, 19 CEV

Reflection

_____

_____

_____

_____

_____

_____

_____

_____

_____

_____

_____

_____

_____

_____

_____

_____

_____

_____

_____

_____

_____

_____

_____

_____

_____

_____

I love
YOU,
LORD
God.

22

Protect Me, Lord

You are my hiding place;
You protect me from trouble.
You surround me with songs of victory.
The LORD says, "I will guide you along
the best pathway for your life.
I will advise you and watch over you.
Do not be like a senseless horse or mule that
needs a bit and bridle to keep under control."
Many sorrows come to the wicked, but unfailing
love surrounds those who trust the LORD.

PSALM 32:7-10 NLT

Reflection

You SURROUND me with *songs* of VICTORY.

23

You Are My Rock

In You, O Lord, do I take refuge;

let me never be put to shame!

In Your righteousness deliver me and rescue me;

incline Your ear to me, and save me!

Be to me a rock of refuge,

to which I may continually come;

You have given the command to save me,

for You are my rock and my fortress.

Psalm 71:1-3 esv

Reflection

You
are my
ROCK
and my
FORTRESS.

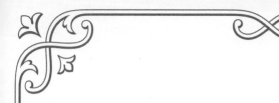

24

You Are Good to Me

There are many who say,

"Who will show us any good?"

LORD, lift up the light of Your countenance upon us.

You have put gladness in my heart.

I will both lie down in peace,

and sleep; for You alone, O LORD,

make me dwell in safety.

PSALM 4:6-8 NKJV

Reflection

YOU have put *gladness* in my *heart.*

25

You Give Me Peace

You will keep in perfect peace
all who trust in You,
all whose thoughts are fixed on You!
LORD, we show our trust in You by obeying Your laws;
our heart's desire is to glorify Your name.
LORD, You will grant us peace;
all we have accomplished is really from You.

ISAIAH 26:3, 8, 12 NLT

Reflection

OUR *heart's* DESIRE is to *glorify* YOUR *name.*

26

Cleanse Me, O God

Have mercy on me, O God,

according to Your unfailing love;

according to Your great compassion

blot out my transgressions.

Wash away all my iniquity

and cleanse me from my sin.

Cleanse me with hyssop, and I will be clean;

wash me, and I will be whiter than snow.

PSALM 51:1-2, 7 NIV

Reflection

_____

_____

_____

_____

_____

_____

_____

_____

_____

_____

_____

_____

_____

_____

_____

_____

_____

_____

_____

Have *mercy* on me, O GOD, according to Your unfailing *love.*

27

Save Me, Lord

I trust in You, Lord;

I say, "You are my God."

My times are in Your hands;

deliver me from the hands of my enemies,

from those who pursue me.

Let Your face shine on Your servant;

save me in Your unfailing love.

Let me not be put to shame, Lord,

for I have cried out to You.

PSALM 31:14-17 NIV

Reflection

SAVE
ME IN
Your
unfailing
love.

28

God Is on My Side

You keep track of all my sorrows.

You have collected all my tears in Your bottle.

You have recorded each one in Your book.

This I know: God is on my side!

You have rescued me;

You have kept my feet from slipping.

Now I can walk in Your presence, O God,

in Your life-giving light.

<small>Psalm 56:8-9, 13 NLT</small>

Reflection

29

Thank You, Lord

It is good to give thanks to the Lord,

to sing praises to the Most High.

It is good to proclaim Your unfailing love in the morning,

Your faithfulness in the evening.

You thrill me, Lord, with all You have done for me!

I sing for joy because of what You have done.

PSALM 92:1-2, 4 NLT

Reflection

I *sing* for **JOY** because *of what* You have **DONE.**

30

Be Exalted, O God

I will praise You, Lord, among the nations;

I will sing of You among the peoples.

For great is Your love, reaching to the heavens;

Your faithfulness reaches to the skies.

Be exalted, O God, above the heavens;

let Your glory be over all the earth.

PSALM 57:9-11 NIV

Reflection

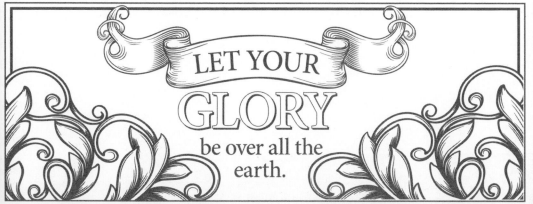

LET YOUR

GLORY

be over all the
earth.

31

You Freed Me

How kind the LORD is! How good He is!

So merciful, this God of ours!

O LORD, I am Your servant;

yes, I am Your servant, born into Your household;

You have freed me from my chains.

I will offer You a sacrifice of thanksgiving

and call on the name of the LORD.

PSALM 116:5, 16-17 NLT

Reflection

You have FREED ME from my chains.

32

Wonderfully Made

Thank You for making me so wonderfully complex!

Your workmanship is marvelous – how well I know it.

You watched me as I was being formed in utter seclusion,

as I was woven together in the dark of the womb.

You saw me before I was born.

Every day of my life was recorded in Your book.

Every moment was laid out

before a single day had passed.

How precious are Your thoughts about me, O God.

They cannot be numbered! I can't even count them;

they outnumber the grains of sand!

And when I wake up, You are still with me!

PSALM 139:14-18 NLT

Reflection

How precious *are* Your *thoughts* about me, O God.

33

Your Righteous Deeds I Proclaim

My mouth will tell of Your righteous deeds,

of Your saving acts all day long –

though I know not how to relate them all.

I will come and proclaim Your mighty acts, Sovereign Lord;

I will proclaim Your righteous deeds, Yours alone.

Since my youth, God, You have taught me,

and to this day I declare Your marvelous deeds.

Even when I am old and gray,

do not forsake me, my God,

till I declare Your power to the next generation,

Your mighty acts to all who are to come.

PSALM 71:15-18 NIV

Reflection

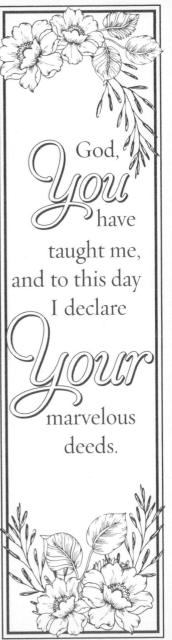

God, *You* have taught me, and to this day I declare *Your* marvelous deeds.

34

Blessed Are Those
Who Trust in You

Hear my prayer, Lord God Almighty;

listen to me, God of Jacob.

Better is one day in Your courts

than a thousand elsewhere;

I would rather be a doorkeeper in the house of my God

than dwell in the tents of the wicked.

For the Lord God is a sun and shield;

the Lord bestows favor and honor;

no good thing does He withhold

from those whose walk is blameless.

Lord Almighty, blessed is the one who trusts in You.

Psalm 84:8, 10-12 NIV

Reflection

The LORD GOD
is a sun and shield.

35

Acceptable to You

The judgments of the LORD are true
and righteous altogether.
More to be desired are they than gold,
Yea, than much fine gold;
Sweeter also than honey and the honeycomb.
Let the words of my mouth
and the meditation of my heart
be acceptable in Your sight,
O LORD, my strength and my Redeemer.

PSALM 19:9-10,14 NKJV

Reflection

Let the *words* of my *mouth* & the meditation of my *heart* be acceptable in Your SIGHT.

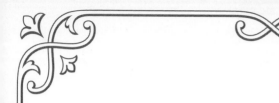

36

You Know Me Best

You have searched me, LORD,

and You know me.

You know when I sit and when I rise;

You perceive my thoughts from afar.

You discern my going out and my lying down;

You are familiar with all my ways.

Before a word is on my tongue

You, LORD, know it completely.

Where can I go from Your Spirit?

Where can I flee from Your presence?

PSALM 139:1-4, 7 NIV

Reflection

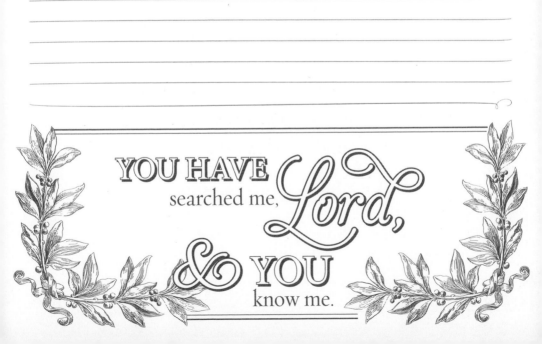

YOU HAVE searched me, *Lord,* & YOU know me.

37

You Are My Strength

The LORD is my strength and my shield;

my heart trusts in Him, and He helps me.

My heart leaps for joy,

and with my song I praise Him.

The LORD is the strength of His people,

a fortress of salvation for His anointed one.

Save Your people and bless Your inheritance;

be their shepherd and carry them forever.

PSALM 28:7-9 NIV

Reflection

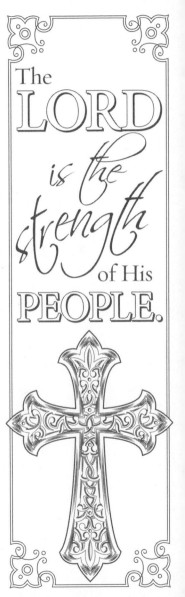

The
LORD
is the
strength
of His
PEOPLE.

38

Never Leave Me

My heart is glad and my tongue rejoices;

my body also will rest secure,

because You will not abandon me

to the realm of the dead,

nor will You let Your faithful one see decay.

You make known to me the path of life;

You will fill me with joy in Your presence,

with eternal pleasures at Your right hand.

PSALM 16:9-11 NIV

Reflection

You make
known to me
the PATH
of LIFE.

39

You Make Me Strong

My heart rejoices in the LORD!

The LORD has made me strong.

Now I have an answer for my enemies;

I rejoice because You rescued me.

No one is holy like the LORD!

There is no one besides You;

there is no Rock like our God.

1 SAMUEL 2:1-2 NLT

Reflection

No one is *holy* like the LORD!

40

I Delight in Your Word

Lord, You know what's happening to me.

Please step in and help me.

Punish my persecutors!

When I discovered Your words,

I devoured them. They are my joy

and my heart's delight,

for I bear Your name,

O LORD God of Heaven's Armies.

JEREMIAH 15:15-16 NLT

Reflection

YOUR WORDS *are my* JOY.

41

You Are Faithful

Your righteousness, O God, reaches to the highest heavens.

You have done such wonderful things.

Who can compare with You, O God?

I will praise You with music on the harp,

because You are faithful to Your promises, O my God.

I will shout for joy and sing Your praises,

for You have ransomed me.

PSALM 71:19, 22-23 NLT

Reflection

You are
faithful
to Your
promises
O MY
GOD.

42

Your Dwelling Place

How lovely is Your dwelling place,

Lord Almighty!

My soul yearns, even faints,

for the courts of the Lord;

my heart and my flesh cry out

for the living God.

Blessed are those who dwell in Your house;

they are ever praising You.

Psalm 84:1-2, 4 niv

Reflection

My heart & my flesh cry out for the LIVING GOD.

43

I Seek the Lord

O God, You are my God; earnestly I seek You;

my soul thirsts for You; my flesh faints for You,

as in a dry and weary land where there is no water.

So I have looked upon You in the sanctuary,

beholding Your power and glory.

Because Your steadfast love is better than life,

my lips will praise You.

PSALM 63:1-3 ESV

Reflection

_____
_____
_____
_____
_____
_____
_____
_____
_____
_____
_____
_____
_____
_____
_____
_____
_____
_____
_____
_____
_____
_____
_____
_____
_____
_____

Your steadfast LOVE is *better* than LIFE.

44

Holy Is the Lord

Holy, holy, holy, is the Lord God Almighty,

who was and is and is to come!

Worthy are You, our Lord and God,

to receive glory and honor and power,

for You created all things,

and by Your will they existed and were created.

REVELATION 4:8, 11 ESV

Reflection

Worthy are You to receive GLORY & HONOR and power.

45

Our Father in heaven,

may Your name be kept holy.

May Your Kingdom come soon.

May Your will be done on earth,

as it is in heaven.

Give us today the food we need,

and forgive us our sins,

as we have forgiven those who sin against us.

And don't let us yield to temptation,

but rescue us from the evil one.

MATTHEW 6:9-13 NLT

Reflection

May
Your

Kingdom
COME
soon.

46

Great Is the Lord

I will praise You with my whole heart;

before the gods I will sing praises to You.

I will worship toward Your holy temple,

and praise Your name

for Your lovingkindness and Your truth;

for You have magnified Your word above all Your name.

In the day when I cried out, You answered me,

and made me bold with strength in my soul.

All the kings of the earth shall praise You, O LORD,

when they hear the words of Your mouth.

Yes, they shall sing of the ways of the LORD,

for great is the glory of the LORD.

PSALM 138:1-5 NKJV

Reflection

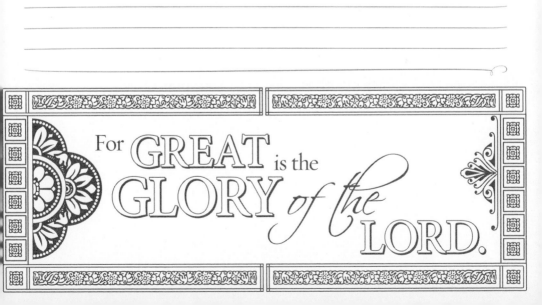

For **GREAT** is the **GLORY** *of the* **LORD.**

47

My Confidence Is in You

You have been my hope, Sovereign Lord,

my confidence since my youth.

From birth I have relied on You;

You brought me forth from my mother's womb.

I will ever praise You.

You are my strong refuge.

My mouth is filled with Your praise,

declaring Your splendor all day long.

Psalm 71:5-8 niv

Reflection

From *birth*
I have *relied*
ON YOU;
You brought
me forth from
my mother's
womb.

48

I Will Exult You

I will give thanks to the LORD with my whole heart;

I will recount all of Your wonderful deeds.

I will be glad and exult in You;

I will sing praise to Your name, O Most High.

For You have maintained my just cause;

You have sat on the throne,

giving righteous judgment.

PSALM 9:1-2, 4 ESV

Reflection

I will be glad & exult in You.

49

Open for me the gates of the righteous;

I will enter and give thanks to the LORD.

I will give You thanks, for You answered me;

You have become my salvation.

The stone the builders rejected

has become the cornerstone;

the LORD has done this,

and it is marvelous in our eyes.

PSALM 118:19, 21-23 NIV

Reflection

You have BECOME my salvation.

50

Deliver Me

Though I walk in the midst of trouble,

You preserve my life;

You stretch out Your hand

against the wrath of my enemies,

and Your right hand delivers me.

The LORD will fulfill His purpose for me;

Your steadfast love, O LORD, endures forever.

Do not forsake the work of Your hands.

PSALM 138:7-8 ESV

Reflection

YOU *preserve* MY *life.*

51

You Are My Shield

I have a lot of enemies, LORD.

Many fight against me and say,

"God won't rescue you!"

But You are my shield,

and You give me victory

and great honor.

I pray to You, and You answer

from Your sacred hill.

I sleep and wake up refreshed

because You, LORD,

protect me.

PSALM 3:1-5 CEV

Reflection

YOU GIVE ME Victory.

52

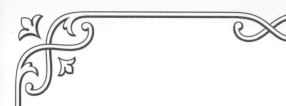
You Are My Security

I will praise You as long as I live,

lifting up my hands to You in prayer.

You satisfy me more than the richest feast.

I will praise You with songs of joy.

I lie awake thinking of You,

meditating on You through the night.

Because You are my helper,

I sing for joy in the shadow of Your wings.

I cling to You; Your strong right hand

holds me securely.

<small>Psalm 63:4-8 nlt</small>

Reflection

I sing for joy in the SHADOW OF YOUR WINGS.

53

Search Me, God

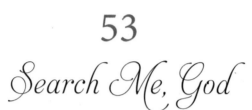

If I go up to the heavens, You are there;

if I make my bed in the depths, You are there.

If I rise on the wings of the dawn,

if I settle on the far side of the sea,

even there Your hand will guide me,

Your right hand will hold me fast.

Search me, God, and know my heart;

test me and know my anxious thoughts.

See if there is any offensive way in me,

and lead me in the way everlasting.

PSALM 139:8-10, 23-24 NIV

Reflection

Your right *hand* will

HOLD
ME.

54

In the Day of Trouble

Be gracious to me, O Lord,

for to You do I cry all the day.

Gladden the soul of Your servant,

for to You, O Lord, do I lift up my soul.

You, O Lord, are good and forgiving,

abounding in steadfast love

to all who call upon You.

Give ear, O LORD, to my prayer;

listen to my plea for grace.

In the day of my trouble I call upon you,

for You answer me.

PSALM 86:3-7 ESV

Reflection

Give ear, O Lord, to my PRAYER.

55

Teach Me Your Decrees

I gave an account of my ways and You answered me;

teach me Your decrees.

Cause me to understand the way of Your precepts,

that I may meditate on Your wonderful deeds.

My soul is weary with sorrow;

strengthen me according to Your word.

Keep me from deceitful ways;

be gracious to me and teach me Your law.

I have chosen the way of faithfulness;

I have set my heart on Your laws.

PSALM 119:26-30 NIV

Reflection

Strengthen
me
according
to
Your
WORD.

56

A New Song

I patiently waited, LORD,

for You to hear my prayer.

You listened and pulled me

from a lonely pit

full of mud and mire.

You let me stand on a rock

with my feet firm,

and You gave me a new song,

a song of praise to You.

Many will see this,

and they will honor

and trust

You, the LORD God.

PSALM 40:1-3 CEV

Reflection

YOU GAVE ME A *new song,* a song of *praise* TO YOU.

57

Lead Me and Teach Me

To You, O LORD, I lift up my soul.

O my God, in You I trust;

let me not be put to shame.

Indeed, none who wait for You shall be put to shame;

they shall be ashamed who are wantonly treacherous.

Make me to know Your ways, O LORD;

teach me Your paths.

Lead me in Your truth and teach me,

for You are the God of my salvation;

for You I wait all the day long.

PSALM 25:1-5 ESV

Reflection

Teach ME Your PATHS.

58

You Redeem Me

In You, O LORD, I put my trust;

let me never be ashamed;

deliver me in Your righteousness.

You are my rock and my fortress;

therefore, for Your name's sake,

lead me and guide me.

Pull me out of the net

which they have secretly laid for me,

for You are my strength.

Into Your hand I commit my spirit;

You have redeemed me, O LORD God of truth.

PSALM 31:1, 3-5 NKJV

Reflection

INTO YOUR
HAND I COMMIT
my spirit.

59

Guide My Steps

The teaching of Your word gives light,

so even the simple can understand.

I pant with expectation,

longing for Your commands.

Come and show me Your mercy,

as You do for all who love Your name.

Guide my steps by Your word,

so I will not be overcome by evil.

Look upon me with love;

teach me Your decrees.

Psalm 119:130-133, 135 nlt

Reflection

The *teaching* OF YOUR *word* GIVES *light.*

60

Send Me Your Light

Send me Your light and Your faithful care,

let them lead me;

let them bring me to Your holy mountain,

to the place where You dwell.

Then I will go to the altar of God,

to God, my joy and my delight.

I will praise You with the lyre,

O God, my God.

PSALM 43:3-4 NIV

Reflection

SEND ME *Your light* & Your faithful CARE.

61

I Love Your Word

Oh, how I love Your law!
I meditate on it all day long.
Your commands are always with me
and make me wiser than my enemies.
I have more insight than all my teachers,
for I meditate on Your statutes.
How sweet are Your words to my taste,
sweeter than honey to my mouth!

PSALM 119:97-99, 103 NIV

Reflection

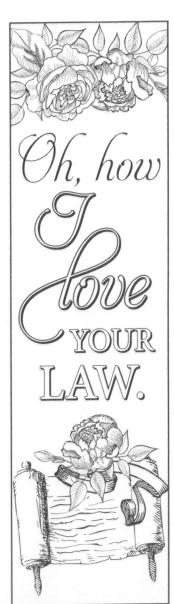

Oh, how *I love* YOUR LAW.

62

Be Attentive to Our Prayers

LORD, the God of heaven, the great and awesome God,
let Your ear be attentive and Your eyes open
to hear the prayer Your servant is praying
before You day and night.
They are Your servants and Your people,
whom You redeemed by Your great strength
and Your mighty hand.
Lord, let Your ear be attentive
to the prayer of this Your servant
and to the prayer of Your servants
who delight in revering Your name.

NEHEMIAH 1:5-6, 10-11 NIV

Reflection

LET YOUR EAR
be attentive to the *prayer*
of this
Your *servant.*

63

Forgive Our Sins

When I was in trouble, L ORD,

I prayed to You, and You listened to me.

From deep in the world of the dead,

I begged for Your help, and You answered my prayer.

But, You, L ORD God, rescued me from that pit.

When my life was slipping away, I remembered You –

and in Your holy temple You heard my prayer.

All who worship worthless idols turn

from the God who offers them mercy.

But with shouts of praise, I will offer

a sacrifice to You, my L ORD.

I will keep my promise, because You

are the one with power to save.

J ONAH 2:2, 6-9 CEV

Reflection

YOU
LISTENED
to
ME.

64

Rescue Me, Lord

I ask for Your help, Lord God,

and You will keep me safe.

Morning, noon, and night

You hear my concerns

and my complaints.

I am attacked from all sides,

but You will rescue me

unharmed by the battle.

You have always ruled,

and You will hear me.

PSALM 55:16-19 CEV

Reflection

YOU WILL keep me safe.

65

A Prayer for Others

I pray that from His glorious, unlimited resources He will
empower you with inner strength through His Spirit.
Then Christ will make His home in your hearts as you trust in Him.
Your roots will grow down into God's love and keep you strong.
And may you have the power to understand, as all God's people
should, how wide, how long, how high, and how deep His love is.
May you experience the love of Christ, though it is too great
to understand fully. Then you will be made complete with
all the fullness of life and power that comes from God.

EPHESIANS 3:16-19 NLT

Reflection

I pray that
CHRIST
will make

HIS
home

in your
hearts.

66

Your Saving Help

You make Your saving help my shield,
and Your right hand sustains me;
Your help has made me great.
You provide a broad path for my feet,
so that my ankles do not give way.
You armed me with strength for battle;
You humbled my adversaries before me.

PSALM 18:35-36, 39 NIV

Reflection

Your
HELP *has made*
me GREAT.

67

I Praise You

The LORD is good to everyone.

He showers compassion on all His creation.

All of Your works will thank You, LORD,

and Your faithful followers will praise You.

They will speak of the glory of Your kingdom;

they will give examples of Your power.

They will tell about Your mighty deeds

and about the majesty and glory of Your reign.

PSALM 145:9-12 NLT

Reflection

Your
faithful
followers
will
PRAISE
YOU.

68

Forgive My Iniquity

Remember, LORD, Your great mercy and love,

for they are from of old.

Do not remember the sins of my youth

and my rebellious ways;

according to Your love remember me,

for You, LORD, are good.

For the sake of Your name, LORD,

forgive my iniquity, though it is great.

PSALM 25:6-7, 11 NIV

Reflection

According
to
Your love
remember me, *for*
You, LORD, are good.

69

Bless This House

O Lord GOD, You are God,
and Your words are true, and You
have promised this good thing to Your servant.
Now therefore may it please You
to bless the house of Your servant,
so that it may continue forever before You.
For You, O Lord GOD, have spoken,
and with Your blessing shall the house
of Your servant be blessed forever.

2 SAMUEL 7:28-29 ESV

Reflection

Bless THE HOUSE OF YOUR servant.

70

May Everyone Know You Are God

Lord God of Abraham, Isaac, and Israel,

let it be known this day that You

are God in Israel and I am Your servant,

and that I have done all these things at Your word.

Hear me, O Lord, hear me, that this people

may know that You are the Lord God,

and that You have turned their hearts

back to You again.

1 Kings 18:36-37 nkjv

Reflection

You *are* the LORD GOD.

71

You Are Our Provision

All creatures look to You
to give them their food at the proper time.
When You give it to them,
they gather it up;
when You open Your hand,
they are satisfied with good things.
When You send Your Spirit,
they are created,
and You renew the face of the ground.
May the glory of the LORD endure forever;
may the LORD rejoice in His works.

PSALM 104:27-28, 30-31 NIV

Reflection

May the glory of the LORD endure forever.

72

Make Your Way Plain to Me

Because of Your unfailing love,

I can enter Your house;

I will worship at Your Temple

with deepest awe.

Lead me in the right path, O Lord,

or my enemies will conquer me.

Make Your way plain for me to follow.

PSALM 5:7-8 NLT

Reflection

Lead me in the
RIGHT PATH,
O LORD.

73

May I Walk in Your Truth

Teach me Your way, O LORD,

that I may walk in Your truth;

unite my heart to fear Your name.

I give thanks to You, O Lord my God,

with my whole heart,

and I will glorify Your name forever.

For great is Your steadfast love toward me;

You have delivered my soul from the depth of Sheol.

You, O Lord, are a God merciful and gracious,

slow to anger and abounding

in steadfast love and faithfulness.

PSALM 86:11-13,15 ESV

Reflection

UNITE
MY
heart
to
fear
YOUR
name.

74

My Inheritance

Keep me safe, O God,

for I have come to You for refuge.

LORD, You alone are my inheritance,

my cup of blessing.

You guard all that is mine.

The land You have given me is a pleasant land.

What a wonderful inheritance!

I will bless the LORD who guides me;

even at night my heart instructs me.

I know the LORD is always with me.

I will not be shaken, for He is right beside me.

PSALM 16:1, 5-8 NLT

Reflection

You alone
are my
cup of
BLESSING.

75

You Reign Forever

God Most High, I will rejoice;

I will celebrate and sing

because of You.

You rule forever, LORD,

and You are on Your throne,

ready for judgment.

You judge the world fairly

and treat all nations with justice.

The poor can run to You

because You are a fortress

in times of trouble.

Everyone who honors Your name

can trust You,

because You are faithful

to all who depend on You.

PSALM 9:2, 7-10 CEV

Reflection

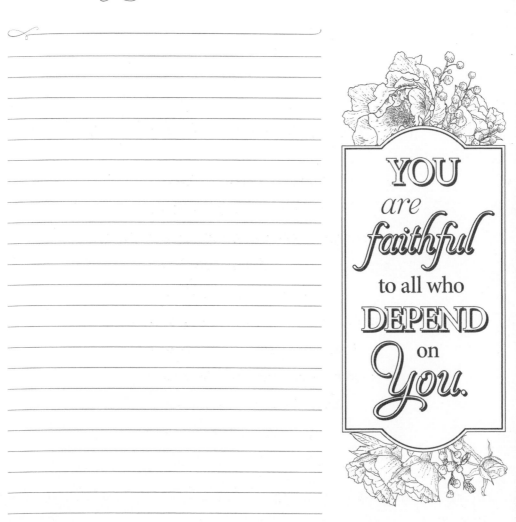

YOU
are
faithful
to all who
DEPEND
on
You.

76

My Salvation Is in You

O Lord, I will praise You;

though You were angry with me,

Your anger is turned away, and You comfort me.

Behold, God is my salvation,

I will trust and not be afraid;

"For Yah, the Lord, is my strength and song;

He also has become my salvation."

Therefore with joy you will draw water

from the wells of salvation.

Isaiah 12:1-3 NKJV

Reflection

I will **TRUST** & not be *afraid.*

77

Bless Us All

O Lord, hear me as I pray;

pay attention to my groaning.

Listen to my cry for help, my King and my God,

for I pray to no one but You.

Listen to my voice in the morning, Lord.

Each morning I bring my requests to You and wait expectantly.

Let all who take refuge in You rejoice;

let them sing joyful praises forever.

Spread Your protection over them,

that all who love Your name may be filled with joy.

For You bless the godly, O Lord;

You surround them with Your shield of love.

Psalm 5:1-3, 11-12 NLT

Reflection

YOU
surround
THEM
with
Your
SHIELD
of love.

78

You Are Wonderful

LORD, our Lord,

how majestic is Your name in all the earth!

When I consider Your heavens,

the work of Your fingers,

the moon and the stars,

which You have set in place,

what is mankind that You are mindful of them,

human beings that You care for them?

You have made them a little lower than the angels

and crowned them with glory and honor.

You made them rulers over the works of Your hands;

You put everything under their feet.

LORD, our Lord,

how majestic is Your name in all the earth!

PSALM 8:1, 3-6, 9 NIV

Reflection

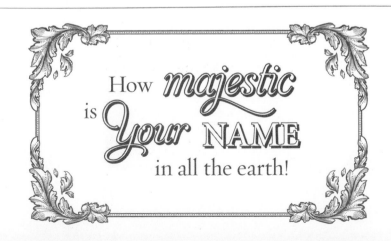

How *majestic* is *Your* NAME in all the earth!

79

The Apple of Your Eye

Hear me, LORD,

my plea is just; listen to my cry.

I call on You, my God, for You will answer me;

turn Your ear to me and hear my prayer.

Show me the wonders of Your great love,

You who save by Your right hand

those who take refuge in You from their foes.

Keep me as the apple of Your eye;

hide me in the shadow of Your wings.

PSALM 17:1, 6-8 NIV

Reflection

KEEP
ME
as the
apple
of
Your
EYE.

80

You Give Me Joy

I will exalt You, Lord,

for You lifted me out of the depths

and did not let my enemies gloat over me.

Lord my God, I called to You for help,

and You healed me.

You, Lord, brought me up from the realm of the dead;

You spared me from going down to the pit.

You turned my wailing into dancing;

You removed my sackcloth and clothed me with joy,

that my heart may sing Your praises and not be silent.

Lord my God, I will praise You forever.

Psalm 30:1-3, 11-12 NIV

Reflection

You removed my
SACKCLOTH &
clothed me with *joy.*

81

May We Always Know Your Goodness

O LORD my God, You have performed many wonders for us.

Your plans for us are too numerous to list.

You have no equal.

If I tried to recite all Your wonderful deeds,

I would never come to the end of them.

May all who search for You

be filled with joy and gladness in You.

May those who love Your salvation

repeatedly shout, "The LORD is great!"

PSALM 40:5, 16 NLT

Reflection

The
Lord
is
great!

82

With You There Is Forgiveness

Out of the depths I cry to You, LORD;

Lord, hear my voice.

Let Your ears be attentive

to my cry for mercy.

If You, LORD, kept a record of sins,

Lord, who could stand?

But with You there is forgiveness,

so that we can, with reverence, serve You.

I wait for the LORD, my whole being waits,

and in His word I put my hope.

PSALM 130:1-5 NIV

Reflection

IN HIS WORD
I put my *hope.*

83

Help the Powerless

LORD, there is no one like You

to help the powerless against the mighty.

Help us, LORD our God, for we rely on You,

and in Your name

we have come against this vast army.

LORD, You are our God;

do not let mere mortals prevail against You.

2 CHRONICLES 14:11 NIV

Reflection

HELP US, *Lord* our *God.*

84

Repent in Dust and Ashes

I know that You can do all things;

no purpose of Yours can be thwarted.

You asked, "Who is this that obscures

My plans without knowledge?"

Surely I spoke of things I did not understand,

things too wonderful for me to know.

You said, "Listen now, and I will speak;

I will question you,

and you shall answer Me."

My ears had heard of You

but now my eyes have seen You.

Therefore I despise myself

and repent in dust and ashes.

Job 42:1-6 niv

Reflection

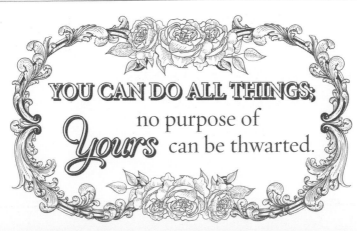

YOU CAN DO ALL THINGS;
no purpose of
Yours can be thwarted.

85

Restore Us

LORD, remember what has happened to us.

See how we have been disgraced!

Joy has left our hearts;

our dancing has turned to mourning.

The garlands have fallen from our heads.

Weep for us because we have sinned.

Our hearts are sick and weary,

and our eyes grow dim with tears.

LORD, You remain the same forever!

Your throne continues from generation to generation.

Restore us, O LORD, and bring us back to You again!

Give us back the joys we once had!

LAMENTATIONS 5:1, 15-17, 19, 21 NLT

Reflection

BRING
US BACK
to
You
AGAIN!

86

Yet I Will Rejoice

LORD, I have heard of Your fame;
I stand in awe of Your deeds, LORD.
Repeat them in our day,
in our time make them known;
in wrath remember mercy.
Though the fig tree does not bud
and there are no grapes on the vines,
though the olive crop fails
and the fields produce no food,
though there are no sheep in the pen
and no cattle in the stalls,
yet I will rejoice in the LORD,
I will be joyful in God my Savior.

HABAKKUK 3:2, 17-18 NIV

Reflection

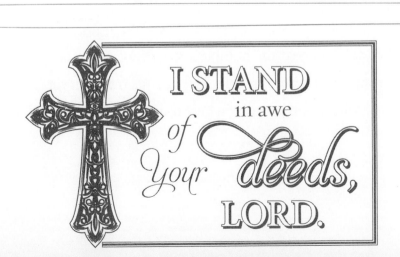

I STAND in awe of your *deeds,* LORD.

87

Hear Our Prayer

O LORD, God of Israel,

there is no God like You

in all of heaven above or on the earth below.

You keep Your covenant and show unfailing love

to all who walk before You in wholehearted devotion.

Listen to my prayer and my plea, O LORD my God.

Hear the cry and the prayer

that Your servant is making to You today.

May You hear the humble and earnest requests

from me and Your people. Yes, hear us from heaven

where You live, and when You hear, forgive.

1 KINGS 8:23, 28, 30 NLT

Reflection

HEAR
us from
heaven...
& *when You*
HEAR,
forgive.

88

Always Near You

One thing I ask from the LORD,

this only do I seek:

that I may dwell in the house of the LORD

all the days of my life,

to gaze on the beauty of the LORD

and to seek Him in His temple.

Hear my voice when I call, LORD;

be merciful to me and answer me.

My heart says of You, "Seek His face!"

Your face, LORD, I will seek.

Do not hide Your face from me,

do not turn Your servant away in anger;

You have been my helper.

Do not reject me or forsake me, God my Savior.

PSALM 27:1-4, 7-9 NIV

Reflection

that I may dwell in the *house* of the LORD.

89

There Is None like You

Lord, there is no one like You!

For You are great, and Your name is full of power.

Who would not fear You, O King of nations?

That title belongs to You alone!

Among all the wise people of the earth

and in all the kingdoms of the world,

there is no one like You.

The Lord is the only true God.

He is the living God and the everlasting King!

JEREMIAH 10:6-7, 10 NLT

Reflection

Lord there is no one LIKE YOU!

90

Bless the Lord

Blessed be Your glorious name,

and may it be exalted

above all blessing and praise.

You alone are the LORD.

You made the heavens,

even the highest heavens,

and all their starry host,

the earth and all that is on it,

the seas and all that is in them.

You give life to everything,

and the multitudes of heaven worship You.

NEHEMIAH 9:5-7 NIV

Reflection

BLESSED

be *Your glorious* NAME.

91

Guide Me in Your Strength

Your right hand, O Lord, has become glorious in power;
Your right hand, O Lord, has dashed the enemy in pieces.
And in the greatness of Your excellence
You have overthrown those who rose against You;
You sent forth Your wrath;
it consumed them like stubble.
You in Your mercy have led forth
the people whom You have redeemed;
You have guided them in Your strength
to Your holy habitation.
You will bring them in and plant them
in the mountain of Your inheritance,
in the place, O Lord, which You have made
for Your own dwelling, the sanctuary,
O Lord, which Your hands have established.

Exodus 15:6-7, 13, 17 NKJV

Reflection

You have *guided them* in Your *strength.*

92

##
Do Not Forsake Us

Although our sins testify against us,
do something, LORD, for the sake of Your name.
For we have often rebelled;
we have sinned against You.
You are among us, LORD,
and we bear Your name;
do not forsake us!
For the sake of Your name
do not despise us;
do not dishonor Your glorious throne.
Remember Your covenant with us
and do not break it.

JEREMIAH 14:7, 9, 21 NIV

Reflection

You are among us,
LORD,
AND WE BEAR
Your name.

93

My Help and Deliverer

Hasten, O God, to save me;

come quickly, Lord, to help me.

May those who say to me, "Aha! Aha!"

turn back because of their shame.

But may all who seek You

rejoice and be glad in You;

may those who long for Your saving help

always say, "The Lord is great!"

But as for me, I am poor and needy;

come quickly to me, O God.

You are my help and my deliverer;

Lord, do not delay.

Psalm 70:1, 3-5 NIV

Reflection

May all
who seek
YOU
Rejoice

94

Light up My Darkness

To the faithful You show Yourself faithful;

to those with integrity You show integrity.

To the pure You show Yourself pure,

but to the crooked You show Yourself shrewd.

You rescue the humble, but Your eyes

watch the proud and humiliate them.

O LORD, You are my lamp.

The LORD lights up my darkness.

In Your strength I can crush an army;

with my God I can scale any wall.

2 SAMUEL 22:26-30 NLT

Reflection

The LORD *lights* up my darkness.

95

I Seek Justice

O LORD of Heaven's Armies,

You make righteous judgments,

and You examine the deepest thoughts and secrets.

LORD, You always give me justice

when I bring a case before You.

So let me bring You this complaint:

Why are the wicked so prosperous?

Why are evil people so happy?

You have planted them,

and they have taken root and prospered.

Your name is on their lips,

but You are far from their hearts.

But as for me, LORD, You know my heart.

You see me and test my thoughts.

JEREMIAH 11:20, 12:1-3 NLT

Reflection

But as for me, **LORD,** *You* know my *heart.*

96

You Are Near to Me

I cry out with my whole heart;

hear me, O LORD!

I will keep Your statutes.

I cry out to You;

save me, and I will keep Your testimonies.

I rise before the dawning of the morning,

and cry for help;

I hope in Your word.

My eyes are awake through the night watches,

that I may meditate on Your word.

Hear my voice according to Your lovingkindness;

O LORD, revive me according to Your justice.

You are near, O LORD,

and all Your commandments are truth.

PSALM 119:145-149, 151 NKJV

Reflection

You are near, O LORD, and all Your COMMANDMENTS are truth.

97

You Are My All

You will light my lamp;

the Lord my God will enlighten my darkness.

For by You I can run against a troop,

by my God I can leap over a wall.

As for God, His way is perfect;

the word of the Lord is proven;

He is a shield to all who trust in Him.

For who is God, except the Lord?

And who is a rock, except our God?

Psalm 18:28-31 nkjv

Reflection

By my

God

I CAN

leap over a

WALL.

98

Overwhelmed by Troubles

Listen to my prayer, O God.
Do not ignore my cry for help!
Please listen and answer me,
for I am overwhelmed by my troubles.
My enemies shout at me,
making loud and wicked threats.
They bring trouble on me
and angrily hunt me down.
My heart pounds in my chest.
Fear and trembling overwhelm me,
and I can't stop shaking.
Oh, that I had wings like a dove;
then I would fly away and rest!
How quickly I would escape –
far from this wild storm of hatred.
Confuse them, Lord, and frustrate their plans,
for I see violence and conflict in the city.

PSALM 55:1-6, 8-9 NLT

Reflection

Oh, that I had **WINGS** like a *dove;* then I would fly away and rest!

99

I Love Your Law

Your compassion, LORD, is great;
preserve my life according to Your laws.
See how I love Your precepts;
preserve my life, LORD,
in accordance with Your love.
All Your words are true;
all Your righteous laws are eternal.
I rejoice in Your promise
like one who finds great spoil.
Seven times a day I praise You
for Your righteous laws.
Great peace have those who love Your law,
and nothing can make them stumble.

PSALM 119:156, 159-160, 162, 164-165 NIV

Reflection

I
rejoice
in Your
promise
like one
who finds
GREAT
spoil.

100

I Promise to Obey

You are my portion, LORD;
I have promised to obey Your words.
I have sought Your face with all my heart;
be gracious to me according to Your promise.
I have considered my ways
and have turned my steps to Your statutes.
I will hasten and not delay
to obey Your commands.
At midnight I rise to give You thanks
for Your righteous laws.
I am a friend to all who fear You,
to all who follow Your precepts.
The earth is filled with Your love, LORD;
teach me Your decrees.

PSALM 119:57-60, 62-64 NIV

Reflection

The EARTH
is filled with
Your love,
LORD.

101

You Hold Me Up

If I say, "My foot slips,"

Your mercy, O LORD, will hold me up.

In the multitude of my anxieties within me,

Your comforts delight my soul.

The LORD has been my defense,

and my God the rock of my refuge.

PSALM 94:18-19, 22 NKJV

Reflection

Your comforts delight my soul.